D1447009

READING STRATEGIES FOR MIDDLE AND SECONDARY SCHOOL TEACHERS

SECOND EDITION

READING STRATEGIES FOR MIDDLE AND SECONDARY SCHOOL TEACHERS

Lou E. Burmeister
University of Texas at El Paso

SECOND EDITION

ADDISON-WESLEY PUBLISHING COMPANY
Reading, Massachusetts
Menlo Park, California · London · Amsterdam · Don Mills, Ontario · Sydney

This book is in the
ADDISON-WESLEY SERIES IN EDUCATION

 Printed in the United States of America. Published simultaneously in Canada. Library of Congress Catalog Card No. 77-088054.

ISBN 0-201-00316-3
DEFGHIJKLM-HA-89876543210

To my mother, Alyce, and Thad
and John W. McFarland,
all of whom made the writing of this book possible

CONTENTS

INTRODUCTION

READING AND THE MIDDLE AND SECONDARY SCHOOL TEACHER

All teachers want students to learn. To promote this goal, almost all teachers use printed materials—books, pamphlets, magazine and newspaper articles—in the classroom. The present book has been written to help teachers and pre-service teachers both choose and utilize printed materials to promote optimal student learning and enjoyment. Throughout the text, the teaching of reading skills and the selection of appropriate reading materials are viewed as means toward helping each student achieve his or her full cognitive and affective potential.

Learning to read, study, and select appropriate reading materials are viewed in this book as continuous processes rather than as skills which can be achieved at one period of time, such as in the elementary grades. The blocks laid and molded into a meaningful base during a person's earliest years form the foundation for an ever-evolving skill structure. Even when students leave our care—upon graduation—they have just begun to develop. At colleges and universities, in the business world—whatever their job—or at home, they must continue to grow. We can help provide a strong background so that they are able and willing to do so.

Those teachers who are most interested in having their students master content—be it science, math, literature, social studies, or anything else—will find that there is in reality no dichotomy between teaching reading and teaching content. When fused with the teaching of content, the teaching of reading skills and the selection of materials appropriate for each student make it possible for students to understand content.

Content area teachers are not expected to teach reading skills in isolation, but they will find that learning is facilitated if they teach those skills which are necessary for understanding their materials. This they can do at the same time that they teach content.

ORGANIZATION OF THIS BOOK

To guide the reader's thinking along these lines, this book has been written. It is divided into four units. Unit One, titled "Adjusting Reading Materials for All Students," deals with such topics as understanding how well students read, judging the difficulty of reading materials, and devising classroom strategies which are helpful in finding the appropriate level of materials for each student and finding materials of interest to each student.

Unit Two, titled "Developing Classroom Strategies for Reading in Content Fields," deals specifically with classroom teaching and organizational strategies which can be used to promote learning and interest. Unit Three, titled "Improving Learning Through Reading Development in Content Fields and Reading Classes," deals with specific ways of developing needed tools for such strategies. And Unit Four, titled "Utilizing School-wide Resources and Staff," deals with strategies for using school resources and extending the program to encompass the whole staff in a cooperative effort.

COGNITIVE AND AFFECTIVE DEVELOPMENT

Two unifying concepts permeate the book. One is concerned with the cognitive development of students; the other, with affective development. *Cognitive development* is intellectual development, the kind of thing teachers have always been interested in. The *cognitive domain,* or intellectual realm, has recently been analyzed, and its components have been arranged in levels according to the degree of intellectual activity necessary at each level. According to Benjamin Bloom, there is a hierarchical continuum of cognitive skills ranging from memory (recall) responses at the lowest level to highly intellectual, critical (analytical)-creative (synthetic)-evaluative thinking at the highest levels.[1]

Affective development relates to the development of a value system, interests, and involvement. The *affective domain,* as delineated by David Krathwohl, describes behavior ranging from simple awareness of an idea at the lowest level to complete internalization of the idea, demonstrated by a state of "characterization," whereby an idea or value permeates a person's whole being.[2]

Although often discussed separately, cognitive and affective behavior normally interact. The processes of valuing, being interested in, and being involved with an idea frequently spark a higher level of cognitive understanding or response to the idea than would otherwise occur. This higher-level intellectual response may, in turn, cause increased affective involvement, and so on.

USE OF THIS BOOK AS A TEXTBOOK FOR A COLLEGE COURSE

This book consists of 12 chapters. In a college class, perhaps one chapter could be studied each week; slightly more time might be spent on some chapters and less on others. Basic related references for further study are listed at the end of each chapter. Also included are suggested activities for students who may wish such guidance. This schedule also provides ample time for giving and discussing two or three examinations.

Relate Reading in This Book to a Content Field Book of Your Choice

It is recommended that readers of this book have at their sides one or more content area textbooks of their choice, at the grade level of their choice. Assignments within some chapters and the suggested activities at the end of chapters can be applied to such texts. Doing such assignments concurrently with the reading of this book should help prepare the student for the implementation of suggested principles and techniques in future teaching.

GRATITUDE EXPRESSED

For their helpful comments and suggestions while she was preparing the second edition of this book, the author wishes to express gratitude to her students at the University of Texas at El Paso. Special thanks are extended to the following graduate assistants: Chuck Sullivan, M. Olivia Roeckl, and Marcy Grenier.

NOTES

1 Benjamin Bloom, *et al. Taxonomy of Educational Objectives: Handbook I, Cognitive Domain.* New York: David McKay, 1956. A more complete discussion of the cognitive domain may be found in Unit Three of this book.

2 David R. Krathwohl, *et al. Taxonomy of Educational Objectives: Handbook II, Affective Domain.* New York: David McKay, 1964. A more complete discussion of the affective domain may be found in Chapter 4 of this book.

UNIT ONE

ADJUSTING READING MATERIALS FOR ALL STUDENTS

Introduction

Unit One consists of four chapters:

Chapter 1
Understanding How Well Students Read

Chapter 2
Judging the Difficulty of Reading Materials

Chapter 3
Finding the Appropriate Level of Materials for Each Student

Chapter 4
Assessing and Building Student Interests in Reading Materials

Unit One has two basic purposes: *first,* to clarify how widely students differ in reading achievement, and *second,* to supply some basic techniques for the appropriate selection of reading materials in relationship to the individual student's reading achievement and interests.

Chapter 1

UNDER-STANDING HOW WELL STUDENTS READ

What is the *range* of reading achievement in a typical classroom?

How well *should* individual students read?

Why is there such a vast range in reading achievement among age-mates?

RANGE OF READING ACHIEVEMENT IN A CLASSROOM

The Facts

Let's imagine that you are teaching a typical class of tenth graders. You are meeting them for the first time and know nothing about the individuals. Let's consider their cognitive development in reading. It's important to know how well they can perform.

Let's say there are 30 teen-agers in the class. How well do you think the best reader reads, and how poorly the poorest? If you don't know, make an educated guess. Circle the grade levels that you think represent the reading achievement of the poorest and best readers in the class:

average

1 2 3 4 5 6 7 8 9 10 11 12 13 14 15 16 17 18

poorest grade best grade

Did you circle 9 and 11, or 8 and 12? If so, you're way off! You're closer to the truth if you circled 6 and 14, or 6 and 15—if it's a good class. If it's a poorer class, you might have circled 5 and 13, or 5 and 14. If it's a typical class, you should have circled *5 and 15.*

Let's try another class—this time a seventh-grade English class. Again, circle the reading-grade level of the poorest reader and that of the best reader:

average

1 2 3 4 5 6 7 8 9 10 11 12 13 14 15 16 17 18

poorest grade best grade

What did you circle? It should have been 3 and 11.

Another? Let's take a twelfth-grade sociology class. Circle the grade score of the poorest reader and that of the best:

average

1 2 3 4 5 6 7 8 9 10 11 12 13 14 15 16 17 18

poorest grade best grade

Did you circle 6 and 18? That's it.

Let's go back to fourth grade. Circle the grade score of the poorest reader and that of the best reader.

average
1 2 3 4 5 6 7 8 9 10 11 12 13 14 15 16 17 18

poorest grade best grade

You should have circled 1 and 7.

Let's look at what we've done. In a typical fourth-grade class, the range is from first to seventh grade:

average
(1) 2 3 4 5 6 (7) 8 9 10 11 12 13 14 15 16 17 18

←4−3→←4+3→

In a typical seventh-grade class, the range is from third to eleventh grade:

average
1 2 (3) 4 5 6 7 8 9 10 (11) 12 13 14 15 16 17 18

←7−4→←7+4→

In a tenth-grade class, the range is from fifth to fifteenth grade:

average
1 2 3 4 (5) 6 7 8 9 10 11 12 13 14 (15) 16 17 18

←10−5→←10+5→

And in a twelfth-grade class, the range is from about sixth to about eighteenth grade:

average
1 2 3 4 5 (6) 7 8 9 10 11 12 13 14 15 16 17 (18)

←12−5.67→←12+5.67→

Formula

The range of reading achievement in a typical class is two-thirds the median chronological age of the students:

$$\text{range in reading achievement} = 2/3\ (\text{C.A.})$$

In fact, the range may be even greater.

To find the ceiling and floor of this range, you may wish to use this formula:

$$\text{range in reading achievement} = \text{grade level} \pm \frac{\text{CA}}{3}$$

Table 1.1 Conversion of grade level to chronological age (formula: Grade + 5.2 = C.A.)

Grade	C.A.	Grade	C.A.	Grade	C.A.	Grade	C.A.
1.0	6.2	4.0	9.2	7.0	12.2	10.0	15.2
2.0	7.2	5.0	10.2	8.0	13.2	11.0	16.2
3.0	8.2	6.0	11.2	9.0	14.2	12.0	17.2

To find the chronological age, add 5 years to the grade level. If you wish to be more precise, add 5.2 *years* to the grade level, as is shown in Table 1.1. Since the chronological age of students increases from year to year, the range from low to high achievement increases as the students move upward in grade level. The approximate range of reading achievement is illustrated in Fig. 1.1.

In *School, Curriculum, and the Individual,* John I. Goodlad states:

> The broad spread from high to low achiever steadily increases with the upward movement of heterogeneous classes (relatively homogeneous in chronological age) through the school. In the intermediate grades, this spread is approximately the number of years designated by the number of the grade-level: that is, by the third grade, three years; by the fourth grade, four years; by the fifth grade,

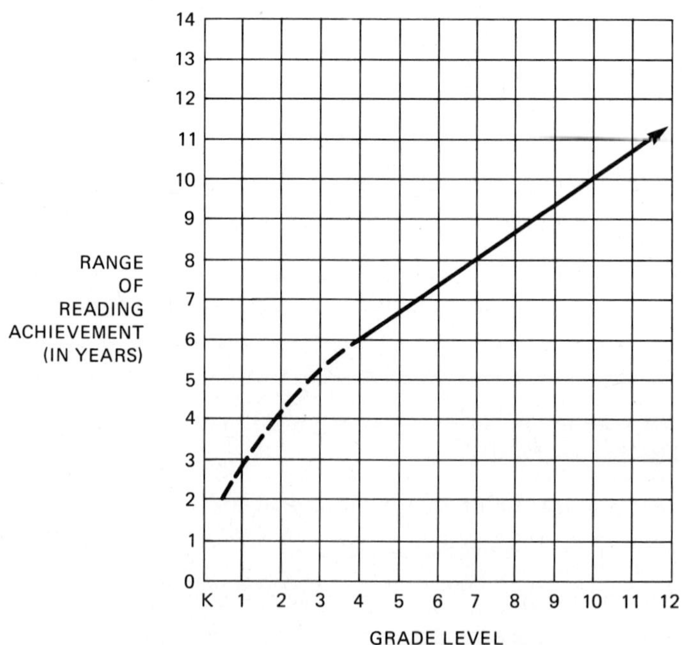

Fig. 1.1 Range of reading achievement in a typical classroom (in years).

> five years. However, since the spread in achievement accelerates slightly faster than a year-per-year of schooling, the overall range in junior high school classes is approximately two-thirds the median chronological age of the groups.
> In subject areas, such as reading and language arts, where children can readily proceed on their own in a variety of out-of-school situations, the spread from high to low achiever frequently is one and one-half to twice the number of the grade level. Hence, in the fifth grade, there frequently is an eight-year spread in reading achievement between the best and the poorest readers. Differentiation in classroom group stimuli to provide for varying levels of accomplishment does not encompass this range, but the encouragement of self-selection of materials for supplementary reading at home and school facilitates highly individualized rates of progress.*

Approximately one-third of the students will read within one to two years of their current grade level. About one-third will read more poorly than this, and one-third will read better. Thus, we often find that the distribution of reading achievement levels among students in classrooms is similar to that shown in Fig. 1.2.

By studying the chart you will notice that the poorest reader gains about two-thirds of a year in reading achievement every year while the best reader gains about twice as much—one and one-third years. Thus the actual difference between the best reader and the poorest reader increases by two-thirds of a year each year. You will also notice that there already is a sizable range in reading achievement (or potential for such achievement) when children enter school in first grade.

Discussion

A teacher should not expect all students in a class to read the same book, for students are very different cognitively, as we can see from the discussion above. Affectively, they also vary greatly—perhaps more than they do cognitively.

"Requiring" everyone in a classroom to read the same book is like expecting everyone to wear the same size shoe. If the shoe is like the glass slipper of Cinderella, it would fit but one foot in a kingdom. Similarly, obliging all students to read the same text bores some and frustrates many more.

If, however, only one textbook is available to a teacher, it must be used with discretion. Provisions must be made, especially for the poorer readers, e.g., possibly, parts of the book could be taped. This would help those students who are able to listen on a higher level than they are able to read at. Often, however, the poor readers are reading as well as they are able to listen. Their problem is one of limited thinking ability (and/or limited background of information and/or limited interests). Supplying the oral counterpart for the

* Reprinted by permission of the publisher, from John I. Goodlad, *School, Curriculum, and the Individual,* © 1966 Xerox Corporation. All rights reserved.

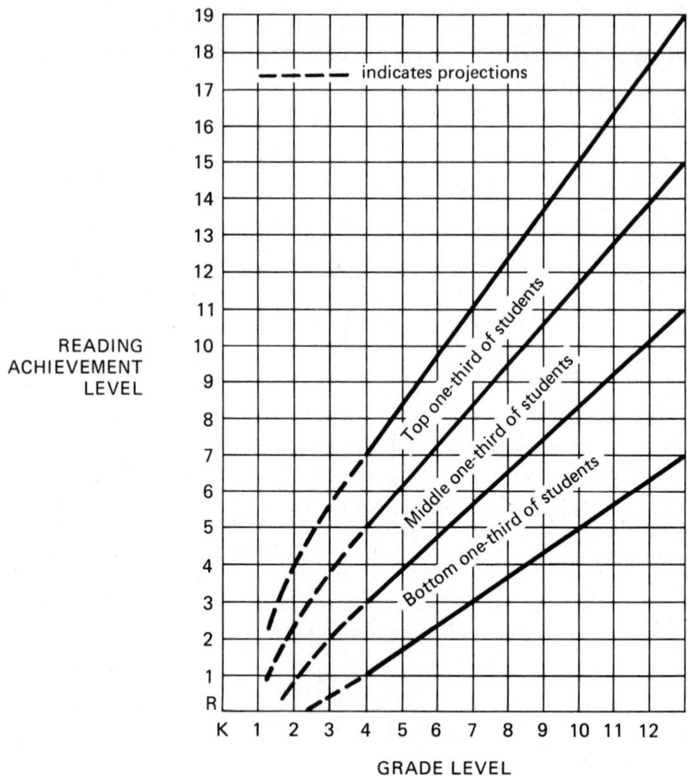

Fig. 1.2 Distribution of reading achievement levels in a typical classroom from grades 4 to 12.9.

printed symbols will not solve their problem; i.e., something other than the textbook is needed to enable them to understand the subject.

Students with normal I.Q.'s who are disabled in reading,* *per se,* however, might benefit from having the book read to them—provided their disability stems from an *oral reading or decoding problem* and not from lack of comprehension skills. This is because when they listen, only the oral counterpart is supplied to them. They still must comprehend the passage.

Some school systems have attempted to alleviate the problem by sectioning students according to reading test scores and possibly by I.Q., too. This decreases the number of levels in a classroom, but it does not eliminate levels. Even the students in the middle group are vastly different. For example, in a tenth-grade classroom, the lowest student in the middle group might be reading at the eighth- (or 8.5) grade level, and the best at the twelfth- (or 11.5) grade

* People are considered *disabled* in reading if they read well below their potential level. They are *retarded* in reading if they read below their grade-placement level.

level—still a wide range. Even two students who have the same total reading score may vary if we consider their relative scores on subtests within a battery. Of two students scoring at the tenth-grade level in reading, for example, one may score grade 8 in vocabulary; the other, grade 12. The first may score grade 10 in comprehension, and the second, grade 11. The first may score grade 12 in rate of reading, and the second, grade 7. They are very different in their reading profiles. They may also vary affectively.

Just as there is a strong trend today toward school integration—socially and racially—there is a trend toward integration academically. We have tried "homogeneous" grouping according to achievement and, at other times, according to I.Q. These techniques solve some problems and create others. Certainly, the poorer student misses much by being deprived of the challenge and activity commonly engendered by average and bright students in a heterogeneous class. Many people think that heterogeneous grouping is lifelike, for youngsters of many ability levels share common interests. There is no easy solution, but no matter how students are grouped, teachers will have to differentiate assignments within the group.

READING EXPECTANCY FOR INDIVIDUALS

At what level might we legitimately expect each student to read? Certainly not at the grade level at which the student is grouped according to chronological age, for some students far exceed that level, and others, no matter what we do, may never reach it.

The level toward which we strive depends partly on our definition of reading. If we think of reading as merely *decoding*, many children should reach the top level by the end of third grade. But if we define reading achievement in relationship to *cognition*, or intellectual development, a top level will never be reached, for our cognitive abilities continue to develop year after year.

Although far from perfect, our best measure of people's present potential for cognitive *achievement* probably is related to their *mental age*, as determined by I.Q. tests that are selected for them in relationship to their ethnic background, reading achievement (if it is a group test), and past educational opportunities. Since such tests are often impossible to find, we compromise by selecting a test that comes close to being a good one, in which case the mental age is only approximate. Or, we use the same test for all students, in which case the mental age any particular student scores might be grossly inaccurate.

Let's hypothesize that we have a good I.Q. test for a student and that the student scored 100 on it. Since an I.Q. of 95 to 105 is average, we would expect a student who scores 100 to be reading at grade level. A student whose I.Q. is above 105 should read above grade level. And it is likely that a student whose I.Q. is below 95 will be reading below grade level.

If we have a student's chronological age and I.Q., it is a simple matter to compute mental age:

$$\text{M.A.} = \frac{\text{I.Q.}}{100} \times \text{C.A.}$$

Thus, for a student whose I.Q. is 110 and whose C.A. is 14, M.A. = (110/100) × 14, or 15.4 years. For one whose I.Q. is 90 and whose C.A. is 14, M.A. = (90/100) × 14, or 12.6 years.

There are various ways of estimating how well a student should read. Writers who feel that M.A. is all-important in estimating reading expectancy recommend the use of the formula:

$$\text{reading expectancy age} = \text{M.A.}$$

This formula gives the *age* score for reading expectancy. To find the *grade* score, subtract 5.2 years from the age score:

$$\text{reading expectancy grade} = \text{M.A.} - 5.2,$$

or simply, reading expectancy grade = M.A. − 5.

Table 1.2, composed by using this formula, gives the approximate expectancy grade-level scores for students of various chronological ages and I.Q.'s. (Rounded off C.A. scores are used.)

Table 1.2 Reading expectancy scores according to I.Q. and C.A., using the formula R.E. (grade) = M.A. − 5.

Usual grade placement	C.A.	I.Q.						
		80	90	100	110	120	130	140
1.0	6.0	R*	R*	1.0	1.6†	2.2†	2.8†	3.4†
2.0	7.0	R*	1.3	2.0	2.7	3.4	4.1	4.8
3.0	8.0	1.4	2.2	3.0	3.8	4.6	5.4	6.2
4.0	9.0	2.2	3.1	4.0	4.9	5.8	6.7	7.6
5.0	10.0	3.0	4.0	5.0	6.0	7.0	8.0	9.0
6.0	11.0	3.8	4.9	6.0	7.1	8.2	9.3	10.4
7.0	12.0	4.6	5.8	7.0	8.2	9.4	10.7	11.8
8.0	13.0	5.4	6.7	8.0	9.3	10.6	12.0	13.2
9.0	14.0	6.2	7.6	9.0	10.4	11.8	13.3	14.6
10.0	15.0	7.0	8.5	10.0	11.5	13.0	14.7	
11.0	16.0	7.8	9.4	11.0	12.6	14.2		
12.0	17.0	8.6	10.3	12.0	13.7	(mature college level)		
12.99	17.99	9.4	11.2	13.0	14.8			

* R = reading readiness

† It would be unrealistic to expect untaught children to be reading at these levels upon entering school.

Harris and Sipay, in the sixth edition of *How to Increase Reading Ability,* recommend instead the use of the following formula to ascertain the expected reading level for students:

$$\text{reading expectancy age} = \frac{2\ \text{M.A.} + \text{C.A.}}{3}.$$

This formula "gives priority to the importance of intelligence, but also recognizes the presence of other age-related characteristics in reading expectancy."[1]

To find the expected reading-grade score, the following formula is used:

$$\text{reading expectancy grade} = \frac{2\ \text{M.A.} + \text{C.A.}}{3} - 5.2.$$

Table 1.3, composed by using this formula, gives the approximate expectancy grade-level scores for students of various chronological ages and I.Q.'s.

Table 1.3 Reading expectancy grade scores according to I.Q. and C.A., using the formula R.E. (grade) = [(2 M.A. + C.A.)/3] − 5.2

Usual grade placement	C.A.	I.Q.						
		80	90	100	110	120	130	140
1.0	6.2	R*	R*	1.0	1.3†	1.7†	2.2†	2.6†
2.0	7.2	1.0	1.5	2.0	2.4	2.9	3.4	3.9
3.0	8.2	1.9	2.4	3.0	3.5	4.1	4.6	5.1
4.0	9.2	2.7	3.4	4.0	4.6	5.2	5.8	6.4
5.0	10.2	3.6	4.3	5.0	5.7	6.3	7.0	7.7
6.0	11.2	4.5	5.2	6.0	6.7	7.5	8.2	8.9
7.0	12.2	5.3	6.2	7.0	7.8	8.6	9.4	10.2
8.0	13.2	6.2	7.1	8.0	8.9	9.7	10.6	11.5
9.0	14.2	7.1	8.0	9.0	10.0	10.9	11.8	12.7
10.0	15.2	7.9	9.0	10.0	11.0	12.0	13.0	14.0
11.0	16.2	8.8	9.9	11.0	12.1	13.1	14.2	
12.0	17.2	9.7	10.8	12.0	13.2	14.3		
12.99	18.19	10.5	11.8	13.0	14.3	(mature college level)		

* R = reading readiness

† It would be unrealistic to expect untaught children to be reading at these levels upon entering school.

Since such formulas are meant to offer only gross, or rough, estimates (since I.Q. tests are not perfect either), it might be wise to select one on a philosophical basis, or a best-fit basis, or use an average of the two. Some school systems have even devised their own formulas.[2]

There are hazards involved in using reading expectancy formulas or charts based on them after a student has reached the chronological age of about 15.

The reason for this is that beyond the age of about 15, mental ability no longer grows in a linear fashion. However, these charts should prove helpful if the scores are used as approximate guidelines rather than as precise expectancy scores.

If you examine these charts carefully by reading on any one horizontal line, you will see that one of the reasons for the wide range of reading achievement in a classroom—where students are grouped by chronological age—is that there is a wide range in I.Q. Therefore, a wide range in reading achievement is inevitable—if teaching is done well. However, the actual range is often wider than the expected range, considering the I.Q.'s of the students in the class. This wider range results from the interaction of a variety of factors which are not considered in such formulas. Some of these factors are facilitative, whereas others are inhibitory.

For example, excellent teaching and the use of materials appropriate to the needs and interests of a student, as well as extraordinary interest and effort on the part of the student, might very likely result in a higher reading score than expected. Additionally, success in an experience such as reading may lead to greater success. Emotional well-being, social adjustment, and an inquiring attitude may support an atmosphere for concentration, which may help improve reading achievement.

On the other hand, a variety of inhibitory factors might interact for the student who attains a lower score than expected. Such factors might be broadly classified as educational, psychological, sociological, and physiological. Restraining factors of these types are frequently found "traveling together" with reading disability; i.e., several, or many, of these factors are commonly characteristic of students who read at levels lower than expected. The presence of such factors gives the teacher clues to what may have caused the reading disability.

A brief description of those factors which are most important for the classroom teacher to be aware of is included here. It is recommended that those students who wish more information about this area study one or more of the sources cited at the end of this chapter.[3]

FACTORS THAT AFFECT READING ACHIEVEMENT

Educational Factors

Educational factors relate to the way a student has been, or is being, taught. It is extremely important for teachers and administrators to face the growing recognition that for most students, achievement depends on the kinds of materials and techniques used in the classroom and that all students do not grow optimally by using the same materials and by being taught in the same ways.

Ernest Horn in "Language and Meaning" argues:

> A single textbook is commonly provided for a grade, in spite of the incontestable evidence of the wide range of knowledge and ability in that grade . . . Investigations have repeatedly pointed out that the typical textbook, even within the limits of its potential usefulness, is much too difficult for the median child in the grade for which it is designed, and it is hopelessly difficult for the children in the lowest quarter of reading ability.*

Bond and Tinker add:

> Frequently, reading disability is largely due to educational factors. Any administrative policy which prevents proper individualization of instruction . . . will prevent effective progress in reading. Failure to acquire the necessary learnings or the acquisition of faulty learnings is most frequently due to ineffective teaching. One or more of the following factors may be involved in the ineffective teaching which brings about reading disability: too rapid progress in the instructional schedule, isolation of reading instruction from other school activities, inappropriate emphasis upon some technique or skill, or treating reading as a by-product of content studies. Frequently, the difficulty occurs because the instructional program has failed to maintain a proper balance in the growth of a large number of skills and abilities.†

Knowledgeable teachers are able to present ideas in a variety of ways, and if only a single textbook is available, they learn to use it as only one of the cores of instruction (see Chapters 4 and 11). They supplement it with paperbacks, pamphlets, magazine and newspaper articles, films and filmstrips, discussions, field trips, etc. They are aware of the kinds of thought processes and reading skills necessary for understanding the content of their courses, and these are the skills they teach their students—in the ways their students can best learn them. Doing this is not a simple task. It is the purpose of this book to help teachers and prospective teachers improve such undertakings.

Some perspectives on the situation

Fourth-grade teachers have for many years been aware of the fact that for some children the transition from the primary grades to the upper-elementary grades has been extremely difficult. Many primary level reading programs focus on "learning to read"; whereas programs above that level often focus on "reading to learn."

---

* Ernest Horn. "Language and Meaning," in *The Forty-First Yearbook of the National Society for the Study of Education Part II, The Psychology of Learning.* Chicago: University of Chicago Press, 1942, p. 390. Reprinted by permission.

† From *Reading Difficulties: Their Diagnosis and Correction,* 2d ed., p. 146. Guy L. Bond and Miles A. Tinker. Copyright © 1967. By permission of Appleton-Century-Crofts, Educational Division, Meredith Corporation.

Many primary level reading programs are designed to teach specific reading skills, for example, sight vocabulary, phonics, reading for detail, main idea, etc. Frequently, such skills are taught in isolation with materials that are designed for the purpose of teaching a specific skill or skills. Skills are sometimes taught in small parcels: a page or two for initial *b*, a page for following directions, a page for main idea, a page or two for syllabication of words spelled with the pattern vowel-consonant-consonant-vowel (tur-key, jour-nal, es-tablish), etc. Children who succeed in such activities in the primary grades and who have not had the advantage of working with a teacher or teachers who integrate the teaching of reading with the teaching of content are frequently unable to cope with the requirements in many upper-grade classes.

Teachers at levels above the primary grades usually feel that one of their major responsibilities is the teaching of content. In the present author's opinion, it is unfortunate that more primary level teachers do not feel this way. In most cases there need be no dichotomy between the teaching of reading skills and the teaching of content. Each should reinforce the other. There are, of course, some instances when a reading skill, *per se*, might be taught, but usually the teaching of a skill can be integrated with the teaching of an idea which is of interest and value to the child. Or, the teaching of a reading skill can grow from the need to have that skill in order to understand ideas. (A swimming instructor might decide to teach children to do the breaststroke because the children want to learn this stroke or because the instructor feels learning the breaststroke is the next step in the children's swimming sequence. The instructor, then, might teach children as they cling to the side of a pool to do the frog kick—over and over until they succeed. But the instructor rarely stops there. An all-important step is to teach the youngsters to integrate the frog kick with the arm stroke. It is not until the leg and arm strokes are synthesized, as well as the proper breathing is learned, that the child is swimming. So, too, in reading. Skill performance in isolation is not reading, though it may be a step toward reading.)

Children may be promoted to the fourth grade having succeeded in achieving the goals of their primary reading program. These goals in some school systems may be the simple attainment of specific reading skills—unrelated or minimally related to the utilization of these skills when reading for content demands their use. Therefore, if the higher-level teachers are to succeed in continuing the education of children, these teachers will have to teach the children to utilize and synthesize appropriate skills when reading for content. Additionally, middle grade and secondary level teachers must extend and refine the teaching of reading skills necessary for understanding content as the children mature in their ability to use such skills. (The swimming instructor does not stop when a child can merely do the breaststroke. The swimming teacher proceeds to teach style and speed, relaxation, the resting backstroke, and the butterfly stroke, as well as alternate strokes, rhythm, water ballet, etc.)

To help middle grade and secondary level teachers better understand the reading backgrounds of children with whom they are working, the following brief description of commonly used approaches to reading in the primary grades is offered.

Approaches to the teaching of reading

Basal reader approach

Basal readers are carefully graded texts designed to be used in the teaching of reading from the pre-primer level (beginning first grade) through sixth grade or even higher. Usually the size of the vocabulary in these books is controlled, with the introduction of a specified number of new words at each level.

The *Teacher's Manual*, which accompanies each basal reader, contains specific instructions for teaching each lesson. Ideas for supplementing the lessons are also included. Additionally, supplementary workbooks for skill development are frequently available.

Extensive studies indicate that at least 95% of primary teachers use basal readers regularly in the teaching of reading. They may use a single text for a whole class, either keeping the class together day by day or pacing the children differently—i.e., having all use the same books but some moving through them more readily than others. Other teachers use a bi-basal or tri-basal program. That is, they use two or three different basal series (usually from two or three different publishing companies). They place each student in the book best suited to his or her reading achievement level.

In the past, basal readers have been criticized because of their limited vocabularies, their narrow range in content, their stereotyping of cultures—both middle class and others, including sex stereotyping—and their almost too systematic attention to the development of specific reading skills.

Although reading experts for many years have deplored round-robin, or circle, reading, saying it was "for the birds" and not for children, this technique persists in classrooms in which basals are used. Thus, children who "learn to read" using the basal approach frequently have been subjected to a great deal of oral reading of the worst type and learn simplistic ideas because of the limited concept load of these books.

It is of utmost importance now to note that many of the newer basals appear to include much more interesting and varied content than the older texts as well as more extensive vocabularies.

Individualized reading approach

Key words for individualized reading are *seeking, self-selection,* and *pacing*: Children *seek* their own interests, *select* their own materials, and *pace* themselves. That is, they decide what they would like to read about (seeking).

From the materials made available to them, they decide which they would like to read (self-selection). And they decide how few or how many they would like to read (pacing).

A wide variety of materials must be available in the classroom. Recommendations run from a minimum of from three to ten books per child. Individual conferences with the teacher on a regular basis are essential, for the teacher's job is to promote growth in taste, diversity and/or intensity of interests, and skill development. The skills taught children are ideally those that they need to understand the materials selected. Such skill development may be accomplished in small group sessions. But all children in the group are there because the need for that skill has arisen from their need or desire to understand the materials selected individually.

For some teachers, record keeping becomes a chore. Many teachers feel inadequately prepared to design individual programs for children. Yet they see distinct advantages in allowing children to read widely. Frequently teachers decide to use a basic program (such as a basal reader program) for skill development and supplement it with individualized (or personalized) reading.

Language experience approach

The language experience approach integrates all of the language arts areas: speaking, listening, reading, and writing. In the beginning stages, the child dictates words, sentences, or short stories to the teacher, who in turn writes them down for the child to read. Thus, the child learns to read what he or she was interested enough in to talk about. Children also talk with one another, share ideas, and dictate stories in groups. They learn to read stories other children have dictated, and in time they learn to write their own stories and read them to the class.

Children normally learn to read sentences before they read individual words. For example, a child may dictate:

I saw a spider on the way to school.

The teacher writes the whole sentence, as above, and reads it with the child. The teacher points from left to right as the child reads the sentence. The teacher makes another copy of the sentence and cuts it into word groups, or phrases, thus:

I saw		a spider
on the way		to school.

The cards are shuffled, and the child learns to place them in order, from left to right. Next the cards are cut so that only one word is on each card. They are shuffled, and the child learns to place them in order from left to right:

I	saw	a	spider	on	the	way	to	school.

Next, the child could learn to substitute words for "I," e.g., the names of the children in his or her class:

Mary saw a spider . . .
John saw a spider . . .
Juanita saw a spider . . .
etc.

And words could be substituted for "spider," e.g., dog, cat, robin, etc.

Elaborations could be added, e.g., *black* spider, *grey* spider, *black widow* spider, etc.

And phonic elements might be taught, e.g., initial "s":

I saw a spider . . .
a s________ . . .
sparrow . . .
squirrel . . .

From such small beginnings, the language experience approach can lead into a full-range reading, writing, speaking, and listening program. Many consider it to be especially useful with culturally different children for whom reading materials of interest are difficult to find. Others criticize it because they feel it limits children to learning to read what they and their peers have experienced. Many combine the use of language experience with other approaches to the teaching of reading.

Linguistic approaches

Various linguistic approaches are used in the teaching of reading. These approaches appear to fall into three major schools: phonology, structure, and psycholinguistics. Those programs that deal with *phonology* deal with sound-symbol relations, but normally avoid the teaching of phonics. Often an alphabetic, or spelling, approach is used, with minimal contrasts to teach "patterns." For example, c-a-t → /cat/, r-a-t → /rat/, f-a-t → /fat/; or the opposite: /cat/ → c-a-t, /rat/ → r-a-t, /fat/ → f-a-t, etc.

Structuralists usually teach using a sentence as a unit. They may choose a specific sentence pattern, e.g., noun-verb (NV), to teach thus:

John runs.	The boy is running.
_____ runs.	The ____ is running.
Mary runs.	The girl is running.
Joan runs.	The dog is running.
________	________
John runs.	The boy is running.
John ___s.	The boy is ____ing.
John sings.	The boy is singing.
John reads.	The boy is reading.
etc.	etc.

In addition, they stress other areas of syntax, e.g., *signal words* (i.e., words that signal, or mark, a structural element such as a noun phrase, verb phrase, prepositional phrase, clause, or question); *word form* changes (e.g., runs → is running, sing → sang, etc.); and *intonation.*

Psycholinguists deal with the psychology of language, the acquisition of language by children, and the thought processes underlying the use of language and growing from the use of language.

Operant conditioning approaches

Programed learning may be used in the teaching of reading at all levels. A task is broken into minute steps, each step is explained, and the learner reacts to a direction and receives immediate reinforcement or correction. *Learning modules* may be used, set up with definite instructions to be followed. *Kits,* or *boxes,* of materials designed to teach specific skills are widely used in the teaching of reading. Also, *criterion referenced* approaches are used. Children's levels of skill development in reading may be assessed, their areas of weakness identified, and materials supplied to them to help them improve in a needed subskill.

Modified orthographic approaches

The use of modified alphabets was widely researched in the 1960s. The *Initial Teaching Alphabet,* known as I.T.A. or i/t/a, utilizes 44 lower-case symbols, presumably one for each phoneme in English. *Unifon* utilizes 40 upper-case symbols. *Words in Color* uses a different color for each of the 44 sounds, but the spelling used is traditional (the 26 letters). Ed Fry's *Diacritical Marking System* utilizes diacritical marks to indicate pronunciation in the text of the reading.

Surely English would be easier to decode if our system were almost completely phonetic. These new alphabets added interest and spice to reading research and could be used with any approach. Yet, the awful truth is that somewhere along the way people who are going to read English have to learn to read it as it's written—with 26 letters. The question is, should they learn the truth in their first attempts to read or later?[4]

Psychological Factors

Among the psychological factors which may affect reading achievement are intelligence, degree and range of interest, emotional and personal adjustment, the student's self-image and the self-fulfilling prophecy, and visual and auditory perception.

Intelligence

Educators are becoming increasingly critical of the use of a single criterion (such as I.Q. or M.A.) to judge the expected level of achievement for youngsters. Because of repeated problems in I.Q. testing—among which are the selection of an appropriate I.Q. test for individual children, the state of health or motivation of the child during the testing period, and the experiential background of the child—it is becoming more and more suspect to rely heavily on one score or type of score in estimating potential for learning.

Although many educators give some consideration to the I.Q. score a student may receive on a test or tests, they also consider other factors in estimating potential for learning. Among these factors are teacher judgment, the professional judgment of other school and nonschool personnel, and even (or especially) the child's own judgment. (The present author has often taken into her special reading classes students whose scores on I.Q. tests indicated no undeveloped potential in relation to reading achievement. These students were eager to read better. Their gain scores in reading achievement were normally comparable to the gains made by students who were invited to take a reading course because of a discrepancy between measured potential and reading performance.)[5]

To do well in a group intelligence test usually requires good reading ability. Poor readers, who cannot read the questions, cannot display their intelligence. When group intelligence tests are given to poor readers, these children are labeled low in intelligence. Thus, they have low *measured* I.Q.'s, and we expect them to read at low levels according to our reading expectancy formulas. A vicious circle is in operation.

A poor reader should be given an individual intelligence test, such as the Stanford-Binet, the WISC (Wechsler Intelligence Scale for Children), or the WAIS (Wechsler Adult Intelligence Scale). Even such tests measure certain reading abilities and many language abilities which may be attained through reading. Also, for culturally different children, the items in general may provide for an unfair evaluation of their potential.

I.Q. testing is fraught with hazards, especially for the poor reader and the culturally different student. Yet for the middle-class student who is an average or good reader, we may have no better gauge of potential at the present time. It would be wise for teachers to be extremely cautious and avoid overreliance on I.Q. test scores.[6] Yet, it may be well to recognize that "intellectually handicapped children are not disabled readers when they read about as well as their intelligence permits."[7]

One of the better substitutes for I.Q. testing to estimate student potential in a classroom situation is explained in Chapter 3 under the heading "Standardized Reading-Listening Tests" and in the discussion of "Capacity Level" as part of the informal reading inventory.

Interests

Interest is probably as important a factor in reading achievement as is intelligence. Most people strive to do a good job of what they enjoy or are interested in. Some people put forth little effort if they do not see an immediate reward. Daniel Fader's *Hooked on Books: Program and Proof* describes this point of view.[8] G. Robert Carlsen's *Books and the Teen-Age Reader* gives many helpful ideas about the natural interests of middle grade and secondary school students and ways of capitalizing on them.[9] Chapter 4 of the present book is devoted to assessing the interests of students in content-related materials.

Emotional, personality, and perceptual problems

A thorough discussion of emotional, personality, and perceptual problems which may inhibit reading growth is beyond the scope of this book. Yet certainly the importance of such problems should not be underemphasized. Many excellent sources are available which contain discussions of these factors. The interested student is advised to begin by reading the references suggested in note 3 at the end of this chapter.

Brief note might, however, be taken here of some of the different types of emotional problems that have been found to be contributory factors in reading disability according to Albert J. Harris and Edward R. Sipay.[10] They are:

1. *conscious refusal to learn.* The child may refuse to learn because he or she may be imitating an admired parent who shows contempt for "book learning." (Even Robert Maynard Hutchins, former Chancellor of the University of Chicago and originator of The Great Books Club, said that he failed mathematics as a matter of "family pride." His father had regularly failed mathematics.) Children may also refuse to learn because of hostility toward parents or teachers or because of hostility toward the cultural values of either.

2. *displacement of hostility.* The child may be jealous of a brother or sister who is a good reader, and this hostility may be transferred to the act of reading, the sibling's strong point. Similarly, a child may be unable to express hostility in an open fashion toward a parent who is an avid reader and believes reading to be important, and may instead express this hostility by refusing to learn to read.

3. *clinging to dependency.* The overprotected child may prefer to remain helpless. Learning to read may suggest to this child self-reliance, a step for which the child may not be ready. To some children success is dangerous.

4. *extreme distractability or restlessness.* The child may be restless and easily

distracted, perhaps because of neurological deviation or because of the need for physical activity.

5. *absorption in a private world.* The child may be preoccupied with concerns beyond the school or with daydreams. According to Harris, "Some of these children, who seem merely to be inattentive so far as the teacher is concerned, are found to have severe mental disturbances. . . ."

The self-fulfilling prophecy

A great deal has been written recently about what is sometimes called "Pygmalion in education" or the "self-fulfilling prophecy." Such books and articles merit the attention of educators.

There appears to be some controversy about the effect of notifying teachers that some students may be "late bloomers" or of predicting "academic blooming" in the near future. In most cases, students who supposedly are to "bloom" are randomly selected. Teachers are notified to expect "great things" from these students, and teachers apparently sometimes do observe and promote greater growth among these randomly selected students than among the unselected ones.[11]

Of major concern to educators should be the school's role in promoting equal opportunity for all children and young people. Perhaps the most vile kind of segregation is that which occurs *within* the classroom, not among classrooms or among schools.

Teachers, like people in general, are saddled with their own biases, prejudices, and value systems. From kindergarten and first grade on, children become victims or benefactors of these biases. Thus teachers may group youngsters in kindergarten or first grade according to the degree to which each child approximates (or fails to approximate) the teacher's "ideal type" and give preferential treatment to youngsters who are most like this "ideal type." Teachers may designate these children as "fast learners" (and others as "slow learners"), may give the favored children more of their time and attention, and may reward their behaviors in positive ways (and reward the other children's behaviors in negative ways).

Children in kindergarten and first grade may thus be grouped on the basis of the father's and/or mother's occupation, the neatness and variety of clothing, grooming of hair and body, ease of interaction with adults, degree of verbalization in Standard American English, and anything else that relates to the teacher's model of the "ideal type" of child.

Children thus grouped soon "learn their place" because of the differential treatment of the teacher toward the groups and of the children in the favored group toward the children in the less favored groups.

If such treatment persists from September to May of the child's first year in school, it frequently continues into successive years—where the next teachers continue to use similar grouping patterns. Also, the children have learned what to expect from themselves and their peers. Thus the teacher's prophecy is frequently fulfilled.* The dye is cast at a very tender age!

Sociological Factors

Students' attitudes toward ideas frequently reflect their family and community background. As explained in greater detail in Chapter 4, people tend to choose reading materials that agree with their point of view. Only the more sophisticated reader will choose to read and consider conflicting ideas.

Also, attitudes toward reading itself often reflect the student's background. Children whose parents rarely read are likely to read little themselves, and such limited reading experience leads to a limited background of experiences and information and possibly to limited aspirations.[12]

The linguistic range of a student is to a great extent dependent on both sociological and educational factors. Many culturally different children get a poor start in school because their home or community language differs from that used in the school.[13]

Physical Factors

Physical factors may also interact and/or be part of the constellation of inhibiting characteristics commonly found in disabled readers. The three physical factors considered here are vision, hearing, and lateral dominance.

Vision

At the present time, the relationship between specific eye defects and reading disability has not been established. Both good and poor readers have been found to have visual defects, although a greater proportion of poor readers often have certain types of defects.

Present research seems to suggest that visual defects alone may not cause severe reading disability, but that when certain visual defects appear along with other inhibiting factors, reading disability may be present. Possibly, visual defects may handicap good readers also, but they are able to compensate for them.

In light of the importance of conserving vision for all, however, care should be taken to protect the eyes of all. Teachers should watch for signs of visual discomfort: rubbing the eyes, excessive blinking, red or swollen eyes, reports of headaches or fatigue resulting from reading, etc. Vision should be checked to determine if certain types of defects appear to be present. Defects that may

---

* See Ray C. Rist. "Student Social Class and Teacher Expectations: The Self-Fulfilling Prophecy in Ghetto Education," in *Harvard Educational Review,* **40** (August 1970): 411–451.

affect reading achievement are *hyperopia, extreme myopia, poor binocular coordination,* and *poor fusion.*[14]

A person who is *hyperopic* (far-sighted) has poor near-point acuity and therefore will find it difficult to see sharp images when reading a book. A person with *extreme myopia* (near-sightedness) may have to hold a book too close to the eyes for physical comfort, and will have difficulty reading the board.

Normally, the two eyes are used together in reading. If the two eyes do not focus simultaneously on the same object, the image may be blurred. Also, the eye lenses must focus with precision on an object if the images seen by the two eyes are to fuse so that only one object is seen.

Unfortunately, the visual test used most frequently by schools, the Snellen Test, will screen out only those students who have myopia. Students with hyperopia normally pass the test, as do students with binocular defects.

The following tests are better for screening these other types of defects:

Massachusetts Vision Test
AO School Vision Screening Test
Keystone Visual Survey Test
Ortho-Rater.[15]

Hearing

Poor hearing may be a contributing factor in reading disability for several reasons. *First,* children normally learn to speak through listening; hence, both the vocabulary and sentence patterns of a person who hears poorly are likely to be inadequate. *Second,* children may be taught to read through an oral approach. Those who cannot hear well cannot auditorily perceive differences in sounds and, therefore, may not learn to read well. *Third,* students of any age who cannot hear well cannot benefit from class discussions, nor can they follow directions given orally by the teacher.

Students who are hard of hearing frequently are not aware that they hear any differently from other students, as they have no standard against which to judge. It is extremely important for students to hear well in school and, therefore, the teacher should be alert to detect any signs of hearing loss, such as inattentiveness, poor pronunciation, frequent misunderstanding of simple directions, turning one ear toward the speaker, etc.

Frequently, the results of an *audiometer* test are available to the teacher and may be found in the student's cumulative folder. According to Harris and Sipay, "a hearing loss of over 25 decibels is almost certain to handicap a child in hearing in classroom situations and is usually accompanied by some indistinctness in speech."[16] A student who exhibits a significant hearing loss should be advised to seek professional help. In the meantime, the student should sit close to the teacher.

Lateral dominance

Most people have a dominant *eye,* a dominant *hand,* and a dominant *leg.* To find which of your eyes is dominant, form a cone with an 8½″ × 11″ sheet of paper. Put a penny on the floor, stand up and hold the cone at arm's length, and look through the *top* of the cone at the penny. Be sure *both* of your eyes are open. First, close your right eye. Do you still see the penny through the cone? If so, you're probably *left-eyed* (for your left eye was open). Then close your left eye. Do you see the penny? If so, you're *right-eyed* (probably). I say probably, because you may go home tonight and repeat the test with the opposite results, in which case, you may have *incomplete eye dominance,* i.e., sometimes the right eye is dominant and sometimes the left.

A. J. Harris, in *The Harris Test of Lateral Dominance,* delineates other tests for eye dominance, hand dominance, and foot dominance.[17]

Many people are dominant on one side of their body. That is, their right eye is dominant, their right hand, and their right leg—or their left eye, left hand, and left leg. By *crossed dominance* we mean that the dominant hand and eye are on opposite sides. By *incomplete dominance* we mean that a person shows nearly equal use of both sides, in either hand or eye dominance.[18]

The concept of lateral dominance has intrigued some reading researchers, who see in it an explanation for *strephosymbolia* (twisted symbols—mirrored vision) or for excessive regressions. It is theorized that people who are right-sided, especially right-eyed, use the left hemisphere of their brain for memory traces for printed words. People who are left-sided, or left-eyed, by contrast, use the right hemisphere of the brain. It is thought that people who have incomplete or mixed dominance, however, may at times see mirror images or twisted symbols, for they may use the left side of the brain at one time and the right side at another. Alas, the theories are intriguing, but accumulated empirical evidence suggests that theories of lateral dominance explain but little in reading disability.

SUMMARY

At first glance, the *range of reading achievement* in the typical classroom seems unbelievably vast. The difference between the reading level of the poorest and the best reader in a classroom where students are grouped principally according to their chronological ages is described by the formula

$$\text{range in reading achievement} = 2/3\ (\text{C.A.}).$$

As children grow older, the range increases—if teaching is done well. Such a range indicates the need for reading materials at many levels.

Reading expectancy for individual students is usually related to their mental ability. The brighter student is expected to read at a higher level than is the average student, and the average student is expected to read at a higher level than is a student with a low I.Q. Several formulas are currently in use for computing the reading expectancy levels of individual students. Two of these are:

$$\text{reading expectancy grade} = \frac{2\ \text{M.A.} + \text{C.A.}}{3} - 5.2$$

and

$$\text{reading expectancy grade} = \text{M.A.} - 5\ (\text{or M.A.} - 5.2).$$

A major problem in using any of these formulas is getting a valid and reliable I.Q. (or M.A.) score, especially for poor readers and culturally different students. Usually, the scored I.Q.'s (or M.A.'s) of these students are vast underestimates of their true potential.

Factors of various types are frequently found to relate to good or poor reading. Such factors can be broadly classified as educational, psychological, sociological, and physiological.

NOTES

1 Albert J. Harris and Edward R. Sipay. *How to Increase Reading Ability,* 6th ed. New York: David McKay, 1975, p. 152.

2 See George D. Spache. "Estimating Reading Capacity," in *The Evaluation of Reading,* ed. Helen M. Robinson, Supplementary Educational Monographs, No. 88. Chicago: The University of Chicago Press, 1958, pp. 15–20.

3 Guy L. Bond and Miles A. Tinker, *op. cit.,* Chapters 4, 5, and 6; Albert J. Harris and Edward R. Sipay, *op. cit.,* Chapters 10, 11, and 12; Theodore L. Harris, Wayne Otto, and Thomas C. Barrett. "Summary and Review of Investigations Related to Reading." *Journal of Educational Research,* February or March yearly, final article: May-June, 1974; Wayne Otto and Richard McMenemy. *Corrective and Remedial Teaching: Principles and Practices.* Boston: Houghton Mifflin, 1966, Chapters 2, 3, and 4; Wayne Otto and Karl Koenke. *Remedial Teaching: Research and Comment.* Boston: Houghton Mifflin, 1969; Helen M. Robinson. *Why Pupils Fail in Reading.* Chicago: University of Chicago Press, 1946; Leo M. Schell and Paul C. Burns. *Remedial Reading: An Anthology of Sources.* Boston: Allyn and Bacon, 1968, Parts 2 and 3; Miles V. Zintz. *Corrective Reading.* Dubuque, Iowa: Wm. C. Brown Co., 1966, Chapter 1; George Spache. *Investigating the Issues of Reading Disabilities.* Boston: Allyn and Bacon, 1976.

4 Numerous references are available on the subject of approaches to reading at the primary level. E.g., Robert C. Aukerman. *Approaches to Beginning Reading.* New York: John Wiley and Sons, 1971. For a general discussion, see George D. Spache

and Evelyn B. Spache. *Reading in the Elementary School.* Boston: Allyn and Bacon, 1973, pp. 39–140.

5 See Bob W. Jerrolds, Byron Callaway, and Wayne Gwaltney. "A Comparative Study of Three Tests of Intellectual Potential, Three Tests of Reading Achievement, and the Discrepancy Scores Between Potential and Achievement." *The Journal of Educational Research,* **65,** No. 4 (December 1971): 168–172.

6 See George D. Spache. "Estimating Reading Capacity," *op. cit.* Also in Schell and Burns, *op. cit.,* pp. 115–121.

7 George D. Spache. *Toward Better Reading.* Champaign, Illinois: Garrard, 1963, p. 117.

8 Daniel Fader and Elton McNeil. *Hooked on Books: Program and Proof.* New York: Berkeley, 1968.

9 G. Robert Carlsen. *Books and the Teen-Age Reader.* New York: Bantam, 1972.

10 Harris and Sipay, *op. cit.,* pp. 300–305.

11 See Robert Rosenthal and Lenore Jacobson. *Pygmalion in the Classroom: Teacher Expectation and Pupil's Intellectual Development.* New York: Holt, Rinehart and Winston, 1968; Ray C. Rist. "Student Social Class and Teacher Expectations: The Self-Fulfilling Prophecy in Ghetto Education," in *Harvard Educational Review,* **40,** No. 3 (August 1970): 411–451; also Jean José and John J. Cody. "Teacher-Pupil Interaction as It Relates to Attempted Changes in Teacher Expectancy of Academic Ability and Achievement," in *American Educational Research Journal,* **8,** No. 1 (January 1971): 40–49. There are numerous other sources.

12 See "Reading Problems" (Part II), in *Improving Reading Ability Around the World,* ed. D. K. Bracken and E. Malmquist. Newark, Delaware: International Reading Association, 1971.

13 See Martin Deutsch. "The Role of Social Class in Language Development and Cognition." *American Journal of Orthopsychiatry* (January 1964): 78–88; *Language Programs for the Disadvantaged.* Report of the NCTE Task Force on Teaching English to the Disadvantaged. Champaign, Illinois: National Council of Teachers of English, 1965; *Language, Reading, and the Communication Process,* ed. Carl Braun. Newark, Delaware: International Reading Association, 1971; *Language and the Higher Thought Processes,* ed. Russell Stauffer. Champaign, Illinois: National Council of Teachers of English, 1965.

14 See Fred W. Jobe. *Screening Vision in Schools.* Newark, Delaware: International Reading Association, 1976; and Helen M. Robinson and C. B. Huelsman. "Visual Efficiency and Progress in Learning to Read," in *Clinical Studies in Reading,* II, Supplementary Educational Monographs, No. 77. Chicago: University of Chicago Press, 1953, pp. 31–63.

15 Massachusetts Vision Test and AO School Screening Test, from American Optical Co., Southern, Mass. Keystone Visual Survey Test, from Keystone View Co., Meadville, Pa. Ortho-Rater, from Bausch and Lomb Optical Co., Rochester, N.Y.

16 Albert J. Harris and Edward R. Sipay, *op. cit.,* p. 288.

17 *Harris Tests of Lateral Dominance.* New York: Psychological Corp.; 1955.

18 After Albert J. Harris and Edward R. Sipay, *op. cit.,* p. 270. You may wish to see pp. 269–281 for a thorough discussion of lateral dominance.

SUGGESTED ACTIVITIES

1. Below are listed reading-grade-level scores obtained from standardized tests given to 24 students in each of four different classes. Tell whether the range in reading achievement in each class is typical, broader, or narrower than usual.

   grade 4 scores: 2.1, 7.6, 3.5, 4.0, 4.1, 4.5, 3.2, 3.8, 2.7, 6.5, 1.9, 1.0, 1.2, 4.0, 6.1, 5.1, 5.7, 5.4, 4.2, 4.2, 4.4, 4.3, 3.7, 3.6

   grade 7 scores: 7.3, 7.1, 6.5, 2.3, 5.7, 8.4, 1.9, 3.2, 9.2, 10.5, 12.3, 12.2, 11.0, 8.1, 4.8, 9.7, 6.7, 5.1, 3.4, 8.5, 11.3, 7.0, 6.6, 7.9

   grade 9 scores: 9.6, 8.5, 7.2, 11.7, 13.8, 4.0, 9.2, 9.2, 8.6, 12.4, 13.5, 6.2, 8.5, 9.6, 7.7, 5.1, 12.3, 11.1, 6.5, 7.2, 4.8, 8.9, 9.1, 9.3

   grade 12 scores: 11.5, 12.8, 9.2, 10.5, 12.1, 13.5, 10.0, 11.7, 16.5, 14.1, 15.2, 10.7, 12.2, 12.4, 11.5, 13.4, 11.1, 12.7, 9.2, 8.1, 5.9, 6.4, 11.8, 12.0

2. Using the following data, indicate the expected reading-grade level for each student according to both the Harris and Sipay criteria and the Simple M.A. criteria.

   a) C.A. = 13.7, M.A. = 13.8   b) C.A. = 13.5, I.Q. = 120
   c) C.A. = 15.2, M.A. = 10.9   d) C.A. = 12.2, I.Q. = 90
   e) C.A. = 9.0, M.A. = 10.2   f) C.A. = 10.2, I.Q. = 130

3 Using the following information, write a brief hypothetical case study for each student, indicating factors which might have interacted to affect the reading-achievement score of each student.

   a) Alan Young, Jr. : C.A. = 14.2, I.Q. = 130, R.G. = 11.8
   b) Juan Gonzalez : C.A. = 9.5, I.Q. = 100, R.G. = 3.1
   c) Tanya K. Onassis : C.A. = 11.3, M.A. = 13.1, R.G. = 5.2
   d) Betty Kissinger : C.A. = 13.0, M.A. = 14.6, R.G. = 9.7
   e) Ray Smith : C.A. = 15.4, I.Q. = 90, R.G. = 6.1

REFERENCES FOR FURTHER READING

Aukerman, Robert C. *Approaches to Beginning Reading.* New York: John Wiley and Sons, 1971.

Bond, Guy L. and Miles A. Tinker. *Reading Difficulties: Their Diagnosis and Correction.* New York: Appleton-Century-Crofts, 1957, Chapter 4, Part 2.

Dechant, Emerald V. *Improving the Teaching of Reading.* Englewood Cliffs, N.J.: Prentice-Hall, 1970, Chapters 3 and 4.

Deutsch, Martin. "The Role of Social Class in Language Development and Cognition." *American Journal of Orthopsychiatry* (January 1964): 78–88.

Goodlad, John I. *School, Curriculum, and the Individual.* Waltham, Mass.: Blaisdell (Ginn), 1966.

Harris, Albert J. and Edward R. Sipay. *How to Increase Reading Ability,* 6th ed. New York: David McKay, 1975, Chapters 10, 11, and 12.

Harris, Theodore L., Wayne Otto, and Thomas C. Barrett. "Summary and Review of Investigations Relating to Reading." *Journal of Educational Research.* February or March yearly to 1973; May-June 1974.

Jerrolds, Bob W., Byron Callaway, and Wayne Gwaltney. "A Comparative Study of Three Tests of Intellectual Potential, Three Tests of Reading Achievement, and the Discrepancy Scores Between Potential and Achievement." *Journal of Educational Research,* **65,** No. 4 (December 1971): 168–172.

Jobe, Fred W. *Screening Vision in Schools.* Newark, Delaware: International Reading Association, 1976.

Otto, Wayne and Richard McMenemy. *Corrective and Remedial Teaching.* Boston: Houghton Mifflin, 1966, Chapter 2.

Otto, Wayne and Richard J. Smith. *Administering the School Reading Program.* Boston: Houghton Mifflin, 1970.

Rist, Ray C. "Student Social Class and Teacher Expectations: The Self-Fulfilling Prophecy in Ghetto Education." *Harvard Educational Review,* **40,** No. 3 (August 1970): 441–451.

Robinson, Helen M. *Why Pupils Fail in Reading.* Chicago: University of Chicago Press, 1946.

Robinson, Helen and C. B. Huelsman. "Visual Efficiency and Progress in Learning to Read," in *Clinical Studies in Reading,* II, Supplementary Educational Monographs, No. 77. Chicago: University of Chicago Press, 1953, pp. 31–63.

Schell, Leo M. and Paul C. Burns (eds.). *Remedial Reading: An Anthology of Sources.* Boston: Allyn and Bacon, 1968, Parts Two and Three.

Shafer, Robert E. "Will Psycholinguistics Change Reading in Secondary Schools?" *Journal of Reading,* **21,** No. 4 (January 1978): 305–316.

Spache, George D. *Investigating the Issues of Reading Disability.* Boston: Allyn and Bacon, 1976.

Strang, Ruth. *The Diagnostic Teaching of Reading.* New York: McGraw-Hill, 1969. Chapters 8, 9, and 11.

Zintz, Miles V. *The Reading Process.* Dubuque, Iowa: Wm. C. Brown Co., 1970.

Chapter 2

JUDGING THE DIFFICULTY OF READING MATERIALS

What factors make printed materials easy or difficult to read?

How do we measure the difficulty of printed materials?

FACTORS THAT INFLUENCE THE DIFFICULTY OF PRINTED MATERIALS

A variety of factors, within both the reader and the printed materials, and the interaction of such factors, account for the difficulty or ease with which a reader can understand written materials. What are some of these factors?

Think of the last time you read something purely for pleasure. Did the zest with which you approached the activity help make it easy for you to understand the material? Did you read something in an area in which you are well versed? If so, your background of information about the subject helped make the printed material readable to you. On the other hand, if you chose to read something foreign to your background, chances are that it was a little harder going, for as you were reading, you came across vocabulary new to you and concepts that took time and effort to assimilate. However, your interest in the ideas helped to carry you along.

Think of other times when you have read, not because you especially wanted to, but because you had to. A basic lack of motivation may have made an assignment difficult for you to understand and remember.

Certainly, the interest that readers bring to the material—their affective involvement—as well as their background of information as it relates to the content of the material are of vital importance in their ability to read the material. For example, an English major may be able to read difficult classical literature but be unable to read a freshman text in physics. A potential high school dropout may be fascinated by *Popular Mechanics* and may understand the contents well; yet may be unable—or unwilling—to read a simple novel. We know that students can and will read difficult (for them) materials if they are vitally interested in them, whereas other materials objectively judged to be at the same readability level may be completely frustrating to them.

Psycholinguistic factors also affect the difficulty level of materials for specific readers. Is the reader familiar with the language patterns used by the writer, e.g., phrasing and syntax, semantics, and the paragraph, chapter, and book organization?

Linguistic factors related to syntax which seem important in readability are sentence patterns and intonation clues. Normal subject-to-predicate patterns (Hortense arrived late) are probably easier to read than are transformations of these patterns (Late arrived Hortense). Sentences in which the oral intonation patterns are clear are easier to read and understand than are those in which the intonation patterns are ambiguous: (*Bob* didn't catch the fish. Bob *didn't* catch the fish. Bob didn't *catch* the fish. Bob didn't catch *the* fish. Bob didn't catch the *fish.*)[1]

Semantics, or word meaning, also needs consideration. What makes a word easy or difficult to read and understand? Is word length a factor? Are multiple or remote meanings a factor? Are denotations easier to understand than connotations?

How are paragraphs organized? What types of headings does the author use? (Has the reader formed the habit of studying headings?) What kinds of illustrations, if any, are used? Do they add to, or subtract from, the intended meanings? (Does the reader notice illustrations?) What size and kind of print is used? (Is it appropriate to the reader?) Is the paper slick or dull? Is the book hardcover or paperback? (Which does the reader prefer?)

All of these factors affect the difficulty of printed materials. In most cases, there is a definite interaction between factors found in written materials and factors found within the person who is reading.

But how do we objectively judge the difficulty of written material? The final section of this chapter deals with techniques that are often used to do this. Such techniques can be used on materials when prospective readers are not available. These techniques are frequently used by publishers, by book-selection committees, and by teachers who want an objective, though restricted, measurement of the difficulty of certain materials. (Chapter 3 deals with techniques that can be used in classrooms to evaluate the difficulty of materials in relationship to the students in the class.)

Teachers are cautioned against accepting at face value readability levels of books as supplied by publishers. Recently the author of this book was asked to conduct a workshop for middle-grade teachers of social studies. She was told that students were having a great deal of difficulty reading some of the assigned texts. No wonder! Upon running readability formulas on these books, she found that the text designed for fourth-grade students had an average readability level of grade 7, with a range from grades 7 to 9.9. The book designed for fifth grades averaged twelfth-grade level, with a range from grades 8 to 16. The book designed for sixth-grade children averaged ninth-grade level, with a range of from 6 to 16. And the book used in seventh grade averaged ninth-grade level in difficulty and ranged from grades 8 to 9.9. These books had been approved for use at these grade levels by several selection committees, including a state committee and a local committee.

MEASURING THE DIFFICULTY LEVEL OF PRINTED MATERIALS

Let's imagine that you have been asked to select one or more textbooks for your students and that you have found four books that seem to be satisfactory in content. Two of these books seem somewhat difficult; the other two seem easier. How can you estimate their *readability levels*; that is, how can you find their levels of difficulty?

There are several readability formulas that you can use to find the approximate grade-level score of written materials, or more accurately, to compare the *relative difficulty* of materials. When using any of these formulas, you will consider two characteristics of printed materials:

1. word difficulty (the greater the number of long or unusual words the selection contains, the harder the selection is likely to be); and

2. sentence length (the longer and more complex the sentences are, the more difficult the selection is likely to be).

It is possible to use two or more formulas on the same passage and get different readability levels. This occurs because *word difficulty* is defined differently in various formulas. Even *sentence length* at times is defined differently.

Is this strange? Not at all! Ask yourself how you would decide whether a word is difficult or easy. You might say that if you know a word well, it is easy; if not, it is hard. You might say that if three-quarters of your students know a word, it is easy for them; otherwise, it is hard. Or, you might say that if a word is short, it is easy; if it's long, it's hard. What other techniques might you use? Would you consider any of them scientific?

Similarly, how would you decide how long the average sentence is in a passage of, say, 100 words? Oh, that's simple, you say. You just count the number of periods, question marks, etc., and divide that number into 100. Not so simple, really!

Consider this brief item: "If the user is good enough, slalom skis are ideal for recreation, for they handle well in every type of snow condition, except powder, and are the best style on any type of ice." One sentence? Now consider this: "If the user is good enough, slalom skis are ideal for recreation, for they handle well in every type of snow condition, except powder. And they are the best style on any type of ice." Two sentences? Finally: "If the user is good enough, slalom skis are ideal for recreation; for they handle well in every type of snow condition, except powder, and are the best style on any type of ice." One or two sentences?

All answers are correct. The first example is one sentence, the second is two sentences, and the third is one sentence according to some formulas and two sentences according to others.

Rudolf Flesch "Reading Ease" Formula

Let us look at how we might use one formula to evaluate the difficulty level of a short passage. The formula that we will use is the Rudolf Flesch "Reading Ease" formula. This formula can be used on materials at the fifth-grade level and above.[2]

Word difficulty

According to Flesch, a word is difficult or easy according to the number of syllables it contains: the more syllables, the harder it is. Flesch recognizes that there are exceptions to this generalization, but he feels that the number of syllables a word contains is usually a good index to its difficulty.

To use the Flesch formula, you count the number of syllables in each 100-word passage you are sampling. You simply count the syllables by saying the words orally and keeping tab.

To make this simple and to allow you to recheck the results, do the following:

1. Count off 100 words in the passage. Put a bracket at the end of the 100th word. (Numbers, like 9,000, are counted as one word. Compounds, whether hyphenated or not, are one word. Names of cities or places like El Paso and Ski Cloudcroft, though not hyphenated, count as one word.)

2. For the "syllables-per-100-word" count, count the number of syllables in a word according to the way you pronounce the word. There is no need to look words up in a dictionary.

To simplify matters, write above each word that contains more than one syllable the number of syllables in addition to one that the word contains. Thus, words of one syllable have nothing written over them. Words of two syllables, like "towers" and "enjoy," have "1" written over them, etc. Words of three syllables, like 9,000, have "2" written above them, etc.

Total these numbers in a 100-word passage, and add 100 to that sum to determine the number of syllables in the sample.

You might try doing this on the following selection:

> Southwesterners who love sunshine and still want the pleasures of wintertime sports in the snow enjoy an ideal situation in the El Paso area, with Cloudcroft less than two hours away. Ski Cloudcroft has become the perfect snow setting for skiers and outdoor enthusiasts who want all their ski pleasures close at hand.
>
> Ski Cloudcroft is found in the nearby Sacramento Mountains of southern New Mexico; it towers to a height of 9,000 feet above sea level, just three short miles from the neighboring town of Cloudcroft. The ski area boasts three lifts and perfectly groomed slopes to accommodate all skiers from beginners who/ have never skied before to experts./
> (100 words)
> (106 words)

Let's check to see if you did it properly:

3 1 1
Southwesterners who love sunshine and still want the pleasures of
2 1 1-2 3 2
wintertime sports in the snow enjoy an ideal situation in the El Paso
1-2 1 2
area, with Cloudcroft less than two hours away. Ski Cloudcroft has
1 1 1 1 1 3
become the perfect snow setting for skiers and outdoor enthusiasts
1
who want all their ski pleasures close at hand.

2 1 3 1
Ski Cloudcroft is found in the nearby Sacramento Mountains of
1 3 1 2 1
southern New Mexico; it towers to a height of 9,000 feet above sea
1 2 1
level, just three short miles from the neighboring town of Cloudcroft.
1-2 2
The ski area boasts three lifts and perfectly groomed slopes to
3 1 2
accommodate all skiers, from beginners who/ have never skied
before to experts. 100

In this 100-word passage, there are about 156–159 syllables.

Now select a 100-word passage in a content area textbook you have chosen to work with. Count the number of syllables in this passage, and write this figure on a piece of paper.

Average sentence length

Flesch instructs:

> In counting sentences, count as a sentence each unit of thought that is grammatically independent of another sentence or clause, if its end is marked by a period, question mark, exclamation point, semicolon, or colon. Incomplete sentences or sentence fragments are also to be counted as sentences. For example, count as two sentences: *What did the minister talk about? Sin.* Count as two sentences: *The Lord is my shepherd; I shall not want.* Count as three sentences: *There are two arguments against this plan: (1) It is too expensive. (2) It is impractical.* Count as two sentences: *Result: Nobody came.* But count as one sentence only: *He registered, but he did not vote.* (Two independent clauses, combined into a compound sentence with only a comma.) Count as one sentence: *There were three people present: Mary, Robert, and John.* (The words after the colon are not a separate unit of thought.) Count as one sentence: *The project is supposed to: (a) provide training; (b) stimulate suggestions.* (No part of this is an independent clause. Count such material as one sentence even if it is paragraphed.)
>
> In dialogue, count the words *he said* or other such tags as part of the quoted sentence to which they are attached. For example, count as one sentence: *He said: "I have to go."* Count also as one sentence: *"That's all very well," he replied, showing clearly that he didn't believe a word of what we said.**

Let us now count the number of sentences in our sample paragraph on pp. 33–34. Counting to the end of the sentence in which the 100th word is found, we have *five* sentences. The first ends with *away,* the second with *hand,* the

* Rudolf Flesch. *How to Test Readability.* New York: Harper & Row, 1951, p. 3. Reprinted by permission.

third with *New Mexico,* the fourth with *Cloudcroft,* and the fifth with *experts.* We have *five* sentences and 106 words (*experts* is the 106th word). Therefore, we have 106 divided by 5, or 21 words in the average sentence in this sample.

Now compute the number of words per sentence in your passage. Write its number on your paper. Use Fig. 2.1 to help you find the reading-ease score. Simply draw a diagonal line from the index number in the *words-per-sentence* column (here 21) to the *syllables-per-100 words* column (here 156–159) in Fig. 2.1. Read the number at the point of intersection in the "reading-ease score" column.

For our sample, the number is about 52–54. This is fairly difficult material according to Flesch. It is comparable in difficulty to magazines such as *Harper's* and the *Atlantic* and is similar in difficulty to materials normally considered to be at grade levels 10 to 12.9 (high school). Table 2.1 gives an interpretation of various reading ease scores. Now follow the same procedure in finding the difficulty level of the passage you have selected.

Caution: Remember, you have sampled only a 100-word passage from your book, and, therefore, you have found the difficulty level of this passage only—not of the complete book. In difficulty, this passage may be typical of the whole book, or it might be quite unusual.

To find the difficulty level of the complete book, you should take 25 to 30 samples at equal intervals throughout the book. You should take these samples *at random*; for example, start with the second paragraph on every tenth page. The mean average *raw score* of these samples should be used to find the difficulty level of the book according to the Flesch criteria.

You may wish to use the same procedure as above but use the Fry graph rather than the Flesch chart. The Fry graph, shown in Fig. 2.2, pinpoints grade level more specifically than does the Flesch chart and is also useful with materials at lower levels.

To use the Fry graph, we must determine the *number of sentences,* rather than the average length of a sentence in a 100-word passage. In our passage, sentence one ends with *away,* two ends with *hand,* three with *New Mexico,* four with *Cloudcroft. Who,* the 100th word in the passage, is the 17th word of a 23-word sentence. Thus this 100-word passage contains 4 17/23 sentences, roughly 4 3/4 sentences.

Next we read the graph to find the point of intersection for 4.75 sentences per 100 words and 156–159 syllables per 100 words. By doing this we find the readability level to be grade 11.

(If the number of sentences in a 100-word passage were 8.3 and the number of syllables in the 100 words were 118, the readability level would be grade 3. If the number of sentences were 6.7 and the number of syllables were 130, the readability level would be grade 6, etc.)

If we were trying to find the average readability level of several, or many, passages, we would compute the *average* number of sentences for each 100-

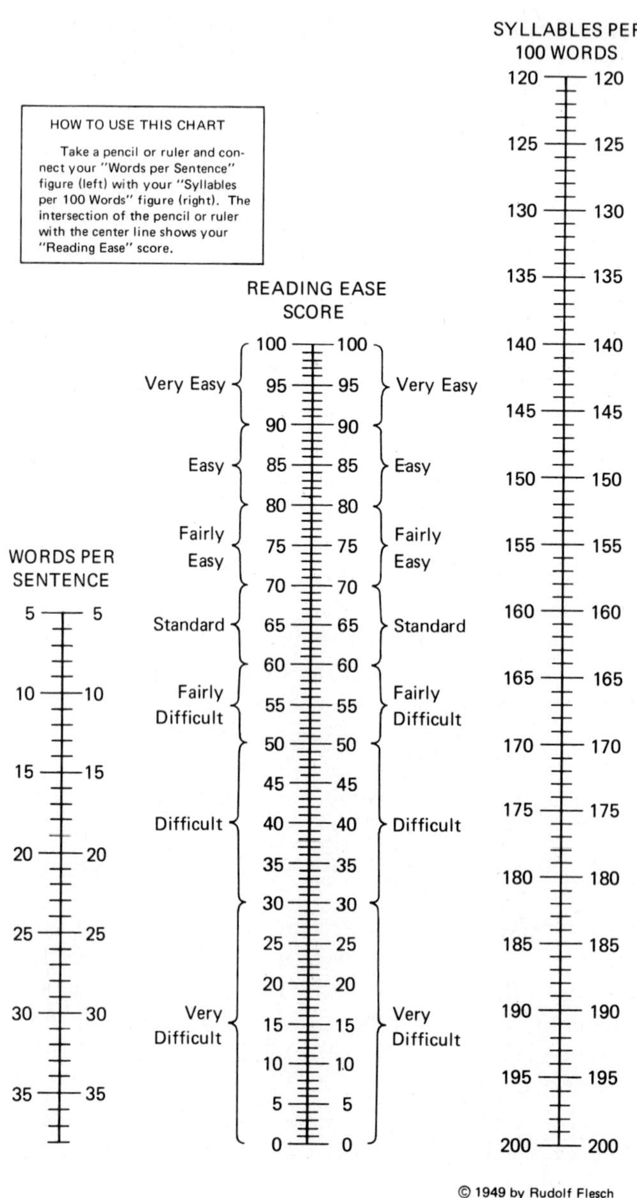

Fig. 2.1 How easy? (Reprinted by permission from *The Art of Readable Writing* by Rudolf Flesch, New York: Harper & Row, 1949, p. 5.)

Table 2.1 Interpretation of reading ease scores. (Adapted by permission from Rudolf Flesch, *How to Test Readability,* New York: Harper & Row, 1951, pp. 6, 43.)

Reading-ease score	Description of style	Typical magazine	Grade
90 to 100	Very easy	Comics	5
80 to 90	Easy	Pulp fiction	6
70 to 80	Fairly easy	Slick fiction	7
60 to 70	Standard	Digests, *Time,* mass nonfiction	8 and 9
50 to 60	Fairly difficult	*Harper's, Atlantic*	10–12 (high school)
30 to 50	Difficult	Academic, scholarly	13–16 (college)
0 to 30	Very difficult	Scientific, professional	College graduate

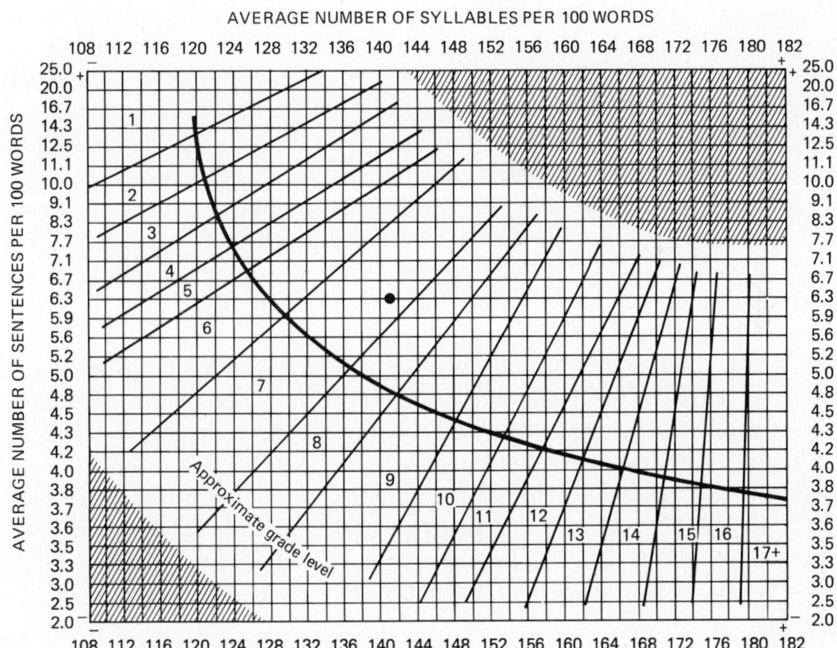

Fig. 2.2 Edward Fry, "Graph for Estimating Readability—Extended"*

* Edward Fry, "Fry's Readability Graph: Clarifications, Validity, and Extension to Level 17." *Journal of Reading,* **21,** No. 3 (December 1977), p. 249, used by permission of the author and the International Reading Association.

word passage and the *average* number of syllables per 100 words and use the graph only once for the *average* readability level.

Factors Within the Material—Affective

Just as Flesch has a "Reading Ease" formula, he also has a "Human Interest" formula, suggesting that he, at least, thinks it is possible to judge the intrinsic interest factor in a piece of writing. His "Human Interest" score is found by counting the percentage of *personal words* (all pronouns other than neuter pronouns, all words that have masculine or feminine gender, and names of people). Also counted are "personal sentences" (spoken sentences, questions, commands, requests, exclamations, and grammatically incomplete sentences). According to Flesch, these factors add to interest; the lack of them causes dullness. By using his scale, one can rank materials from dull to interesting to dramatic.[3]

Other Readability Formulas

There are, of course, other readability formulas which might be used. Two such formulas are the Spache readability formula, useful on material at grade levels 1–3.9, and the Dale-Chall formula, to be used on material at the fourth-grade level and above. Since a somewhat different readability level might be found by using one of these formulas rather than the Flesch or Fry, you might wish to try one of them also to find the difficulty level of your materials.

The basic reason that the difficulty levels might vary from one type of formula to another is that the Flesch and Fry type estimate difficulty of words according to the number of syllables per 100 words. The Spache and Dale-Chall formulas use word lists—words on the appropriate list are easy; words not on the list (with some exceptions) are difficult.

In general, however, formulas are not meant to pinpoint the exact grade level of passages. Instead, they are designed to show the relative difficulty of passages and/or to give the range of difficulty among passages.

Although this book does not contain either the Dale-Chall or the Spache formulas, it does include in Appendix A charts for use with these formulas so that it will not be necessary for you to make mathematical computations to determine readability levels. The explanatory materials must be found in the original sources or in other sources where they have been reproduced. (See Appendix A.)

Those readers interested in estimating the readability levels of materials in languages other than English might wish to refer to the article by George R. Klare, "Assessing Readability," listed among the references at the end of this chapter. Explanations of and references to formulas for materials in French, Dutch, Spanish, Hebrew, German, Hindi, Russian, and Chinese are included.

It is, of course, possible that the Fry and/or Flesch techniques might be used on foreign language materials.

SUMMARY

Factors that influence the difficulty of printed materials as they relate to readers of such materials were discussed. Such factors include the readers' interest in the content of the materials and their background of information as it relates to this content. Also important is their familiarity with the kind of language which is used—in terms of syntax, semantics, and organizational patterns. If utilized by the reader, section and paragraph headings and illustrations might add to ease of reading. Additionally, the type and size of print, the kind of paper used, and the type of cover might influence the readability of the material.

The use of two readability techniques, the Flesch "Reading Ease" formula and the Fry graph, were explained. By using these techniques, one can estimate the approximate level of difficulty of written materials.

NOTES

1 John Dawkins. *Syntax and Readability*. Newark, Delaware: International Reading Association, 1975.

2 Rudolf Flesch. *How to Test Readability*. New York: Harper and Brothers, 1951.

3 Rudolf Flesch, *op. cit.*

SUGGESTED ACTIVITIES

1. Compute the readability level of a 100-word passage in a content area book by using the Flesch formula and/or Fry graph. Listed below are the steps to follow:

   a) Make a copy of a passage at least 100 words long from a content area textbook.

   b) Count off 100 words. Draw a slash after the 100th word, and write 100 above it.

   c) Write the number of syllables in addition to one above each word in the 100-word passage.

   d) Count the total number of syllables in the 100-word passage. Write the number on the worksheet.

   e) Count the number of sentences in the 100-word passage. Write down the number.

f) Use the Flesch "How Easy?" chart to get the "reading-ease score." Write the score on your sheet. Write the grade level(s) down. And/or write the grade level from the Fry graph.

2. Compute the readability level of the same passage by using another formula, possibly one suggested in this chapter.

3. Compare the results of the two formulas. Are they similar or quite different in terms of grade-level scores? If they are different, what factors within the formulas caused the scores to differ? Which formula do you prefer for use with your book? Why?

4. You have computed the readability level of only one short passage within your book. Design a reasonable strategy for computing the readability level of the whole book.

5. Explain why factors other than word difficulty and sentence length have not been included in most readability formulas. Using your content area book, explain what additional characteristics of the book might make the book readable. Which characteristics of the same book might make it less readable than the formula score indicates?

6. Comment on the following statement: "Jane and George both received the same score on the standardized reading test recently given at school. Yet George finds my textbook, *Biological Science,* easy to read, but Jane has a constant struggle with it." (Assume that the standardized test score for each is valid.)

REFERENCES FOR FURTHER READING

Dale, Edgar and Jeanne Chall. "A Formula for Predicting Readability," *Educational Research Bulletin* (January 21, 1948): 11–20, 28.

Dale, Edgar and Barbara Seels. *Readability and Reading: An Annotated Bibliography.* Newark, Delaware: International Reading Association, 1966.

Dawkins, John. *Syntax and Readability.* Newark, Delaware: International Reading Association, 1975.

Flesch, Rudolf. *How to Test Readability.* New York: Harper and Brothers, 1951.

Fry, Edward. "Fry's Readability Graph: Clarifications, Validity, and Extension to Level 17," *Journal of Reading,* **21,** No. 3 (1977): 242–252.

Goodman, Kenneth S., *et al. Choosing Materials to Teach Reading.* Detroit: Wayne State University Press, 1966.

Harris, Theodore L. "Making Reading an Effective Instrument of Learning in the Content Fields," *Forty-seventh Yearbook, Part II: Reading in the High School and College.* Chicago: National Society for the Study of Education, 1948, p. 129.

Klare, George R. "Assessing Readability," *Reading Research Quarterly,* **X,** No. 1 (1974–1975): 62–102.

Klare, George R. *The Measurement of Readability.* Ames, Iowa: Iowa State University Press, 1963.

Koenke, Karl. "Another Practical Note on Readability Formulas," *Journal of Reading,* **15** (December 1971): 203–208.

Lorge, Irving. *The Lorge Formula for Estimating Difficulty of Reading Materials.* New York: Bureau of Publications, Teachers College, Columbia University, 1959.

McLaughlin, G. Harry. "SMOG Grading—A New Readability Formula." *Journal of Reading,* **12** (1969): 639–646.

Spache, George D. *Good Reading for Poor Readers.* Champaign, Illinois: Garrard Publishing, 1974, pp. 195–207.

Chapter 3

FINDING THE APPROPRIATE LEVEL OF MATERIALS FOR EACH STUDENT

What level of materials can students read independently?

What level of materials can students read when they have the help of a teacher?

What level of materials frustrates students?

INTRODUCTION

This chapter deals with some techniques that can be used to assess the cognitive reading achievement of students. Our purpose is to explore a variety of procedures that will give us an intelligent estimate of the level of materials which individual students can read successfully.

Cognitive reading achievement can be measured by using both standardized tests and informal (nonstandardized) instruments or techniques. Standardized tests are especially valuable in helping us compare our students' reading achievement with that of students in a national norming group. Informal reading tests are especially helpful in determining which of our available materials are best suited to the needs and achievement of individual students in our classes. By using informal tests, we can determine which of our available materials are on a student's frustrational reading level, which are on that student's instructional reading level, and which are on his or her independent reading level.

Materials that are on a student's *frustrational reading level* are normally too difficult for the student to read, even with the help of a teacher. Materials that are on the *instructional reading level* are suitable if the student has guidance from a teacher. Materials on the *independent reading level* are easy enough for the student to read independently.

Ideally, textbooks and other materials read by students under the guidance of a teacher should be selected at each student's instructional level. Other materials, such as supplementary materials which the student reads with little or no guidance from the teacher, should be at the student's independent reading level. Only rarely, and only when the student is strongly motivated, should a student read materials at the frustrational reading level.

Unfortunately, many teachers do not have at their disposal multilevel materials. If such is the case, it is still of value to know:

1. for which students the available material is well suited
2. for which students the material is too difficult for them to succeed with—even with the help of the teacher
3. for which students the material is quite easy—perhaps too easy and unchallenging.

The proper use of an informal reading inventory will give the teacher such information.

Both standardized tests and informal reading inventories can also be used in another way. It will be explained in this chapter how they can be used, under certain circumstances, as a valid substitute for an I.Q. test in determining the potential, or capacity (reading expectancy), level for a student.

First, let us look at standardized reading tests.

STANDARDIZED READING TESTS

Let's say that you are a classroom teacher in the tenth grade. You know that in a typical tenth-grade classroom, you will expect to find a range in reading achievement of about ten years ($\frac{2}{3}$ of $15 = 10$). The poorest reader may be reading at the fifth-grade level; the best, as well as an average university junior. But you don't know the *actual reading-grade level* of each student. How will you find it?

Probably the best way of finding the reading-grade level of a student is by administering a standardized reading test and using the grade score supplied by the publisher. This seems like a very simple task. However, the more you examine the many standardized reading tests available for your use, as well as the interpretation of grade scores supplied by publishers, the more complex your decisions become.

Different reading tests do not measure the same reading skills. There are two *broad* categories for classifying reading tests: oral and silent. Some very reputable oral reading tests measure *only* oral reading—no comprehension questions are asked. Obviously, different types of reading skills are being measured when students take such a test and when they take a silent reading test in which they are asked to indicate synonyms or antonyms for words as well as to respond to study skill and comprehension questions.

To get the maximum amount of usable information from a reading test, a wise choice of tests must be made. As a teacher, you must ask yourself what you most want to know in relationship to a student's reading achievement.

Oral Reading Tests

Do you want to know how well your students compare with students nationally in oral reading? If so, give a good standardized oral reading test. (Some of these tests are listed at the end of the chapter.)

If you have been trained in giving an oral reading test, you may also be able to derive valuable *diagnostic information* from it. By observing a student's oral error patterns, you can set up a program for correcting these errors. Thus, you might look at such behavioral characteristics as:

1. mispronunciations—are there patterns to the mispronunciations, e.g., syllabication errors, certain types of vowel errors, errors principally in word endings, etc.? (Dialectal variations are not considered to be errors.)
2. substitutions—does the student misread words, usually putting in a synonym for the word given by the author?
3. omissions—does the student skip words?
4. insertions—does the student include words that are not in the passage?

5. regressions—does the student repeat words or phrases?
6. hesitations—does the student pause for long periods of time?
7. punctuation errors—does the student ignore punctuation?

By observing the *types of errors* a student makes in oral reading, a reading teacher is able to set up a program for the correction of these errors.

Some teachers may wonder about the value of oral reading tests—especially for junior and senior high school students. Theoretically, the value lies in an assumption that the kinds of errors students make when they read orally serve as a clue to the kinds of errors they make when they read silently. The assumption is that if they ignore punctuation when they read orally, they also do so when they read silently. If they mispronounce words when they read orally, they really don't know the meanings of these words when they read silently, etc.

Such assumptions may or may not be valid. Many students who read rapidly when they are reading silently find it difficult to shift gears. When they read orally, therefore, they often skip words and may also appear to be ignoring punctuation. Also, they may know meanings of words they cannot pronounce.

Oral reading tests may serve as valuable diagnostic tools for some students —especially students who are reading at the elementary school levels. For all students, such tests may give us *clues* for designing programs for reading improvement, especially if used in conjunction with silent reading passages used to evaluate comprehension.

Silent Reading Tests

You are probably more interested in knowing how well students comprehend when they read silently. Since silent reading tests vary among themselves, you should select the test that requires the student to do the kind of reading you are interested in assessing. Not every test will give you this information.

You may wish to refer to the end of this chapter, where there is an annotated list of available tests. From this list, you may wish to select a few tests to order for further examination. Most tests used in schools have been critiqued in Buros' *Mental Measurements Yearbook.* If you wish to be somewhat sophisticated in selecting a test, you should refer to these reviews, which are written by experts in the field of the test.

Precautions

When an oral reading test is administered by a well-trained person, *diagnostic information* which could be used in setting up a corrective reading program might be obtained. However, silent reading tests are rarely diagnostic because too few items of any one type are given in any one test. Standardized silent-reading tests are usually *survey tests,* i.e., they yield a grade score or a percentile score.* But despite what some manuals say, they usually do not give reliable information, though they may give clues, for designing a reading program for an individual student.

Also, most silent reading tests, especially those used above the primary level, *inflate* the grade-level scores. The grade score usually indicates the *frustrational* level for the student. That is, the grade score a student gets on a silent reading test tells you the student's breaking point.† You must drop back a year or more to find the student's *instructional level,* the level at which the student can successfully learn—*with your help.* You must drop back even further to find the *independent level,* the level at which the student can read material without outside help.[1]

Standardized Reading-Listening Tests

At the present time there are two standardized reading-listening test batteries on the market. These are the Durrell Reading-Listening Test, for intermediate grades (3.5–6) and advanced (7–9), and the Brown-Carlsen Reading-Listening Test. Each of these tests contains parallel subtests, one of which is read *by* the student and one of which is read *to* the student.

Usually, the student will score the same on both subtests. However, some students receive a higher score on the test read to them than they receive on the test that they themselves must read. If the listening test score is significantly higher than the reading test score, it is assumed that the student has an undeveloped capacity for reading. That is, it is assumed that the student has greater mental capacity than he or she is using in the reading situation. It is also assumed that the student is disabled in reading and needs help principally in oral reading, possibly including phrasing, because the only skill supplied in the listening test that is not supplied in the reading test is oral reading.

INFORMAL (NONSTANDARDIZED) TECHNIQUES

Although standardized tests may give us information about a student's—or a class's—reading-grade or percentile levels, such tests fall short of providing all of the information we need in assuring ourselves that the student is able or unable to read the materials that are available in our classroom. Major values

---

* A percentile score indicates the percentage of students who score at a lower level than the person receiving that score. A percentile score of 60 means that 60% of the norming group scored more poorly than the person receiving that score. A score of 30 means that 30% scored at a lower level.

† The Flesch readability formula included in Chapter 2 of this book also indicates frustrational level of materials. A passage found to be at the sixth-grade level according to this formula would frustrate the average sixth-grader. In other words, the grade score for a passage is an indication of the break-off point for the passage. Flesch has another formula which can be used to find the instructional level of a passage, but that formula is rarely used.

of standardized silent reading tests are: (1) they allow us to compare our students' reading achievement with national norms or other norming groups, and (2) they provide us with an easy way to grossly rank our own students from strongest to weakest.

However, results of standardized reading tests can rarely be used to indicate whether or not a particular book is at the *frustrational, instructional,* or *independent* reading level for a particular student. The problem is compounded because readability formulas used by various publishers differ, and no one formula is equally valid on all types of materials. Thus, for example, if there are two books of equal difficulty, one publisher might say its book is at the tenth-grade level, and the other might grade its book at the eighth-grade level.

What techniques can *you* use to give you reasonable assurance that your students are placed at their optimal levels in reading materials in your class? This question is particularly important in relationship to the textbook they are expected to read, since the textbook normally is used regularly throughout a semester or year, and so much of a student's course work is dependent on success with the textbook.

Using a type of informal reading inventory is probably the answer. Two types are explained here: a modification of the standard IRI and the Cloze readability technique.

A Modification of the Informal Reading Inventory

The standard informal reading inventory, widely discussed in the literature, consists of two parts—one oral and the other silent. Since the value of an oral reading test given to students who read above the fifth- or sixth-grade level is widely questioned and since giving an oral reading test is extremely time-consuming and impractical for a classroom teacher, it is not recommended that the oral part of an informal reading inventory be given to most middle grade and secondary school students. For these reasons, only the silent reading part of the inventory is described here. The oral part of the test is explained briefly in Appendix B. Teachers may prefer to use miscue analysis techniques for oral testing.[2]

Procedure

Ideally, the teacher will have at his or her disposal several books at various levels of readability. From each of these books, the teacher will select a passage of about 1500 to 3000 words (shorter passages for middle grade children, longer ones for older students) that appears to be fairly representative of the book, or at least the beginning of it.

The teacher carefully reads each passage to determine what kinds of reading skills are necessary for a student to have in order to understand it. The teacher then selects about four skills. For example, one teacher might select these skills:

1. ability to derive meanings of words from context
2. ability to grasp and remember important details
3. ability to recall main ideas and sequence
4. ability to interpret and use what is read.

Next, the teacher composes five questions in each of these categories. An IRI on a passage from a science textbook might look like this:

Book: *Science Today* Name____________________

Part 1. *Vocabulary*
Before reading, examine the following five key words. See if you can recall having heard them. Do you know what they mean? For each key word, *underline* the meaning which you think is correct. Then read the passage. When you finish reading, you will return to this section and *circle* the meaning which you may recall from the passage.

1. *hypothesis:*
   a) a statement you are sure about
   b) the side opposite the right angle of a triangle
   c) your best guess
   d) your religion
2. *technique:*
   a) one who does things well
   b) an object having three sides
   c) a systematic procedure for accomplishing a task
   d) a principle to be evaluated
3. *ingredient:*
   a) element, part
   b) color, shade
   c) odor, scent
   d) temperature
4. *controlled experiment:*
   a) a series of activities done regularly
   b) a carefully designed testing procedure
   c) the use of instruments to guide production
   d) a converter used to change processes
5. *attack* ("a carefully designed *attack* on the question"):
   a) force used against answering the question
   b) procedure to follow to get results
   c) initial harmful act in solving the question
   d) assault

Part 2. Do not read this part until you have finished reading the assignment.

Noting details (Circle T or F)

6. T–F: To test a hypothesis on molding bread, you would need two pieces of bread from the same loaf.
7. T–F: The author suggests that you should examine each piece of bread every second day.
8. T–F: The author suggests that one of the best ways to organize your materials for experiments in this course is to store results in stacks and put them in the same box.
9. T–F: You should date and enter in a ledger (book) every observation at the time it is made.
10. T–F: Later in this course you will be asked to refer to data collected early in the course.

Main ideas and sequence

11. Where or how does an experiment begin?
12. Number the following steps of a controlled experiment in the order in which they occur:

    ____ a hypothesis is formulated

    ____ results are acted upon

    ____ a question is asked

    ____ a plan of attack is followed

13. Can a single experiment answer the question, "What causes bread to mold?" *yes-no.* If "no," why not? If "yes," which experiment?
14. Give—in order—the four steps the author suggests you follow to find out if moisture produces molding in bread.

    a)______________________________

    b)______________________________

    c)______________________________

    d)______________________________

15. Why does an entire experiment depend on the nature of the hypothesis?

Interpretation and application

16. About how many days do you think it will take to complete the experiment discussed in your book? Why?

17. What do you think might be some causes (other than moisture) of molding in bread? Suggest at least two.
18. How might you set up an experiment to test the effect of one of these on molding?
19. From your knowledge of natural ingredients and preservatives (often avoided by health enthusiasts), comment on the relative duration of freshness of white breads with preservatives as opposed to whole grain breads without preservatives.
20. Why do all experiments begin with the same step?

Introducing the IRI

The IRI should be thought of as part of a sample lesson. Thus, the IRI should be introduced to the students in a manner similar to one a teacher would use if instructing students. The validity of an IRI is determined by the extent to which it approximates an actual teaching-learning experience. Its purpose is to find an optimal three-way match between teacher, student, and material. Therefore, it should be introduced to students by the teacher who will be teaching them, and in the normal way in which the teacher instructs.

The previous IRI might be introduced this way:

First, the teacher might call attention to the vocabulary terms in the inventory. He or she might ask the students to look at Part 1 of the activity. The teacher might ask if anyone can pronounce the first word (*hypothesis*). Then the teacher might ask students to underline the best definition of the word. The same would be done with the remaining words.

Of course, no attempt is made to define any of these terms before reading occurs. But the attention of the students is called to important words and expressions. (When students finish reading, they will circle the correct meanings. Only circled responses are scored.) A very positive effect of this kind of activity occurs when students underline the wrong answer but circle the right one. Students thus learn that they themselves can derive meaning from context.

Next, the teacher might lead the students in paging through the assignment and noting main and subheadings of sections. The teacher might write the main heading and subheadings of one or more sections on the board:

Specific Steps Are Followed in a Controlled Experiment:

A question is asked

A hypothesis is formulated

A plan of attack is followed

Results are acted upon:

Results are observed	Results are tabulated	Results are interpreted

Then the teacher might stress, or draw from the students, that the discussion proceeds in time-order and then complete a flow chart:

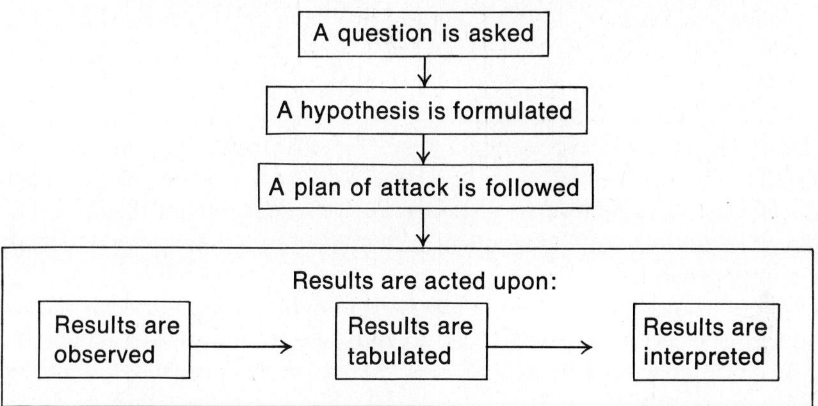
Specific Steps Are Followed in a Controlled Experiment:
A question is asked
A hypothesis is formulated
A plan of attack is followed
Results are acted upon:
Results are observed
Results are tabulated
Results are interpreted

Finally, the teacher might elicit from the class some questions which might be answered in the author's discussion. For example, students might ask:

1. Why is a question asked first?
2. What is a hypothesis? How does one state a hypothesis?
3. What kind of attack is followed? Does the attack differ from experiment to experiment? What kind of attack would be followed in the testing of the molding of bread? (They have surveyed the complete passage, although this flow chart covers only part of it.)
4. How are results acted upon? How might we observe the molding of bread? How might we tabulate results? How can we interpret results? Do such results hold for the molding of all kinds of bread?

By this time the students should be ready to read. They do so silently, reading directly from their books. Before answering the questions, they close their books.

Interpretation of results

Both survey and limited diagnostic information can be gained from this IRI. The following reading levels can be identified:

independent level—95–100% correct
borderline (high)*—90% correct
instructional level—70–85% correct
borderline (low)*—55–65% correct
frustrational level—0–50% correct.

Thus, students who score 95–100% correct probably need a more difficult and challenging book for instructional purposes. This book (or at least this part of the book) is at their *independent level*; that is, it is easy enough for them to read without the help of a teacher.

This book is at the *instructional level* for students who scored 70–85% on this IRI. The book is at the proper level for these students if the teacher introduces other lessons in a way similar to the way in which this lesson was introduced. Additionally, these students are in need of follow-up activities after the reading is completed.

Students who scored 50% or below will probably be frustrated if required to read this book. It is too difficult for them to use even with a teacher's help.

If an additional book is available on an easier level, those students who scored on the frustrational level should be similarly tested with it. If they score 70%–85% correct on this second book, it is on their instructional level and is the book they should use—with teacher guidance.

If an additional book is available on a higher level, those students who scored on the independent level should be similarly tested with it. If they score 70%–85% correct on it, it is on their instructional level.

Thus, it is suggested that if multilevel materials are available, the initial test be given on the materials of middle level in difficulty. Those who score below 70% on this test should be given a test on easier materials. Those who score 90% or better should be given a test on the more difficult materials.

Capacity level can also be determined if the teacher orally reads a passage and the questions to the student or to a group of students. If a student scores 70%–80% correct using such a procedure, the material is said to be on his or her capacity (reading expectancy) level. Teachers who wish to use this technique normally read passages from a book that was found to be at a student's frustrational reading level. Students whose instructional level is found to be considerably below their capacity level should be referred to a remedial reading teacher for further diagnosis and help.

Besides looking at the total percentage score, it is often interesting to look at patterns of both errors and correct responses, but this can be done only if

* Traditionally, the independent level is defined as the level at which students score 90–100% correct, and the instructional level is the level at which they score 55–90% correct according to some authors and 70–90% correct according to others. Thus, a score of 90% correct falls in both the independent and instructional level categories and might more clearly be called borderline. Also, 55–65% correct is considered by some writers to be instructional level; whereas others consider it to be frustrational level.

there is a sufficient number of questions of the types analyzed. Students might be considered deficient in a skill if they miss two or more out of five items in a category. They might be considered strong in a skill if they score 100 percent in a category. From such an analysis, a teacher might get *clues* as to what types of items need emphasis among certain groups of students.

The teacher might wish to compose a chart, such as the following, for each student for each IRI taken.

Book ______________________ Student ______________________

Readability of Passage ______________

Survey information:

Independent level 100–95	Borderline 90	Instructional level 85–80–75–70	Borderline 65–60–55	Frustrational level 50–45–40—

Diagnostic information:

v v v v v * o	d d d d d * o	m s m s m * o	i i i i i * o

For one student, the teacher might complete the chart thus:

Book *The Modern Scientific World* Student *John Jacobs*

Readability of Passage *7–8*

Survey Information

Independent level 100–90	Borderline 90	Instructional level 85–80–75–70	Borderline 65– (60) –55	Frustrational level 50–45–40—

Diagnostic information:

(v)(v) v v v * (o)	(d) d d d d * o	(m)(s)(m) s m * (o)	(i)(i) i i i * (o)

By reading this chart, we can see that this student scored 60% on this IRI. For him, this book is bordering on the frustrational level. The student should be tested on an easier book. We can also see that he made two errors in vocabulary, one in details, three in main idea and sequence, and two in interpretation. He has no strong area in comprehension when using this level of material and has three weak areas (according to this test).

After identifying the instructional level for each student, the teacher might compose a chart for either the entire class or the group of students who are using a particular book. Table 3.1 shows hypothetical charts for a science classroom in which three books are being used.

Other comprehension skills, such as critical-creative reading skills, could be added to these charts a little later—after the students have used the books and the teacher has had an opportunity to observe each student's strengths and weaknesses in these areas of reading achievement. In addition, the teacher might at regular intervals time students when they read passages from the book. These rate scores could also be recorded on the master sheet.

Table 3.1 (a) ***Science Today*****—readability level: grades 5–6**

Instructional level for	Vocabulary	Details	Main idea, sequence	Interpretation, application	Add other skills later
Armstrong, Henry	o	*		o	
Bardet, Marie		*	o		
Dorsey, George	o	o	*	*	
Klein, Baron	*		*	o	

Table 3.1 (b) ***The Modern Scientific World*****—readability level: grades 7–8**

Anderson, John	o		*	*	
Jones, Carolyn	*	o			
Martinez, Maria		o	*		
Rollins, James	o	*		o	

Table 3.1 (c) ***Earth Science*****—readability level: grades 9–10**

Calabresa, Betty	*		*	o	
Fignewton, Jeremy	*	o	*		
Hodges, Mary	o	*	o	*	
Jahnke, Eleanor	o	o	*		

Comprehension: * = strength; o = weakness

The charts shown in Table 3.1 can be very useful; by reading across a line, the teacher can identify relative strengths and weaknesses of each student. If each student is placed in a book at the appropriate instructional level, he or she will have missed from three to about six questions. Thus, each student is likely to have a profile. Therefore, by giving an IRI of this type, teachers are able to get a limited amount of diagnostic information. Since diagnosis should be continuous, teachers can constantly add to their understanding of students' needs. The IRI is just a beginning.

Also, by reading down the columns, the teacher is able to identify those students who are most in need of help in a particular skill area. The teacher can also identify those who are strong and might serve as peer leaders. Thus, by reading this chart, we can see that the following students might need special help in vocabulary development as it relates to the unit on experiments in science: Henry Armstrong, George Dorsey, John Anderson, James Rollins, Mary Hodges, Eleanor Jahnke. And the following students might be peer leaders if they wish: Betty Calabresa, Jeremy Fignewton, Carolyn Jones, and even Baron Klein, though he's reading the easiest book.

Thus a teacher might design a skill center for teaching the vocabulary of this unit. (Chapter 6 in this book will give you ideas about how to design such a center.) Those who need vocabulary development most would be given time to work in this center. A skill center should also be designed to teach the important details of this unit, and other centers would be designed to reinforce main ideas and sequence, and interpretation and application of ideas of this unit. Unit Three in this book is designed to show you how to develop such skill centers.

Other centers, of course, should be added later, such as a center to develop critical-creative skills, in which materials are available from a variety of sources. Students would be taught how to select appropriate sources, how to compare ideas from various authors, how to identify biases, how to synthesize ideas from many sources, and how to evaluate ideas. Ideas which should be helpful in doing this will be found in Chapter 9 of this book. In addition, the teacher might wish to develop interest centers. Ideas for doing this are explained in Chapter 4.

Bormuth Cloze Readability Technique

The Bormuth Cloze readability technique may be used as a substitute, or partial substitute, for the previously explained informal reading inventory.[3] The Cloze technique is elegant in its simplicity. Once a passage is selected that is representative of the book upon which the student is to be tested, the procedure is simple to use. However, selection of the passage is more complex. This will be explained last.

Let us say that we have the representative passage. It will be 250 words of continuous writing, and *every fifth word* will be "CLOZED." That is, every fifth word will be omitted, and in its place will be an underscoring. Each underscoring must be of uniform length (about 12 typewriter spaces). All students in a class can be given the same passage at the same time. They are asked to write in the *exact* word that has been omitted. There is no time limit.

In a 250-word passage, there are 50 clozures since every fifth word is deleted. Each correct response counts for two percentage points. To be correct, the student must supply the author's *exact* word, though it might be misspelled. That is the way the procedure has been standardized, and that is the way the passage must be scored. Credit is *not* given for synonyms—what one person may consider a synonym, another may not.

The percentage score a student receives is used to determine his or her reading level for the passage:

58%–100% correct—independent level
44%– 57% correct—instructional level
0%– 43% correct—frustrational level.

For the logic behind the "CLOZE" procedure, see Bormuth's article. This procedure is becoming increasingly popular with reading experts, for hidden in the correct response is an understanding of the author's style and technique as well as a revelation of the background of information and syntactic ability of the student being tested.

Selection of a passage that is representative of the book

Obviously, the passage which is selected is of utmost importance. It must come very close to being representative of the book of which it is a part. Bormuth instructs that originally *12* passages should be selected from a book. If the book appears to be of uniform difficulty throughout, the passages are selected at equal page intervals throughout, e.g., every 50 pages. If the book becomes progressively more difficult, the 12 passages are selected from the beginning of the book, again at equal intervals, perhaps every eighth page.

Each passage is 250 words long and need not end with the last word of a sentence. The passage is the first 250-word passage of continuous writing that is found on or after the designated page number. Each *fifth* word is clozed to the end of the sentence in which the 250th word occurs. Only the first 50 clozures are scored.

The passage is typed on a single sheet of paper and should look something like the following:

Learning all we can ____________ all that we observe
____________ surely an important phase ____________
science and, consequently, a ____________ of the scientist.

Think, ______, of the vast amount ______
information we could assemble ______ of how difficult
it ______ become to find a ______ item of this
information ______ we did not group ______ in
some convenient manner. ______ how much simpler our
______ will be if we ______ the objects we
are ______ into classes or kinds ______ we begin
to gather ______ data. By doing this ______
may generalize about many ______ of the group after
______ careful study of only ______ few
members. In effect, ______ did this in our ______
on the single sugar ______ when we grouped our
______. We said that in ______ trials a spot
appeared ______ 34 and no spot ______ 66.
This classification made ______ simpler to describe what
______ had observed and easier ______ us to
evaluate our ______ in order to draw ______
about what could not ______ observed directly. This
grouping, ______ sorting, activity is the ______
of classification; it is ______ taxonomy.
Classification is a ______ operation and can be
______ according to many different ______.
The plan we use ______ on our purpose. The
______ of sorting also varies ______ the
situation. Your grocer ______ certain kinds of food
______ in the store for ______ shopping
convenience and for ______ convenience in restocking
supplies. ______ cans of food you ______ at
(250 words)
home may be ______/ in the cabinet with ______,
vegetables, and soups on ______ shelves, or at different
______ on a single shelf.

The clozed passage is reproduced so that all students have their own copy, and they fill in the blanks. Numbers and answer sheets cannot be used, for this would invalidate the results. (Each blank filled in serves as a clue to another blank. An answer sheet would make these clues more difficult to recognize.) Each of the 12 passages is given to at least 30 students. If six classes of 30 students each were being used, each student would be given only two passages.

To ensure a random distribution of passages, teachers should refer to the alphabetical listing of students in their grade book. They divide the list into six equal parts, or count off students 1, 2, 3, 4, 5, 6 / 1, 2, 3, 4, 5, 6, etc., and designate the groups as 1, 2, 3, 4, 5, 6. Each of the 12 passages is also numbered. The chart that follows can be used for the distribution of passages to students:

Student groups	*Passages*
1	4 and 7
2	3 and 12
3	6 and 11
4	1 and 8
5	5 and 10
6	2 and 9

After each passage has been scored, the mean average (arithmetic average) for the passage is computed by adding all of the percentage scores and dividing by the number of students who were tested on the passage. Thus, we might have the following average scores for the passage:

Passage	*Mean average*
1	40
2	26
3	70
4	36
5	52
6	58
7	40
8	65
9	43
10	48
11	36
12	54

Next, the mean of the means is computed. For these passages it would be:

$$\frac{40+26+70+36+52+58+40+65+43+48+36+54}{12} = \frac{568}{12} = 47.3.$$

The passage whose mean is closest to the mean of the mean is selected as representative of the book. In this case it would be *passage 10,* whose mean is 48.

Now, all students (except those in group 5, who have already had it) are given this passage. Also, whenever testing is done on this book in the future, this passage should be used. Therefore, the "selection of passage" procedure is no longer necessary for this book.

Comment

All of the percentages given for use with the modification of the IRI and the Bormuth technique are meant as *guidelines* only. They are *not meant to serve as rigid cutting-off points.* Teachers must carefully observe their students in other ways to be certain that the books they are using are appropriate.

Students vary greatly in their ability and desire to cope with easy and/or difficult materials. A student with a great deal of interest in a subject may not mind being frustrated a bit. Another who lacks interest may find material which is considered to be on the appropriate instructional level too difficult to be worth the effort. Indeed, the affective dimensions of reading must also be considered.

SUMMARY

Standardized and informal techniques are commonly used in order to assess students' cognitive level of reading achievement. Usually, *standardized reading tests* provide us with information that (1) allows us to compare our group of students with a national norming group, and also (2) allows us to roughly rank order our students. If we know how to administer a *standardized oral reading test,* and if we are working with children who read at about the fifth-grade level or below, we may get valuable information that will help us design a partial reading program for children to whom we have given the test. Few, if any, *standardized silent reading tests* give us enough diagnostic information for preparing a program of study in needed comprehension and study skills. *Standardized listening-reading tests* help us to locate students who may be disabled in reading.

It is difficult to know the exact meaning of the grade-level scores supplied by text publishers. The grade scores students get on a standardized silent reading test frequently suggest their *frustrational level,* the lowest level at which they cannot succeed, even with the teacher's help. Their instructional level is usually one or two years below this. The scores a student receives on a standardized listening-reading test are meant only for comparing the level of the two skills; if the listening score is sufficiently higher than the reading score, the student may need corrective or remedial help in reading.

In order to determine which reading materials at our disposal are at the correct level for individual students, *informal techniques* are the most useful. Among these techniques are (1) a modification of the Informal Reading Inventory, especially appropriate for use in the content areas, and (2) the

Bormuth CLOZE Readability Technique. Each of these techniques enables us to intelligently estimate the student's *independent, instructional,* and *frustrational reading levels* in relationship to the materials used in testing. The IRI also enables us to estimate the student's capacity level. Only one of these techniques need be used by a content area teacher.

NOTES

1 See Joseph L. Vaughan, Jr. "Interpreting Reading Assessments," *Journal of Reading*, **19**, No. 8 (May 1976): 635–639.

2 See, for example, Kenneth S. Goodman (ed.). *Miscue Analysis—Applications to Reading Instruction.* Urbana, Illinois: National Council of Teachers of English, 1973.

3 John Bormuth. "The Cloze Readability Procedure," *Elementary English,* **XLV** (April 1968): 429–436.

SUGGESTED ACTIVITIES

1. Design an Informal Reading Inventory for use with your content area textbook, following the model explained in the section of this chapter titled "A Modification of the Informal Reading Inventory."
2. Plan a microteach session to last for about five minutes, demonstrating exactly how you would introduce the timed section of your IRI to your class. In this session briefly relate the ideas of the passage to the students' past experiences, and lay the foundation for your students to anticipate ideas which will be covered in the reading material. Tell them what you want them to think about while they are reading.
3. Explain the value of giving an IRI if you have multilevel materials available in your classroom. What is its value if you have only one set of materials?
4. Using your context area textbook, tell from which pages you would select the 12 passages to be used initially with the Bormuth Cloze Readability Technique. Give the 12 page numbers and the first four words of each passage. Remember to begin each passage at the beginning of a paragraph.
5. Set up the first passage, clozing every fifth word.
6. Compare the IRI and the Bormuth Cloze Readability techniques. Which is easier to set up initially? Which is easier to administer? Which gives you more diagnostic information? Which do you think you would prefer to use?

REFERENCES FOR FURTHER READING

Blanton, William, Roger Farr, and J. Jaap Tuinman (ed.) *Reading Tests for the Secondary Grade: A Review and Evaluation.* Newark, Delaware: International Reading Association, 1972.

Bond, L. and Miles Tinker. *Reading Difficulties: Their Diagnosis and Correction.* New York: Appleton-Century-Crofts, 1967, Section 3.

Bormuth, John. "The Cloze Readability Procedure," *Elementary English,* **XLV** (April 1968): 429–436.

Buros, Oscar (ed.). *Mental Measurements Yearbook.* Highland Park, N.J.: Gryphon Press.

Farr, Roger (ed.). *Measurement and Evaluation of Reading.* New York: Harcourt, Brace and World, 1970.

Farr, Roger. *Measurement of Reading Achievement* (an annotated bibliography). Newark, Delaware: International Reading Association, 1971.

Goodman, Kenneth S. (ed.). *Miscue Analysis—Applications to Reading Instruction.* Urbana, Illinois: National Council of Teachers of English, 1973.

Guszak, Frank J. *Diagnostic Reading Instruction in the Elementary School.* New York: Harper & Row, 1972.

Hafner, Lawrence E. (ed.). *Improving Reading in Middle and Secondary Schools, Selected Readings,* 2d Edition. New York: Macmillan, 1974, Section 7.

Harris, Albert J. and Edward R. Sipay. *How to Increase Reading Ability.* New York: David McKay, 1975, Chapters 8 and 9.

Johnson, Marjorie Seddon and Roy Kress. *Informal Reading Inventories.* Newark, Delaware: International Reading Association, 1965.

Karlin, Robert (ed.). *Teaching Reading in High School—Selected Articles.* Indianapolis: Bobbs-Merrill, 1969, Chapter 4.

Leibert, Robert E. (ed.). *Diagnostic Viewpoints in Reading.* Newark, Delaware: International Reading Association, 1971.

Olson, Arthur V. and Wilber S. Ames (eds.). *Teaching Reading Skills in Secondary Schools.* Scranton, Pa.: International Textbook, 1970, Section 4.

Strang, Ruth. *The Diagnostic Teaching of Reading.* New York: McGraw-Hill, 1969, Chapters 2–7 and 10.

Taylor, Stanford E. *Listening: What Research Says to the Teacher.* Washington, D.C.: National Education Association, 1973.

Viox, Ruth G. *Evaluating Reading and Study Skills in the Secondary Classroom.* Newark, Delaware: International Reading Association, 1968.

Zintz, Miles V. *The Reading Process.* Dubuque, Iowa: Wm. C. Brown Co., 1970, Chapter 3.

SILENT READING TESTS (STANDARDIZED)

California Reading Test, 1957 edition with 1963 norms. Grades 4–6, 7–9, 9–14. Three scores: vocabulary, comprehension, total. California Test Bureau, Del Monte Research Park, Monterey, California 93940.

Davis Reading Test, 1962. Grades 8–11, 11–13. Two scores: level of comprehension and speed of comprehension. Psychological Corporation, 304 East 45th St., New York, New York 10017.

Gates-MacGinite Reading Tests, 1965. Grades 4–6, 7–9. Three scores: speed and accuracy, vocabulary, comprehension. Teachers College Press, Teachers College, Columbia University, New York, New York 10027.

Kelley-Greene Reading Comprehension Test, 1955. Grades 9–13. Five scores: paragraph comprehension, directed reading, retention of details, reading rate, total. Harcourt, Brace and World, Inc., 757 Third Ave., New York, New York, 10017.

Nelson Reading Test, 1962. Grades 3–9. Three scores: vocabulary, paragraph comprehension, total reading score. Houghton Mifflin Co., 2 Park Street, Boston, Mass. 02107.

Nelson-Denny Reading Test: Vocabulary—Comprehension—Rate, 1960. Grades 9–16. Four scores: vocabulary, comprehension, total, rate. Houghton Mifflin Co., 2 Park Street, Boston, Mass. 02107.

Reading Comprehension: Cooperative English Tests, 1960. Grades 9–12, 13–14. Four scores: vocabulary, level of comprehension, speed of comprehension, total. Cooperative Test Division, Educational Testing Service, Princeton, N.J. 08540.

SRA Achievement Series: Reading, 1967. Grades 4–9 (multilevel). Three scores: comprehension, vocabulary, total. Science Research Associates, Inc., 259 East Erie St., Chicago, Ill. 60611.

Sequential Tests of Educational Progress: Reading, 1963. Grades 4–6, 7–9, 10–12, 13–14. Cooperative Test Division, Educational Testing Service, Princeton, N.J. 08540.

Stanford Achievement Test: High School Reading Test, 1964. Grades 9–12. Harcourt Brace Jovanovich, Inc., 757 Third Ave., New York, New York 10017.

Stanford Diagnostic Reading Test, 1974. Levels I, grades 2^2–4^1, scores in comprehension, vocabulary, auditory discrimination, syllabication, beginning and ending sounds, blending, sound discrimination; Level II, grades 4^2–8^1, scores in comprehension (literal and inferential), vocabulary, syllabication, sound discrimination, blending, rate of reading; Level III, grades: high school and early college, scores in comprehension, vocabulary, decoding, and rate. Harcourt Brace Jovanovich, Inc., 757 Third Ave., New York, New York 10017.

Tests of Reading: Cooperative Inter-American Tests, 1963. Grades 1–3, 2–3, 4–7, 8–13, 10–13. A series of parallel tests in English and Spanish. Three or four scores depending upon level: vocabulary, comprehension, total; or level of comprehension, speed of comprehension, vocabulary, total. Guidance Testing Associates, 6516 Shirley Ave., Austin, Texas 78752.

ORAL READING TESTS (STANDARDIZED)

Diagnostic Reading Scales, by George Spache, 1963. Grades 1–8 and retarded readers in grades 9–12. California Test Bureau, Del Monte Research Park, Monterey, Calif. 93940.

Durrell Analysis of Reading Difficulty, New Edition, by Donald Durrell, 1955. Grades 1–6. Harcourt, Brace and World, Inc., 757 Third Ave., New York, New York 10017.

Gates-McKillop Reading Diagnostic Tests, by Arthur Gates and Anne S. McKillop, 1962. Grades 2–6. Teachers College Press, Teachers College, Columbia University, New York, New York 10027.

Gilmore Oral Reading Test, by John Gilmore. Grades 1–8. Harcourt, Brace and World, Inc., 757 Third Ave., New York, New York 10017.

Gray Oral Reading Test, by Wm. S. Gray and Helen Robinson, Grades 1–Adult. Bobbs-Merrill Co., Inc., 4300 West 62nd Street, Indianapolis, Indiana 46206.

Chapter 4

ASSESSING AND BUILDING STUDENT INTERESTS IN READING MATERIALS

Why do people choose to read?

What do students choose to read?

How can we measure a student's intensity of involvement in a school subject?

INTRODUCTION

Teachers have always been concerned with the degree of interest students display in their school subjects. Most teachers can immediately tell an inquirer which students seek extra tasks, which always do the prescribed assignments well, which do as little as possible, and which do almost nothing in or out of class.

To measure the degree of involvement a student has in a course is perhaps not as difficult as to explain why one student is interested and another is not. Some students have *limited aspirations* in life and have little desire to continue an academic education. Others are interested in only specific areas of the curriculum. Still others are vitally concerned with many courses, and for them interest is easily sparked.

Some students are inflexible in their rate of reading. Some relatively rapid readers do well in literature and history classes but cannot slow down enough to seek out the details of mathematics and science and to plot courses of action that solving a mathematics problem and following a science experiment require. Still others read everything slowly. These students may find the preciseness of mathematics and science well suited to their reading habits, but they find that reading a novel is a tedious job.

Over several years' time those students whose reading habits lead them to success in mathematics and science and to less than success in history and literature will undoubtedly find that their backgrounds of experience are rich in some areas and deficient in others. Further, their reading skills are unevenly developed; they may find that courses in which literal comprehension skills are stressed are to their liking (because they do well in these). But they may find that courses in which discussions center on higher level cognitive skills—such as deciding on motives of characters or real people or judging the worth of a novel or biography—are dull. Similarly, the opposite type of reader exists.

So, accumulated experiences in a variety of courses may in itself channel students. Yet, in most classes, a wise teacher can somewhat circumvent an otherwise almost certain poor showing for some students—and can build achievement in areas where students are weak and capitalize on areas of strength—by allowing students, at least sometimes, to pick their favorite genre (novel, biography, essay, poetry, newspaper or magazine article, documents, etc.) and also their area of interest, probably within prescribed boundaries.

The remainder of this chapter will help you understand: (1) why people choose to read; (2) techniques to use to find out what *specific students* are interested in and/or choose to read and ways of developing interest; and (3) a taxonomy of affective involvement, which enables us to judge the intensity of interest a student has in a subject. It is hoped that these explanations will help you to better meet the interests of your students.

REASONS FOR READING

Understanding what *motivates* students to read may help us to make willing readers of them. That is, if we know their basic drives and can satisfy these drives, we will get students involved.

Given time, why do people *choose* to read? Waples, in his book *What Reading Does to People*, gives us five reasons.[1] He says that people read for: (1) the instrumental effect, (2) prestige, (3) reinforcement of an attitude, (4) vicarious aesthetic experiences, and (5) respite. Let us look at each of these reasons in a little detail. You may wish to refer to Waples' book for more complete explanations.

Instrumental Effect

According to Waples, people read for the instrumental effect when they have a problem to solve, a test to pass, a speech to give, a cake to bake, a model airplane to build, etc. They seek printed materials that are lucid and to the point. If one set of materials—such as a textbook, a magazine or newspaper article, a set of directions, a biography, etc.—is not complete, they seek supplementary materials. Usually, they are looking for books or articles that help them to work efficiently.

After they have read the materials and used their ideas to solve the problem, pass the test, give the speech, etc., they have attained the instrumental effect. Given another problem, another test, another speech, they're back at it again—seeking and reading lucid materials that will help them to achieve another goal.

Prestige Effect

People also choose to read for prestige—especially to improve their own self-image. Some adults read all of the books on the "best seller" lists to enhance their own egos. Other read the sports pages regularly, or the society pages, or certain magazines or journals—so that they are not caught short when asked a question.

Students frequently read, or pretend to read, the classics, not because they enjoy or appreciate them, but because such reading impresses the teacher. Encouraging students to read for such a reason is unwise. Such reading does *not* build a permanent interest in reading. We are rapidly developing a nation of people who can read but will not!

However, another facet of this category may lead to worthwhile goals, although it may also lead to self-deception. The deception enters if the stories chosen are pat, slick, stereotyped, and biased. If the stories have substance and truth, such reading can be therapeutic and inspiring. Choice of materials is therefore all-important.

The idea here is that people often choose to read the kind of story that glamorizes their real-life situation. A boy chooses a sports story in which the leading character is like him—a football hero but a poor student. This reader may resolve his anxieties about his poor scholarship by seeing his hero in the book succeed despite poor grades in school. More easily done in a book than in real life? The reader, especially if he concentrates on such books, may be in for a shock later on.

Similarly, a poor girl may read romantic stories about other poor girls who grew up to marry wealthy prince charmings. All well and good if such reading leads the reader to self-improvement, but even so, she may be in for a letdown, for there may not be enough prince charmings to go around.

But what of the budding scientist who reads authentic biographies of scientists? Through such reading, he or she may begin to understand how the scientific mind works—how scientists got their starts and how they continued to grow in creative ability. Or, a young home economist might read about Julia Child or the *Cordon Bleu* and thereby become involved. The lives of Einstein, Schweitzer, Frank Lloyd Wright, Florence Nightingale, Lincoln, Benjamin Franklin, Madame Curie, Thoreau, Georgia O'Keeffe, Sarah Caldwell, Rachel Carson, Agatha Christie, Ann Sexton, Jacques Cousteau, Helen Keller, and hundreds of others could inspire our young to travel a creative route if they see something in the lives of these people with which they can empathize and which they might emulate.

Reinforcement of an Attitude

People sometimes choose to read in order to reinforce their opinions or feelings. They "know" they believe in something—their political party, their religion, their styles, or even their superiority—but they may not know exactly why, or they may not have all the latest arguments at their fingertips. They read to reinforce their attitude, possibly even to give themselves ideas for their next verbal encounter.

This is fine—perhaps. Certainly we can all learn more about many things we honestly believe in. But, and this may not surprise you, people tend to choose to read only those books and articles which *reinforce* their beliefs. If, for example, each of two local newspapers leans toward a different political party, it is likely that readers will choose to read the one that backs their favorite party, for they would find it distressing to read the other paper. Only the very sophisticated reader chooses to look at the other side of an issue.

Many people by nature build and strengthen one point of view and are unaware of any logical arguments on the other side. They even "tune off" people who speak on the other side, frequently becoming so emotional that they are unable to listen.

The duty of our schools is to present multiple points of view—to help students see that there may be other ideas worth considering. Students should learn to weigh, to compare, to evaluate. Of course, conversion may occur if a student considers another point of view.

Schools, themselves, are guilty of presenting biased points of view. If only a single textbook is available, for example, students get a one-sided argument. Textbooks differ in what they include. Even mathematics and science textbooks differ. What the author and publisher consider to be important is included, and that's all. History texts, for instance, are summary statements of the author's ideas. The statements often are broad, and the details included are those the author wished to include. Compare a textbook written by a Southerner about the Civil War and one written by a Northerner. Certainly multiple reading materials are needed to help students see many points of view. Fiction, biography, essays, and poetry are necessary to enable the student to empathize with course content.

Frequently, literature anthologies include the same selections edition after edition. (Note the "staying power" of *Silas Marner* in tenth-grade texts, etc.) Also, the very *organization* of anthologies channels thought, *e.g.*, consider the different kinds of thinking and relating that are likely to occur when one studies a chronological presentation, a genre presentation, an area to area presentation, or a thematic presentation.

Vicarious Aesthetic Experience

People may choose to read for vicarious aesthetic experiences. An author can state ideas more clearly, more forcefully, more beautifully, than most readers can. Through the words of a writer, people can see clearly what another age was like or what another country is like.

Classical writers have uncommon insights, and they have the ability to portray these visions through words. We grow in depth and breadth by reading Stevenson, Milne, Kipling, E. B. White, Jonathan Swift, Saint-Exupéry, Shakespeare, Cervantes, Chaucer, Molière, Byron, Keats, and others. We learn about human nature—about what motivates people. By reading, we can live in all ages—past, present, and future. And we can live in all places—on earth, on the moon, in a harem, under the sea, atop mountains, in a palace, in a ghetto, in a submarine, in a chemistry laboratory with the Curies, as an observer, or even as a member of the President's cabinet. We can live vicariously as almost anyone—anywhere. We can learn to understand a variety of personalities. We can experience the full range of human emotions. Unfortunate is the man who does not read, for his life is lived within restricted boundaries—of places, ages, and people.

Respite

We also read for respite—for temporary relief from pain or sorrow, or for escape. We must all escape sometimes, and reading is a ready avenue of escape. The further removed reading matter is from our actual experience, the greater our ability to escape is likely to be.

It is well known that English professors and college presidents love to read mysteries. They enjoy books they can read just for pleasure and then forget. By doing such reading, they get a short vacation. Why deny such pleasure to our students?

Surely, teachers in all content areas can find books for their students to read that are pure pleasure. *They should be allowed to read them in class sometimes.* Science fiction, sea stories, historical mysteries, delightful biographies, historical fiction, and mathematical puzzles are some appropriate categories.

As teachers, we needn't feel guilty if we set aside class time—even one hour a week—for such "free" reading. We may be giving some students the therapy they need, and we may be lighting flames in many. Students may even begin to *enjoy* our classes—and why not? Surely *we* enjoy them.

Comment

If one of our goals is to have students *enjoy* reading (so that they will become readers), we must avoid asking them too many questions. Sometimes just a simple inquiry, "Did you like it?" is enough. And an answer of yes is enough from them. Perhaps you can see that they enjoyed a book just by watching them while they were reading it. What do we think we—or they—are gaining by having them answer so many questions?

Many students will *wish* to share what they have learned or experienced through reading. There are many ways in which they might do this: telling about it, reading a passage to the class, pantomiming, being in a skit or a member of a panel, drawing a mural, etc.

WHAT STUDENTS CHOOSE TO READ

In addition to knowing what motivates students to read, it is helpful to know what kinds of things they like to read. Of course, students' reading interests are as diverse as are the students themselves. Some like to read one kind of book and others, another. Yet it is possible to describe types of books that appeal to a large number of students at various chronological age levels.

It is important to note that chronological age, rather than mental age (or I.Q.), is a major factor in determining a student's reading interests. Bright students tend to enjoy the same types of stories as do average students of the same chronological age. Young adolescents, no matter how bright, usually do not seek out adult fiction. In general, they like stories about young people—their age-mates. Yet, surely, no one can generalize about individual students.

Numerous studies have been conducted about the reading interests of students. One of the most complete and readable guides is *Books and the Teen-*

Age Reader by G. Robert Carlsen.[2] Carlsen carefully describes the "stages of reading development" which students frequently progress through—from early adolescence (grades 5–9), to middle adolescence (grades 9–11), to late adolescence (grades 11–college). He also discusses numerous books that appeal to teenagers. You would do well to study this and other similar sources carefully.

Yet, knowing the interests of adolescents in general is not the same as knowing the interests of specific adolescents—your classes of students—or of a specific student. How can you discover what a specific student likes?

Self-Selection

One of the best ways known to find out what book a specific student will like is to use a very simple technique. Lay out a banquet table, and see what the student selects. Bring to your classroom a wide variety of books, and see which ones he or she takes. Like the good child who would prefer the chocolate cake but takes spinach because mother is watching, a student or two or three may select a book for the prestige effect. Be alert to this!

Be sure that the atmosphere is free. And be sure that you *don't* compliment students for having made a wise (or good or any other kind of a) choice.[3] Anything goes in a self-selection situation as long as the students are happy. Remember, you're trying to find out what the students are interested in, not whether they will read books you want them to read. You can, of course, control some factors, for you may bring to class only certain kinds of materials, but be *as broad as possible* in your choices and include a variety of genre (biography, essays, poetry, fiction, newspaper and magazine articles, documents, etc.), a variety of themes, when possible, and a wide range in level of difficulty.

Some students may pile selected materials high on their desks, whereas others may find nothing they like. You may wish to take some students to the school library, where there may be a greater range of materials.

To add variety, you may from time to time give "book talks," introducing something by reading it to the class or to a group of students. Then set it aside and see who takes it. Students, too, may wish to give "book talks" or to use some other technique to interest their classmates in a particularly interesting book or article.

Such activities should go on in *all* content area courses, not just in English class. And they should occur frequently.

Questionnaire Technique

If you wish to survey the reading interests and/or favorite activities of a group of students, you might use one, or several, questionnaire techniques. A simple technique to use is an open-ended questionnaire.

QUESTIONNAIRE

Name ____________________

1. Do you read a newspaper regularly? ____

2. Which parts of a paper are your favorites:

____ news stories	____ funnies
____ sports pages	____ crossword puzzles
____ editorials	____ astrology
____ fashions	____ inspirational articles
____ society pages	____ art, theater, movie critiques
____ ads for ____	____ other: ____________________

3. Do you read any magazines regularly? ____ If so, name them: __________
____

4. Do you enjoy reading comic books? ____ Which are your favorites?
____
____

5. Name some of the favorite books you have read:

______________________________	______________________________
______________________________	______________________________
______________________________	______________________________

6. If you could read about *anything*, what would you read about? __________
____

7. Number in order of preference your favorite kinds of reading materials and put a zero before those you dislike:

____ short stories	____ essays
____ novels	____ plays
____ biographies or autobiographies	____ science fiction
	____ mysteries
____ poetry	____ comic books
____ newspaper article—news	____ "how to do it" materials
____ newspaper article—sports	____ religious articles or books
____ newspaper article—society	____ other: (name)
	____ other: (name)

8. Name any T.V. programs you watch regularly:

______________________ ______________________

______________________ ______________________

______________________ ______________________

9. Do you watch any news program regularly? ______________________

10. How do you most enjoy spending your free time?

______________________ ______________________

______________________ ______________________

Another type of questionnaire is one which might reveal reading attitudes toward such things as free and organized reading in the classroom, reading in the library and at home, and recreational and general reading. The Heathington Intermediate Scale, which follows, is such a questionnaire.

HEATHINGTON INTERMEDIATE SCALE*

Name ______________

Blacken the box for each number to indicate how you feel about each statement, using this system:

SA = strongly agree U = undecided D = disagree
A = agree SD = strongly disagree

SA	A	U	D	SD		
☐	☐	☐	☐	☐	___	1. You feel uncomfortable when you're asked to read in class.
☐	☐	☐	☐	☐	___	2. You feel happy when you're reading.
☐	☐	☐	☐	☐	___	3. Sometimes you forget about library books that you have in your desk.
☐	☐	☐	☐	☐	___	4. You don't check out many library books.
☐	☐	☐	☐	☐	___	5. You don't read much in the classroom.
☐	☐	☐	☐	☐	___	6. When you have free time at school, you usually read a book.

* Betty S. Heathington. "Heathington Intermediate Scale," in *Attitudes and Reading,* by J. E. Alexander and R. C. Filler. Newark, Delaware: International Reading Association, 1976, pp. 30–32. Reprinted with permission of the author and the International Reading Association.

SA A U D SD

☐ ☐ ☐ ☐ ☐ ___ 7. You seldom have a book in your room at home.

☐ ☐ ☐ ☐ ☐ ___ 8. You would rather look at the pictures in a book than read the book.

☐ ☐ ☐ ☐ ☐ ___ 9. You check out books at the library but never have time to read them.

☐ ☐ ☐ ☐ ☐ ___10. You wish you had a library full of books at home.

☐ ☐ ☐ ☐ ☐ ___11. You seldom read in your room at home.

☐ ☐ ☐ ☐ ☐ ___12. You would rather watch TV than read.

☐ ☐ ☐ ☐ ☐ ___13. You would rather play after school than read.

☐ ☐ ☐ ☐ ☐ ___14. You talk to friends about books that you have read.

☐ ☐ ☐ ☐ ☐ ___15. You like the room to be quiet so you can read in your free time.

☐ ☐ ☐ ☐ ☐ ___16. You read several books each week.

☐ ☐ ☐ ☐ ☐ ___17. Most of the books you choose are not interesting.

☐ ☐ ☐ ☐ ☐ ___18. You don't read very often.

☐ ☐ ☐ ☐ ☐ ___19. You think reading is work.

☐ ☐ ☐ ☐ ☐ ___20. You enjoy reading at home.

☐ ☐ ☐ ☐ ☐ ___21. You enjoy going to the library.

☐ ☐ ☐ ☐ ☐ ___22. Often you start a book, but never finish it.

☐ ☐ ☐ ☐ ☐ ___23. You think that adventures in a book are more exciting than TV.

☐ ☐ ☐ ☐ ☐ ___24. You wish you could answer the questions at the end of the chapter without reading it.

Scoring of each item can be done in the blanks just before the numbers. Five points are given for a very positive response, 4 for a positive response, 3 for an undecided response, 2 for a negative response, and 1 for a very negative response.

On nine of the items (items 2, 6, 10, 14, 15, 16, 20, 21, 23) a response of "strongly agree" is very positive and receives 5 points. On all of the other items, a response of "strongly disagree" indicates a very positive attitude and receives 5 points. The possible range of scores is 5×24 (120) to 1×24 (24).

The Intermediate Scale also has groups of questions which can be used by classroom teachers to diagnose specific areas of reading attitudes. They are as follows:

1. free reading in the classroom (items 5, 6, 15)
2. organized reading in the classroom (items 1, 24)
3. reading in the library (items 3, 4, 9, 17, 21)
4. reading at home (items 7, 10, 11, 20)
5. other recreational reading (items 12, 13, 23)
6. general reading (items 2, 8, 14, 16, 18, 19, 22)

A third type of questionnaire, or inventory, might correlate well with specific content being studied. We all know that textbooks supply a limited amount of information—and frequently no enjoyment to the student. Textbooks tend to contain summary statements. A great deal is covered in limited space. By reading textbooks, students frequently get an overall view, but rarely does a reader empathize with a textbook.

To know what it was like to live in another age, another area, another dimension, one must "live" in that age, area, dimension. One can hardly accomplish this by reading a textbook, but one can by reading good literature.

Dwight Burton says, "A lifetime is too long a time to find out what it's like to live."* One might even say, "A lifetime is not long enough to find out what it's like to live." Indeed, how much can we learn *directly*—that is, through direct experience? Compare that with what we can learn—and enjoy and appreciate—by living *vicariously,* for example, through reading.

By reading we can live many lives, limited only by our choice of books and our reading ability. We can each choose our own books and combinations of books *ad infinitum.* (Quite different from the limitations of television, movies, and even the theatre in our area—not that these do not sometimes offer excellent opportunities for expanding horizons.)

Through reading, we can see creative genius at work, and we can also see the diabolic developing. We can watch specific influences on people's lives and thus guide our own better.

We can know what it's like to be black—in the South and in the North. We can know what it's like to be Chinese, Japanese, British, French. We can know what it's like to struggle with adversity and also to live a life of ease and harmony.

We can live many lives through reading. In reality we can live but one.

Imagine how dull a classroom would be where only textbooks and pamphlets and factual materials are read. Not that these are not important, for they are. But compare such a classroom with one that uses those materials plus biography and imaginative literature. Trade books of many types can be used as an integral part of *all* courses—and of most units within these courses.

---

* Dwight Burton, *Literature Study in the High Schools.*

The vital teacher of any course is already well acquainted with numerous trade books related to the content of the course. All teachers might wish to consult Chapter 11 in this book to identify references for locating additional materials.

Physical education teachers sometimes say, "Ah, but how does this apply to me?" And a fellow teacher says, "Your students might read biographies of Lou Gehrig, Hank Aaron, the Four Horsemen. Your students might want to teach younger children to swim, to play basketball, or tennis. They'll need a book to learn how to teach these. They might want to read about famous sports events of the past—real or fictional. They might want to read about careers in the sports field, etc."

And a math teacher might say, "How does this apply to me?" Consider the atmosphere of a class where only problems are worked with that of a class where practical applications are explained in the areas of a student's interest, for example, in engineering, in architecture, in a supermarket, at a pool table. In math one might also read about famous mathematicians to find out how mathematics became what it is today. A mathematics student might want to work math puzzles, etc.

A mathematics teacher might gather a wide variety of materials, perhaps 40 or more books that relate to the course being taught. The teacher might introduce these to the class by using an interest inventory, such as the following:

GEOMETRY

Name ____________________

Would you like to read a book about (circle Yes or No):

1. Yes–No: the history of math as it marches through time beginning in 600 B.C. under Greek influences and progressing through the Middle Ages and Renaissance up to 1908? (W. W. Rouse Ball: *A Short Account of the History of Mathematics*)

2. Yes–No: a proof that shows a right angle equal to an obtuse angle or that 1 = 2? (W. W. Rouse Ball: *Mathematical Recreations and Essays*)

3. Yes–No: geometry's place or existence in our everyday lives with illustrations to explain the terminology used? (Anthony Ravielli: *An Adventure in Geometry*)

4. Yes–No: how to draw an octogon using a square, or to draw parallel lines, one-point perspectives, and other designs using the tools of a draftsperson? (J. R. Walker and E. G. Plevyak: *Industrial Arts Drafting*)

5. Yes–No: creating geometric designs? (Adolf Lorch: *Modern Geometric Design*)

6. Yes–No: the advantages and disadvantages of being an architect, the qualifications, job opportunities, and a self-evaluating test? (Richard Roth: *Your Future in Architecture*)

7. Yes–No: the intuitive understanding of geometric principles rather than logical relationships? (D. Hilbert and S. Cohn-Vossen: *Geometry and the Imagination*)

8. Yes–No: the math of primitive humans, progressing to the new math, with interesting sketches and pictures to accompany the history? (James T. Rogers: *The Pantheon Story of Mathematics for Young People*)

.
.
.

40. Yes–No: different types of kites, along with their history and construction, that can contribute to the development of measurement, comparison, and geometric ideas? (H. Waller Fowler, Jr.: *Kites*)

In a history class where students are studying World War II, an inventory such as the following might be used:

WORLD WAR II (HISTORY)

Name ____________________

Would you like to read a book or article about (circle Yes or No):

1. Yes–No: Norwegian children who helped smuggle millions of dollars out of Norway to America to keep it from their German captors? (Marie McSwigan: *Snow Treasure*)

2. Yes–No: a Jewish girl who spent several years in an attic room in Amsterdam to escape the Nazis? (Anne Frank: *Diary of a Young Girl*)

3. Yes–No: a hunchback who sailed the British Channel to rescue stranded soldiers in Dunkirk who were being forced into the sea by the Nazis? (Paul Gallico: *Snow Goose*)

4. Yes–No: five men who lived through the atomic attack on Hiroshima and tell their story? (John Hersey: *Hiroshima*)

5. Yes–No: a Japanese girl who saw her mother die in the atomic attack on Hiroshima and later fell in love with an American soldier—her dilemma? (Edita Morris: *Flowers of Hiroshima*)

6. Yes–No: an insane genius who feared he was part Jewish (one grandparent) and was determined to exterminate Jews and rule the world? (John Toland: *Hitler*)

7. Yes–No: the coup of World War II: the breaking of the German code which allowed the Allies to read most of the signals between Hitler and his generals throughout the war? (F. W. Winterbotham: *The Ultra Secret*)

8. Yes–No: life for a Russian in a Stalinist workcamp after he allowed himself to be captured by the Germans in 1945 and escaped? (Alexander Solzhenitsyn: *One Day in the Life of Ivan Denisovich*)

.
.
.

40. Yes–No: a possibly true account of attempted surrender by the Japanese before the dropping of the atom bomb? (William J. Caughlin: "The Great Makusatsu Mistake—Was This the Deadliest Error of Our Time?" *Harper's Magazine,* March 1953)

The next inventory is one designed for a science class in which students are studying animals of the Southwest.

SCIENCE—ANIMALS OF THE SOUTHWEST

Name ____________________

Would you like to read a book about (circle Yes or No):

1. Yes–No: the big and small animals of the Cichuahan, Sonoran, Mohave, and Great Basin deserts as well as some personal experiences encountered by the author in his research? (Edmund C. Jaeger: *Desert Wildlife*)

2. Yes–No: some of our more interesting neighbors in the desert by the name of javelina, armadillo, ring tails, and others, told in a storylike form? (B. F. Beebe: *American Desert Animals*)

3. Yes–No: one man's personal adventures in a year of studying and living with the coatimundi? (Bil Gilbert: *Chulo*)

4. Yes–No: some of our feathered friends and the land they live in, with color photographs of the area and the birds? (Roland H. Waver: *Birds of the Big Bend National Park and Vicinity*)

5. Yes–No: deadly vertebrates and invertebrates common to the Southwest? (Charles T. Vorkies: *Poisonous Animals of the Desert*)

6. Yes–No: 16 different families of fish and the common as well as scientific names of the members of each family? (William J. Koster: *Guide to the Fishes of New Mexico*)

7. Yes–No: the part the coyote played in the first eclipse and the Flood, along with other Navajo myths? (Dobie J. Frank, editor: *Coyote Wisdom*)

8. Yes–No: the creatures that inhabit one of the most beautiful national parks in America? (Vernon Bailey: *Animal Life of the Carlsbad Caverns*)

.

.

.

40. Yes–No: the history, some personal tales, and beliefs about animals? (Clayton Williams: *Animal Tales of the West*)

Rather than selecting books because of subject matter, a teacher, especially an English teacher, might wish to select them because of literary genre, or form. The next inventory is of this type.

HUMOR AND SATIRE

Name ____________________

Would you like to read a book (circle Yes or No):

1. Yes–No: of jokes, anecdotes, and stories about topics ranging from advertising to the generation gap and history, by one of America's wittiest writers? (Bennett Cerf: *The Sound of Laughter*)

2. Yes–No: about the funny exploits of seven men who undertake the perilous climb of the world's largest mountain? (W. E. Bowman: *The Ascent of Rum Doodle*)

3. Yes–No: about the evolution of American humor, including short tales, poems, and ballads from the different periods of American history? (Constance Rourke: *American Humor—A Study of the National Character*)

4. Yes–No: that allows one to enjoy the rarely seen humorous side of prominent English and American politicians from the eighteenth century to the 1960s? (Leon A. Harris: *The Fine Art of Political Wit*)

5. Yes–No: about 3 good friends who buy each other's clothes at a rummage sale, and including 28 other humorous plays? (Robert Fontaine: *Humorous Skits for Young People*)

6. Yes–No: about the cowboy who fell asleep during duty hours and was awakened by a tarantula, and including other humorous antics, tall tales, and jokes of and about cowboys? (Stan Hoig: *Humor of the American Cowboy*)

7. Yes–No: about the development of American literature as never explained by your teachers? (Richard Armour: *American Lit Relit*)

8. Yes–No: on the history of American humor, with numerous references to humorists and their works? (Willard Thorp: *American Humorists*)

.
.
.

40. Yes–No: about the adventures and misadventures of a man who suddenly finds himself thrust back into the sixth century in Camelot? (Samuel L. Clemens: *A Connecticut Yankee in King Arthur's Court*)

Such a technique is similar to the "self-selection" technique, except that it's possibly more efficient and also includes brief descriptions of reading materials. A classroom teacher may wish to vary the technique, alternating the types used.

Ring-a-Bell Technique

Have enough *different* books related to the theme or literary genre being studied so that there is one copy for each student in the group or class. You may supply these books, or you may ask each student to bring in one book. Distribute a book to each student and allow each student to read his or her book.

After five minutes, ring a bell. All students *must* pass their book to the person next to them. Allow five minutes again for the examination of the new book. Then ring the bell, and the students must pass their second book on to another student. Continue for thirty minutes.

At the end of thirty minutes, allow students to choose their favorite and continue reading it until the end of the hour. They may sign it out if they wish to take it with them. Work out some plan in case several want the same book.

Letter of the Alphabet

An enjoyable activity might be to send a group of students to the library for an hour to research and prepare a report about something of their choice that begins with a certain letter of the alphabet—say *h*. In a science class students might choose: harp seal, Halley's comet, hummingbird, hartebeest, hairball, hoot owl, etc. In English: Hindi, hyperbole, Huxley, haiku, Hesse, hillbilly, Helen of Troy, etc. In social studies: handgun, Harry Truman, Ho Chi Minh, habeas corpus, The Hague, horoscope, hitch hiking, or even hanky-panky in Washington, D.C., etc. In mathematics: hyperbola, hypotenuse, hemisphere, heptagon, or Einstein (for those who prefer another letter, since it's mostly for fun anyway). In home economics: hairdo, hamburger, hors d'oeuvres, hot fudge, handiwork, haberdasher, etc. In physical education: halfback, handball, hall of fame, half gainer, horse shoe, etc.

Variations might be that each student is given a different letter of the alphabet. Or students might be asked to research something that lives in the desert, in the sky, in the water, on mountains, etc.

Choral Reading

Choral reading, or reading in unison, is very popular among young people. Teachers may choose poetry and have the whole class read orally together or have groups of students take parts. Poetry can be found that is appropriate to any content area subject at any level.

Read-In

Nationally, Read-Ins are becoming more and more commonplace at all educational levels. Read-Ins occur when the program of the whole school stops and everyone—the principal, librarian, guidance counselor, janitor, teachers, and students—chooses a book to his or her liking and reads it for pleasure. Teachers do not grade papers or read textbooks. They read adult books they enjoy. This may be the only time a student sees an adult read for pleasure.

Some schools set aside an hour a week for a Read-In. Others set aside a half-hour daily. However it is scheduled—at a fixed time or at random—a Read-In is sure to be a success.

Some schools call this technique USSR: Uninterrupted Sustained Silent Reading.

MEASURING INTENSITY OF INTEREST

David Krathwohl is the senior author of the book *Taxonomy of Educational Objectives: Handbook II, Affective Domain.*[4] An article titled "Evaluating the Affective Dimension of Reading," by David W. Darling, delineates this domain and gives excellent suggestions of ways to develop interests of students through the use of printed materials.[5]

```
         R
        RECEIVING
         S
         P
         O
         N O
         D R
     VALUING
         N A
         G N
           I
CHARACTERIZING
           I
           N
           G
```

Affective Levels

The taxonomy gives us a "hierarchical continuum" of the affective domain. By using this taxonomy and observing student behavior, we can recognize the affective level of each student as it relates to our classroom activities. Such recognition may, when necessary, encourage us to provide more appealing materials and ideas. Thus, we may raise the level of involvement of some students. According to Krathwohl *et al.*, there are five major levels of affective involvement, and these form the basis of the present author's elaboration in the sections that follow.

Receiving

If students are not receiving information or ideas, they are not affectively involved, even at the lowest level. One can spot such students easily: they may be reticent, daydreaming, or highly aggressive. To know the reason for their noninvolvement, however, may be more difficult. They may display several of these characteristics: they may be hard of hearing; their vision might be inadequate; they may read English poorly; they may already know the ideas being imparted or may lack the background to understand them; their friends or family may discourage them from learning; or their family may push them too much. Some of these factors can be remedied more easily than others. Frequently, the help of a specialist is required.

Students who are at the lowest end of the affective continuum—in the *receiving* category—will be seen to listen and observe, but not to respond. Their eyes and ears follow the teacher and the class discussion, but they are only mildly involved. They may be merely *aware* of what is going on; or better, they may be *willing to receive* ideas; or better still, they may exhibit *controlled attention.* It is sometimes difficult to know the degree of their reception or even their sincerity.

> Some students appear to be receiving when they are not, for they have developed a facial set which gets them through many—to them—dull or frustrating experiences. Other students are timid and shy and observe intensely, but with a sort of hidden interest. A good number of students—especially teenage boys—*pretend a lack of interest* by squirming and wiggling, and may display what at first appears to be dislike for a subject or book. But on second glance, a teacher can see that their souls are alive. When they're alone with the teacher, they may not be able to keep up the pretense, and the teacher may find that they are really *committed!*
>
> When I first began teaching reading in high school, I was fooled a few times by such boys. Later, I saw a pattern, and instead of being disturbed by such overt behavior, I appreciated it and even hoped for it. Such boys in my class usually had records of juvenile delinquency and/or were often in the vice-principal's office for discipline. Some-

how, they all got to take reading (they were disabled readers, of course). Like the boys in *Hooked on Books,* they usually *could* read, but would not.

Well, they read in my classes, where they were given free choice from an extensive classroom library. These boys (like Lester in *Hooked on Books,* who read *The Scarlet Letter*) read—amazingly—books like *Cry, the Beloved Country, To Kill a Mockingbird, Old Man and the Sea,* etc. They might, however, hide such a book in a school notebook so their classmates would not catch on to them. But they would come to my reading center, even if I had a class, during their study halls and read more of such books. They knew immediately that I was on to them, though I never told them or asked them questions. I just gave them passes to come and had enough books I knew would interest them.

Such boys only *appeared to be merely at the receiving level.* Many teachers, thinking these students were basically lacking in interest or were hostile, easily provoked their hostility. I did, too, when I first started teaching—until I found that hidden under that toughness was a rarely awakened sensitivity and interest.

Responding

However, when a stimulus is given, we usually look for more than simple receiving. We hope for some type of response. In fact, the stimulus-response theory of learning is widely respected. Students who progress beyond the receiving category can be further classified by the type of responding behavior they display—those who *acquiesce in responding,* those who are *willing to respond,* and those who display *satisfaction in responding,* replying, or reacting.

It is simple to observe which students must be strongly encouraged to openly react in class. They must always be called upon, and their answers are usually brief and half-hearted. Some may, however, be interested but insecure, and this may account for their *acquiescence* in responding.

Other students know they should respond in class, so they do—but with little satisfaction. Their hands are up because they want a better grade or because they want to fill in a time gap, not because they feel they have a fascinating idea or because they love to share their thoughts with others. These students are *willing* to respond.

Others, however, are enthusiastic about a book they read or an idea that just flashed through their mind—or they may find that they learn by sharing ideas. They volunteer and are *satisfied* by responding.

Valuing

A level above responding is valuing. Some students may value the act of reading, and thus they will be readers (provided that satisfactory materials are available), and/or some students may value subject matter (perhaps in a specific area) enough to pursue this interest. In other words, they may be devoted to reading, *per se,* or they may be devoted to specific ideas they get through reading.

Again, there are three sublevels in this category of behavior. The lowest level is *acceptance of a value*—the student approves of reading or of what he or she learns through reading. A higher level is *preference for a value*—when given a choice of alternatives, the student chooses to read or to read certain things. An even higher level is *commitment to a value.* To evaluate commitment by observing external behavior characteristics, "the teacher should look for (a) constant reading, (b) depth reading in special areas, and (c) a dependence on reading as a means of recreation as well as a means of becoming informed."[6]

Students can be helped to recognize their own value system if the teacher asks them such questions as: " 'What books [or activities] did you reject before settling on this one?' Or, 'Why did you decide to major in English rather than math, science, or history?' (*preference level*). Or, 'Are you willing to recommend that author [or book, idea] to the class?' (*commitment level*)."[7]

Retrospective-introspective questions might be utilized to help students recognize their degree of valuing. Such questions as the following might help them recognize their own value system.

Retrospective

1. How long have you enjoyed mathematics (science, history, literature, music, manual arts, home economics, art, etc.)?
2. During your study periods, when your homework is finished, have you frequently thought of your mathematics (etc.) problems—and perhaps of ways of using your math (etc.) out of school?
3. Have you used what you have learned *in mathematics,* for example, in building a cabinet or other piece of furniture; *in literature* in figuring out why someone acted as he or she did; *in social studies* in analyzing propaganda; *in history* in seeing similarities between what has happened in the past and what is happening now; *in science* in seeing how a plant in your yard grows; *in home economics* in cooking at home?
4. Have you ever found yourself dreaming about mathematics (science, literature, writing, history, music, etc.) and thinking of unique problems or ways of using it?

Introspective

1. Why do you enjoy mathematics (science, history, literature, etc.)?
2. Under what conditions do you think you will continue to enjoy it?

3. Have you noticed that you find time to read about and/or study mathematics (science, history, literature, etc.) when there are other things you might be doing? Is this desirable or is it inconsistent with your present and/or future needs?

When such retrospective and introspective questions are suitably answered by students, they may move into the *organizing* level, the level at which they display a conscious awareness of their value system and see a value as part of their life structure.

Organizing

If students have a well-organized value system, they are aware of what they value, and there is a degree of consistency in their value system. The two areas within the organizing category, thus, are *conceptualization of a value* and *organization of a value system.*

Retrospective and introspective questions help them become aware of, and thereby *conceptualize,* their values. Questions that will lead students to analyze whether this value is consistent with their philosophy of life and with their immediate and future goals are important here. For example, students might be asked how long they have felt the way they do about reading (or the content). If the content is science, for example, they might be asked if they feel they have the ability and means to become a scientist—if they think of science as a vocation or avocation, if they are especially interested in a specific area of science. They might be asked if they think that interest is temporary or permanent.

Characterization by a Value or a Value Complex

People who reach the very highest level—characterization—are completely devoted to a value or group of values. They embody the value in an internally consistent way. Actors and actresses sometimes temporarily *become* the person they are portraying. Students sometimes become scientists, mathematicians, poets, or lovers of poetry. These people have reached the highest level of affective involvement. Unfortunately, sometimes youngsters *become* delinquents or dropouts because they have not learned to love anything the school offers and, therefore, they must look elsewhere.

Some people find the affective domain difficult to understand. Perhaps an example will help clarify it.

Imagine that it is your birthday. A family member or friend has given you a gift—a tennis racket and some balls. (Throughout this example, remember that ideas—such as ideas one gets in class—are gifts too.)

You had never thought much about playing tennis. Perhaps you're not sure you want to learn to play. At this point, you have several choices: You might reject the gift. You might accept it, examine it, and then exchange it for something more to your liking. Or you might accept it and examine it carefully and perhaps decide to keep it.

So far, at most you are at the *receiving* level of the affective domain. You have begun at the point of *awareness*—you recognize that your gift is a tennis racket and balls. You may, or may not, have progressed to the point where you are *willing to receive* this gift. But if you are willing to do so, you may progress to giving your gift your *controlled attention;* i.e., everything else is of no importance at this point.

If you are to progress, your next step will be in the *responding* category. You may thank the donor because you know you must (*acquiescence in responding*) or you may begin using your racket because you know you should. You may, instead, willingly and somewhat happily play around with the racket and ball and say a cordial "thank you" for it (*willingness to respond*). You may progress to find yourself very satisfied with your gift and volunteering to play tennis, perhaps a bit to your surprise (*satisfaction in responding*).

Next, you may be observed to become warm toward the game (*acceptance of a value*). Those around you will notice that when given a choice of activities, you sometimes choose to play tennis rather than other tempting things (*preference for a value*). Soon you regularly choose to get out on the court (*commitment to a value*).

But you, yourself, may not have noticed how devoted you are to the game. Once this recognition flashes through your mind, you're in the *organizing* level: you've *conceptualized the value.* By now you may find yourself in some trouble. You're playing tennis all the time and ignoring your homework and who knows what all. It's time to get organized! (Or as the famous college cartoon says: "*Next* week, I've got to get organized.") Soon you may put things in perspective: some tennis, yes, but not tennis always. Stick with it, and you are at the *organization of a value system* level. (Perhaps you've decided you'll be a tennis pro or enter Wimbledon, in which case tennis may deserve a major part of your time—of your value system.)

Whether you've decided to give tennis major or minor priority, you may move up one step to the *characterization* level. Playing tennis is an integral part of your behavior. You may be characterized by loving to play tennis (*characterization by a value*) or by loving to play tennis but also enjoying other things a great deal too (*characterization by a value complex*).

Discussion

We may compare our tennis enthusiast with our students or perspective students. Let us note that a decision was made at the very first stage about whether or not to accept the gift. Had the gift been rejected, no progress would have been possible. Of course, rejection is possible at any level, and it is not possible for everyone to be characterized by everything we hope to teach.

We may feel that the content we think we must teach is more important than the interests of our students. We may feel that we must cover the syllabus or the textbook—whether the students like it or not. If we feel this way, we may "cover the material" even though our students are not listening. If students are not "plugged in" and willing to receive—willing and, perhaps, anxious to respond and react—willing to pursue and value what they are learning, we are failing. In most cases it is *we* who are doing something wrong and thereby failing both them and society. If they do not receive, they should be elsewhere. If they do not react, they are robots. If they do not value, they do not enjoy, they do not continue to grow and prosper, they do not love: they are devoted to nothing.

Affective Chart

Teachers might like to use the following chart to record the affective involvement of their students in particular units of study. They may wish to use a new chart for each unit so that they might compare the degree of interest of specific students, and the class in general, from unit to unit. Units in which students display high interest might serve as models for those that elicit less interest among students.

A different color or symbol might be used each time an observation is made. It seems reasonable to expect individual students to move up the affective ladder as the unit progresses and students become more familiar with the ideas. If this does not happen, teachers might ask questions such as:

1. Why is interest not growing?
2. Am I using materials appropriate to the reading achievement levels of individual students?
3. Am I diversifying materials enough?
4. Am I building skills necessary for understanding the concepts of the unit?
5. Am I varying my approaches to teaching?
6. Am I allowing students free time to read unit-related materials of their choice?
7. Am I allowing students to share their ideas with one another if they wish?
8. Etc.

AFFECTIVE CHART

Unit Title: Courage as Displayed in Literature Dates: Oct. & Nov.

AFFECTIVE LEVELS

	RECEIV-ING			RESPOND-ING			VALUING			ORGAN-IZATION		CHARACTER-IZATION
NAMES	awareness	willingness	controlled attention	acquiescence	willingness	satisfaction	acceptance	preference	commitment	conceptualization	organization	characterization
1. Betty Allen	1		2									
2. John Brady			1				2					
3. Judy Clark		1	2									
4. Mary Dick	1					2						
5. Dennis Flack								1	2			
6. Catherine Fox	2		1									
7. José Herrera						1		2				
8.												
9.												
10.												

By reading this chart, we can see by looking at the first observations (marked "1") that most students were in the *receiving* category, but Dennis Flack was already at the *valuing level*. He was already highly interested, perhaps because of previous reading about the subject. José also had ideas to offer to the class, and he enjoyed sharing them.

At the second recorded observation (marked "2"), we see that most students moved up in interest. However, Catherine Fox regressed. One would wonder why. Perhaps she hadn't found the "right" book for her.

SUMMARY

If we wish to encourage students to read, it is helpful to know why they might choose to read. Waples explains that people read: (1) for the *in-*

strumental effect, (2) for the *prestige effect,* (3) to *reinforce an attitude,* (4) for *vicarious aesthetic experience,* and (5) for *respite.* Frequently, such motives are in harmony with the goals of a content area classroom, and a wise teacher can capitalize on them. The kind of student reporting, if any, done after such reading should be related to the purpose.

To find out what types of materials individual students choose to read, one need only observe what they select when given a wide choice and when no value judgments are made by an authoritarian figure such as a teacher or parent. Questionnaire techniques, possibly of a general nature, or perhaps geared to specific materials related to course work, might also be used.

An affective taxonomy was explained to help teachers more fully develop their ability to observe the intensity of interest which students display toward course work. Typical student behavior at each level ranges from *receiving* to *responding* to *valuing* to *organizing* to *characterizing.*

NOTES

1 Douglas Waples. *What Reading Does to People.* Chicago: University of Chicago Press, 1967.

2 G. Robert Carlsen. *Books and the Teen-Age Reader.* A Bantam Book, H3468, 1972.

3 See David Darling. "Evaluating the Affective Dimensions of Reading," in *The Evaluation of Children's Reading Achievement,* ed. Thomas C. Barrett. Newark, Delaware: International Reading Association, 1967, pp. 127–141.

4 David Krathwohl. *Taxonomy of Educational Objectives: Handbook II, Affective Domain.* New York: David McKay, 1964.

5 David Darling, *op. cit.*

6 *Ibid.*

7 *Ibid.,* p. 138.

SUGGESTED ACTIVITIES

1. Waples gave us five reasons why people choose to read. In terms of your content area subject and the amount of class time available, evaluate the relative worth of each reason as deserving of class time. That is, which do you feel is most deserving of class time? Least deserving? Why?
2. Describe four interest centers you would like to have in your classroom when you are teaching a specific concept or set of concepts. What specific printed materials would you hope to have in each center? What other materials would you like to have? When would your students use these centers?

3. Design an interest inventory in which you include brief descriptions of 40 books, pamphlets, or articles which relate to a theme or genre you might teach in your content area. Use a format similar to the 40-item inventory models given in this chapter. Use the reference aids explained in Chapter 11.
4. Describe the behaviors—in class and out—that you feel would characterize one of your students who is at the lowest end of the *receiving* category of the affective domain. What behaviors would a student display if he or she were at the preference level in your course (valuing level: preference for a value)? How does the latter's behavior differ from the behavior of a student who has reached the *characterization* level?
5. Explain what you would do if you found that one or more students in your class were at the lowest level of the affective domain. Would you change your teaching methods? Materials? What would you do if many students reached the responding level but apparently were not going to move any higher?

REFERENCES FOR FURTHER READING

Alexander, J. Estill, and Ronald Claude Fuller. *Attitudes and Reading*. Newark, Delaware: International Reading Association, 1976.

Andresen, Oliver. "Evaluating the Author's Theme in Literature," in *Corrective Reading in the High School Classroom*, ed. H. Alan Robinson and Sidney J. Rauch. Newark, Delaware: International Reading Association, 1966, pp. 64–74.

Burton, Dwight L. *Literature Study in the High Schools*, 3rd ed. New York: Holt, Rinehart and Winston, 1970.

Carlsen, G. Robert. *Books and the Teen-Age Reader*. New York: Bantam, H3468, 1972.

Cooper, Charles R. *Measuring Growth in Appreciation of Literature*. Newark, Delaware: International Reading Association, 1972.

Darling, David. "Evaluating the Affective Dimension of Reading," in *The Evaluation of Children's Reading Achievement*, ed. Thomas C. Barrett. Newark, Delaware: International Reading Association, 1967, pp. 127–141.

Fader, Daniel. *Hooked on Books*. New York: Berkeley Publications, 1968.

Hafner, Lawrence E. (ed.). *Improving Reading in Secondary Schools, Selected Readings*. New York: Macmillan, 1967, Section 11.

Huus, Helen. *Children's Books to Enrich the Social Studies for the Elementary Grades*. Washington, D.C.: National Council for the Social Studies, 1966.

Jennings, Frank. *This Is Reading*. New York: Bureau of Publications, Teachers College, Columbia University, 1965.

Krathwohl, David R., *et al. Taxonomy of Educational Objectives: Handbook II, Affective Domain*. New York. David McKay, 1964.

Massialas, Byron and Jack Zevin. *Creative Encounters in the Classroom: Teaching and Learning Through Discovery.* New York: John Wiley, 1967.

Monson, Dianne L. and Betty J. Peltola. *Research in Children's Literature—an Annotated Bibliography.* Newark, Delaware: International Reading Association, 1976.

Painter, Helen W. *Reaching Children and Young People Through Literature.* Newark, Delaware: International Reading Association, 1971.

Reid, Virginia M. (ed.). *Reading Ladders for Human Relations.* Washington, D.C.: American Council on Education, 1972.

Sargent, Eileen E., Helen Huus, and Oliver Andresen. *How to Read a Book.* Newark, Delaware: International Reading Association, 1970.

Torrance, E. Paul and R. E. Myers. *Creative Learning and Teaching.* New York: Dodd, Mead, 1970.

Waples, Douglas. *What Reading Does to People.* Chicago: University of Chicago Press, 1967.

Reprinted by permission of The Washington Star Syndicate, Inc.

INTEREST INVENTORIES

Austin, Mary C., C. L. Bush, and M. H. Huebner. *Reading Evaluation.* New York: The Ronald Press, 1961.

Harris, A. J. *How to Increase Reading Ability*, 5th ed. New York: David McKay, 1970, pp. 462–466.

Heathington, Betty S. "Primary and Intermediate Scales for Measuring Attitudes," in *Attitudes and Reading*, by J. Estill Alexander and Ronald Claude Filler. Newark, Delaware: International Reading Association, 1976.

Karlin, Robert. *Teaching Reading in High School.* Indianapolis: Bobbs-Merrill, 1964, pp. 212–215.

Strang, Ruth. *The Diagnostic Teaching of Reading*, 2d ed. New York: McGraw-Hill, 1969, pp. 110–117.

Witty, Paul. *Reading in Modern Education.* Boston: D. C. Heath, 1949.

UNIT TWO

DEVELOPING CLASSROOM STRATEGIES FOR READING IN CONTENT FIELDS

Chapter 5 focuses on:

(1) the teacher's responsibility in presenting a reading assignment and in providing for post-reading activities. Skills needed for reading, and purposes for reading, in four content areas—science, mathematics, social studies, and English—are listed, with cross-references to chapters, or sections within chapters, of this book where more complete explanations and techniques for teaching are given.

(2) a technique designed for independent study of expository material, including two variations of the technique, one for use in reading science materials, and the other for use with mathematics problems.

(3) classroom management in terms of grouping procedures, including whole class instruction, personalized instruction, and small group instruction.

Chapter 5

TEACHING STRATEGIES FOR CLASSROOM USE

What is the teacher's responsibility in presenting a reading lesson to a group of students?

What guidelines, or models, can be used in presenting a lesson?

What can a teacher do to provide for, and encourage, individualized and/or group reading following a required assignment?

What are some grouping procedures commonly used in content area classrooms?

INTRODUCTION

The focus of this chapter is on the responsibility of teachers in presenting a reading assignment, their role in the discussion which follows the reading assignment, and their role in helping students extend their interests. Also included is a discussion of some grouping procedures commonly used in content area classrooms.

The *directed reading activity,* a five-step plan, is explained first. This plan includes pre- and post-reading activities. It is these activities, which the teacher should plan well for, that allow students to successfully read on their *instructional level,* a higher level than their independent level.

SQ3R, also a five-step plan, is designed especially for mature students, although many of its provisions are also useful for other students. Teacher guidance in the use of SQ3R will aid many students to attain independence in the skillful study of expository materials.

Whenever students read assigned lessons, it is hoped that they will wish to pursue interests which have grown in this reading. To help this occur, teachers should follow certain procedures. Among them are helping students clarify their interests, helping students locate varied materials, providing class time for the pursuit of such interests, and providing opportunities for making full use of what is learned.

There will be times when students and teachers will recognize the need for further skill development. Opportunities for this should also be provided. Such activities may find nourishment in class-wide sharing, but at other times individualization, or personalization, of instruction will be desirable. Also, there are many times when group activities are most useful.

The final section of this chapter deals with classroom management as it relates to class-wide, individual, and group procedures.

DIRECTED READING ACTIVITY

The directed reading activity (DRA) is a five-step lesson plan especially designed to help those students who are reading materials that are on their *instructional,* rather than *independent,* reading level. It is designed to be used in a group or class-wide situation, for this plan is too lengthy to be used with individuals.

Step 1

Explore students' backgrounds in regard to *information* related to the reading assignment and *skills* the students will need in order to understand the assignment. *Build students' backgrounds* when it is apparent that they have insufficient *information* to be able to understand the assignment and/or insufficient *skills.* Relate the assignment to their previous learning. Part of this step and the next is to *motivate* students so that they will wish to read the assignment.

The following kinds of activities might be useful in accomplishing Step 1:

1. Review a previous chapter and/or related readings or experiences.
2. Review, or teach for the first time, a necessary word attack skill such as a syllabication generalization, a type of context clue, the meaning of morphemes that relate to the assignment, etc. (See Chapter 6 of this book.)
3. Possibly list new vocabulary words on the board. *If desirable,* explain their meanings, if possible by using illustrations or models. (See "Dimensions of Vocabulary" in Chapter 6. You may wish to use one of the teaching techniques suggested in Chapter 6, e.g., see pp. 138–139.) Such techniques can be used before the chapter is read by the students. Some of the other techniques might legitimately be used after the chapter has been read by the students.*
4. Review, or teach for the first time, a comprehension skill such as outlining (see Chapter 7: "Sequence") which is necessary for understanding the assignment.
5. Review, or teach for the first time, a critical-creative skill, such as an area of semantics (connotations, etc.) or propaganda analysis, fallacies of reasoning, syllogistic reasoning, etc., synthesis activities, or evaluation. The skill that should be reviewed or taught is the one that is necessary for the understanding of the assignment to be read. (See Chapter 6: "Connotations" and Chapter 9: "Analyzing, Synthesizing, and Evaluating Ideas Through Reading.")
6. Show a film or filmstrip to build the students' background of experience so that they can better understand the assignment and/or so that they gain interest in it.
7. Show the class a picture or real object—especially in science or mathematics—so that they can better visualize what is being discussed in the assignment.
8. Have someone who is knowledgeable about the subject or a related subject —a student, another teacher, a parent, a member of the community, etc.— talk to the class.

---

* According to George G. Mallinson, "The lists of key words . . . should not be studied *before* the materials in the chapter are covered. Otherwise, the student will acquire a number of atomistic definitions that are out of context. These lists may well be studied for post-testing, but hardly for pre-study." From "Methods and Materials for Teaching Reading in Science," in *Sequential Development of Reading Abilities,* ed. H. M. Robinson. Supplementary Educational Monographs, No. 90. Chicago: University of Chicago Press, 1960, pp. 145–149.

All of the above are never done in one lesson. Following is an example of how a teacher might introduce a lesson on space travel. Here the teacher might engage the class in "brainstorming." The teacher might ask students to suggest as many ideas as they can that relate to space travel.

Students might volunteer these random ideas:

> Mars—"When do you think we'll send a person to Mars?"
> the moon—"We've been there!"
> Venus
> Pluto
> Saturn—"Saturn is dark. It has a ring around it."
> money—"The cost of it all."
> time astronauts
> distance cosmonauts
> exciting green people on Mars
> "I saw Neil Armstrong take his first step on the moon."
> "I saw Alan Shepard's trip."
> "Russia beat us into space."
> "Do you think we'll find rare metals in space?"
> "Do you think there are living things in space?"

(The teacher prods: "What else do you know about travel in space? What other questions do you have?")

> "What are we doing in our space program now?"
> "I'd like to travel in space. I want to go to another universe."

The teacher might continue to probe for additional comments. Then he or she would ask students to begin to group ideas into general concepts or broad categories. For example, some categories might be:

1. *planets or where we might go in space:* Mars, Pluto, Saturn . . . beyond our universe . . . "Do you know any other planets or places we might travel to?"
2. *reasons for space travel:* excitement, we might find metals . . . "What are other reasons? . . . educational value, scientific value . . . others?
3. *people who have traveled in space:* Alan Shepard, Neil Armstrong . . . "Who are some others? . . . Would *you* like to travel in space?"
4. *When have we traveled in space?*

While the class is classifying the ideas suggested by the students and is adding to these from the background of information the students have, the teacher might sketch a chart like the following on the board:*

* The spoke graph is useful with materials organized in an expository (logical) order. Time lines, flow charts, and tree charts are better for materials in time order. Maps and sketches are appropriate for material organized in space order. Chapter 7 of this book includes examples of such illustrations.

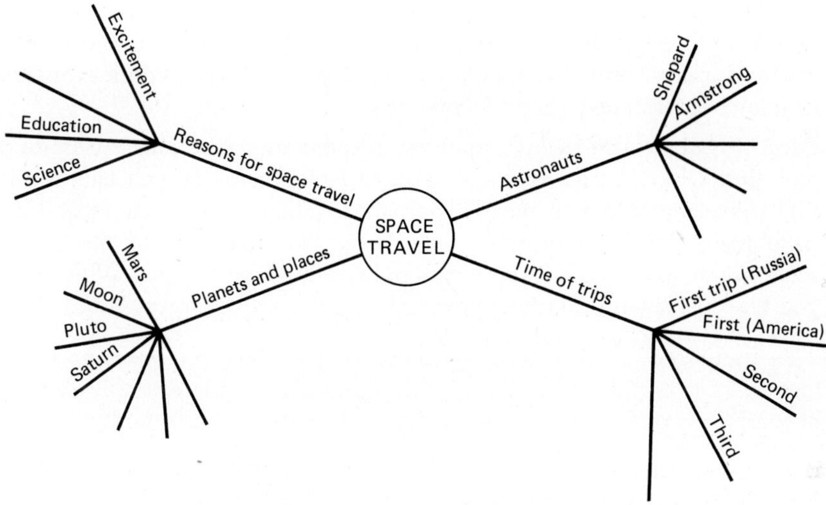

Next, the teacher might show the students an illustration of the earth and the distances of the planets from it. He or she might also show pictures of some of the astronauts and cosmonauts and highlight some of their trips.

Then the teacher might list several words that may be new to students in this assignment. The words would be pronounced and their meanings clarified if the context of the assignment did not clarify them.

Step 2

The second step includes: (1) *previewing* the assignment, (2) *clarifying purposes* for reading the assignment, and (3) possibly making a statement about the *rate of reading* that is appropriate for the assignment. The purpose of this is to give definite guidance to learning. Purposes should be stated clearly and should be suited to the content of the materials and to affective goals of instruction. First, *preview* the assignment by using a survey technique. (See "S" in SQ3R in this chapter and "Skimming" in Chapter 10.)

Second, *state purposes for reading* the assignment, or better still, *have students state purposes.*

1. Purposes might include the acquisition of literal information, for example, getting meanings of specific words from context, getting main ideas, sequence, theme (if stated), following directions, etc., and translation activities. (See Chapters 6 and 7.)
2. Purposes might also include a specific question about interpretation (e.g., What will happen if what the author recommends does occur? etc.) (See Chapter 8.)

3. Purposes might also include eliciting critical-creative reactions. (Are any fallacies of reasoning used? Is there card stacking? Is there one idea that you find useful? By what standards would you evaluate the ideas included in this chapter? etc.) (See Chapter 9.)
4. Purposes might also include affective responses or reactions: How do you feel about . . . ? Would you like to have been there? Which character, or real person, would you most like to be? When would you most like to have been the protagonist? Least? Does the resolution of the problem seem fair to you? Which topic was most interesting to you? Why? Would you like further information about any topic? (See Chapters 4 and 11.)

The importance of stating the purpose, or purposes, for reading as a pre-reading activity cannot be overemphasized. Consider, for example, how you might read a chapter on space travel if your purpose were to find:

1. What country was first to launch a man in space. Second? What country is likely to be next? Why? What events led Russians and Americans to compete to be first? What kinds of feelings about educational systems were apparent in Russia and the United States at the time of the initial launchings?

Would you read the assignment differently if your purpose were, instead, to find:

2. Why we travel in space. Do we travel for an educational value? If so, what is the educational value of space travel? Is it worth the money spent? Do we travel for a scientific value? A communications value? Are there other reasons for space travel? Which value is most important according to the author? Which value is most important to you?

Or, your purpose might be to read it for another reason, which would require another focus on your part. For example, you might read it to find:

3. Who the astronauts have been, in chronological order of their trips in space. Who have the cosmonauts been—in order? You might wish to arrange the astronauts' and cosmonauts' trips together in one time line. How have our astronauts been selected and trained? How do the Russians select and train their cosmonauts? Are there similarities in the two selection processes? Differences? Have either the Russians or Americans sent a woman into space? Is your background similar to that of any astronaut? Do you think you could become an astronaut if you wished to?

It becomes obvious that the stated purpose helps to focus thought during reading. Although readers will gather information other than that asked for in the statement of purpose, they are likely to concentrate on the kind of information that is requested.

The teacher might state purposes such as one or more of those above. Or the teacher might draw from the students purposes for reading such an assignment that are particularly interesting to them. The purposes might grow out of the discussion as suggested in Step 1.

A teacher might, instead, specify certain sets of questions for certain students, perhaps according to student interest. If several texts or materials are being used (varying the materials according to student reading levels), the teacher might assign one set of purposes to one group and another set of purposes to another group, etc.—the purposes being appropriate to the content discussed in the specific materials being read by the various groups of students.

Third, if desirable, make a statement about an appropriate *rate of reading* to use for the assignment. (See Chapter 10.)

Step 3

Students read silently. (This might be homework.)

Step 4

Students *discuss* the assignment or in some other way respond to it (by writing about it, by doing what is suggested in it, by drawing a picture or other illustration about it, etc.). They carry through and/or are helped in carrying through the activities whose foundations were laid and whose purposes were stated in Steps 1 and 2, respectively, of the DRA. At this time, students might read aloud brief statements from the assignment to prove an answer they have given to a question. Additional useful activities might emerge from student thought and discussion during or after the reading of the assignment.

This fourth step is extremely important. The teacher must decide just how this sharing activity is going to be carried on. Many possibilities are available. Among them are:

1. *a teacher-directed discussion or quiz:* This might be best when certain kinds of learnings are to be achieved by the student, and the teacher is interested in ensuring that such is the case. This is particularly useful when convergent thinking is desired. Normally, questions are asked by the teacher, and students respond to them—orally, in writing, or by performing an activity.
2. *a nondirective, or inquiry-centered, discourse:* This is best when the teacher does not pose as an authority figure. Students are free to respond to, and question each other about, the assignment.

   The teacher's job might be one of prodding students to explore and test alternatives, to encourage students to defend any statements they make, to ask for the clarification of points made by students, to raise additional questions at a time of impasse, to legitimize creative expression, to perform certain managerial tasks such as recognizing students, planning many of the topics that will be explored, spacing and sequencing topics, locating materials, introducing materials and topics, serving as a springboard for inquiry and discussion, and summarizing discussions.[1]

Step 5

Extend the activity. This might mean going on to the next chapter or having students do related reading or other activities.

The original assignment might lead to reading related materials, including newspaper and magazine articles and pamphlets, biography, poetry, fiction, etc. (See "The Unit Plan" in this chapter, "Using Library Resources" in Chapter 11, and "Assessing and Building Student Interests in Reading Materials" in Chapter 4.)

It might lead to an interview with another person, or seeing a play, a movie, or a T.V. show. It might lead to writing an original communication or work of art, such as a skit, which might be performed for the class. (See Chapter 9: "Synthesis.") It might lead to the setting up of an experiment and performing it.

Assignment: Keep the steps of the DRA clearly in mind as you read the next five chapters of this book. After you finish these chapters, you will be asked to write your own DRA for a chapter in your content area book.

Skills Needed for Reading in Specific Content Areas

The most commonly needed skills for reading in specific content areas are described in the following pages. You will note that general areas are similar but that the specifics may differ.

Science

Vocabulary

1. learning and recognizing terms that are unique to science, e.g., photosynthesis, phylum, stromata, multicellular (see Chapter 6: "Denotations of words, meanings of new words" and "Morphology" and "Phonic Syllabication");
2. learning scientific meanings of common words, e.g., culture, power, belt (see Chapter 6: "Denotations of words, multiple meanings of simple words");
3. learning scientific and mathematical symbols and abbreviations, e.g., H_2O, Fe, $<$, $>$, Σ (see Chapter 6: "Symbols and Abbreviations);

4. understanding how new words enter our language or are coined, e.g., television, astronaut, sputnik (see Chapter 6: "Diachronic Linguistics");
5. consider also: over-heavy vocabulary load (see Chapter 2: "Judging the Difficulty of Reading Materials" and Chapter 3: "Finding the Appropriate Level of Materials for Each Student").

Comprehension

1. selecting significant details, recognizing main ideas, classifying convergently, following directions, getting sequence, recording information in outline, graph, map, and chart form, and reading outlines, graphs, maps, and charts (see Chapter 7 and "Skimming" in Chapter 10);
2. formulating main ideas from evidence, classifying, seeing likenesses and differences, assuming cause-effect relationships, retrospecting and anticipating, applying ideas to new situations (see Chapter 8);
3. dissecting, analyzing information, establishing validity of source of information, determining author's purpose, establishing cause-effect relationships, syllogistic reasoning, synthesizing ideas, divergent production, evaluating (see Chapter 9).

Comprehension and appreciation

4. developing the habit of extensive and intensive reading in science—for greater cognition and appreciation (see Chapters 4 and 11).

Speed of comprehension

1. developing the ability to adjust speed according to the purpose for reading and the difficulty of materials (see Chapter 10).

Mathematics

Vocabulary

1. learning and recognizing terms that are unique to mathematics, e.g., perpendicular, quadrilateral, congruent, numerator (see Chapter 6: "Denotations of Words, meanings of new words" and "Morphology" and "Phonic Syllabication");
2. learning mathematical meanings of common words, e.g., square root, improper fraction, reduce (see Chapter 6: "Denotations of Words, multiple meanings of simple words);
3. learning mathematical symbols and abbreviations, e.g., bu, pk, ÷, $\surd$ (see Chapter 6: "Symbols and Abbreviations");

4. consider also: over-heavy vocabulary load (see Chapter 2: "Judging the Difficulty of Reading Materials" and Chapter 3: "Finding the Appropriate Level of Materials for Each Student").

Comprehension

1. selecting significant details, classifying convergently, following directions, recognizing main ideas, recognizing sequence, recording information in graph and chart form, and reading graphs and charts (see Chapter 7);
2. seeing likenesses and differences, anticipating approximate answers, applying ideas to a new situation, formulating main ideas (see Chapter 8);
3. analyzing information, recognizing irrelevant information, establishing validity of a source of information, syllogistic reasoning, synthesizing ideas, evaluating (see Chapter 9).

Comprehension and appreciation

4. developing the habit of extensive and intensive reading in mathematics—for greater cognition and appreciation (see Chapters 4 and 11).

Speed of comprehension

1. developing the ability to adjust speed according to the purposes for reading and the difficulty of materials (see Chapter 10).

Social Studies

Vocabulary

1. learning and recognizing terms that are unique to social studies, e.g., communism, democracy, imperialism, centralization (see Chapter 6: "Denotations of Words, meanings of new words" and "Morphology" and "Phonic Syllabication");
2. learning social studies meanings of common words, e.g., race, bill, cabinet, left and right (see Chapter 6: "Denotations of Words, multiple meanings of simple words");
3. learning word connotations, understanding figurative language and allusions, e.g., liberal, hot potato, money talks, modern David (see Chapter 6: "Word Connotations and Figurative Language");
4. understanding that words change in meaning, e.g., propaganda, melting pot, unique (see Chapter 6: "Diachronic Linguistics");
5. understanding how new words are coined or how they enter our language, e.g., smog, UNESCO, NATO, SALT, zapped (see Chapter 6: "Diachronic Linguistics");

6. consider also: over-heavy vocabulary load (see Chapter 2: "Judging the Difficulty of Reading Materials" and Chapter 3: "Finding the Appropriate Level of Materials for Each Student").

Comprehension

1. selecting significant details, classifying convergently, following directions, selecting main ideas, recognizing sequence, recording information in outlines, graph, map, chart form, and reading outlines, graphs, maps, charts (see Chapter 7 and "Skimming" in Chapter 10);
2. formulating main ideas from evidence, classifying, anticipating and retrospecting, assuming cause-effect relationships, inferring time and place, determining motives of real people, applying information to new situations (see Chapter 8);
3. analyzing information, establishing authenticity of sources of information, analyzing propaganda, recognizing fallacies of reasoning, synthesizing ideas, evaluating (see Chapter 9).

Comprehension and appreciation

4. developing the habit of extensive and intensive reading in social studies materials—for greater cognition and appreciation (see Chapters 4 and 11).

Speed of comprehension

1. developing the ability to adjust speed according to the purpose for reading and the difficulty of materials (see Chapter 10).

English

Vocabulary

1. learning and recognizing terms that are unique to English, e.g., adjective, apostrophe, ballad, antihero (see Chapter 6: "Denotations of Words, meanings of new words" and "Morphology" and "Phonic Syllabication");
2. learning English (literary or grammatical) meanings for common words, e.g., romantic, comedy, subject, feet, act (see Chapter 6: "Denotations of Words, multiple meanings of simple words");
3. learning word connotations and understanding figurative language and allusions, e.g., lemon, two peas in a pod, Narcissus, Pygmalion (see Chapter 6: "Word Connotations and Figurative Language");
4. understanding that words change in meaning and pronunciation, e.g., "lewd and nice," criticism, perfect, poem, family (see Chapter 6: "Diachronic Linguistics");

5. understanding how new words are coined or how they enter our language, e.g., motel, SNAFU, morpheme, antsville (see Chapter 6: "Diachronic Linguistics");
6. consider also: over-heavy vocabulary load (see Chapter 2: "Judging the Difficulty of Reading Materials" and Chapter 3: "Finding the Appropriate Level of Materials for Each Student").

Comprehension

1. selecting significant details, classifying convergently, following directions, selecting main ideas, recognizing sequence, recording information in outline, graph, map, chart form, and reading outlines, graphs, maps, charts (see Chapter 7 and "Skimming" in Chapter 10);
2. formulating main ideas from evidence, recognizing theme, classifying, anticipating and retrospecting, making comparisons, inferring time, place, mood, and motives of characters, responding to imagery, empathizing, applying ideas to new situations (see Chapter 8);
3. recognizing semantic devices, making judgments about the authenticity of sources of information, distinguishing between fact and opinion, analyzing propaganda, detecting fallacies of reasoning, synthesizing, writing unique communications, evaluating (see Chapter 9).

Comprehension and appreciation

4. developing the habit of extensive and intensive reading in language arts materials and literature—for greater cognition and appreciation (see Chapters 4 and 11).

Speed of comprehension

1. developing the ability to adjust speed according to the purpose for reading and the difficulty of materials (see Chapter 10).

SQ3R

SQ3R can serve as a student directed substitute for a teacher directed reading activity when students are working on the *independent reading level.*[2] It can also serve as an alternative DRA, to be used as a teacher guided activity in a group or class-wide situation to achieve certain purposes when students are working at their *instructional reading level.*

It is especially helpful as a *teacher directed activity* in introducing and reviewing a textbook. And it is especially helpful as a *student directed activity* for mature readers who are reading non-narrative material without the aid of a teacher's guidance in the form of a DRA. Parts of it can even be built into a DRA.

The following flow chart illustrates the SQ3R process. The steps are explained below.

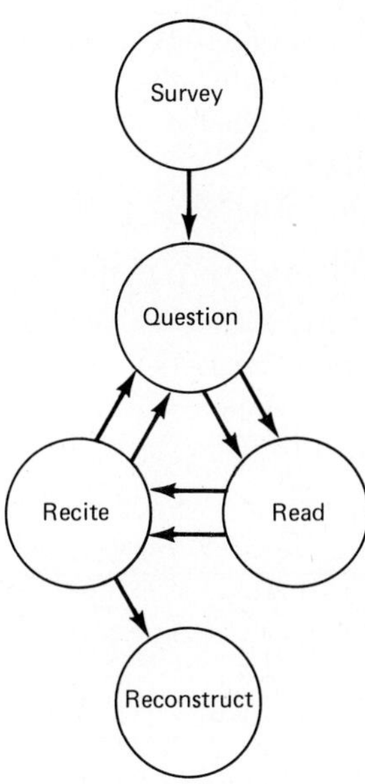

S = Survey[3]

Read the title of the book. Read the author's name. What are the author's credentials? Is he or she likely to be biased? Is a particular school of thought likely to be represented? Are there other schools of thought to be compared with this one?

Study the Table of Contents. From it you can get an outline of the whole book. Is there card stacking? Are any important major ideas not included? (Of course, no book can include everything on a topic.) Must I consult other sources to get a complete view?

Read the Introduction and/or Preface. What is the author's point of view? For whom is the book written?

Survey each of the chapters in the following way: read the title, the introductory statement, and all main headings in order. Study illustrations, and read the concluding statement or summary. Try to recall the outline of the chapter before going on to survey the next chapter.

Glance through the Glossary and Appendixes to see what additional information is given.

Finally, when you begin to read the book chapter by chapter, survey each chapter again before reading it. Try to construct an outline in your mind—or on paper—before studying the chapter. Also ask questions, e.g., Is anything important omitted?

For example, the chapter might be about dialects of American English. The main headings within the chapter might be organized in a spatial pattern, thus: Eastern Dialects, Southern Dialects, Midwestern Dialects, Southwestern Dialects, Northwestern Dialects.

In your mind, you might visualize a pattern such as the following. You might even sketch it on paper.

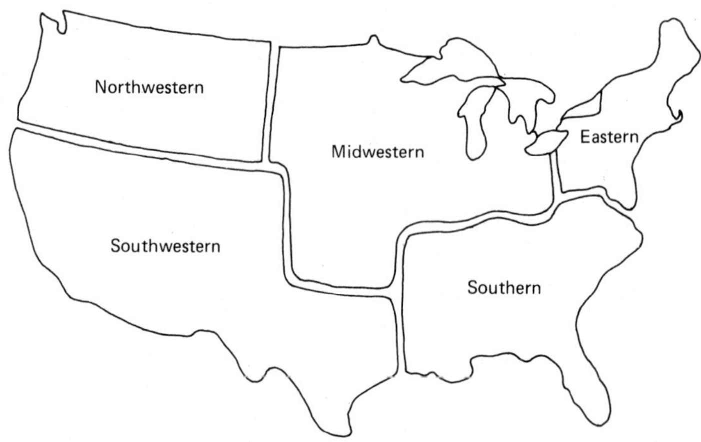

Q = Question

Look at the first main heading. Ask yourself what it means. Ask yourself questions that you think might be answered in the section. For example, ask yourself, "What are the characteristics of Eastern dialects that differentiate them from other dialects? Why is there a unique dialect group in the East? Is this dialect likely to specialize more in the future, or is it likely to become more like "general American" because of T.V., the radio, movies, etc.? Ask similar questions about the other dialects as you proceed in your reading.

R_1 = Read

Read to find the answers to your questions. If the answers are not there, you may wish to find them somewhere else. These are good questions to ask in class or to go to find the answers to in the library.

R_2 = Recite

Recite the answers to yourself to help you remember them. Ask yourself if the answers given by the author make sense. Ask yourself if you have a new idea which you can use—perhaps in a written assignment or in conversation or in performing a task, etc.

Q, R_1 R_2 = Go to the next heading and repeat: Question, Read, Recite. Then go to the next heading and repeat, etc., until you have finished the chapter.

R_3 = Review or Reconstruct

Review the whole chapter in a "survey" fashion, but with the details filled in. Then reconstruct the outline in your mind or on a piece of paper. Try to recall important ideas the author has discussed. Ask yourself some interpretive level or critical-creative-evaluative level questions. Also try to think of applications of the ideas learned.

At this point you may wish to *extend* your reading to find additional sources which give you information in greater depth or give you another point of view. Even reading of a tangential nature may be interesting.

Variations of SQ3R

Variations of the SQ3R technique have been suggested in the literature. One is for science; the other, for mathematics.

Science

For science, George Spache suggests the use of the PQRST technique.[4]

Preview:	rapidly skim the total selection
Question:	raise questions to guide the careful reading to follow, in terms of the study purposes
Read:	read the selection, keeping the questions in mind
Summarize:	organize and summarize the information gained
Test:	check your summary against the selection.

Mathematics

For problem reading in mathematics, Leo Fay recommends the use of the SQRQCQ technique.[5]

Survey:	read the problem rapidly to determine its nature
Question:	decide what is being asked, what the problem is
Read:	read for details and interrelationships

Question: decide what processes should be used

Compute: carry out the computation[6]

Question: ask if the answer seems correct, check the computation against the problem facts and the basic arithmetic facts.

EXTENSION ACTIVITIES

Whenever reading is done in any one source or in a limited number of sources, there is the distinct possibility that it may be desirable to read and study other materials. The original source may be so interesting that it will lead to in-depth related readings. Or, the source may be incomplete, and other materials are needed so that more answers can be found. It is possible that the original source is biased, and other points of view may be needed to round out the discussion. Whatever the reason, and that reason may vary from person to person, additional sources are often needed or desired.

The wise teacher provides for such additional reading or research. Such activities fan out into group work, individual study, or possibly to whole class activities. The activities are usually *student-inspired,* although the teacher may provide guidelines.

Guidelines

The teacher may follow certain guidelines in providing for extension-type activities. Among them are:

1. *The teacher helps students clarify and extend interests.* Students may wish to study additional materials, but may have hazy ideas about focusing on a topic. Without teacher help, they may waste a great deal of time because of their naiveté in self-direction. The teacher should provide guidance to those who need it, helping them explore possibilities for extended activities and possibly helping them in formulating an outline of how to proceed.

2. *The teacher helps students locate varied materials,* or at least makes sure that the students are knowledgeable about using resource aids and materials. The teacher may have varied materials available in the classroom. Even some of these, such as dictionaries, almanacs, *Who's Who,* atlases, encyclopedias, etc., require the student to have reference techniques for their proper use. The card catalog, Dewey decimal system, *Reader's Guide to Periodical Literature,* and such other indexes as the *Agricultural Index, Art Index, Industrial Arts Index,* etc., are useful tools each student should know about. The teacher's job is to ensure that students know how to use these tools and/or to teach their effective use. (See Chapter 11 for further information about library use and reference aids.)

3. *The teacher provides class time for group or individual work.* At more advanced levels, the teacher may provide "homework time" for such activities. During this time the students might go to the library, to an experimental room, to small seminar rooms or special areas of the classroom for discussions, or use the classroom library. Individual students might just read their books in class or perform some creative activity.

4. *The teacher provides opportunities for making full use of what is being learned or experienced.*[7] The teacher allows students to share—informally or otherwise—what they have learned. He or she may provide help in organizing the information, in relating it to other ideas they have, in critically responding to it, and in creating with it. Also, the teacher helps students in assessing their growth through these extended activities. The teacher may also provide help in further extending in-depth or wide-reading activities.

CLASSROOM MANAGEMENT—GROUPING PROCEDURES

The following types of grouping plans within the classroom are useful at various times.

Whole Class Instruction

There are many occasions when everyone in a classroom will benefit from the same instruction or activity. When new ideas or skills are being introduced, the whole class could be oriented together. Often, the whole class will read the same chapter in a book. A film or filmstrip might be shown or a recording or possibly a speaker listened to. There might be classroom discussions, panel discussions, debates, choral reading, etc.

Even middle grade and teenage "show and tell" activities could be very rewarding: a student might bring an important newspaper article or editorial to any class—or a recipe in home economics, a floor plan in manual arts for arts and crafts class, a political cartoon in social studies, etc. Or, objects might be brought by travelers or just by those who carefully observe the neighborhood in science class.

There are many occasions when it would be mutually profitable for students to share with the whole class what they have learned individually or in small groups. Such sharing may happen spontaneously, or it may be carefully planned for, as when a unit of study is being completed. There is no need for such sharing to be stiff, stilted, or stereotyped. There are numerous creative ways for students to share ideas with one another.

Some students might prepare bulletin boards. Some might highlight an interesting story. Others might write news items for a class paper—in any class. Some might work on mathematical models or puzzles—or prepare crossword puzzles for their classmates. Such possibilities are infinite. Many students themselves will pleasantly surprise the class with unique ideas.

Let's look at a model for whole class instruction. The *English* or *history* teacher might lead a discussion about men and women who have displayed *courage* in order to get the students ready to read individual or group selections related to the theme of courage (in English class) or a particular period, e.g., the Revolutionary War period, in history. Students might contribute examples of courageous acts they have observed, read about, or even seen on television. Some students might even tell about their own most courageous acts.

Following this, the class might engage in the choral reading of a poem depicting a relevant courageous act. Parts might be assigned for a short play, which could be read orally to the class. Even a film might be shown and perhaps a recording played, for example, Churchill's "blood, sweat, and tears" speech. Hypothetical cases might be advanced: "What would you do if . . . ?" Also, cases that relate to available reading materials might be stated: "What would you do if . . . ?" And after students answered, they read to find out what really (real or fictional) happened.

When a whole class does read the same selection—a chapter in a textbook, a poem, a pamphlet, an article—a discussion usually precedes the reading. This discussion usually takes the form of a directed reading activity, discussed earlier in this chapter.

Many examples have been given for class-wide activities. In all classrooms, there ought also be frequent opportunities for individual work.

Individualized and Personalized Instruction

Often, it is advantageous for students to work individually. If we call this *individualized instruction,* we mean that individual students *seek* their own area of interest, *select* their own reading materials, and *pace* themselves, i.e., they do as much reading as they themselves wish to do. "Seeking, self-selection, and pacing" are key words advanced by Olson to describe modern, individualized reading programs.[8]

In such programs, the student is given free rein (although there are frequent pupil-teacher conferences). Such freedom of choice in interest areas is usually not possible in content area subjects, where the range of topics is limited. Individualized instruction, such as Olson describes, might be found in reading class and in English or language arts classes at times, but only rarely in other classes.

In content area classrooms, however, *complete freedom* of choice in interest areas may not be possible. But within a certain range—within a particular theme or genre or skill—students (at least sometimes) should be given a choice. When there are limitations placed on the "seeking, self-selection, and pacing," many term the kind of reading that occurs *personalized reading,* rather than individualized reading.

Students might contract to do certain units, but within the units, different students might read different things (self-selection and pacing principles). *Work centers* might be organized around the classroom, each featuring a different area of interest or a different skill and each containing a *variety of materials.* Students could choose the materials they wish to work with within the unit. They might freely choose their units (if they are interest units) or possibly be assigned to them (if they are skill units).

At other times, personalized reading in a content area classroom might be freer. In a mathematics classroom, for example, students may freely *choose* to read almost anything that relates to the course work. Some may choose biographies of mathematicians, or of architects or scientists, or even artists or musicians who are known to have used related mathematical principles. Still others may look for immediate practical applications of the mathematical principles—in a purchasing situation, or in building a cabinet, designing a room divider, multiplying or dividing a recipe, or converting from one measuring system to another. Still others may look for relationships in nature—for balance and structure in sea shells, trees, flowers, and so on.

In history class, if the Civil War period is being studied, some students might also wish to read biographies of Lincoln, Lee, Grant, or Mrs. Lincoln, etc. Some may wish to read *Uncle Tom's Cabin, Gone with the Wind, Red Badge of Courage, Spoon River Anthology,* etc. Still others may wish to study documents, to read poetry of the period, essays, or even newspaper accounts. A variety of materials should be available from which students may choose. Even filmstrips could be viewed and music listened to.

Surely, there is no dearth of materials available for use in a science class. If the class is studying animal or plant life, magazines such as *Ranger Rick, National Wildlife,* and *National Geographic* are available. Biographies and science fiction are also available. Many library books suggest experiments some students might wish to try.

There is much excellent material available for the English teacher. Among the best sources are *Books and the Teen-Age Reader* by G. Robert Carlsen, *Literature Study in the High Schools* (third edition) by Dwight L. Burton, *Reading Ladders to Human Relations* by Virginia M. Reid, *Good Reading for Poor Readers* by George Spache, and *Hooked on Books* by Daniel Fader. Prepared collections of paperbacks—for personalized and/or unit reading—are also available. In addition, "club memberships" are available for the purchase of paperbacks by students.

Most of the discussion in this section has revolved around the development and extension of *interests* by using a personalized approach. A *skills* approach is also possible, and often necessary. Usually, however, the teacher must know which skills the individual student is in need of improving: is it rate, flexibility of rate, word attack, vocabulary, main idea and sequence, critical reading, study skills—or what? Students should work on the skills appropriate to *their needs*. They usually do not know what their needs are, and therefore they need guidance from the teacher to channel them to the correct area of skill development.

Practical suggestions for improving reading and study skills will be given in later chapters. All teachers should give aid to students in the development of such skills—as a means of helping them to understand the content area subject.

Small Group Instruction

When students have common *reading achievement* levels, common *skill needs*, or common *interests*, they can be grouped together. Frequently, such grouping is fluid: groups are formed, students work together for a short period of time, and when a goal is reached, the groups disband. Then, other groups are formed and soon disbanded, etc.

Achievement grouping

For example, several textbooks or trade books may be available on a variety of *levels*—one set quite difficult, another easier, and another quite simple. Students might be grouped together to read the materials they are capable of reading, as revealed by the informal reading inventory they were given. Thus, students might be grouped homogeneously according to their level of reading achievement.

Sometimes, it might be useful to group students heterogeneously according to reading achievement, as, for example, in pupil-team teaching, where one student may read to the other. Or, cross-grade grouping may be used, where a poor reader in a higher grade may be unashamed of reading "easy books" to a younger student, and both may learn.

Skill grouping

But some students in each achievement group may need help in a particular *skill*, such as how to use a microscope, how to use the *Reader's Guide to Periodical Literature* or the *Art Index*, how to divide words into syllables, etc. When this skill is being taught, the teacher could group these students together for instructional purposes. As soon as the skill is learned, there is no need for this group, so its members will scatter and need not meet together again. Then, other skills will have to be taught, and new groups will be formed, only to disband when the skill is learned.

Interest grouping

A group of students may share similar *interests.* They may or may not wish to, or be able to, read the same materials, but they may desire to share their learnings with one another. Thus, temporary interest groups may be formed for sharing ideas of interest to all, but possibly not of interest to the whole class. For example, several students might be interested in reading war stories; other may wish to read plays. Some may wish to study weather maps (in science), or products of a particular region, etc. Or, students might be grouped together because they have *diverse interests.* For example, a Republican and a Democrat might be paired off to discuss an imminent election, etc.

Social grouping

In some classrooms *social grouping* can be used. A social studies teacher might group together students who have similar social backgrounds, so that they can work together, for example, in planning a budget. Or, students who are socially diverse might be grouped together to help them understand one another better. They might discuss ways holidays are celebrated, their favorite foods, or their feeling about how well or how poorly they are accepted by other groups of people.

Discussion

We have just discussed four basic criteria by which students might be grouped in classes: achievement, skill, interest, and social factors. We have briefly discussed both *homogeneous grouping* and *heterogeneous grouping* according to each criteria.

Try now to fill in the cells in Table 5.1, showing the pros and cons of homogeneous grouping and the pros and cons of heterogeneous grouping according to each criterion. Each cell should be completed.

Constellation Grouping—The Unit Plan

Constellation grouping provides for the logical and meaningful combination of all of the previously mentioned forms of grouping. For example, whole class activities may lead to small group activities and/or personalized activities. These, in turn, may lead back to whole class activities, and the cycle may begin again. This is what happens if we use the *unit approach.*

Table 5.1 Pros and cons of homogeneous and heterogeneous grouping according to various criteria

Criteria for grouping	Grouping			
	Homogeneous		Heterogeneous	
	Pros	Cons	Pros	Cons
Achievement				
Skill				
Interest				
Social				

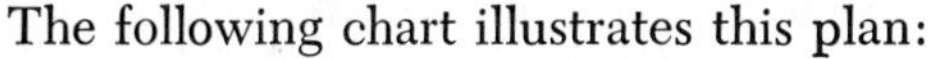

The following chart illustrates this plan:

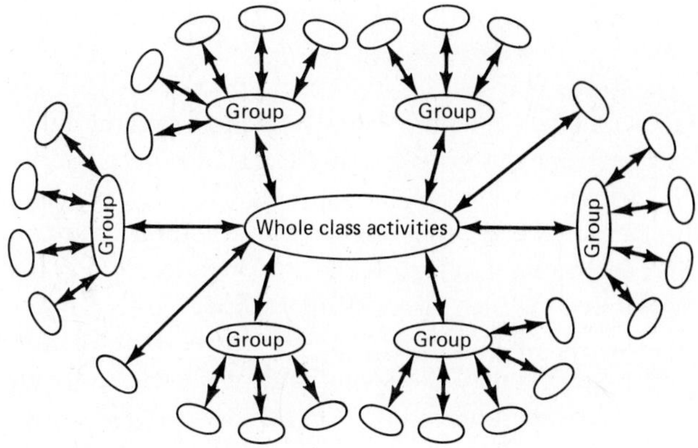

A unit may be developed around a *theme,* i.e., a particular idea, such as ecology, the next election, drug addiction, people who survived against great odds, careers, a weekly menu, foods around the globe, building home furniture, tennis, golf, sportsmanship, weather prediction, controlling harmful pests in the garden, the Revolutionary War period, the Vietnam war, mathematical principles in music and art, one aspect of solid geometry, etc. Or, a unit may be developed around a *genre,* i.e., a literary form, such as biography and autobiography, the essay, poetry, novels, short stories, newspaper articles, etc. In addition, a unit might be developed around a needed *skill,* such as how to use various machines in the woodwork shop, how to develop vocabulary and word power, how to punctuate, how to get the main idea and sequence of a selection, how to use various instruments in science class, how to multiply using various number systems, how to use the library, etc.

A unit usually consists of four phases:

Phase 1—class-wide activities orienting the student to the unit.

Phase 2—small group activities built around interests, skill needs, social factors, or achievement which flow from the class-wide activities and reinforce and more fully develop the unit according to group needs or interests.

[If at this point the teacher plans to use multiple textbooks, there is no need to concern herself or himself about the fact that various textbooks on the same subject do not cover exactly the same ideas. In fact, it might be desirable for the teacher to select textbooks that have only the basics in common and that elucidate and exemplify these basics in different ways. Thus the students in all groups may find the basics explained, but each group will be able to offer to the class unique examples. Students in all groups, therefore (even students in the slowest group), find they are able to add to the discussion in a dimension that others cannot.

For example, students in a science class might be studying about the propagation of plants and trees. Those using one book might find in it explicit examples about the propagation of fruiting trees and the possibility of grafting on to one trunk various members of the same family (e.g., peach, apricot, plum, to produce the famous "fruit cocktail" tree). Another group, using another book, might find instructions on growing an avocado from the stone to be a valuable contribution to the class. Still another group may demonstrate propagating African violets and other popular house plants. Thus each group—slow, average, fast—can contribute something of worth, and each student can maintain a high degree of pride.]

Phase 3—personalized activities which flow from the small group activities, but which pinpoint individual needs or interests more accurately than can group work. [Teachers often feel that it is too expensive to provide a wide variety of books to meet individual interests. Such teachers may wish to explore the possibility of participating in the RIF program (Reading Is Fundamental), in which matching funds are made available to groups.[9]]

Phase 4—sharing of interests and/or learnings with the groups of Phase 2 and/or the whole class.

Keep the following principles in mind when planning and working on a unit.

I. Planning the unit
   A. Determine the reading levels and abilities of students.
   B. Identify suitable materials for reading.
      1. Select materials in harmony with unit objectives.
      2. Use a systematic method of estimating the difficulty of materials.
      3. Furnish a variety of materials, including reference and supplementary materials of different levels of difficulty.
   C. Provide a suitable environment for reading.
      1. Plan both socialized and individualized reading experiences.
      2. Plan suitable physical conditions for reading.

II. Producing the unit
   A. State concretely the purposes for reading and for preparatory activities to reading, relate the purposes to student experience, and help students formulate their own purposes for reading.

B. Explore and clarify the experience background of students through class discussions, pretests, autobiographies, conferences, special reports, etc.

C. Extend and enrich the background of students through the judicious use of instructional aids such as illustrative flat pictures, projected still pictures, motion pictures, phonograph records, the radio, oral reading, objects, field trips, excursions, etc.

D. Discuss with students the location of materials and the use of reference aids to guide wide reading activities.

E. Suggest the use of appropriate general methods of reading, text signals, and other more specific aids to reading in the content field.

III. Developing the unit

A. Aid students in actually locating materials and using library aids effectively.

B. Assist students in adjusting their method of reading to varying purposes, materials, and abilities.

C. Help students practice organizing, remembering, and applying what they read through the use of such techniques as intent to remember, self-recitation, outlining, making summaries and précis, and the use of the whole-part-whole approach to reading.

D. Continue those activities suggested in introducing the unit as they are needed.

IV. Concluding the unit

A. Provide for both student and teacher evaluation of the effectiveness of the learning activities.

B. Encourage students to apply the results of their learning to new problems, activities, and situations.*

SUMMARY

The teacher has definite responsibilities in presenting a reading assignment in any content area. When the whole class or a group of students is being instructed, a plan that has proved highly effective might be used. It is called the directed reading activity (DRA).

There are five steps in the DRA. Step 1 involves *exploring the backgrounds* of students as they relate to the reading material—in terms of both ideas and skills—and it involves pointing out relationships between what they know and

* Theodore L. Harris. "Making Reading an Effective Instrument of Learning in the Content Fields," in *Reading in High School and College*, N.S.S.E. 47th Yearbook, Part II. Chicago: University of Chicago Press, 1949, pp. 133–134. Reprinted by permission.

what they are about to learn. It also includes *building the background,* when necessary, and motivating the students to learn. Step 2 involves *setting up purposes* for reading to direct the students to focus on points of major importance. Step 3 involves *silent reading* of the assignment, and might be done as a homework assignment. Step 4 deals with *follow-up activities,* which might be *teacher-directed* or *inquiry-centered.* Step 5 relates to *extending the activity.*

Skills commonly needed for reading in four different content areas were listed, with cross references to chapters, or sections within chapters, where theory and techniques for teaching them are explained in greater detail.

SQ3R was also explained. S stands for *survey;* Q stands for *question;* R_1 represents *reading;* R_2 means *reciting;* and R_3 means *review,* or reconstruct. It is hoped that mature students will learn to use this study skill independently. Variations of this technique, known as PQRST in science, and SQRQCQ in mathematics, were also noted.

In addition to providing for whole class learning, the teacher's job includes encouraging and providing for extended (often individual or group) learnings. To help students go beyond the assigned lesson, the teacher should help students clarify individual or group interests as they relate to the assignment and help them locate materials which warrant further perusal or study. The teacher should provide class time for such pursuits and opportunities for sharing and using what has been learned.

In order to capitalize on the diverse abilities and interests of students, and to help develop students as individuals, it is necessary to use a variety of classroom organizational plans. Groups formed in the classroom should be *fluid* rather than fixed. Students gather together and disburse as their needs and interests develop and change.

Whole class instruction and sharing can and should be used frequently. There are numerous occasions when all students can learn together. This may happen when the group is being oriented to new ideas and skills. It may occur when a film is being shown, a recording listened to, a story or chapter read. It may take the form of choral reading, of a game or activity, of the spontaneous sharing of an idea by someone. There may be panel discussions, skits, bulletin board displays, even "show-and-tell."

But there are also times for *personalized instruction,* when individuals want to, or need to, "do their own thing." This may be true for skill development and/or interest development. Olson's principles of "seeking, self-selection, and pacing" are well worth considering for "letting things happen" in a prepared way.

Frequently, students might form *small groups*—either homogeneously or heterogeneously—in the classroom. They may group according to *interests* (similar or diverse), *skill needs* (similar or pupil-team), *social characteristics* (similar or different), or *achievement* (similar or pupil-team).

Constellation grouping is especially useful in content area subjects, where the unifying force may be supplied by a *theme* (or a chapter in a textbook), a *genre,* or a *skill.* All students are oriented together (Phase 1); they then select or are assigned to a group that takes off from the whole (Phase 2); next, individuals orbit around their groups (Phase 3) in personalized activities; finally, they return home (Phase 4) to share their discoveries. Although such flexible grouping may seem difficult, it is really easier—and more profitable—for all (including the teacher) than continual whole class work.

NOTES

1 Byron G. Massialas and Jack Zevin. *Creative Encounters in the Classroom—Teaching and Learning through Discovery.* New York: John Wiley, 1967, pp. 25–26. This excellent book contains classroom examples of this technique in action in most content areas.

2 For the rationale of this technique see Francis P. Robinson. "Study Skills for Superior Students in Secondary School." *The Reading Teacher,* **25** (September 1961): 29–33+.

3 Also see David Ausubel and his discussion of the "advanced organizer," in *The Psychology of Meaningful Verbal Learning.* New York: Grune & Stratton, 1963, pp. 85–87.

4 George Spache. *Toward Better Reading.* Champaign, Illinois: Garrard, 1963, p. 94.

5 After Leo Fay. "Reading Study Skills: Math and Science," in *Reading and Inquiry,* ed. J. Allen Figurel. Newark, Delaware: International Reading Association, 1965, p. 93.

6 In this book it is recommended that an estimate be made before the actual computing is done (see Chapter 8: "Anticipation").

7 These four points are taken from "Individualized Reading: More than New Forms and Formulas," by Alexander Frazier. *Elementary English,* **XXXIX** (December 1962): 809–814.

8 Willard Olson. "Seeking, Self-Selection, and Pacing in the Use of Books by Children," in *The Packet.* Boston: D. C. Heath, Spring 1952, pp. 3–10.

9 For information, write to Reading Is Fundamental, Inc., Smithsonian Institute, L'Enfant 2500, Washington, D.C. 20560.

SUGGESTED ACTIVITIES

1. Design a 10- to 15-minute microteach in which you do the prereading activities of a Directed Reading Activity designed to introduce a specific chapter or section of your content area book. You may wish to use the "brainstorming" technique suggested in Step 1 of the DRA.

2. Compare the conditions under which you feel a teacher directed discussion or quiz is a highly appropriate follow-up activity to a reading assignment with those conditions under which you feel that a nondirective discourse is preferable in your content area.

3. Review the section in this chapter that relates to the skills needed for reading in your content area. React to the following questions: Is the list complete? Are there some irrelevant items? Do you see the teaching of such skills as a means of implementing the understanding of content in your subject? Why or why not?

4. Do you use the SQ3R technique when you study? If not, try it for a month. Begin by surveying a complete textbook. Then SQ3R each chapter as you study it. After doing this for one month, evaluate the strengths and/or weaknesses of the approach.

5. Evaluate the strengths and weaknesses of the unit approach. In setting up the criteria against which you will evaluate the unit approach, consider the range of reading achievement in a typical classroom, the range of interests, and any other factors you feel are important. Then consider the possibilities within the unit approach for satisfying these criteria. Would you like to use the unit approach in your teaching? If so, when?

6. Write to RIF headquarters, as given in Note 9 in this chapter. Using the information provided by them, describe a situation within which you might apply for matching funds from them for the purchase of books for a hypothetical group of youngsters to help make possible the individualization of instruction in a classroom situation.

REFERENCES FOR FURTHER READING

Amidon, Edmund and John Hough (eds.). *Interaction Analysis: Theory, Research, and Application.* Reading, Mass.: Addison-Wesley, 1967.

Ausubel, David. "Learning by Discovery: Rationale and Mystique," *Bulletin of the National Association of Secondary Principals,* 1961, pp. 18–58.

Ausubel, David. *The Psychology of Meaningful Verbal Learning.* New York: Grune and Stratton, 1963.

Bruner, Jerome. *The Process of Education.* New York: Vintage Books (Random House), 1960.

Fay, Leo. "Reading Study Skills: Math and Science." *Reading and Inquiry,* ed. J. Allen Figurel. Newark, Delaware: International Reading Association, 1965.

Hafner, Lawrence E. (ed.). *Improving Reading in Middle and Secondary Schools.* New York: Macmillan, 1974, Sections 10, 11, and 12.

Harris, Theodore L. "Making Reading an Effective Instrument of Learning in the Content Fields," in *Reading in High School and College,* N.S.S.E. 47th yearbook, Part II. Chicago, University of Chicago Press, 1949, Chapter 7.

Herber, Harold (ed.). *Developing Study Skills in Secondary Schools.* (Perspectives in Reading #2). Newark, Delaware: International Reading Association, 1965, Chapters 3 and 4.

Herber, Harold. *Teaching Reading in Content Areas.* Englewood Cliffs, N.J.: Prentice-Hall, 1970, Chapters 3 and 4.

Howes, Virgil M. (ed.). *Individualizing Instruction in Reading and Social Studies.* New York: Macmillan, 1970.

Karlin, Robert. *Teaching Reading in High School—Selected Articles.* Indianapolis: Bobbs-Merrill, 1969, Chapter 13.

Laffey, James L. (ed.). *Reading in the Content Areas.* Newark, Delaware: International Reading Association, 1972.

Marksheffel, Ned D. *Better Reading in Secondary School.* New York: The Ronald Press, 1966, Chapters 2 and 10.

Massialas, Byron and Jack Zevin. *Creative Encounters in the Classroom.* New York: John Wiley, 1967.

Olson, Arthur V. and Wilber S. Ames. (eds.). *Teaching Reading Skills in Secondary Schools.* Scranton, Pa.: International Textbook Co., 1970, Sections 6 and 7.

Rickards, John P. "Processing Effects of Advanced Organizers Interspersed in Text." *Reading Research Quarterly,* XI, No. 4 (1975–1976): 599–622.

Robinson, Francis P. "Study Skills for Superior Students in Secondary School." *The Reading Teacher,* **25** (September 1961): 29–33+.

Smith, James A. *Creative Teaching of Reading and Literature in the Elementary School.* Boston: Allyn and Bacon, 1967.

UNIT THREE

IMPROVING LEARNING THROUGH READING DEVELOPMENT IN CONTENT FIELDS AND READING CLASSES

Unit Three focuses on the skills necessary for understanding reading materials in all content areas of the curriculum. Explanations of major skills are given, usually followed by examples of techniques which might be used to teach each skill. Examples are drawn from the following content areas: science, mathematics, social studies, and English.

Chapter 6

TEACHING CONCEPTS THROUGH VOCABULARY BUILDING

How large are the vocabularies of students?

How can we teach denotations and multiple denotations of words?

Which morphemes are important in your content area? How can they be taught?

How can we teach connotations and literary uses of words?

How can we teach students about the fluidity of English, i.e., its ever-changing quality?

What are our three phonic syllabication generalizations? How can they be taught?

INTRODUCTION

Vocabulary power is an extremely important facet of reading power, and vocabulary study for many is intriguing. To help our students develop a strong vocabulary, a variety of techniques can be used.

Content area teachers, of course, are most interested in building vocabulary strength and diversity in their fields. Indeed, this is one of their responsibilities. In order to succeed in their duty, content area teachers should choose the words and techniques best suited to promoting growth in the understanding of the materials students explore and read for their classroom. An understanding of diverse ways of doing this will help the teachers make the wisest choice.

In this chapter several facets of word power are examined. An attempt is made to answer the question, "How large are the vocabularies of children and young people?" Thereafter, the discussion proceeds from the examination of denotations (literal meanings) of words, to connotations (interpretive meanings) of words and figurative language, to diachronic linguistics (changes in language), to a brief consideration of phonic syllabication generalizations, which might help students pronounce multisyllabic words.

VOCABULARY SIZE

How large is your vocabulary? That seems like a simple question, doesn't it? Ask a few friends—or the students in one of your classes. Chances are that after a short deliberation, they will give you a few answers—like 5000 words or 15,000 words, perhaps 20,000 words, or even 80,000 words. Then you will probably be asked which of these estimates is closest to being correct.

The question about vocabulary size is deceptively simple. It is not as difficult a question to answer as "What is truth?" But it possibly has not been answered satisfactorily as yet.

Multiple Denotations

But why not? Ask yourself just what it means to "know" a word or even to "know the meaning of" a word. For example, what does the word *run* mean? To move rapidly? Surely not in these sentences:

Charles will *run* for class president.
There's a *run* on the bank.
These towels *run* long.
Try not to *run* up a bill.
Jack made a home*run*.

There are at least 130 different definitions of the word *run* in most collegiate dictionaries. How many of these meanings must you know before you can say that you know what the word *run* means? One—or the majority—or all? And so on for other words with multiple denotations.

Connotations

You know what a *plum* is, don't you? Of course, you had one for breakfast yesterday. But what is "a *plum* of a job?" If you do not know the figurative meaning of *plum*, do you really know the word?

Two Types of Vocabulary

We all have two types of vocabularies—*receptive* and *expressive*. Our receptive vocabulary is composed of the words we recognize through reading and listening. This vocabulary is usually several times larger than our expressive vocabulary, which is made up of the words we use when we speak and write. Our total vocabulary is composed of the words we recognize and/or use in receptive and expressive ways.

Basic and Total Vocabularies

Let me ask you another question: "What is a word?" Simple, you say. It's made up of a letter or letters (when it's written, that is) and has space on both sides of it. Does someone say it's a free morpheme? Or a bound and a free morpheme? Wait, you're ahead of the game.

Let me ask the question this way: Is *sing* a word? Of course! But is *sang* another word? And what about *sung* and *sings* and *singer* and *singing?* Do we have one word or six words? And what about *air?* Is that a word? And *port*—another word? Then what about *airport?* Is that a third word? If we are going to estimate the size of someone's vocabulary, we must define a word. We might talk about the size of our *basic vocabulary*—or the size of our *total vocabulary*, including derivatives and compounds. Obviously, if we talk about the basic vocabulary, the word count will be much smaller than if we talk of the total vocabulary.

Size of Basic Vocabulary

Perhaps an analogy will help you understand what is meant by "knowing" a word in research studies. If I should ask you if you know a certain person, say Marie Ashworth, and you reply yes, I would expect you at least to be able to point her out to me if she were in a small group of people. You might, of course, know her well and be able to tell me many things about her—but this is not necessary when you just say that you know her.

When a researcher says that someone "knows" the meaning of a word, he usually means that the person can select, from several choices, a correct meaning of the word. In-depth meaning is rarely tested. Another technique used is

Table 6.1 Estimates of the average size of children's and young people's basic vocabulary

	Dale*	Smith †	Seegers and Seashore ‡
Grade 1	2,500–3,000	17,000	
Grade 6	8,000	32,000	
Grade 12	14,000–15,000	47,000	
College	18,000		58,000

* Edgar Dale. "Vocabulary Measurement: Techniques and Major Findings," *Elementary English* (December 1965): 895–901, 948.

† M. K. Smith. "Measurement of the Size of General English Vocabulary through the Elementary Grades and High School," *Genetic Psychology Monographs,* **24** (1941): 313–345.

‡ J. C. Seegers and R. H. Seashore. "How Large Are Children's Vocabularies?" *Elementary English* (April 1949): 181–194.

to count the number of different words people say and/or write. Table 6.1 shows the average size of the *basic vocabulary* of children and young people as estimated by various researchers.

You can see that there is a wide variation in the estimates of vocabulary size. Dale's study suggests that school children learn about 1000 *new words* per year, or about three new words per day (365 days of the year). Smith's and Seashore's studies suggest that children learn approximately 3000 *new words* per year, or about eight new words per day. Which seems more realistic to you?

Whichever you choose, what is of extreme importance to you as a teacher is that you be committed to improving the word power of your students—*in your content area.* Your approach must be varied to maintain interest. Let us look at some aspects of vocabulary and some ways of enriching our students' vocabularies.

DENOTATIONS OF WORDS

When we talk about the denotation of a word, we are talking about the literal meaning of the word. If the word has a physical referent, that object represents the denotation. The denotation of the word *cat,* for example, is a four-legged animal, usually with a tail. The denotation of the word *lemon* is a small, yellow citrus fruit. The denotation of *green* is the color we call green.

Denotations are very different from connotations, for connotations of words are interpretive meanings—poetic, emotional, colored. Consider the meaning of the word *cat* in the following sentence: Mrs. Glowgruber is a *cat.* What does *lemon* mean in: This T.V. is a *lemon.* And what is the meaning of *green* in: Leslie turned *green* when she heard Joanna had won. Can you think of other ways of using these same three words *connotatively?*

One of the most fascinating tales is one that can be told only because a certain word is ambiguous. It may be the horror story of all time. First reported in *Harper's Magazine,* March 1953, the account is by William J. Caughlin and is titled "The Great Mokusatsu Mistake—Was This the Deadliest Error of Our Time?"

Mokusatsu is a Japanese word that has no direct English counterpart. In English it can mean "refrain from comment" or "ignore." According to the story, Premier Suzuki, when questioned about the Japanese cabinet's response to the Potsdam Declaration, said that his cabinet "was holding to an attitude of *mokusatsu.*" Mistranslated, news flashed to the Western world that the Japanese chose to "ignore" the ultimatum. Thus were triggered the first two atomic attacks the world has ever known, for "to ignore" is quite different diplomatically from "to refrain from comment."

Certainly of lesser impact on the world is the fact that most words have more than one denotation. A serious vocabulary problem in content area subjects grows from words that have restricted and specific meanings peculiar to a particular subject matter field.

Because students can pronounce a word, and because they know a meaning or two for that word, they may think they know the word every time they see or hear it. Imagine their confusion when they come across the word *root* (which to them means the part of a plant that is underground) in the following sentences:

> Find the square *root* of 9.
> What is the *root* of the word unhappy?
> We must find the *root* of his problem.
> The love of money is the *root* of all evil.

Teaching Strategies

1. Give words with very common meanings in Part 1 of an activity. In Part 2, cloze the word and use sentences with the unique meaning. Have students fill in the clozure. Such an activity could be done as a reinforcement, after students have been introduced to the special meaning. Below are examples from several content areas:

Mathematics

Each italicized word in Part 1 below has a special meaning specific to a mathematics class. Select the appropriate italicized words from sentences in Part 1 to insert in the blanks in Part 2. You may change the part of speech, if necessary.

Part 1

Term	*Common meaning*
1. difference	What *difference* does it make?
2. division	Dad was in the 32nd Army *Division.*

3. product	Many artistic *products* come from Mexico.
4. sign	A cloudy sky is a *sign* of possible rain to come.
5. times	These are sad *times.*
6. reduce	John's mother promised to *reduce.*
7. pound	Don't *pound* too hard on the nail.
8. foot	I cut my *foot.*
9. rod	The curtain *rod* broke.
10. yard	Jack cleaned the *yard.*
11. peck	The bird *pecked* on the orange.
12. figure	How do you *figure?*
13. base	Jim is at the air *base.*
14. center	The youth *center* closed.
15. point	It's not polite to *point.*
16. side	Whose *side* are you on?
17. power	America is a world *power.*
18. mean	John didn't *mean* that!
19. mode	What *mode* of clothing do you prefer?
20. root	The *root* of the plant was dry.

Part 2

1. The (*mean*) is the arithmetic average.
2. Two (*times*) three equals six.
3. The (*product*) results when two factors are multiplied together.
4. A number greater than zero has a positive (*sign*).
5. An arch's radius goes from a point on the circle to the (*center*) of the circle.
6. 2/4 can be (*reduced*) to 1/2.
7. Sixteen ounces is equivalent to one (*pound*).
8. The square (*root*) of sixteen is four.
9. To find the area of a square, any two (*sides*) of the square are multiplied together.
10. The inverse operation of multiplication is (*division*).
11. The area of a triangle equals the (*base*) times the height.
12. A square, a triangle, and a rectangle are all examples of geometric (*figures*).
13. The subtraction operation finds the (*difference*) between two numbers.
14. Four to the second (*power*) is equal to sixteen.

15. A line segment is an infinite number of (*points*).
16. One (*foot*) is equal to twelve inches.
17. The number occurring most often in a sequence of numbers is called the (*mode*).
18. A (*peck*) is a measure of volume equaling about eight quarts.
19. A measure of length of about sixteen and one half feet is a (*rod*).
20. Three feet are equivalent to one (*yard*).

Science

Each italicized word in Part 1 below has a special meaning specific to a science class. Select the appropriate italicized words from sentences in Part 1 to insert in the blanks in Part 2. You may change the part of speech, if necessary.

Part 1

Term	*Common meaning*
1. culture	The *culture* of the Southwest is unique.
2. root	Find the square *root.*
3. seal	*Seal* the envelope.
4. iron	Mother will *iron* tomorrow.
5. soil	Please don't *soil* your clothes.
6. mine	That book is *mine.*
7. belt	My *belt* was tight.
8. pole	The boys were practicing *pole*-vaulting.
9. mouth	Sue has a small *mouth.*
10. port	The sailors were on *port* side.
11. rapid	Bob is a *rapid* reader.
12. sound	What does it *sound* like to you?
13. cape	The lawyer's *cape* had to be shortened.
14. power	Raise six to the eighth *power.*
15. graft	There is much *graft* in the government.
16. cell	The prisoner returned to his *cell.*
17. matter	That doesn't *matter.*
18. boil	Henry was *boiling* mad.
19. base	The *base* of the triangle was three inches.
20. colon	A *colon* indicates that something is to follow.

Part 2

1. The (*root*) of a plant is normally in the ground.
2. Transferring skin from one part of the body to another in an operation is called a skin (*graft*).

3. The United States space missions are launched from (*Cape*) Kennedy in Florida.
4. A sample of bacteria grown in a laboratory is called a (*culture*).
5. A (*seal*) is a mammal who spends much time underwater.
6. Water will (*boil*) at 100° centigrade.
7. A river empties into a larger body of water at its (*mouth*).
8. Extremely cold weather conditions exist at the Earth's (*poles*).
9. Precious (*soil*) is lost if conservation measures are not used by farmers.
10. (*Iron*) is a valuable natural resource used in the steel-making process.
11. An amoeba is an example of a one- (*cell*) form of life.
12. Atomic (*power*) is being developed as an energy source for the future.
13. The Midwest is the food (*belt*) for the United States and much of the rest of the world.
14. Rough areas of water in a river are called (*rapids*).
15. The (*colon*) is part of the large intestine.
16. Anything which occupies space can be classified as (*matter*).
17. A body of water connecting two large bodies is called a (*sound*).
18. A city which has a harbor is a (*port*).
19. The family of chemical compound called the hydroxides is an example of a (*base*).
20. Working in a coal (*mine*) can be a very hazardous job.

Social Studies

Each italicized word in Part 1 below has a special meaning specific to a social studies class. Select the appropriate italicized words from sentences in Part 1 to insert in the blanks in Part 2. You may change the part of speech, if necessary.

Part 1

Term	*Common meaning*
1. race	Who won the *race*?
2. cabinet	Our kitchen *cabinet* needs a new door.
3. union	His *union* suit was torn.
4. act	I wish Sue would *act* logically.
5. bill	Don't forget to pay the *bill*.
6. article	The magazine *article* was interesting.
7. motion	John made a jerky *motion*.
8. duty	It is your *duty* to go.

9. power — The telescope is *power*ful.
10. civil — Try to be *civil.*
11. ticket — Did you get a parking *ticket*?
12. trust — I *trust* that you enjoyed the movie.
13. class — The *class* met on Monday and Wednesday.
14. right — Your answer is *right.*
15. left — He *left* before she came.
16. graft — Will the skin *graft* take?
17. period — Put a *period* at the end of a sentence.
18. stable — The horse *stable* burned.
19. movement — We observed the *movement* of the stars.
20. draft — There was a *draft* in the room.

Part 2

1. His conservative voting record indicates that he is a member of the (*right*) wing.
2. The congressperson introduced a (*bill*) to reform the tax laws.
3. The United States has gone through a (*period*) of great social change since 1960.
4. The defense lawyer proposed a (*motion*) for a mistrial.
5. Communist party members are usually in the (*left*) wing of the political spectrum.
6. You must pay (*duty*) on that article.
7. Democratic party pros felt that their (*ticket*) was certain to be elected.
8. The House of Lords in England is composed of members of the upper social (*class*).
9. In the early twentieth century, big industries formed (*trusts*) to evade antimonopoly laws.
10. When a politician is elected president, his party is in (*power*) for the next four years.
11. The military (*draft*) was used to induct men into the armed services.
12. A (*stable*) currency is essential to economic well-being in a country.
13. The president-elect began his task of selecting (*cabinet*) members for his new government.
14. Office holders have to be careful to avoid (*graft*) in their government.
15. The (*Civil*) Rights Act was passed in 1964.
16. The (*Articles*) of Confederation preceded our present constitution.

17. The antiwar (*movement*) had an effect on presidential politics in the 1960s.
18. Workers join together into a labor (*union*) and bargain collectively with their employer.
19. Many cities were victimized by (*race*) riots in the 1960s.
20. An (*act*) of Congress gave 18-year-olds the right to vote in 1972.

English

Each italicized word in Part 1 below has a special meaning specific to an English class. Select the appropriate italicized words from sentences in Part 1 to insert in the blanks in Part 2. You may change the part of speech, if necessary.

Part 1

Term	*Common meaning*
1. draft	He was *draft*ed when he became twenty.
2. period	What do you think is the most interesting historical *period?*
3. root	The love of money is said to be the *root* of all evil.
4. appendix	Her *appendix* gave her trouble.
5. foot	A *foot* is 12 inches long.
6. act	It would take an *act* of Congress to change that.
7. romance	Many people like books about *romance.*
8. novel	What a *novel* idea!
9. article	What is that *article* of clothing called?
10. dash	*Dash* to the store.
11. subject	What is your favorite school *subject*?
12. sentence	The judge announced the *sentence.*
13. future tense	The *future* looks *tense;* the past, imperfect.
14. first person	Jack was the *first person* in line.
15. third person	Who was the *third person* in line?
16. critic	You're always *critic*al!
17. style	The flower's *style* was broken.
18. case	Where is your suit*case*?
19. stem	The rose's *stem* was long.
20. scene	What a *scene* she made!

Part 2

1. An autobiography is often written in (*first person*).
2. A (*foot*) is a metric unit of poetry.

3. The ending of a sentence in a piece of writing is denoted by a (*period*).
4. A (*critic*) is a person who evaluates a work of art.
5. E. E. Cummings wrote much of his poetry using unconventional, lower (*case*) type.
6. The novel's (*appendix*) contained information on events discussed in the story.
7. She sent a (*draft*) of her play to the producer.
8. The magazine contained (*articles*) of interest to everyone in the class.
9. The author's (*style*) of writing is both intriguing and puzzling.
10. A lengthy, fictional work is called a (*novel*).
11. A sentence must have both a (*subject*) and a predicate.
12. The (*root*) of the word imperfection is perfect.
13. A biography is often written in (*third person*).
14. Most plays are written with three (*acts*).
15. A (*scene*) is an element of an act in a theatrical production.
16. (*Romantic*) writing is a form of literature which highlights pleasant occurrences and happy endings.
17. A paragraph is composed of one or more (*sentences*).
18. Prefixes and suffixes are added to a (*stem*) to make new words.
19. A side-thought or incidental occurrence in a paragraph is punctuated by a (*dash*).
20. Some science fiction and stream of consciousness writers make use of the (*future tense*) to present their story.

2. Use the word in a sentence. Have the student select the correct definition from a dictionary:

   Jack Snowden is a *left*-winger, whereas his brother leans to the *right.*

   left—definition number ________

   right—definition number ________

   left (left): 1. of or designating that side toward the east when one faces south. 2. a liberal or radical position or political party. 3. past participle of *leave.*

   right (rīt): 1. straight. 2. in accordance with law. 3. correct. 4. suitable. 5. a conservative or reactionary political position or party.

3. List four sentences, each containing the word being taught. Two of the sentences should use the word in the same way, and this should be the

definition that is being taught. Have the student indicate the two sentences that use the word in the same way.

Rod

a) Jim lost his fishing *rod.*
b) A *rod* is a measure of length equal to $5^1/_2$ yards.
c) The thieves beat their victim with an iron *rod.*
d) Translate the length of a football field from yards to *rods.*

(b, d)

Compact

a) A bilateral *compact* was signed by England and France.
b) Ann took out her *compact* to powder her face.
c) Parking a *compact* is simpler than parking a large car.
d) The *compact* was broken by the four nations concerned.

(a, d)

4. Use illustrations or real objects. Have students draw lines from the sentences to their correct illustrations.

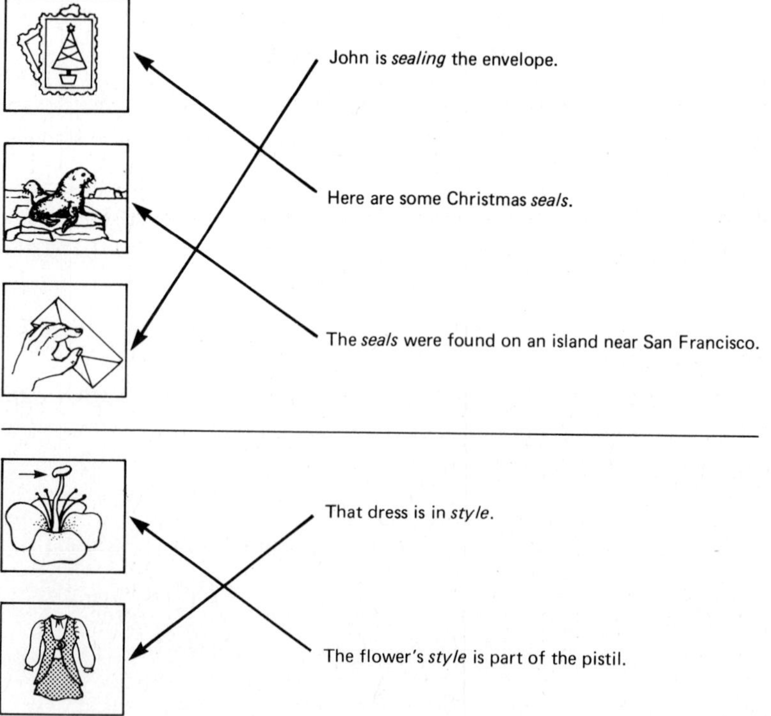

John is *sealing* the envelope.
Here are some Christmas *seals*.
The *seals* were found on an island near San Francisco.
That dress is in *style*.
The flower's *style* is part of the pistil.

5. Havė the class play a game.

   a) First, ask the students to write as many sentences as they can using the word *run* (or another word of your choice) with a different meaning each time. Give them between three and five minutes to do this.

   b) Next, randomly divide the class into six groups by having the students count off: 1 - 2 - 3 - 4 - 5 - 6; 1 - 2 - 3 - 4 - 5 - 6; etc. Group all one's together, all two's together, etc.

   c) Each group in turn contributes one sentence using *run* in a way it has not been used before by another group. The first time around, each group giving a correct response gets one point. The second time around, each group gets two points for a correct response; the third time around, three points, etc. Students police this, not the teacher. So students must listen carefully to all group responses.

   d) The group having the highest score wins.

6. A similar game can be played with *overused words,* e.g., *said.* Students supply words that could be used instead of *said,* e.g., replied, responded, retorted, questioned, hissed, commented, shouted, etc. You might expect 150–200 different words to be suggested, so allow enough time.

   Another technique is to list a variety of words in categories. Examples might be means of locomotion, e.g., ran, hopped, flew, waltzed, tangoed, swam, etc.; announcement that one team beat another team, e.g., stopped, edged, conquered, whipped, incapacitated, dumped, obliterated, mauled, etc.; words related to plants, e.g., daisy, rose, stem, petal, roots, cactus, etc. This is similar to the "brainstorming" technique. Next, students could classify the words. Each time a student or group of students can name a main idea and give the subpoints that belong under it, they are given a point.

7. Use a nonsense word to substitute for a new word being taught. Familiar uses of the word must be given in the other sentences. For example:

   a) Mom bought a new electric *flam.*

   b) The forest *flammer* sighted a fire.

   c) There was a wide *flam* in the price of motorcycles from city to city.

   d) The *flam* in reading achievement in a classroom is two-thirds the chronological age of the children.

   e) The mountain *flam* was 200 miles long.

flam = ________

The new use of the familiar word is given in *sentence d.* In which sentence is the word used in the same way? ________ What does flam mean in *sentence d?* ________________________________

____

____

Meanings of New Words

Often, of course, it is not multiple meanings that are being taught, for the word is completely new. Teachers should be sure that the students can pronounce each new word. They might pronounce the word for the class, or have the students use their phonics skills on the word—when the word is phonetic. The following techniques might prove helpful for teaching meanings of new words.

Teaching Strategies

1. Supply a picture of the object the new word represents.

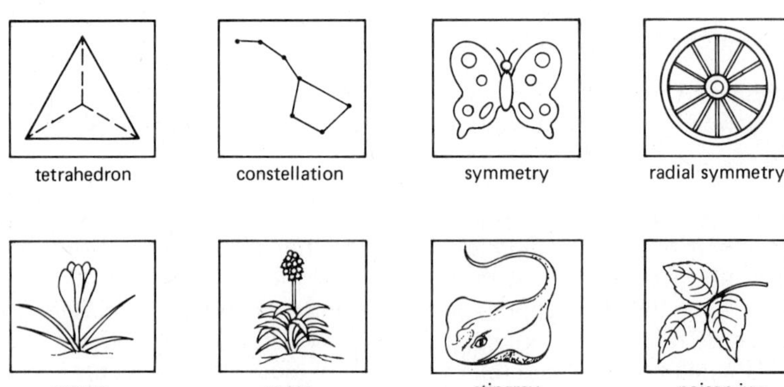

2. Better still, display the real object or a three-dimensional model of it, or take the students on a field trip, or show a film.

3. If context clues are clear in the passage to be read, list on a dittoed sheet the new words, followed by multiple-choice items from which students make a selection of the answers they think are correct *before* they read the passage. Then, while they are reading, or after they have finished, they make corrections. The more corrections, the better, for they are learning that context can serve as a clue to understanding new words.

   Since this is a teaching rather than a testing technique, it is helpful to make the correct multiple-choice item fairly obvious, i.e., obvious after the reading has been done. All choices should grammatically suit the syntax of the sentence, but only one of the choices should make sense semantically.

   epitomize: vocalize typify gratify harmonize
   vintners: villains expungers wine merchants miners
   esquires: administrators strong men questioners horseback riders
   envoy: escorter of ships artery diplomat refugee
   lyrics musical patterns words of poetry ballads songs of nature

Passage

Chaucer's life and career seem to epitomize the history of the later Middle Ages. His name, being French for *shoemaker* (the French *chausseur* means "cobbler"), suggests that his family had followed that trade, but for as far back as his ancestors can be traced on English soil, they had been vintners. As the son of a well-to-do wine merchant living in London, and later as a customs official, Chaucer was a member of the rising middle class.

Most of his life Chaucer was associated in one way or another with the royal household. Through his father's court connections, he probably was given his first position as page in the service of Elizabeth, Countess of Ulster, daughter-in-law of Edward III. While still in her service, he went as a soldier to France in the division of Prince Lionel, Elizabeth's husband and third son of the King. Here, he had the misfortune to be captured by the French, but he was soon ransomed by King Edward. Later Chaucer became one of the King's esquires, which in those days meant that he worked in the administrative department of the King's government. One of his duties was to act as a government envoy on foreign diplomatic missions, carrying on such work as that performed by embassies of our day. His diplomatic missions took him first to France and later to Italy. While in France Chaucer came in contact with French literature, and from his very earliest writings through 1370 a French influence is noticeable. To the French period can be assigned many of his lyrics, which follow models laid down by earlier and contemporary French poets.*

4. Ask the students to list (on cards, a sheet of paper, on the board) all major words related to a chapter or unit just studied. If students are using different textbooks, ask each group to compose its own list. Then compare lists. You might notice that some authors do not include ideas other authors may feel are very important. For example, lists that might have come from three different textbooks for a unit on government might be:

Book 1	*Book 2*	*Book 3*
socialism	matriarchy	autonomy
communism	patriarchy	federal
dominate	dictatorship	regent
coercion	regent	republicanism
despotism	liberty	liberty
absolutist	hierarchy	hierarchy
dictatorship	totalitarianism	manage
liberty	Nazi	democratic
totalitarianism	axis	communism
bolshevism	communism	socialism
despotize	socialism	statism
democratic	collectivism	municipal
collectivism	autocracy	
autocracy	kaiserism	
czarism	Caesarism	
	theocracy	

* From *England in Literature* by Robert C. Pooley, *et al.* Copyright © 1968 by Scott, Foresman and Company. Reprinted by permission of the publisher.

By examining such lists, students might notice that the books have different focal points, different flavors. They might identify these focal points and learn terms and concepts from students in groups other than their own.

Also, the class might consult a thesaurus, especially one of the newer ones organized in dictionary form. They could look up the term *government* to identify government-related terms not used in any of the books or not listed in any of the student lists. They might note that they had omitted some important terms the author used. They might also notice that authors do not discuss *everything* related to a topic—perhaps because of bias or space limitations, etc. They might conclude that they must read many sources for a more complete discussion of the topic.

For example, some government terms listed in a thesaurus but not used in any of the above books are:

empire	oligarchy
executive branch	fascism
legislative branch	bolshevism
judicial branch	sovietism
absolutism	terrorism
monocracy	feudalism
benevolent despotism	imperialism
paternalism	federalism
aristocracy	etc.
fellow traveler	

5. A more detailed study of sentence patterns might help students understand how many authors use context clues.[1] Sentence-pattern context clues are usually of the following types: (a) definition or explanation, (b) restatement, (c) examples, (d) contrast. Examples are given below.

A. Definition or explanation

1. N_1 Lv N_2: Noun_1 = word being taught (here in italics)
   Lv = linking verb (here circled)
   Noun_2 = the known, i.e., the definition, etc. (here underlined)

   a) Remember ≠ (is read) "is not equal to."

   b) The term *set* (means) a group or collection.

   c) A *hybrid plant* (is) the offspring of two parent plants which have opposite or different characteristics.

2. N_2 Lv N_1

   a) Fish that feed on the bottom of the ocean

are known as *ground fish.*

b) The stockholder's share of the company's profits is called a *dividend.*

c) Persons who ridicule each other good-naturedly are known as *banterers.*

B. Restatement of meaning in other words

1. Unknown word in basic sentence, appositive introduced by using the word *or*, or an article—*a, an,* or *the*, or *other signal words* (here circled).

   a) The problem of *farm surpluses*, or having more food than is needed, is one of the major agricultural problems of the U.S.

   b) Many mackerel are caught by *seining*, or snaring with nets.

   c) There the Indians had built their homes on *piles*, or long timbers, above the water near the shores of the lake.

   d) Such an airship is called a *dirigible*, a word that means steerable.

   e) We will begin our discussion of the parts of a cell with the *nucleus*, the control center of all cell activity.

   f) *Barbados*, an eastern island of the Lesser Antilles, is one of the most crowded lands on earth.

   g) *Sieve tubes* are the most prominent, appearing as rows of rather large living cells that have thin walls and protoplasm but no nucleus.

   h) A current of this kind is part of a *convection current*, that is, a current that carries heat.

   i) The guards were ordered to be *neutral*, that is, they were not to take sides in the fight.

2. Unknown word given in the appositive

   a) Each section, or *stage*, is a rocket with its own fuel and burning chamber.

   b) Inside the cortex lies the innermost layer of bark, the *phloem.*

   c) There are six different arrangements, or *permutations*, of the letters x, y, and z.

C. Examples help clarify a family name (here underlined)

1. Family name given first, followed by examples

a) *Ground fish*, including cod, hake, haddock, and halibut, are caught along the Atlantic coast.

b) *Condiments*, such as cinnamon, nutmeg, and paprika, were once too expensive for most people.

c) Eyesight is well developed in the *primates*—gorillas, chimpanzees, orangutans, gibbons, monkeys, marmosets, and lemurs.

2. Examples given first, followed by the family name

a) Rats and mice are among the most common *rodents.*

b) The cow, ox, bison, sheep, goat, antelope, camel, llama, giraffe, deer, elk caribou, and moose are all *ruminants.* These animals have four-chambered stomachs.

c) $3 + \square = 7$ and $10 - \square = 6$. This sentence is neither true nor false because *both clauses are open. (open clause)*

D. Contrast—tells what the word does not mean, not necessarily what it does mean

1. Contrasting phrase introduced by the word *not* (here circled)

a) This is a *survey*, (not) a diagnostic, test.

b) This is a *nebulous*, (not) a clear, statement.

c) Mr. Jones was noted for his *caustic*, (not) gentle, remarks.

2. Compound sentences—contrasting independent clause introduced by the word *but* (here circled)

a) The older folk were eager to go home, (but) the children were *reluctant* to leave the beach.

b) Much of the land in the Maracaibo Basin is swampy, (but) the *cultivable* land is fertile.

c) The mountain goat looks clumsy, (but) he is remarkably *nimble.*

6. Students might keep files of *flash cards* for learning and reviewing words. Three-by-five cards might be cut into four or five pieces. On one side of the card, the student could write the new word and also use it in a sentence. On the other side of the card, the meaning should be given. For example:

amphibious The amphibious craft was seen on the shoreline.	compunction Roseanne felt no compunction after telling the lie.
↕	↕
amphibious (ăm-fib´ ĭ-ŭs): able to live or navigate both on land and in water	compunction (kŏm-pungk´ shŭn): regret, a sense of guilt

Such cards can be flexibly used. One a day might be taped to a bathroom mirror, or students might clip a different one on their notebook each day—or until they learn it. The cards could be kept in several files—one file for words they think they know well. These might be reviewed monthly. Another file could be composed of words they are not sure of, to be reviewed weekly. New words could be in another file—to be studied daily. Rubber bands or paper clips around each file should be sufficient to keep the cards together. Things should be kept simple so the cards can be stuck into a pocket or purse. At times, students might pair off, or work in larger groups, quizzing each other on their words.

7. Cards of formerly known and new words could be filed according to some classification system. This technique is known as *card sorting* and is a useful technique for *concept development* and for laying the foundation for *breaking the stereotype,* an area of critical thinking.

   For example, in how many *different* ways could a set of words (ideas) be grouped? (Note that each different way of grouping results from stressing different aspects, or facets, of the words (ideas). Unusual classifications result from creative thinking, i.e., synthesis level of the cognitive domain—divergent production. Common classifications result from convergent thinking.)

8. In a content area classroom, there could be a *card bank,* a container with a hole large enough for a hand to go through. Each student could insert one or more cards per week with content area words he or she knows. Periodically—or at the end of the hour when time permits—a "worddown" could be held. One student would draw the words and write them on the chalkboard. The student whose turn it is must pronounce the word correctly, use it in a sentence, and define it—or else sit down and let the chance go to the other team. (When the word is picturable, the student might sketch it on the board, possibly in lieu of defining it.)

Morphology

Morphology is an area of descriptive linguistics. *Morpheme* is a useful new word for a very useful old idea. A *morpheme* (often called a *morph,* for short) is the smallest unit (eme) of meaning (morph) in our language. The word *cat* is a morpheme, as are the words *dog, fish, octopus, rhinoceros,* and *blotch.* The following are also morphemes: *un-, re-, super-, trans-, -ful, -less.*

It can be seen from these examples that there are two kinds of morphemes —*free* morphemes and *bound* morphemes. Free Engish morphemes are uninflected English words (cat, dog, rhinoceros, etc.). Put two together and you have a compound word: airport, oatmeal, housewife, scarecrow.

A bound morpheme (formerly known as a prefix or suffix, or possibly a root), on the other hand, must be attached to another morpheme—*either free or bound*—to form a word.* Examples of a bound morpheme combined with a free morpheme to compose a word are: *un*kind, *re*make, thought*ful.* Examples of two bound morphemes combined to form a word are: *geo graphy, philo sophy,* and *in ert.* The simplest such formations for children to understand are combinations of a bound morpheme with a free English morpheme.

Teaching Strategies †

Sequence in teaching morphology might progress from:

1. *First*—teaching simple compounds, such as:

milkman	postman	mailman	fireman
boxcar	oatmeal	airport	windmill
sandbox	baseball	toothbrush	flagpole
houseboat	birthday	horseshoe	classmate

It should be pointed out to children that these words are divided into syllables between the two morphemes (words).

Activity

Select compound words from the children's reading materials or simply compounds you wish to teach. If you have about 10 or 12 compounds, you might prepare materials for a concentration game. Take cards of a uniform size. Write one root on each card. If a root appears in two or more words, a card must be written for each one. Your cards might look like this:

---

* Some linguists do not consider all suffixes to be morphemes. Some suffixes such as *-ing, -ed, -ly, -er,* and *est* are still referred to as inflections, having little or no meaning, serving principally to alter the part of speech. Other suffixes, such as *-less* and *ful,* which function principally to change meaning, are considered morphemes. At the present time it appears to this writer a waste of time to split hairs over this terminology—except for linguistic researchers who are formulating our base for reorganized thinking in linguistic terms.

† Some of these strategies first appeared in Lou E. Burmeister. "Vocabulary Development in Content Areas Through the Use of Morphemes." *Journal of Reading* (March 1976): 481–487. Used by permission of the International Reading Association.

milk	man	base	ball
box	car	birth	day
sand	box	mail	man
house	boat	air	port
post	man	tooth	brush
oat	meal	horse	shoe

Shuffle the cards well. Then turn them over and number them consecutively on the back. Then arrange cards in order with the number side up.

About six to eight children can play. The first child gives two numbers. The cards corresponding to these two numbers are turned with the word side up. If they compose a word and the child recognizes the word and can use it in a sentence, he or she keeps the cards and gets another turn. When the child is unable to make a word, the next child goes. The child with the greatest number of cards wins.

2. *Second*—teaching simple bound morphemes attached to *free* English morphemes, such as:

unwrap	dislike	refill	incorrect
__fair	__loyal	_turn	_human
__paid	__agree	_write	_born
__happy	__honest	_count	_laid
__known	__appear	_open	_formal
__like	__own	_pay	_field
__lock	__trust	_name	_doors
__broken	__please	_call	_land

Students should be taught that the bound morphemes have meanings. For example, *un-* means *not,* or *do the opposite of. Un-* means *not* when combined with: fair, paid, happy, known, like, broken. But *un-* means *do the opposite of* when used with: wrap and lock. *Dis-* means *not* when combined with like, loyal, agree, honest, trust, and please. But *dis-* means *do the opposite of* when used with appear and own, etc. Students should also be taught to syllabicate between a prefix and a root.

Activity

The teacher prepares blank wordo (bingo) cards like the following so that each student can have one or two.

		FREE		

The teacher lists on the board, or elsewhere, "families of words" having a morpheme in common, such as those above. For this activity the teacher should use about four to six such "families."

On small pieces of paper the student writes the morpheme that all members of the family have in common. Here students would write *un* on several slips, *dis* on several, *re* on several, and *in* on several slips.

Next the children would write in random order 24 of the free morphemes in the spaces on their wordo cards. For example, one child might have a card that looks like this:

wrap	appear	like	field	fair
agree	formal	count	honest	human
loyal	happy	FREE	laid	born
trust	write	name	pay	lock
broken	land	correct	own	please

The game is played thus: The teacher gives a clue to the word the student is to form, e.g.:

1. The party was *not formal . . . not formal.*
   (The child covers *formal* with a slip that has *in* on it.)
2. The decision was *not fair . . . not fair.*
   (The child covers *fair* with *un*.)
3. The ball was hit *within the field . . . within the field.*
   (*field* + *in*)

Etc. Sometimes, of course, the child will not be able to go even if he or she knows the word because the free morpheme is not on his or her card.

Rules are stated before each game, e.g.: one column up, down, or diagonally wins. Picture frame, four corners, black out, etc.

Another activity such as the following might also be helpful.

Prefixes

1. anti—against
2. ante—before
3. pro—forth, for
4. trans—across
5. dis—not
6. ex—out of, from
7. sub—under
8. auto—self
9. hyper—above, more than
10. tele—far, distant
11. non—not
12. re—again
13. circum—around
14. pseudo—false
15. contra—against
16. a—not, without
17. uni—one
18. mono—one
19. bi—two
20. tri—three
21. poly—many
22. omni—all
23. pan—all
24. semi—half
25. hemi—half
26. inter—between
27. intro—into
28. in—not
29. in—into, within
30. post—after
31. pre—before
32. homo—same

Word	*Prefix*	*Prefix meaning*	*Word meaning*
1. antisocial	anti	against	against society
2. anteroom			
3. proceed			
4. transport			
5. dislike			
6. extract			
7. submarine			
8. automobile			
9. hyperactive			
10. telegraph			
11. nonconformist			
12. return			
13. circumference			
14. pseudonym			
15. contradict			
16. atypical			
17. unicycle			

Word	*Prefix*	*Prefix meaning*	*Word meaning*
18. monocle			
19. bigamy			
20. trilateral			
21. polytheism			
22. omnipotent			
23. pan-American			
24. semicircle			
25. hemisphere			
26. international			
27. introspect			
28. indecisive			
29. inborn			
30. postgraduate			
31. prefix			
32. homogeneous			

3. *Third*—words composed of two bound morphemes are more difficult. But learning such words is very helpful to students because each of the morphemes can be combined with many others. Knowing the meaning of just one of the morphemes in a new word is often enough to unlock the meaning of the whole word if that word is found in context.

   Words that content area teachers feel responsible for teaching are those that their students use when they think and talk about, listen to, write, and read in that content area. These words can be found simply by looking through textbooks and other materials in that content area.

   There are many teachers who might find identifying morphemes difficult at the beginning. Because of this, Appendix C is included in this book. You might wish to refer to it in order to get going. Another technique that might help you begin is this: Page through one of your content area books, and write down *just four* words that are composed of two bound morphemes. For example, a social studies teacher might write these:

   monogamy, atheism, autocracy, telegraph

   Next, branch out by writing five additional words with each morpheme, e.g.:

(one) *mono gamy* (marriage)		(not, without) *a the*ism (god)	
*mono*theism	poly*gamy*	*a*typical	poly*the*ism
*mono*poly	miso*gamy*	*a*social	*the*ocracy
*mono*mania	bi*gamy*	*a*moral	*the*ologian
*mono*lingual	a*gam*ic	*a*sexual	*the*ocentric
*mon*archy	hetero*gamy*	*a*mnesty	apo*the*osis

(self) *auto cracy* (governing)

*auto*graph	theo*cracy*
*auto*biography	pluto*cracy*
*auto*mobile	Dixie*crat*
*auto*nomy	demo*cracy*
*auto*matic	techno*crat*

(far off) *tele graph* (to write)

*tele*pathy	bio*graph*y
*tele*photo	auto*graph*
*tele*vision	poly*graph*
*tele*communication	photo*graph*
*tele*scope	di*graph*

This is a good activity for students, too, especially when performed as a class-wide activity in which all students might suggest words.

4. When a widely used morpheme occurs in a reading assignment or in a class discussion, take time to write it on the board. Ask students if they know the meaning. Next, ask them if they can suggest any other words that use the same morpheme. Write these on the board, and then, if possible, branch off as illustrated below. The teacher should be able to fill in when necessary.

   For example: The morpheme is *-nym*, as in the word synonym.

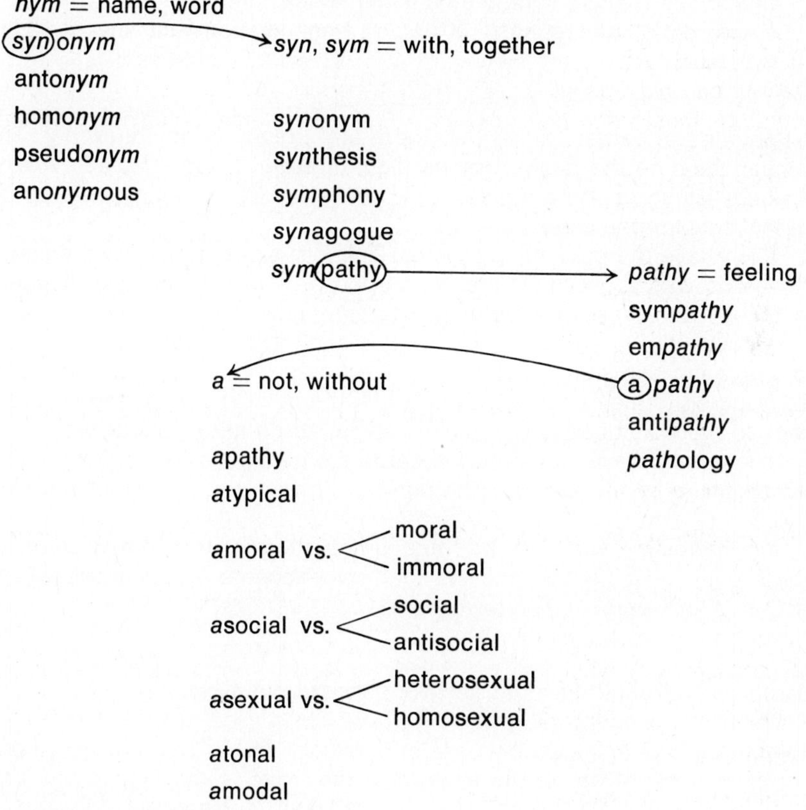

And that's enough for one day.

5. Morpheme concentration (as explained in number 1, above) can also be played with combinations of bound and free morphemes as well as with words composed of two bound morphemes. Words used in this game are best selected directly from the reading assignments of the students, but the following is offered as a "starter":

for English: colon, non, semi, eu, logue, critical, chrono, biography, phony, dict, logue, lingual, phile, bi, auto, climax, para, epi, biblio, graph, verbal, hyper, contra, anti

for social studies: crat, poly, demo, bi, crat, anti, logy, bellum, philo, mono, demo, ante, theosis, sophy, sonic, pathetic, trust, auto, apo, anthropo, a, war, poly, cameral

for science: verge, ped, epi, nutrition, body, chrono, meter, logy, centi, pede, anthropo, bi, here, co, bi, oid, mal, anti, sect, con, a, symmetric, dia, zoo

for mathematics: octo, sect, metry, semi, kilo, a, phery, group, bola, meter, circle, angle, sphere, hemi, quadr, tri, sym, peri, geneous, modal, hetero, sub, gon, para

Shuffle the cards. Those given here are already in random order. Then number them on the back. Arrange them in order of the numbers, with the numbers facing up, on a table or in a pocket chart. (You may wish to have several sets for one classroom.)

Then have the students play thus: The first student gives two numbers. The cards with these numbers are turned around, and the player sees if he or she can make one word using these morphemes. If so, the player must define the word and/or use it in a sentence. If the player is able to do this, he or she keeps the cards. If the player fails at any point, the cards are returned to their original position with the number side facing up. Player number two continues in the same fashion, as do all other players.

The game is over when all the cards are gone, or when no more words can be made by the players. The player with the greatest number of cards wins.

An interesting variation is to encourage students to make up their own words combining the morphemes that are exposed; e.g., *monosophy* (the wisdom of one person), *polybellum* (many war periods), etc.

6. Morpheme baseball: In a hat, box, or fishbowl put slips of paper, each one of which has a bound morpheme on it which is used in the subject being studied. Let's imagine that we are in a science class. The following bound morphemes might be on the slips: bio, zoo, retro, semi, logy, trans, ultra, bi, chrom, co, epi, dia, morph, para, mal, poly, uni, and so on.

A baseball diamond is drawn on the floor, or chairs are placed to indicate bases. The class is divided into two teams. One team is out in the field, and the other is up to bat. The pitcher shuffles the slips and holds the container so that the batter can draw a slip. To get to first base, the batter must define the morpheme (e.g., *chrom* means *color* or *pigment*). To go on to second base, he or she must give a word in that content area which uses the morpheme (e.g., *chromosome*). To get to third base, the batter must define the word and/or use it in a sentence (e.g., Chromosomes are thought to be responsible for the determination and transmission of hereditary characteristics). And to get home, he or she must give another word using the morpheme (e.g., *achromatic*).

Players might progress on their own to first, second, or third base, but they might be brought home by a teammate. If they do not get to first base on the first try, however, they are out. Three outs, and the other team is up to bat.

Rules should be made with regard to the ability of students in the classroom. The game should not be so easy that everyone gets a homerun. Neither should it be so difficult that almost no one can get to first base.

7. Content area wordo: Wordo, as explained in number 2 above, can also be played with content area words composed of two bound morphemes. In this case, however, clues are often more difficult to state since the caller is working with all *bound* morphemes. Therefore, the caller might simply say morphemes which might be on the cards, and players cover each called morpheme with a slip of paper which has a morpheme on it, the two of which would compose a word. For example, if *bio* were called and the player had it on his or her card, the player could cover it with *logy* if that were one of the "family" morphemes for this game.

   Included are "families" for specific content areas. (Students write on their wordo card the morphemes that are not italicized. They write on slips of paper the italicized morphemes.)

For English

pre:	*logy:*	*mono:*	*para:*
*pre*view	tri*logy*	*mono*cycle	*para*dox
*pre*fix	ideo*logy*	*mono*graph	*para*graph
*pre*face	dialecto*logy*	*mono*theism	*para*phrase
*pre*mise	apo*logy*	*mono*syllabic	*para*chute
*pre*judice	grapho*logy*	*mono*lingual	*para*meter
*pre*caution	philo*logy*	*mono*logue	*para*bola
*pre*literate	bio*logy*	*mono*graph	
*pre*date		*mono*gamy	

(Some words come from other content areas to help students understand that the same morpheme may be found in many areas.)

For science

logy:
bio*logy*
physio*logy*
zoo*logy*
geo*logy*

epi:
*epi*center
*epi*demic
*epi*morphosis
*epi*gram
*epi*cotyl
*epi*crisis
*epi*dermis

multi:
*multi*lateral
*multi*angular
*multi*cellular
*multi*ethnic
*multi*ply

retro:
*retro*grade
*retro*rocket
*retro*spect

tele:
*tele*scope
*tele*pathy
*tele*binocular

ultra:
*ultra*modern
*ultra*sonic
*ultra*violet

For mathematics

gon:
penta*gon*
octo*gon*
hexa*gon*
poly*gon*
deca*gon*

meter, metry:
para*meter*
centi*meter*
kilo*meter*
peri*meter*
geo*metry*
sym*metry*
asym*metry*

circum:
*circum*ference
*circum*vent
*circum*scribe
*circum*navigate

bi:
*bi*ped
*bi*annual
*bi*cycle
*bi*modal
*bi*sect
*bi*cameral
*bi*lateral

tri:
*tri*angle
*tri*sect
*tri*gonometry
*tri*cycle
*tri*pod
*tri*plet

quad, quadri, quadru:
*quadri*lateral
*quad*rangle
*quadru*plet
*quadri*partite

For social studies

auto:
*auto*cracy
*auto*graph
*auto*biography
*auto*didact
*auto*hypnosis
*auto*mat
*auto*nomy

bi:
*bi*cameral
*bi*lateral
*bi*gamy
*bi*annual
*bi*sect
*bi*partisan
*bi*racial
*bi*lingual
*bi*polar
*bi*ped

dem(o):
*demo*cracy
*demo*graphy
*dem*agogue
*demo*phobia

epi:
epicenter
*epi*cycle
*epi*demic
*epi*gram
*epi*logue
*epi*crisis

gamy:
bi*gamy*
poly*gamy*
miso*gamy*

the(o):
a*the*ism
poly*the*ism
mono*the*ism
*theo*cracy

8. Morpheme discs can be designed easily by the students or the teacher. Pick morphemes that are frequently used in your subject. For example:

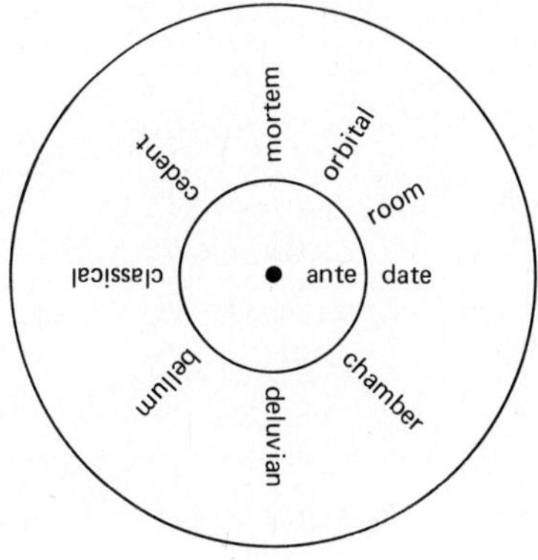

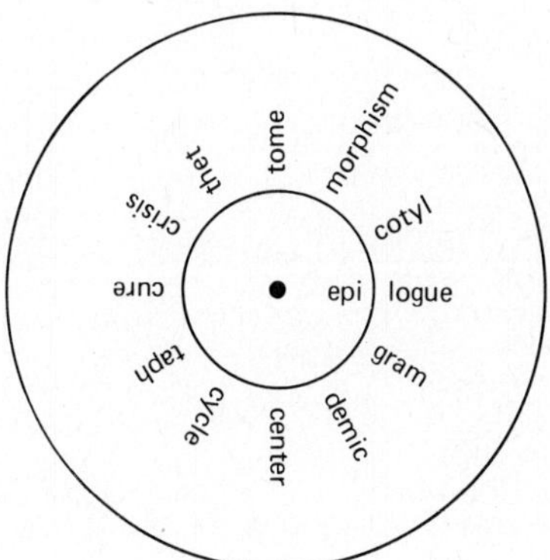

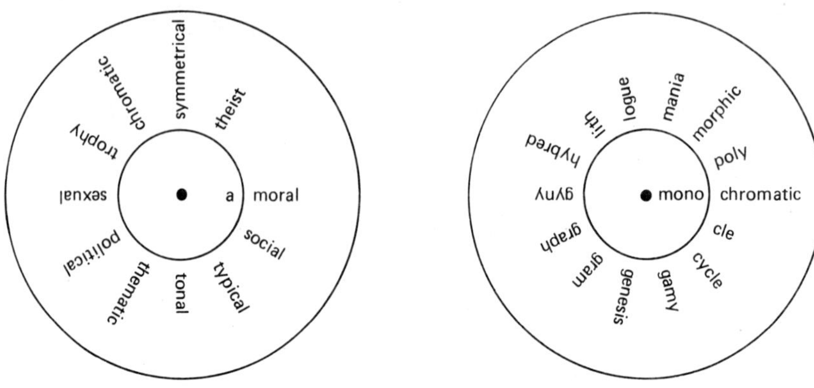

Divide the class into several teams. Turn the morpheme discs upside down, and have each team select one. Team 1 gives one word using its disc, gives the meaning of the word, and uses it in a sentence. If the team can do so, it gets one point. Team 2 does the same with its disc, etc. At the end of the round, the discs are shuffled and turned upside down, and each team draws another disc. The game proceeds for another round. In the entire game, no word may be repeated if a point has been received for using that word. The team with the greatest number of points wins.

9. Use spiral-bound cards:

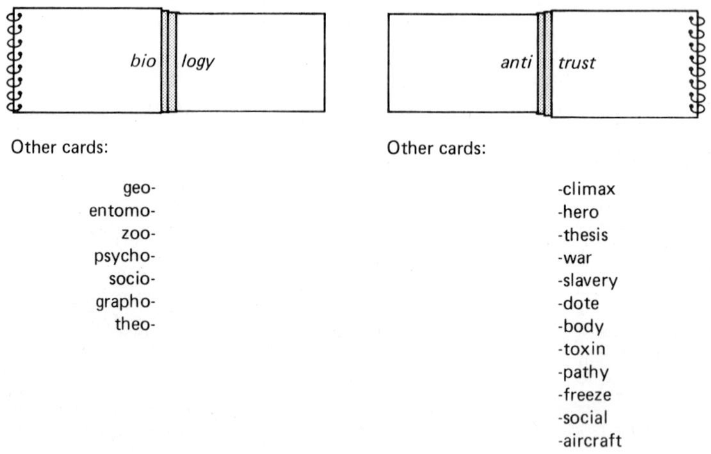

10. Use fold-ins:

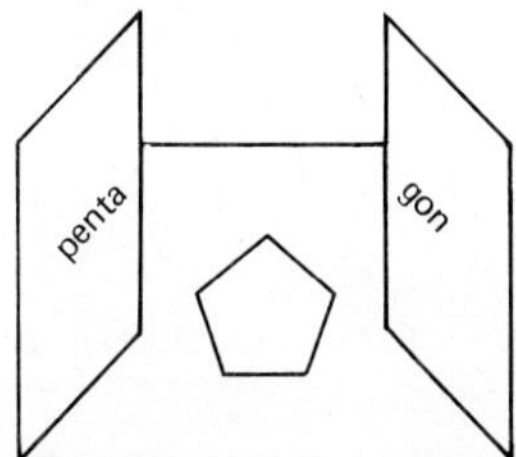

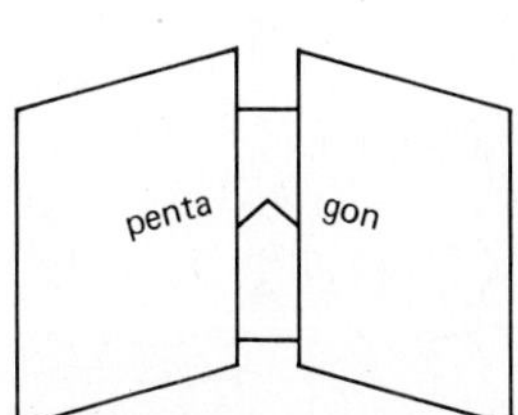

11. Use crossword puzzles. They're easy to make. Keep a supply of graph paper and use only infrequent crossovers. For example, if you wish to use the words telegram, telephone, teletype, telescope, phonograph, stenography, photography, geography, cablegram, autograph, fill them in on your graph paper, thus:

					G								T								
					E				T				E								
					O				E		T	E	L	E	S	C	O	P	E		
					G				L				E								
			C		R				E				P		P						
			A		A	U	T	O	G	R	A	P	H		H						
			B		P				R				O		O						
			L		H				A				N		N						
T	E	L	E	T	Y	P	E		M		S	T	E	N	O	G	R	A	P	H	Y
			G												G						
			R						P	H	O	T	O	G	R	A	P	H			
			A												A						
			M												P						
															H						

Next, clip this sheet over a ditto master and use a ruler to draw in the needed boxes. Take off the graph paper and number the boxes. Write the key on the bottom of the page, thus:

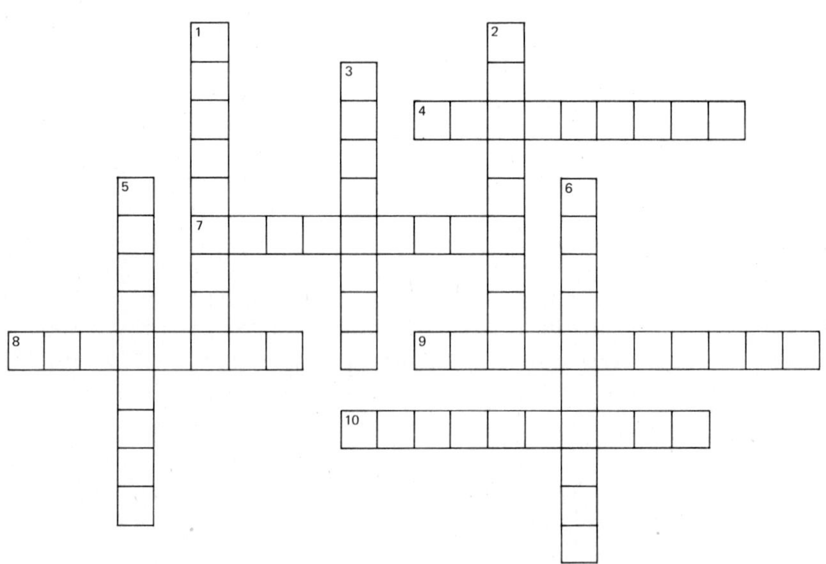

Across:
4. instrument for "seeing from far"
7. the writing of one's own name
8. typing from far
9. writing in shorthand
10. picture writing, "light writing"

Down:
1. "earth writing," study or writing about the earth
2. "sound from far"
3. "writing from far"
5. message sent through an underwater tube
6. "sound writing"

12. Use seek-and-find puzzles, thus: Compose a seek-and-find rectangle using bound morphemes from your content area which, when combined with another morpheme, make up a word. Ask students to draw a ring around the morpheme in the puzzle and insert it in the correct blank in the activity below. (In seek-and-find puzzles morphemes can run horizontally, vertically, or diagonally in any direction.)

E.g.:

S	E	M	I	H	A	C	B	S	H
D	O	E	E	N	I	M	R	Y	S
I	S	M	R	D	A	U	Q	M	K
L	I	F	Q	A	R	C	O	J	M
L	N	P	(I	L	Y	E	T	S	U
I	X	W	R	F	K	N	G	U	C
M	N	E	T)	A	Z	T	J	B	R
N	X	M	T	I	C	I	B	L	I
V	O	N	U	D	I	O	Y	E	C
B	E	P	I	O	T	C	O	L	D
P	O	L	Y	H	N	O	N	G	P

1. ______(tri)angle A geometric figure with three sides.
2. ______meter The measure through the center of a circle.
3. ______ference The boundary line of a circle.
4. ______finite Not ending, going on and on.
5. ______gon Having many sides, many angles.
6. ______gon Having five sides, five angles.
7. ______linear Points not in a straight line.
8. ellips______ A geometric surface having all plane sections in either circles or ellipses.

9. multi ________ "Many-fold"; to increase in amount.
10. ________ meter A thousandth of a meter.
11. ________ meter A hundredth of a meter.
12. ________ sect To cut in two.
13. ________ metry "Like-measure"; equivalence, mirrored image, balance.
14. ________ sine The function of an acute angle that is the ratio of the adjacent side to the hypotenuse.
15. ________ angle Having four angles, four sides.
16. ________ circle Half of a circle.
17. ________ set A set within a set.
18. ________ sphere Half of a sphere.
19. ________ gon Having eight sides, eight angles.
20. ________ mathematics "Behind or transcending mathematics"; the study of the principles and consistency of mathematical systems.

13. For fun, have students make up new words by combining morphemes. Have them either define the new word or illustrate it. Remind them that there are many newly coined words: astronaut, cosmonaut, aquanaut, television, etc.

Busalogue

Three new words were recently minted by the Army in a single written order: *embus, debus* and *reembus,* meaning, respectively, to get on, to get off and to get back on a motor bus. Splendid! If the Army doesn't mind, we'd like to play too. How about *suprabus,* meaning to ride on top? Or *subbus,* to travel hanging on to the crankcase like a hobo under a coal car? A platoon that has reached its destination in a single vehicle might be said to *monobus;* but if the platoon had to transfer, it would *bibus.* (The driver from whom the soldiers obtained their transfers was obviously a *busagogue.*) If the weather was pleasant, the scenery beautiful and the bus not overcrowded, the platoon *eubussized* the trip; if contrary conditions prevailed, and there was a blowout in the left hind *busotrope,* the trip would probably be *dysbustic* for one and all. A soldier who turned bus-happy and rode on them to excess would *hyperbus,* while a soldier who hated buses and didn't use them enough for his own good would *hypobus.* Soldiers arriving at a new post by bus would be *imbusogrants;* any rookie who *misbussed* would be sure to get good and chewed by his sergeant. To *heterobus* clearly means to get on a bus containing members of the opposite sex; after the GIs met up with the Wacs, the vehicle would be a *zoobus,* a bus filled with life. Any love affairs that resulted would be *busogenic* in origin; any crackups, *busomatic.* What the Army needs is a less inhibited *busicographer.**

* From *Life,* December 1, 1952. Copyright, 1952, by Time, Incorporated. Reprinted by permission.

How logical are the words presented here? Can you add further *bus-* words, such as *busophile* (or *-phobe*)?

14. Morpheme tree: You may wish to make a morpheme tree for your bulletin board, or you may wish to make a free-standing one, like a Christmas tree. Students can bring leaves, or fruit, or ornaments to complete it. For example:

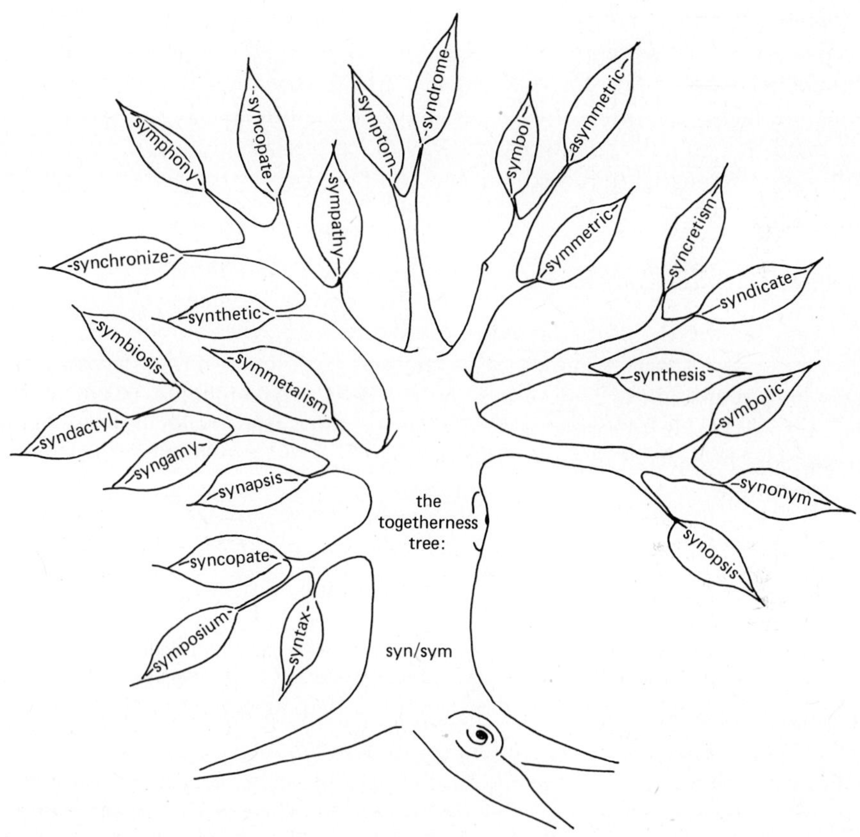

15. Select words composed of two or more morphemes from the reading materials of the students. Write each word on a slip of paper and throw the slips in a hat.

    Divide the class into five or six teams. A student from team 1 picks a slip and reads the word (e.g., *biology*). The student must define the word and/or use it in a meaningful sentence. He or she then gets one point. Team 2 must give another word using one of the morphemes (e.g., *theology*) and define it or use it in a sentence to get a point. Team 3 suggests a word using one of these morphemes (e.g., *theocracy*), etc. When one team cannot suggest a word, it loses its point, and the next team draws a new word from the hat.

Symbols and Abbreviations

Symbols and abbreviations have a unique place in vocabulary-concept development. Symbols are not an alphabetic, or phonic, counterpart for the oral word or words they represent. Abbreviations may or may not be shortened alphabetic counterparts for their words. An abbreviation is higher level abstraction than is the printed word because it is a shortened way of representing the word. A symbol is an alternative way of expressing an idea; a symbol does not necessarily signal the word, but may, in fact, bypass the word to signal the idea.

Symbols

Many of the "words" of mathematics are symbols, i.e., the symbols represent an idea, possibly a process. They may or may not represent (in the reader's mind) their *oral* counterpart. Thus, for some students, the symbol is easier to read than are the words it represents. For other students—those who go from symbol to oral counterpart—it is more difficult.

For example, does a student who sees

$$6 + 2 = ?,$$

automatically respond 8, or does the student think "6 plus 2 equals" 8? Does a student who sees

$$5 - 3 = ?,$$

automatically respond 2, or does the student think "5 minus 3 equals" 2?

In other words, does the student go from symbol to concept, or from symbol to word to concept? The symbol is not an alphabetical representation of the oral word; however, most printed words are. So, the student in mathematics needs a type of paired-associate skill that those who read in other fields do not need.

A student of mathematics who sees

$+$, must think *plus* (i.e., the word and/or the concept)

$-$, must think *minus*

$=$, must think *equals*

$\neq$, must think *does not equal.*

A student who has not memorized these symbols is unable to supply the oral counterpart. Phonics cannot be used. Yet some students find that reading symbols is easier than reading the words. The important point here is that the task is different.

How many of the following commonly used mathematics symbols do those of you who are not in mathematics remember:

$$+ \quad - \quad = \quad \neq \quad < \quad > \quad \sim \quad \cong \quad \Sigma \quad \div \quad \% \quad @ \quad '' \quad ' \quad \times$$

$$\pm \quad \surd \quad \pi \quad // \quad \triangle \quad \perp \quad \odot \quad ▱ \quad \square \quad \angle \quad ∟ \quad \therefore$$

Abbreviations

Certain abbreviations commonly used in some content area subjects may cause problems among students. Some examples follow.

in mathematics:	bu, doz, ft, gal, hr, in., lb, min, oz, pk, pt, qt, sq, wk, yd, yr
in English:	e.g., i.e., *ibid.*, *op. cit.*, *viz.*, A.S., Fr., Sp., etc.
in chemistry:	Ag, Al, As, B, Ba, Bi, Br, C, Ca, etc.

Teaching Strategies

1. A concentration game, as explained in the section on morphology, could be prepared. Here, the symbol or abbreviation would be on one card to be matched with a card on which the meaning or complete word or phrase is given.
2. A spell-down technique could be used. Symbols or abbreviations could be given by the caller. The responder would explain the symbol or give the complete word for the abbreviation.
3. Crossword puzzles, such as the following, could be used.

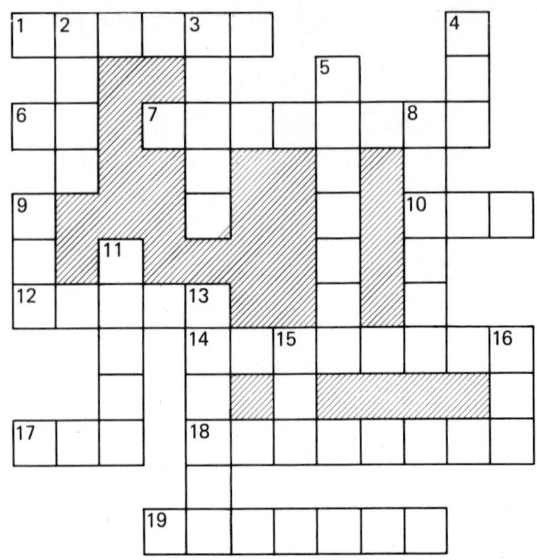

Across:

1. A part of #4, down
6. π
7. --, the process
10. $\rightarrow$, as in AB
12. --
14. $24 \div 6 = \boxed{4}$. The number 4 is a ___________
17. 1
18. +, the process
19. .1 or .02 or .80, etc.

Down:

2. an individual, group
3. =
4. { }
5. $2 \times 3 = \boxed{6}$. Six is the ________
8. the term for $\odot$
9. $2 + 3 = \boxed{5}$. Five is a ________.
11. $<$
13. □
15. The numbers 1, 3, 5, 7, 9, 11 . . . are __________.
16. 10

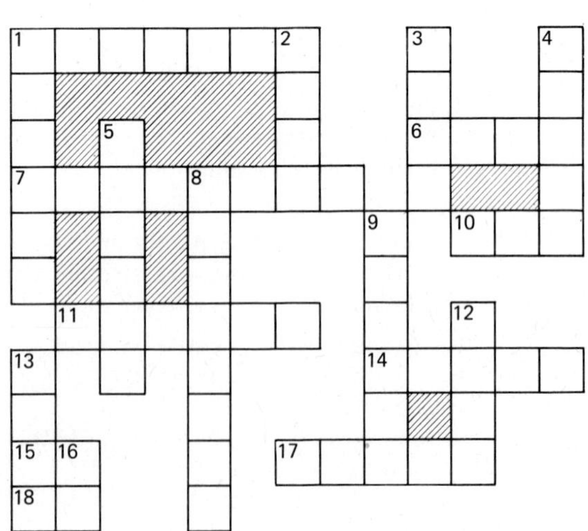

Across:

1. Si
6. Pb
7. F
10. Sn
11. Cs
14. B
15. Sodium (symbol)
17. Xe
18. Cesium (symbol)

Down:

1. S
2. Ne
3. Au
4. Rn
5. Cu
8. Rb
9. C
12. Fe
13. Zn
16. Arsenic (symbol)

This format might also be used in social studies for names of states and abbreviations, and in English for language abbreviations and contractions.

WORD CONNOTATIONS AND FIGURATIVE LANGUAGE

When we talk about denotations of words, we are referring to the literal, or scientific, meanings of words. But when we talk about *connotations* of words, we are referring to the interpretive meanings of these words—the poetic and emotional meanings.

Most science and mathematics books are written to convey precise information. The words selected by the authors are usually those that suggest very specific meanings—ones that are generally agreed upon by all who write and read in the field. However, the language of the poet or other literary writer, as well as the language of many social scientists and newspaper writers, is intended to sway our feelings or to convince us of a particular point of view. Words chosen by such writers are frequently being used connotatively, and the connotative meanings may vary from individual to individual.

For example, what is your idea of a *liberal*? Ask your friends what they think it means to be liberal. Do the same for the word *conservative*. Is it "good" to be a liberal in politics and a conservative in religion? What does it mean to have *liberal* moral values? What about *radical*? *Conservative*? *Reactionary*? Are you to the *left* in some ways, to the *right* in others? What do *you* mean by *left* and *right*? What does your neighbor mean? What does a particular historian mean? Remember, something you might consider to be the greatest thing in the world, someone else might scorn:

Reprinted through the courtesy of the Chicago Tribune–New York News Syndicate, Inc.

Simple Connotations

Children might be introduced to the idea of connotative language by being taught denotative meanings of words with their connotative counterparts. For example, denotatively, blue is a color. Connotatively, *blue* might mean sad (Upon hearing the news, they felt blue) or regal (blue blood).

Ask students to give the denotations and some possible connotations of the following words: *dog, monkey, yellow, pink, peach, apple.* Point out that denotations are scientific, literal meanings; where there is a *physical referent,* the denotation is synonymous with it. Connotations are emotional meanings—and may be pleasant or unpleasant.

A delightful verse that appeared in *The Saturday Evening Post* might serve to introduce young people to the idea of connotations and to the pleasant and unpleasant associations words used connotatively might suggest.

Semantics
by John Donovan

Call a woman a kitten, but never a cat;
You can call her a mouse, cannot call her a rat;
Call a woman a chicken, but never a hen;
Or you surely will not be her caller again.

You can call her a duck, cannot call her a goose;
You can call her a deer, but never a moose;
You can call her a lamb, but never a sheep;
Economic she likes, but you can't call her cheap.

You can say she's a vision, can't say she's a sight;
And no woman is skinny, she's slender and slight;
If she should burn you up, say she sets you afire,
And you'll always be welcome, you tricky old liar.*

Teaching Strategies

1. Ask students to suggest as many *animal names* as they can that are used connotatively. For example:

cat	duck	lamb	worm
kitten	goose	sheep	tiger
mouse	deer	monkey	fox
rat	moose	beaver	wolf

Have students use these words connotatively in sentences or phrases.

2. Ask students to suggest as many *growing things* as they can that are used connotatively. For example:

peach (He's a peach.)
peachy (Everything's peachy.)
apple (apple of his eye)
plum (plum of a job)
nut (What a nut she is.)
egg (good egg, bad egg)
banana (top banana)
lemon (The car's a lemon.)
potato (hot potato)
pea (two peas in a pod)
violet (shrinking violet)
pansy (He's a pansy.)
vegetable (She is a vegetable.)

---

* Reprinted with permission from *The Saturday Evening Post*, © 1946 The Curtis Publishing Company.

3. Ask students to suggest as many *colors* as they can that are used connotatively. For example:

green (with envy)	pink (glowing)
green (naive)	red (anger)
blue (sad)	red (communism)
white (with fear)	red (in the red—losing money)
white (purity)	rosy (happy)
yellow (cowardly)	brown (brown-nose)

4. Contrast the connotative meanings of colors with the ideas the visual image of the same colors represents, for example, in national and school flags. For example:

red (anger, communism)	red (valor)
white (with fear, purity)	white (purity, hope, truth)
blue (sad)	blue (justice, loyalty, sincerity)

5. Design an activity in which words are used denotatively in Part 1 and connotatively in Part 2. For example:

Social Studies

Each italicized word in the first group of sentences below has a special meaning when used connotatively. Select the appropriate words from the sentences in Part 1 to insert in the blanks in Part 2.

Part 1 (Denotative use)

1. *Red,* white, and blue are the colors of the American flag.
2. The *potato* crop was poor this year.
3. British aristocrats often enjoy *fox* hunts.
4. My *pink* petunias are especially pretty.
5. I wish my grass would turn *green.*

Part 2 (Connotative use)

1. Nations in close geographical proximity to communistic countries often turn __________ or __________.
2. __________ is a term used for communism.
3. The Cuban situation turned into a hot __________.
4. Rommel was known as the Desert __________.
5. He hasn't held a public office for long enough. He's too __________ to run for President.

Mathematics

Each italicized word in the first group of sentences below has a special meaning when used connotatively. Select the appropriate words from the sentences in Part 1 to insert in the blanks in Part 2. You may change singulars to plurals, and plurals to singulars.

Part 1 (Denotative use)

1. A *square* is a four-sided figure with all sides equal.
2. When you *add* two and three, you get five; two *plus* three equals five.
3. Two, four, six, and eight are even *numbers*.
4. The cube *root* of eight is two.
5. *Zero* is a numerical concept which denotes the absence of quantity.

Part 2 (Connotative use)

1. Her explanation just doesn't ______________ up. She will not be a ______________ to our committee.
2. Although he had a high opinion of himself, the girls all thought he was a ______________.
3. She had such old-fashioned ideas, that everyone considered her a ______________.
4. She was pleased when, at the end of the performance, they asked her to do another ______________.
5. He yanked out hair by the ______________ in frustration over his math problems.

Physical Education

Each italicized word in the first group of sentences below has a special meaning when used connotatively. Select the appropriate words from the sentences in Part 1 to insert in the blanks in Part 2.

Part 1 (Denotative use)

1. The *cat* is a popular house pet.
2. *Trench* warfare was a big part of World War I.
3. Every community needs a *fireman* to protect it from fires.
4. Spring is a good time to thoroughly *clean up* the house.
5. The small-town arsonist was arrested because he was a *barn burner*.

Part 2 (Connotative use)

1. The offensive and defensive linemen in football battle it out in the ______________.
2. The fourth hitter in a baseball line-up is called the ______________ hitter.
3. Last Sunday's pro football playoff was a real ______________.
4. A relief pitcher is known in baseball circles as a ______________.
5. The agile basketball player was all over the court like a ______________.

6. Design a similar activity as that above, but list words at top. These words are to be inserted in Part 1 with their denotative meanings and in Part 2 with their connotative meanings. For example:

Science

backbone   fish   electricity   heart   boiling point

Part 1 (Denotative use)

1. The ______________ of water is 100° C.
2. A vertebrate is an animal with a ______________.
3. The ______________ pumps blood to all parts of the body.
4. ______________ live primarily in water.
5. ______________ is needed for many modern household appliances.

Part 2 (Connotative use)

1. It was said she lacked ______________ in making her decisions.
2. The football team was outclassed but still played with a lot of ______________.
3. The hot-tempered boy had a low ______________.
4. There was ______________ in the air among the crowd at the big game.
5. He was considered a real ______________ among his poker-playing partners.

English

act   scene   myth   dangling   case

Part 1 (Denotative use)

1. The subject of a sentence is in the nominative ______________.
2. A sentence with a ______________ participle is often ambiguous.

3. The second ____________ of the play had to be revised.
4. Act three, ____________ two began at midnight.
5. Each day for a month we studied a different Greek ____________.

Part 2 (Connotative use)

1. She lost her temper and made quite a ____________.
2. He had a hard time putting his ____________ together.
3. She had a ____________ on him, but he didn't know she existed.
4. His excessive lying made us believe he was a ____________ omaniac.
5. She left him ____________, being unable to make up her mind.

7. Connotations can be pleasant or unpleasant. Ask students to tell how the writer or speaker feels about situations or people as indicated by word choice.

   Directions: Write an L in the space provided before each sentence if the writer likes the person or situation. Write a D if the writer dislikes the person or situation.

   D 1. Jake gabs a lot.
   L 2. Jake is a fluent speaker.
   ___ 3. Betty likes soft, neutral colors.
   ___ 4. Betty is mousy.
   ___ 5. Mrs. Jones' house is full of old junk.
   ___ 6. Mrs. Jones collects antiques.
   ___ 7. He's the town gossip.
   ___ 8. He's the best informed person in town.
   ___ 9. What a shrewd businessperson Mrs. Patrick is.
   ___ 10. Mrs. Patrick is a crook.

Figurative Language

"Figures of speech" are a form of connotative, or nonliteral, language. Some of the most commonly used figures of speech are *similes, metaphors, personification,* and *allusions.* Such figures of speech are commonly found in literature and in slanted writing. Frequently, figurative language is used to clarify a difficult idea.

Similes

A simile is an analogy in which two dissimilar things are shown to be alike, at least in one respect. In a simile, the word *like* or *as* is used. For example:

"*Words are like leaves,*
And where they most abound
Much fruit of sense beneath
Is rarely found. . . .

"But *true expression,*
Like the unchanging sun
Clears and improves
Whate're it shines upon."

Joseph Addison, "Essay on Criticism"

"The kingdom of heaven is like to a grain of mustard seed . . ." (Matt. 13:31)

"The kingdom of heaven is like unto leaven, which a woman took, and hid in three measures of meal, till the whole was leavened." (Matt. 13:33)

"The bluejay shouted like a noisy politician."

"Airplanes roar like demons tearing through the sky to strike at their foes."

Metaphors

Metaphors, like similes, are analogies, but the word *like* or *as* is not used.

They are two peas in a pod.

Theresa is a vegetable.

He is a peacock.

"Merry larks are ploughmen's clocks."

"All the world's a stage."

"Dry leaves are little brown kites riding the wind."

"The clouds are fairy castles in the sky."

Personification

Personification is the technique of representing a thing or an animal as a person. For example:

The flames ate the house.

Fear lit flames of horror in her eyes.

Money talks.

The ocean threatens with the voice of an angry giant.

The pages of my book speak to me with many voices.

Allusions

An allusion is an indirect reference to a person—real or mythical—or to a place or a thing. For example:

1. Someone once said, "The only thing wrong with Shaw's *Pygmalion* is its

name." Although the title describes the play perfectly, most people do not understand the allusion.

Pygmalion, of course, was a Greek sculptor who carved an ivory statue of a maiden and then fell in love with it. Mere human women could not compete, in Pygmalion's eyes, with his own creation. He therefore prayed to the goddess Aphrodite for a wife who would resemble the statue. Aphrodite brought the statue to life.

In Shaw's play, Professor Henry Higgins is Pygmalion, and Eliza Doolittle is the statue—molded not from ivory, but from "a squashed cabbage leaf." It is fascinating to follow the allusion through the play, including the Epilogue, in which Shaw comments that Eliza should not marry the professor, but rather Freddie. Why does Shaw say this? Remember the *allusion.*

2. Research relating to mythology is interesting.
   a) Is *January* an appropriate name for the first month of the year? Who is *Janus?*
   b) Is *cereal* named appropriately? Who is *Ceres?*
   c) Was the ship *Titanic* appropriately named? Who is *Titan?*
   d) Have you ever been *tantalized?* Who is *Tantalus?*
   e) Where does *hypnotize* come from? Who is *Hipnos?*
3. Biblical allusions also abound.
   a) What was meant when Moishe Dayan was called a modern *David?*
   b) Who was *Job,* as in Job's Daughters?
   c) What does it mean to "raise *cain*"?
   d) Have you ever felt like *Daniel?*
   e) "East Pakistanis engage in mass *exodus.*" Exodus?
   f) The *genesis* of the idea—Genesis?
4. Modern allusions are also common.
   a) Have you ever heard of anyone called an *Einstein?*
   b) Did anyone ever say to you that "if you take that job, you'll be going to *Timbucktu*"?
   c) He's met his *Waterloo.* To what does this refer?
   d) She's a modern *Florence Nightingale.*

DIACHRONIC LINGUISTICS

One very enjoyable area of language that is often overlooked is the area of diachronic linguistics. Use your morphology to figure out what diachronic means. *Dia-* means "through," as in diameter (measure through), diathermy (heat through the skin), diagnose (to know, or see through). *Chron-* means "time," as in chronological (time order), chronic (lasting a long time), and chronometer (a highly accurate kind of clock). Diachronic, therefore, means through time, and diachronic linguistics is a description of language as it changed through time.

The English language has changed in several major ways. One such change has been in *sentence patterns.*[2] English has evolved as a language of very straightforward syntax—NV, NVAd, NVN, NVNN, NVNA, VLvN, NLvA, NLvAd, and transformations and elaborations of these patterns. *Sound patterns* of words have also changed, and correspondingly, so have many spellings. *Meanings* of some words have changed. *New words* have been added to our language.

The study of diachronic linguistics for students below the college level ought to be pure pleasure. There is no need to be overly technical about it. The major stress ought to be to make children and young people *aware* of the fact that *language grows and changes*—all living languages do. Such a concept cannot be taught in the abstract. Numerous examples are needed to make the point clear.

Students are fascinated by finding the many ways our language has grown and is presently growing. Language, like human behavior, changes continuously. Only dead languages, like Latin, do not change. Let us look at some simple and enjoyable ways of making this point.

Sound Changes

English has undergone a "great vowel shift" from Old English to Middle English to Modern English. This shift, though regular, is quite complex, too much so to hold the interest of most precollege students. However, if you are an English teacher, your class would enjoy comparing Chaucer in the original with modern translations of the same passages.

The consonant shift, however, is much easier to grasp and demonstrates some major changes in sounds of English. Frequently referred to as *Grimm's law,* after one of the brothers Grimm, who described the change, it is also often called the *First Germanic Consonant Shift,* the only Germanic consonant shift which affected English.

Broadly stated, what happened was:

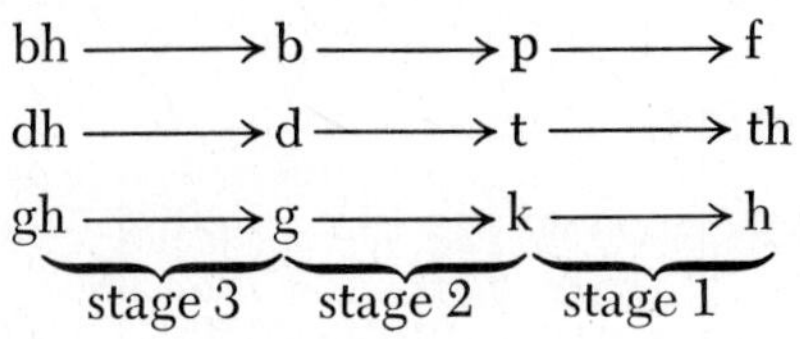

bh ⟶ b ⟶ p ⟶ f
dh ⟶ d ⟶ t ⟶ th
gh ⟶ g ⟶ k ⟶ h
stage 3 stage 2 stage 1

Each original set of consonants changed only once; for example, the *b, d, g* that resulted from the shift of *bh, dh, gh* did not shift further. Indeed, had they done so, the words formerly distinguished by these sounds would have fallen together as homophones, losing distinction and producing much confusion. The whole process is understood to have taken place in three stages; after *p, t,* and *k* had shifted, it was possible for *b, d,* and *g* to shift without producing homophones.*

Table 6.2 shows the alteration of some words according to Grimm's law. Note that these changes involve only consonant shifts. Some vowels shifted later.

Table 6.2 Sound and spelling changes occurring as a result of Grimm's law

Grimm's law describes these sound and spelling shifts which occurred in the Germanic languages, including the ancestor of Old English.		From the language named, English later borrowed a cognate and used it in more formal words, such as the following:	
Original	New	Language	Words
dent	tooth, teeth	Latin	*dent*al, *dent*ist, in*dent*
gno	know	Greek	dia*gno*se, a*gno*stic, pro*gno*sis
pater	father	Latin	*pater*nal, *patr*icide
mater	mother	Latin	*mater*nal, *matr*ix
ped	foot, feet	Latin	*ped*al, *ped*estal, tri*pod*
centum	hundred	Latin	*cent, cent*ipede
pisces	fish	Latin	*pisc*ary, *Pisces*, *pisc*iculture
kardiakos	heart	Greek/Latin	*cardiac, cord*ial, *cour*age
canis	hound	Greek/Latin	*canine*
corn	horn	Latin	*corn*ucopia, uni*corn*, tri*corn*
tris	three	Greek/Latin	*tri- (tri*angle, *tri*cycle)
host	guest (circular shift)	Latin	*host, host*el, *hos*pital, *hos*pitality, *host*age

Another interesting sound shift is one that is occurring today. If you listen to yourself—and other people—speaking, you will notice that very often in words of three syllables, the middle vowel, and therefore the middle syllable, is being dropped. We just do not say it. Of course, some people do—but enough do not. The change is widespread nationally. Following are some of the words that are changing.

* Stuart Robertson and Frederic G. Cassidy. *The Development of Modern English,* 2d. ed. Englewood Cliffs, N.J.: Prentice-Hall, 1954, p. 29. Reprinted by permission.

rest*au*rant	fam*i*ly	prob*a*bly
om*e*let	av*e*rage	comp*a*ny
int*e*rest	min*e*ral	diff*e*rence
gen*e*ral	crim*i*nal	po*e*m

Try to think of other examples. Ask your students to help you. You might be able to list hundreds of them.

Changes in Meaning

We can also look back to see how meanings of words have changed. Some common types of changes are *amelioration* and its opposite, *pejoration*; also, *generalization* and its opposite, *specialization*. Today is an age of both *euphemism* and *antieuphemism* and of *hyperbole*.

Amelioration

Meanings of some words have ameliorated, or elevated. For example, at one time, any youth was a *knight,* and a minstrel was what we consider a buffoon today. A *minister,* now a servant of God, was a common servant. If one was *enthusiastic,* it meant he or she was fanatical. And *nice* meant ignorant.

Pejoration

The opposite trend is perhaps more common. Pejoration means degradation. Meanings of more words seem to pejorate than to elevate. For example, a *villain* was a person from a villa, a farm servant, rather than a scoundrel. *Lust* meant pleasure or joy. A *lewd* person was a lay person, unlearned, but not indecent or obscene. Chaucer once described someone as “lewd and nice,” i.e., unlearned and ignorant. *Lewd* has pejorated, whereas *nice* has ameliorated. A *pirate* was one who adventured. And any boy was an *imp.* Today *propaganda* is pejorating, as is *criticism.* Can you think of examples?

Generalization

Some words broaden, or extend, in meaning. Once upon a time, when one *shipped* something, one sent it by ship. Logical? But today, we “ship” by plane, truck, train, car, or any other way we can find. If we *sailed* the Atlantic, we *sailed*—but not today! We might “sail” to Europe, but does anyone think we’re taking a sailboat?

At one time only men were described as *virtuous.* To call a lady virtuous was disastrous—like calling a woman *virile* today (the same root). And once, a *picture* was a painting only—not a photograph, a collage, a print, etc.

Specialization

Word meanings also change in the opposite way. And, no doubt, more words specialize than generalize. A *girl* used to be a young boy or girl. Starving meant dying, but today it is just one way of dying. *Meat* was any food, not just the flesh of an animal. And *coast* was any border.

When there are two or more words in our language that mean the same thing, all but one will drop out, or the words will diverge in meaning. At one time there were three words meaning "small animal": animal, beast, and deer. Today, *animal* is the general term, *beast* often means a brutal creature, and *deer* is a particular kind of small animal.

Divergence and specialization lead to preciseness in definition. For example, one speaks of a *pack* of wolves, but a *herd* of cattle, and a *flock* of sheep, a *school* of fish, and a *swarm* of bees. One speaks of the *aroma* of coffee, but the *bouquet* of wine, and the *fragrance* or *perfume* of flowers.

To call a person *fatherly* is different from calling him *paternal* (though the words are cognates). And *motherly* differs in meaning from its cognate, *maternal.*

Much new terminology is now being used in mathematics—in the new math. Also, new terminology is used in English classes—especially in relation to linguistics. In both cases many of the words are not new, but they are being used in specialized ways. In some cases the terms *are* new, possibly newly coined, e.g., grapheme, phoneme, and morpheme.

Euphemism and antieuphemism

If we wish to be delicate in our speech, we use euphemisms—at times. If we wish to be direct, and possibly harsh, we use antieuphemisms—at times. A euphemism is a pleasant term for what may be a very unpleasant idea. Since the idea is unpleasant, the euphemism remains a euphemism only for a time and then it, too, becomes unpleasant, and a new euphemism is needed.

Note the names for women's sizes: junior, misses, women's half-sizes, petites. Women's blouses are sized large, so that almost anyone can take size 12, 14, or 16, but skirts are smaller, so that most can take size 8, 10, or 12. Stretch stockings are not sized small, medium, large, and extra large, but short, average, long, and extra long. This pleases milady, for no woman wants to be considered extra large, but extra long is fine.

For awhile, one rarely used the term *to die,* but instead used *to pass away.* To die has returned, however, especially if we are speaking of a person who is not close to us. Cemetery has become memorial park. And sometime during World War II, "replacements" no longer were sent into battle; instead, "reinforcements" went in. We all felt better about it. And the draft has become the selective service.

Another example is the word *symphony,* which caught on briefly as a euphemism for melting pot. What do the contributions of individual instruments of a symphony orchestra suggest to you that might be similar to contributions of various peoples in our society? Does *melting pot* suggest something quite different?

Hyperbole

Hyperbole is an overstatement, an obvious exaggeration. With some people, things are never fine or good, but *grand, superb, perfect, gorgeous, fantastic*—or *dreadful* or *horrid. Unique,* which used to mean one of a kind or without equal, has been replaced by *absolutely unique.* Some things are *quite unique.*

New Words Enter Our Language

How do new words come into our language? Chiefly by coining and by borrowing (stealing?).

Coining

We can coin new words in a variety of ways:

1. We *combine morphemes* in new ways:

   aquanaut   cosmonaut   astronaut   television

2. We *blend* the first part of one word with the last part of another:

*sm*oke + f*og*	= smog	*str*ong + so*ft*	= stroft
*br*eakfast + l*unch*	= brunch	*ca*ttle + buff*alo*	= catalo
*mot*or + hot*el*	= motel	*beef* + buff*alo*	= beefalo
*bo*at + hot*el*	= botel	*sl*ip + gl*ide*	= slide
*fl*oat + hot*el*	= flotel	*tw*ist + wh*irl*	= twirl
*sk*irt + sh*ort*	= skort	*fl*ash + bl*ush*	= flush (flush of pride)
*squ*eeze + cr*ash*	= squash		

3. *Acronyms* are words formed from the first (or first few) letters of several words:

   UNESCO—*U*nited *N*ations *E*ducational, *S*ocial, *C*ultural *O*rganization

   SNAFU —*S*ituation *N*ormal: *A*ll *F*ouled *U*p

   What do these represent? In time, we forget because the acronym is enough to convey meaning.

WAVES	RADAR	NATO
WACS	SONAR	SCUBA
CARE	SALT	MOPED (*mo*torized + *ped*als)

4. Slang words or expressions come and go. Occasionally, however, one stays. What do these mean?

   dinged zapped waxed mushroom people

   Her heels were on fire = she was in a hurry

   Antsville = a place full of people

   Pile up the z's = go to sleep and snore

   Stable your horse = park your car

   Slang is novel, fresh, and picturesque when it enters our language. Too soon, however, it brands its user as stereotyped and unimaginative—unless the user has a *new* slang expression.

Borrowing

Fortunately, we do not have to spend Washingtons (American dollars) for the words we borrow from our neighbors around the world—or we would really be broke. Both the English and Americans have been heavy borrowers, and that is one reason our language is extremely rich and colorful.

Page through a well-illustrated dictionary. Whenever you see an interesting picture, check to see from which language the word came. Here are some samples:

American Indian	*Spanish*	*Italian*
pecan	patio	violin
totem pole	maize	cameo
moccasin	potato	volcano
tepee	chocolate	piano
toboggan	mosquito	opera
raccoon	taco	vest
chipmunk	llama	

French	*German*	*Hindi*
pork	dachshund	cheetah
venison	otter	bungalow
genie	wiener	shampoo
humor	dollar	pajamas
croissant	house	jungle
calendar	edelweiss	

Greek	*Scandinavian*	*Australian English*
alphabet	sister	kangaroo
circus	teeter totter	boomerang
octopus	sky	
Arabic	*Russian*	*Eskimo*
candy	sputnik	kayak
algebra	babushka	igloo
sugar		
Turkish	*Persian*	*Japanese*
coffee	caravan	kimono
yogurt		

Teaching Strategies

1. Collect as many euphemisms as possible. Contrast them in meaning with the words for which they are substitutes.
2. Collect as many acronyms as you can. See if you can coin some new ones.
3. Make your own exercises, like the following one for mathematics, using words in your content area.

Greek	*Latin*	*Arabic*	*Hebrew*	*Chinese*
geometry	triangle	zero	abacus	tangram
tetrahedron	set	algebra		
labyrinth	tangent	zenith		
octagon	square			

Write the language from which the words for the following illustrations come:

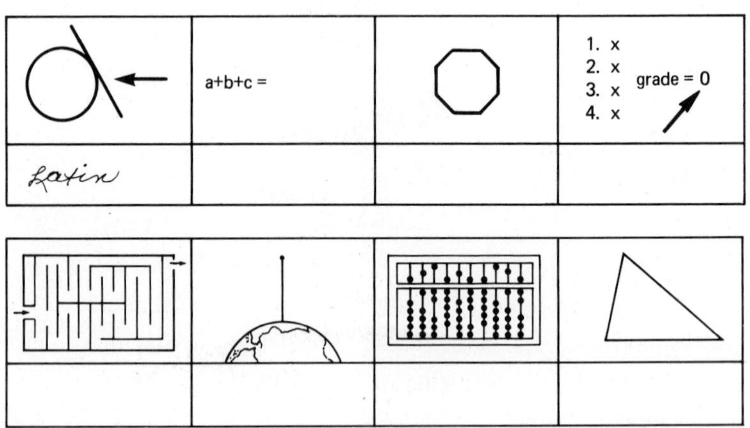

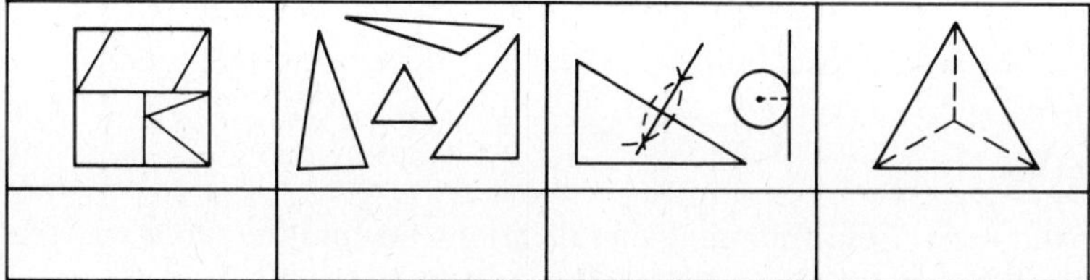

4. Prepare "books" of four cards each. Each book should contain the word that has evolved as described by Grimm's law, plus three words which have been borrowed later from another language and maintain the old spelling. Examples of books are:

   teeth, dental, dentist, indent
   know, diagnose, agnostic, prognosis
   father, paternal, patricide, patriarchy
   mother, maternal, matrix, matriarchy
   feet, pedal, tripod, pedestal
   hundred, centipede, cent, centennial
   fish, Pisces, piscary, piscivorous
   horn, cornucopia, unicorn, tricorn
   three, triangle, trilogy, trinity
   heart, cardiac, cordial, courage
   guest, hospitality, hostage, host
   hound, canine, kennel, Canary Islands

   Put in an odd card, and play like "Old Maid." Students must give the meanings of the words in order to lay the books down.

5. Design an activity like this:

   strong + ____________ = stroft
   ____________ + fog = smog
   cattle + buffalo = ____________
   etc.

PHONICS

Sometimes students know a word orally, but are unable to pronounce it when they see it in print. Most English words are phonically regular, and if students know and can apply fewer than 20 phonic generalizations which have proved useful, they are able to decode these "regular" words. Thus, they would be able to pronounce words they see in writing and, if they have them in their listening vocabulary, they would be able to derive meaning from the written symbol. They would save time by not having to refer to the dictionary so often.

Syllabication

Among the most useful phonic generalizations for middle grade and secondary students to know are those that relate to syllabication. English and English language arts teachers might wish to teach these to their students directly. Teachers of other subjects may wish to study these so that when they are teaching new words to their classes, they can reinforce the use of these generalizations.

The methodology for teaching these generalizations progresses from teaching: (1) *auditory discrimination* of syllables, to (2) *visual discrimination* of syllables, to (3) actual syllabication according to three generalizations.

Teaching Strategies

1. Ask students to say several one-syllable words, then two-syllable words, then three-syllable words (auditory discrimination).
2. Ask students to number from 1 to 30 on a sheet of paper. *The teacher reads the following words,* each accompanied by its number. The student writes the number of syllables each word contains (auditory discrimination). Students *do not* see these words in print.

1. October	11. remote	21. rose
2. March	12. any	22. daisy
3. June	13. concern	23. complete
4. apple	14. elephant	24. statue
5. number	15. dinosaur	25. window
6. professor	16. coffee	26. piñata
7. main	17. pitcher	27. organ
8. linguistics	18. lamp	28. cello
9. ornament	19. carpet	29. phonograph
10. ten	20. garden	30. mouse

   The teacher checks individual papers to see which students have made errors. Any student who has made *more than three errors* needs extra help.

3. Next, the teacher writes the same 30 words on the board and explains that each time we have a *single vowel,* a *vowel pair,* or a final *vowel-consonant-e,* we have a syllable (visual discrimination). Students are asked to circle each vowel grapheme. (A *vowel grapheme* is composed of the number of vowels it takes to spell an unbroken vowel sound. In general, English vowel

graphemes are spelled with *one vowel,* as in *cat, me, and, strong,* or with *vowel pairs,* as in *coat, main, meet, coin,* or with a *vowel and a final e,* separated by a consonant, as in *cake, Pete, cute,* and *hide.*)

1. O c t o b e r
2. M a r c h
3. J u n e
4. a p p l e
5. n u m b e r
6. p r o f e s s o r
7. m a i n
8. l i n g u i s t i c s
9. o r n a m e n t
10. t e n
11. r e m o t e
12. a n y
13. c o n c e r n
14. e l e p h a n t
15. d i n o s a u r
16. c o f f e e
17. p i t c h e r
18. l a m p
19. c a r p e t
20. g a r d e n
21. r o s e
22. d a i s y
23. c o m p l e t e
24. s t a t u e
25. w i n d o w
26. p i ñ a t a
27. o r g a n
28. c e l l o
29. p h o n o g r a p h
30. m o u s e

4. Next, students are supplied with "hypothetical words" and are asked to circle each vowel grapheme and write the number of syllables the word contains (visual discrimination):

v = vowel c = consonant l = l e = e

1. v c v c v c ____
2. c c v c c v v c ____
3. v v c v v c c ____
4. c v c v v c v c e ____
5. c c v c v v ____
6. v c c v c c v v ____
7. v c v c c v v c e ____
8. c v c c v c v v c ____
9. v c v v ____
10. c v c e ____
11. c c v c v v c l e ____
12. v v c v c c ____
13. c v c c v c c l e ____
14. v c v v c v ____
15. v c c v c c v v c v c ____
16. v v c ____
17. v v c e ____
18. c v c l e ____
19. v c v v c v c e ____
20. c c c v c ____

answers:

1. (v) c (v) c (v) c	3	*11. c c (v) c (v v) c l (e)	3
2. c c (v) c c (v v) c	2	12. (v v) c (v) c c	2
3. (v v) c (v v) c c	2	13. c (v) c c (v) c c l (e)	3
4. c (v) c (v v) c (v) c e̸	3	14. (v) c (v v) c (v)	3
5. c c (v) c (v v)	2	15. (v) c c (v) c c (v v) c (v) c	4
6. (v) c c (v) c c (v v)	3	16. (v v) c	1
7. (v) c (v) c c (v v) c e̸	3	17. (v v) c e̸	1
8. c (v) c c (v) c (v v) c	3	18. c (v) c l (e)	2
9. (v) c (v v)	2	19. (v) c (v v) c (v) c e̸	3
10. c (v) c e̸	1	20. c c c (v) c	1

* A *final e* is pronounced only when it is preceded by a *consonant* + l (-cle), in which case the *e represents a schwa sound* and is pronounced before the *l*: ta*ble* = ta*bəl*, princi*ple* = princi*pəl*.

5. Next, students are supplied with "nonsense words" and asked to circle each vowel grapheme and then write the number of syllables the word contains (visual discrimination):

1. s p e e n o t	____	11. v o n e	____
2. r o a z z l e	____	12. c r o y k l e	____
3. n e a s e	____	13. a w s e m m a b	____
4. n e i s e	____	14. s c h l a m p s	____
5. d o a l l y	____	15. p s y r d	____
6. m o u s s o p t	____	16. d o m i k	____
7. d e m m i n	____	17. p u b m y	____
8. f a i t s u d	____	18. b l y	____
9. r o n d l e	____	19. s a t h p h a	____
10. b o i j a u d t a l	____	20. a m n e s e	____

answers:

1. s p (e e) n (o) t	2	5. d (o a) l l (y)	2
2. r (o a) z z l (e)	2	6. m (o u) s s (o) p t	2
3. n (e a) s e̸	1	7. d (e) m m (i) n	2
4. n (e i) s e̸	1	8. f (a i) t s (u) d	2

9. r (o) n d le	2		15. p s (y) r d	1
10. b (o i) j (a u) d t (a) l	3		16. d (o) m (i) k	2
11. v (o) n ~~e~~	1		17. p (u) b m (y)	2
12. c r (o y) k le	2		18. b l (y)	1
13. (a w) s (e) m m (a) b	3		19. s (a) t h p h (a)	2
14. s c h l (a) m p s	1		20. (a) m n (e) s ~~e~~	2

6. Next, students are taught the three phonic syllabication generalizations:
   a) *situation: v c c v* When two vowel graphemes are separated by two consonants, divide between the consonants: as-ter, sil-ver, tar-get, but-ler.
   b) *situation: v c v* When two vowel graphemes are separated by one consonant, the consonant may go with the first or the second vowel. Try it both ways. If you know the word orally, you will know which one is correct: liz-ard, lem-on, wag-on; ra-zor, spi-der, ti-ger.
   c) *situation: -c l e* When a word ends in consonant l-e, these three letters compose the final syllable: bi-ble, ea-gle, bun-dle, tur-tle, noo-dle.

7. Next, ask students to divide the *hypothetical words* and the *nonsense words* into syllables (visual discrimination):

answers:

*1. (v) ′c, (v) ′c, (v) c	3		11. c c (v) ′c, (v v) /c l (e)	3
2. c c (v) c/c (v v) c	2		12. (v v) ′c, (v) c c	2
3. (v v) ′c, (v v) c c	2		13. c (v) c/c (v) c/c l (e)	3
4. c (v) ′c, (v v) ′c, (v) c ~~e~~	3		14. (v) ′c, (v v) ′c, (v)	3
5. c c (v) ′c, (v v)	2		15. (v) c/c (v) c/c (v v) ′c, (v) c	4
6. (v) c/c (v) c/c (v v)	3		16. (v v) c	1
7. (v) ′c, (v) c/c (v v) c ~~e~~	3		17. (v v) c ~~e~~	1
8. c (v) c/c (v) ′c, (v v) c	3		18. c (v) /c l (e)	2
9. (v) ′c, (v v)	2		19. (v) ′c, (v v) ′c, (v) c ~~e~~	3
10. c (v) c ~~e~~	1		20. c c c (v) c	1

* Use ′c, to indicate that division may come *before* or *after* the single consonant.

answers:

1. s p (e e) ′n, (o) t	2		3. n (e a) s ~~e~~	1
2. r (o a) z/z l (e)	2		4. n (e i) s ~~e~~	1

5. d o a l/l y	2	13. a w ′s, e m/m a b	3
6. m o u s/s o p t	2	14. s c h l a m p s	1
7. d e m/m i n	2	15. p s y r d	1
8. f a i t/s u d	2	16. d o ′m, i k	2
9. r o n/d l e	2	17. p u b/m y	2
10. b o i ′j, a u d/t a l	3	18. b l y	1
11. v o n e	1	**19. s a t h/p h a	2
12. c r o y/k l e	2	20. a m/n e s e	2

** The following are consonant digraphs (one sound spelled with two letters) and are never divided: *ph, sh, th, ch.*

8. Now we are ready for *real words.* To review the generalizations, do the following:

   a) *Clue 1:* vc - cv

ram - page	as - ter	mas - cot
vc - cv	vc - cv	vc - cv
har - dy	cal - cine	plain - tiff
vc - cv	vc - cv	vc - cv

   When two vowel sounds are separated by two consonants, divide between the consonants.

   b) *Clue 2:* v - cv or vc - v

E - gypt	par - a - noid	lem - on
v - cv	vc - v - cv	vc - v
lei - sure	rem - i - fy	frig - ate
v - cv	vc - v - cv	vc - v

   When two vowel sounds are separated by a single consonant, divide either before or after the consonant.

   c) *Clue 3:* - cle

cy - cle	poo - dle	ten - a - ble
ma - ple	snif - fle	tem - ple

   When a word ends in *-cle*, divide before the consonant.

9. When a real word is to be taught in a content area and it is phonetic:
   a) Write it on the board, perhaps in a sentence.
   b) Ask the students to try to pronounce it.
   c) If they cannot do so, ask how many syllables it has and where the syllabic

divisions are. Mark them on the board. Then ask students to pronounce it. If they still cannot do so:

d) Reinforce appropriate vowel generalizations or consonant generalizations by listing several easy words that have the troublesome vowel or consonant grapheme. (See below.)

e) Ask them to pronounce the word, or pronounce it for them. Have them repeat it orally.

f) Define it and/or use it in a sentence. Use an illustration if possible.

Teachers of students who have more serious problems in recognizing grapheme-to-phoneme relationships might need to diagnostically teach other phonics generalizations. It is beyond the scope of this book to explain the methodology for doing this. However, the generalizations which are commonly taught in modern phonics programs are listed below. The reader may wish to study methodology for teaching in one or more of the sources listed at the end of this chapter.[3]

Particularly Useful Grapheme-to-Phoneme Relationships*

I. Consonants

A. Single consonants

1. Each consonant (except c, g, s, and x) is highly consistent in representing one sound.
2. When *c* or *g* is followed by *e, i,* or *y,* it represents its soft sound (city, certain, cycle; gem, agile, gym). When followed by anything else, or nothing, it represents its hard sound (cake, coat, cup, clash, cram, attic; game, goat, gum, glass, grip, flag). Omit *ch* and *gh.*
3. The letter *s* usually (86% of the time) represents its own sound (swim, soft, solo). Its next most frequent sound (/z/—11%) is found in words such as resort, raisin, music, desire, treason. Omit *sh.*
4. The letter *x* represents the sounds found in the following words (/ks/ or /k/ + /s/): ax, box, tax; foxy, taxi, vixen, and (/g/ + /z/): exact, exempt, exist, example.

B. Double consonants (and triple consonants)

1. Consonant blends—When two unlike consonants appear side by side, usually the sound represented is a blend of the sounds represented by each (*bl*ock, *cl*own, *dr*own, *gr*ow, *sm*ile, *sp*ook, *spl*ash, etc.).
2. Consonant digraphs—Although spelled with two consonants, consonant digraphs function as single consonants. They are *ch, sh, th,*

---

* From Lou E. Burmeister. "Content of a Phonics Program Based on Particularly Useful Generalizations," in *Reading Methods and Teacher Improvement,*" ed. Nila Banton Smith. Newark, Delaware: International Reading Association, 1971, pp. 27–39. Used by permission of the International Reading Association.

ph, *ng*, and *ck*. *Ch* represents three sounds: /ch/ child, chop (63%); /k/ chorus, christen, orchid (30%); and /sh/ chef, chute, mustache (7%). *Sh* represents /sh/, as in should, ship, shed. *Th* represents two sounds: voiced, as in this, they, rhythm (74%); and voiceless, as in think, thick, youth (26%). *Ph* represents /f/, as in elephant, photo. *Ng* represents /ŋ/, as in sing, wing, young. *Ck* represents /k/, as in chick, package, cuckoo.

3. Consonant clusters that represent only one sound
   a) Like consonants—When two like consonants are side by side, they represent only one sound, e.g., ball, egg, guppy, guerilla, tattoo. (This is not true of *cc* or *gg* when followed by *e*, *i*, or *y* —success, suggest.)
   b) Unlike consonants—When certain consonants are side by side in the same syllable, only one sound is represented. This is true of the following pairs (the only pairs which occur at least once per thousand running words): *initial kn-*, as in kneel, knot; *initial ps-*, as in psalm, pseudo; *initial wr-*, as in wrap, write; *final -dg(e)*, as in dodge, bridge; *final -gn*, as in sign, reign, but also *initial gn-*, as in gnat, gnome; *final -lm*, as in calm; palm; *final -mb*, as in bomb, comb; *final -tch*, as in catch, witch.

II. Vowels

A. Definitions: The five vowels (*a*, *e*, *i*, *o*, *u*) and two "semivowels" (*y* and *w*) are used singly and in pairs and in the final "vowel (consonant) *e*" position to represent a variety of sounds. The most common sounds are the vowel's own short sound (h*a*t, p*e*t, h*i*t, h*o*t, h*u*t), the long sound (m*ai*n, m*ea*t, s*i*z*e*, *oa*k, c*u*t*e*), a schwa (*a*bout, cam*e*l, penc*i*l, lem*o*n, circ*u*s, marr*ia*ge), an *r* modified sound (c*ar*, c*are*, h*er*, h*ear*, f*or*), a diphthong (*ou*t, c*ow*, c*oi*n, b*oy*), a *broad a*, i.e., *circumflex o*, (*au*to, *aw*ful, b*a*ll), a long and short double *o* (r*oo*ster, b*oo*k).

B. Single vowel graphemes

1. Closed syllable (syllable that contains a single vowel and ends with a consonant)—A single vowel in a closed syllable represents its own short sound, its *r* controlled sound when it is followed by an *r*, or a schwa sound.
2. Open syllable (syllable that contains a single vowel in a final position)—If the single vowel in an open syllable is an *e*, *o*, or *u*, it usually represents its own long sound; if the vowel is an *a*, it may represent a schwa (53%), a long *a* sound (32%), or a short *a* sound (12%); if the vowel is *i*, it may represent a schwa (49%), a short *i* sound (37%), a long *i* sound (14%).
3. Final *y*—If a word ends with a consonant + *y*, the *y* will represent a long *i* sound if the word is monosyllabic (try, my, thy, cry), but the *y* will represent a short *i* (long *e*) sound if the word is polysyllabic (baby, balcony, century, city).

C. Vowel pairs

There is no generalization that can be taught to cover a majority of instances of vowel pair grapheme-to-phoneme relationships. A particular generalization, however, may be taught to cover specific vowel pairs. The vowel pairs listed below need description in a phonics program.

1. Long sound of first vowel—If the vowel pair is *ai, ay, ea, ee, oa,* or *ow,* the most frequent sound is the long sound of the first vowel (main, pay, meat, meet, boat, crow). But *ea* often represents a short *e* sound (bread), and *ow* often represents a diphthong (cow).
2. Diphthongs—The vowel pairs *oi* and *oy* represent a diphthong (coin, boy). The pairs *ou* and *ow* often represent a diphthong (mouse, cow). However, when *ou* is in a suffix, it represents a schwa sound (dangerous, wondrous).
3. Broad *a* (circumflex *o*)—The pairs *au* and *aw* represent the "broad *a*" sound (auto, awful), just as does *a* when followed by *ll* (ball, fall).
4. Long and short *oo*—The pair *oo* represents two sounds (rooster, book).
5. *Ei* and *ie*—The most common sound *ei* represents is long *a* (neighbor, weigh). Otherwise *ei* and *ie* represent the following sounds, in order of frequency: long *e* (c*ei*ling, f*ie*ld), short *i* (for*ei*gn, lass*ie*), long *i* (s*ei*smic, d*ie*).
6. *Ey* represents a short *i* sound, as in hon*ey,* or a long *a,* as in th*ey.*
7. *Ew* represents a long *u* sound, as in n*ew*s, or an $\bar{o}\bar{o}$ sound, as in fl*ew.*

D. Final vowel-consonant-e

1. When a word ends with a *single-vowel,* single consonant, and an *e,* the vowel sound is usually the long sound of the first vowel (cape, Pete, pipe, hope, cute).
2. Groups of exceptions are (1) *i-e* words in which the *i* represents a short *i* sound: l*i*v*e*, g*i*v*e*, off*i*c*e*, prom*i*s*e*; (2) *i-e* words in which the *i* represents a long *e* sound: mar*i*n*e*, magaz*i*n*e*; (3) *a-e* words in which the a represents a short *i* sound, especially *-ace, -age, -ate* words: surf*ace*, pal*ace*; aver*age*, cour*age*; sen*ate*, delic*ate*.

E. Consonantizing of *i*

When *io* or *ia* follows a *c, t,* or *s,* the consonant plus the *i* combine to represent a /sh/ or /zh/ sound: racial, social; mention, caution; pension, mansion; vision, fusion.

SUMMARY

To help students build diverse and powerful vocabularies, many considerations are necessary. Words must be looked at in several ways—denotatively and connotatively. Techniques for building vocabulary in each of these areas are numerous.

Words rarely have only one *denotation*. Some words have over 100. It is not unusual for people to think they know the meaning of a word and not be aware of other nuances or meanings and, therefore, misinterpret or misrepresent a passage.

Of unsuspected difficulty sometimes are *simple words with specialized or technical meanings* in the content areas. The importance of using *context clues* was stressed. Students should be taught to examine words to see if the meanings they are associating with these words make sense in the sentence and paragraph in which they are found. Authors of textbooks frequently lead readers by the hand to help them understand new words or new meanings of old words. Several techniques the teacher might use to guide students and to make vocabulary study enjoyable were given. The study of *morphology* develops word power rapidly. And it is interesting.

Symbols and *abbreviations* add variety, but may also burden the reader. We must be sure that students understand the symbols and abbreviations used in our books.

Different from word denotations are word *connotations*, the interpretive meanings of words. Young children can be taught to grasp *simple connotations*. In fact, they thoroughly enjoy working with connotations for animal names and growing things. Later, they can work with *figurative language: similes, metaphors, personification,* and *allusions*.

Diachronic linguistics is an area often overlooked. Yet to study some aspects of how language has changed is both pleasurable and helpful. Especially interesting are *sound changes* that have occurred in the past, such as the *First Germanic Consonant Shift,* and the present tendency to drop medial vowels in some three-syllable words. *Meaning changes* also fascinate some of our young. These changes can be classified today into certain patterns: *amelioration* and *pejoration, generalization* and *specialization, euphemism* and *antieuphemism,* and *hyperbole*. New words are continually being added to our language by *coining: combining morphemes* in new ways, *blending,* forming *acronyms,* and *slang*. The English and American languages have also borrowed heavily from languages around the globe.

Many secondary school students would benefit from being taught phonic syllabication generalizations. These generalizations can help them pronounce many polysyllabic words which already are in their listening vocabularies. Three generalizations were given and ways of teaching them were explained. Also, other phonic generalizations were listed.

NOTES

1 Additional references include: Wilbur S. Ames. "The Development of a Classification Scheme of Contextual Aids," *Reading Research Quarterly,* **II** (Fall 1966): 57–82; A. S. Artley. "Teaching Word-Meaning Through Context," *Elementary English Review,* **XX** (1943): 140–143; K. L. Dulin. "New Research on Context

Clues." *The Journal of Reading,* **XIII** (1969): 33–38; Constance M. McCullough. "Learning to Use Context Clues," *Elementary English Review,* **XX** (1943): 140–143.

2 See Carl Lefevre. *Linguistics and the Teaching of Reading.* New York: McGraw-Hill, 1964.

3 For further elaboration, see Lou E. Burmeister. *Words—from Print to Meaning: Classroom Activities: for building sight vocabulary, for using context clues, morphology, and phonics.* Reading, Mass.: Addison-Wesley, 1975; also Thaddeus M. Trela. *Sensible Phonics.* Belmont, Calif.: Fearon, 1975.

SUGGESTED ACTIVITIES

1. Design four different kinds of vocabulary exercises or activities that would be useful for teaching words in your content area.
2. Design a bulletin board display using morphemes important in your content area.
3. Compose a chart using the following format, which includes bound morphemes important in your content area.

morpheme	meaning	words in my field using the morpheme	words in other fields using the morpheme

4. Design one exercise or activity to help students understand the process of language change (diachronic linguistics) as it relates to your content area.
5. Syllabicate the following nonsense words:

a n s a m	t r e f l e	w a u n m o p
d o m c l e	v o a g g a d	z e f g o n e
p a i s o d	b o l e	c l o o m p
t u n n o i k	u s m o u t h	d r e s c l e

REFERENCES FOR FURTHER READING

Altick, Richard. *Preface to Critical Reading.* New York: Holt, Rinehart and Winston, 1969, Chapters 1 and 2.

Ames, Wilbur S. "The Development of a Classification Scheme of Contextual Aids," *Reading Research Quarterly,* **II** (Fall 1966): 57–82.

Artley, A. S. "Teaching Word-Meaning Through Context," *Elementary English Review,* **XX** (1943): 68–74.

Burmeister, Lou E. "Content of a Phonics Program Based on Particularly Useful Generalizations," in *Reading Methods and Teacher Improvement,* ed. Nila Banton Smith. Newark, Delaware: International Reading Association, 1971, pp. 27–39.

Burmeister, Lou E. *Words—from Print to Meaning: Classroom Activities: for building sight vocabulary, for using context clues, morphology, and phonics.* Reading, Mass.: Addison-Wesley, 1975.

Cole, Luella. *The Teacher's Handbook of Technical Vocabulary*. Bloomington: Illinois Public School Publishing Co., 1940.

Davis, Nancy B. *Basic Vocabulary Skills*. New York: McGraw-Hill, 1969.

Dulin, K. L. "New Research on Context Clues," *Journal of Reading*, **XIII** (1969): 33–38.

Fries, C. C. *Linguistics and Reading*. New York: Holt, Rinehart and Winston, 1963.

Hafner, Lawrence E. (ed.). *Improving Reading in Middle and Secondary Schools, Selected Readings*. New York: Macmillan, 1974, Sections 3 and 5.

Harris, Albert J. *How to Increase Reading Ability*. New York: David McKay Co., 1970, Chapters 13, 14, 15.

Hayakawa, S. I. *Language in Thought and Action*, 2d ed. New York: Harcourt, Brace and World, 1964.

Herber, Harold. *Teaching Reading in Content Areas*. Englewood Cliffs, N.J.: Prentice-Hall, 1970, Chapter 8.

Karlin, Robert. *Teaching Reading in High School*. Indianapolis: Bobbs-Merrill, 1964, Chapter 5.

Karlin, Robert (ed.). *Teaching Reading in High School—Selected Articles*. Indianapolis: Bobbs-Merrill, 1969, Chapter 5.

Laffey, James L. (ed.). *Reading in the Content Areas*. Newark, Delaware: International Reading Association, 1972.

Laird, Charlton. *The Miracle of Language*. New York: Harcourt, Brace and World, 1953.

Lefevre, Carl. *Linguistics and the Teaching of Reading*. New York: McGraw-Hill, 1964.

McCullough, Constance M. "Learning to Use Context Clues," *Elementary English Review*, **XX** (1943): 140–143.

Olson, Arthur V. and Wilber S. Ames (eds.). *Teaching Reading Skills in Secondary Schools*. Scranton, Pa.: International Textbook Co., 1970, Section 5.

Pei, Mario. *The Story of the English Language*. Philadelphia: J. P. Lippincott, 1967.

Roberts, Paul. *Modern Grammar*. New York: Harcourt, Brace and World, 1968.

Robertson, Stuart and Frederic Cassidy. *The Development of Modern English*. Englewood Cliffs, N.J.: Prentice-Hall, 1964.

Schubert, Delwyn and Theodore Torgerson (eds.). *Readings in Reading—Practice, Theory, Research*. New York: Thomas Y. Crowell Co., 1968, Section 4.

Spache, George. *Toward Better Reading*. Champaign, Illinois: Garrard, 1963, Chapter 20.

Trela, Thaddeus M. *Fourteen Remedial Reading Methods*. Belmont, Calif.: Fearon, 1968.

Trela, Thaddeus M. *Sensible Phonics*. Belmont, Calif.: Fearon, 1975.

Chapter 7

DEVELOPING LITERAL COMPRE-HENSION OF READING MATERIALS

What is the cognitive domain?

What are the seven levels of the cognitive domain?

What is the place of literal comprehension activities in the cognitive domain?

What are four common literal level reading skills?

Which of these skills are important in your content area?

How can each of these be taught at the recall level? At the translation level? What are the possibilities for teaching such skills at higher cognitive levels?

INTRODUCTION

This chapter and the next two deal with the development of students' comprehension skills and abilities. Chapter 7 is concerned with literal comprehension. Chapter 8 deals with interpretation skills as well as those that relate to the application of ideas in practical situations. Chapter 9 presents ways of teaching what is commonly referred to as critical-creative reading.

These skills are considered to be cognitive skills. *Cognition,* or the processes of knowing and perceiving, relates to the intellectual development of a person or society. Much has been written lately about the *cognitive domain,* that is, the domain, or realm, of the intellect—that part of a person's development commonly referred to as intellectual development. Cognitive qualities are measured on I.Q. tests and on many school tests.

It has long been an aim of teachers to develop students intellectually. There is an ever-evolving body of knowledge in most subject areas that the schools have felt a need to pass on to youth: to have them learn it, digest it, react to it, and possibly create with it.

Society often dictates that educated people know certain facts, and people are often judged by the amount and kind of knowledge they possess. Often, people succeed in business in relationship to their knowledge, their ability to *think*—to apply what they know to old and new situations, and to judge, create, and evaluate intellectually.

There is little doubt that the intellectual development of students is important—both in general and in relation to subject matter areas. Yet though we have long talked about such development, it is only recently that a clear structure of the *cognitive domain* has been provided for our use.

If we understand the structure of this domain, we will be better able to understand what we are doing—or perhaps what we ought to be doing—in the classroom to foster our students' thinking ability. If we understand the various *levels of cognition,* we may be better able to balance our classroom activities in order to avoid an overemphasis on one or more levels and an underemphasis on or omission of others.

THE COGNITIVE DOMAIN

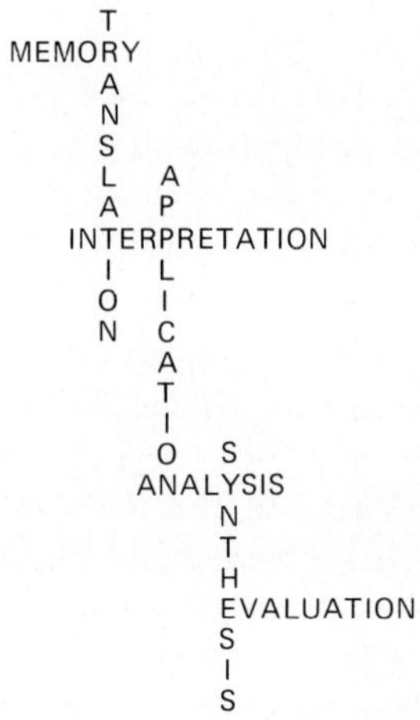

Benjamin Bloom is the senior author of a book titled *Taxonomy of Educational Objectives: Handbook I, Cognitive Domain.* Using this volume as source material, Norris Sanders wrote a very practical and lucid book, *Classroom Questions—What Kinds?* in which he outlined seven levels of the cognitive domain. In the discussion that follows, the seven levels are taken from Sanders. The descriptions of the levels are partly Sanders', but largely the work of the present author, who gathered her ideas from numerous sources. The seven levels are:

1. *Memory*—remembering or recognizing just what the author has said. Common types of questions or activities at the memory level relate to recalling, identifying, or recognizing: (a) facts, dates, definitions, (b) main ideas as given by the author, (c) sequence of events, commonly called the story line, and (d) directions as given.

2. *Translation*—putting information or knowledge into another form. For example, a student might: (a) paraphrase a definition or passage, (b) take information from a paragraph and put it into graph, map, or chart form; or the opposite—take information from a graph, map, or chart and put it into sentence or paragraph form, (c) put a story into skit form or a play into story form, (d) actually follow directions exactly as given.

3. *Interpretation*—recognizing, or seeing, *unstated relationships,* such as: (a) given the cause, determining the effect; or, given the effect only, understanding the cause, (b) anticipating what might happen next, (c) formulating a main idea when none is given—inductive reasoning, (d) making deductions from generalizations supplied, (e) relating to characters—real or imaginary—

and understanding what motivates them, (f) imagery—being able to live vicariously—being able to see, feel, smell, hear, and taste through the imagination.

4. *Application*—a relatively high level of cognition which involves the ability to *both* (a) recognize an instance when a principle applies and also (b) apply it with success. College students taking a reading methods course might ask themselves if they could recognize what kind of help each student in a class needs and whether they could successfully give this help. But that is not enough. They must do it.

5. *Analysis*—the knowledgeable dissection of something and the examination of the parts that compose the whole. We may analyze propaganda, for example, by answering such questions as: (a) Who is the author and whom is he or she serving? (b) What are the author's purposes? (c) What techniques does the author use? (d) To what need is the author appealing? Or, we may analyze poetry, noting (a) rhyme, rhythm, meter, (b) the period in which it was written and whether it is exemplary of that period, (c) mood and tone. Or, we may learn to recognize fallacies of reasoning. Or, we may reason deductively by using syllogisms or inductively by using necessary and/or sufficient conditions, etc. Or, we may look at the steps as outlined for a chemistry experiment and logically question what the result of following them would be —or we might recognize that if we did not follow them *exactly*, something disastrous might happen.

6. *Synthesis*—the integration, reorganization, or fusion of ideas, usually from various sources. J. P. Guilford, in *Structure of the Intellect*, uses the terms *convergent* and *divergent* production.[1] In *convergent production*, ideas or materials are integrated in a conventional way. In *divergent production*, ideas or materials are organized or produced in a unique, or unusual, way. Divergent production also includes elaboration and fluency.

7. *Evaluation*—the formulation of a standard and the judging of an idea or object in relationship to that standard. For example, if we decide what characterizes a good modern play, we can then critique a play according to these standards. Of course, new standards may be evolving.

Discussion

When we are teaching in the content areas, we may feel that our textbook and other materials at our disposal at least partially dictate the cognitive level at which we will expect our students to perform. It is true that sometimes the cognitive level is well determined by the material or occasion. For example, the following people might be best off to follow directions precisely as given: the cook who is baking a cake, the chemist who is performing a given experiment, the engineer who is building a bridge (memory-translation level).

At other times these same people might perform at higher levels: the cook who decides to add poppy seeds to the cake, the chemist who is experimenting in the hope of discovering something new, or the engineer who is designing a bridge (analysis, synthesis, and evaluation levels).

It is often not only the material, but also the way *we* view the material that determine the level at which we expect students to perform. Do we view the ideas contained in a textbook as completely objective? If so, perhaps it is best to work at the lower levels. Or, do we think the author is biased, presents just one point of view, and is too general or incomplete? If so, we are likely to work at higher levels and to send our students in search of additional information.

The way we view our students may determine the levels at which we work. Perhaps we think that the brighter students should work at the higher levels and the less bright at the lower levels. Yet certainly the brightest students need to know some facts, and they must be able to understand exactly what an author is saying before they react to it. And the slowest students need these skills, too, but they must also learn to reason, analyze, synthesize, and evaluate as best they can, though certainly with simpler materials and ideas than the bright student would use. It may just be that it is *our* knowledgeability and *our* point of view toward the material and students that determine the levels at which we work.

Literal Comprehension

It is the purpose of this chapter to discuss four major literal comprehension skills and, when possible, to demonstrate ways of helping students achieve these skills. Brief suggestions will be made to indicate that some of these skills can and should, at times, be taught at higher levels also. The teaching of these skills at higher levels will be explained more completely in the following two chapters.

Readers of this book should recognize that as teachers, they are the ones who decide which reading skills are important—or which kinds of questions they will ask—to help develop the understandings they feel are important in their courses at a particular time. No one else can do this for them, for only they know their students and how they relate, or are able to relate, to the materials and ideas of their courses.

Teachers should understand the full range of cognitive skills—or thinking levels and activities—so that their decisions are made wisely. They should also understand the capabilities of their students. Their goals, or objectives, as well as their activities, should be designed so that they are appropriate to both the students and also the content of the subject. The following skills are considered to be at the literal level:

following directions as given
recalling facts, dates, etc.
recognizing and recalling main ideas
recognizing and recalling the pattern and sequence of ideas

Students can engage in these activities at what Sanders calls the memory and/or translation levels. At the *memory level,* they recall or identify exactly what the author has said, in the author's words. At the *translation level,* they recall what was said, but they respond by using their own words or by engaging in some other type of "translation" activity, such as drawing an illustration, putting words into graph, map, or chart form, putting a story into skit form, actually following directions as given, etc.

FOLLOWING DIRECTIONS AS GIVEN

Following directions is obviously a very important skill, not only as it relates to reading, but also as it relates to many other in-school and out-of-school activities. Yet, students frequently learn to ignore directions for several reasons: directions are often poorly given, the same directions are repeated so often that students know they will be given again and again, and students learn to "mask" directions with the hope that someone else will do the job—and often someone else does!

Much of the student's behavior in relation to following directions is molded at home; however, a teacher cannot bemoan this fact. Positive action must be taken. What can a teacher do? Of utmost importance is establishing the practice of *giving directions only once* and expecting them to be followed. Of course, it is necessary that the directions be given clearly and unambiguously. If they are complex, it helps to present them in written form.

With students who do not follow directions well, the following procedure can be used. First, be sure you have the student's attention. Second, present only one direction at a time, e.g., "Open your book to page 29." Wait for it to be followed. Then, present another single direction, e.g., "Read the title of the chapter." Wait for this to be done. Then, give another single direction, e.g., "Read the first main heading." Wait for this to be done. Give another single direction, e.g., "Formulate several questions that you expect to be answered in this section," etc.

After students are able to follow one direction at a time, give them two to be followed consecutively ("Open your book to page 29, and read the title of the chapter"). When this has been done, follow with, "Read the first main heading and formulate several questions that you think will be answered in this section," etc. When students are able to follow two consecutive directions well, give them three consecutive directions. Later, give them four and then five. If they wish, allow them to write the directions down.

Remember that when you give directions, you must have the attention of the students to whom they are given. The directions must be clearly stated and in the students' realm of understanding. It must be possible for the students to carry out the instructions.

Teaching Strategies

It can be interesting, enjoyable, and worthwhile to give students in a classroom a list of directions to follow. Be sure the reference materials are available so that they can find the answers. Time students when they are doing the exercise.

In English

1. Look up the word "genre" in your dictionary and write the first two definitions given.

   ____

   ____

2. Look in your dictionary to find in what year Thomas Gray was born and in what year he died. Write the dates here: born ________, died ________.
3. Complete the following sentence by inserting two adjectives that make sense in it:

   The ________ ________ building collapsed when the tornado struck.
4. Insert two common nouns and any additional words necessary to complete the following sentence:

   ________ and ________ tied in the race.
5. If all the words in the following sentence are spelled correctly, circle every third word in this complete item; if not, circle every second word: "The dinosaur is a prehistoric animal."

.

.

.

10.

time: ________

In mathematics

1. Circle names of objects that are three-dimensional and underline names of objects that are two-dimensional:

   circle triangle sphere parallelogram

   square cube cone hexagon
2. Put a box around the number that is the cube root of 64. If it is not given, put a triangle around each number:

   1 2 4 5 7 8 16

3. Draw an illustration of a pentagon in the box below.

4. If 5 zos 7 = 12,
   and 8 zos 9 = 17,
   and 12 zop 2 = 10,
   and 4 zop 1 = 3,
   what does 6 zos 8 zop 5 equal? ________

5. What real word does *zos* stand for? ________

6. What mathematical symbol does *zos* represent? ________

7. What real word does *zop* stand for? ________

8. What mathematical symbol does *zop* represent? ________

9. If quadruped means four-footed, *quadrilateral* means four-sided, and *biped* means two-footed, what is the word for two-sided? ________

10. Octopus (really octo*ped*) means what? ________

time: ________

In science

1. On what page(s) in your textbook will you find information about air pollution? ________

2. Circle names of members of the primate order. Cross out other names:

man	elephant	monkey	spider	chicken
lemur	zebra	orangutan	lion	ape
deer	tiger	dinosaur	gorilla	dog

   (Common knowledge? Otherwise, a chart should be in sight.)

3. If 32° Centigrade equals 0° Fahrenheit, circle every word that starts with a vowel; if not, underline every word that starts with a *c* or an *s*. (Common knowledge? Otherwise, a chart should be available.)

4. Look at the chart in the front of the room. Find the planet which is nearest the moon. Write its name here: ________

5. Look in the Glossary of your textbook. Write the author's definition of the word polarize: ____

____

.

.

.

10.

time: ________

In social studies

1. Look at the map on page 192 of your book. Circle the states that fought on the side of the South in the Civil War; underline the states that fought on the side of the North. Cross out the states that did not fight.

New York	Arizona	Louisiana	Florida
Alabama	Texas	Wisconsin	Iowa
Indiana	Maine	California	Alaska
Michigan	Kentucky	Missouri	Pennsylvania
Virginia	West Virginia	Ohio	Nevada

2. Using the same map, locate the states that fought for the South that are not listed in item 1. Write their names here: ____________________

____

____

3. Find the jacket for the book *Black Like Me* on the bulletin board. Write the name of the author here: __________________________________

4. Use your dictionary to find what the word *apartheid* means. Write the definition here: ____

____

5. Use the Biographical Sketches part of your textbook to find the date of the original publication of *Uncle Tom's Cabin,* by Harriet Beecher Stowe. Write it here: __________

.

.

.

10.

time: ________

The first student finished with a perfect paper could write a set of directions appropriate to the content field for the next similar activity, perhaps to be held the next week. (Any one student would do this only once.) By writing such directions, the student would get practice in stating instructions lucidly and unambiguously. If the student does a poor job, it might be better for the teacher to allow the student's peers to correct him or her at the time of the activity rather than for the teacher to correct the student before time.

Caution

Students should know that it is not always wise to follow directions. When students follow directions as given, they may be operating on the literal level of thinking. If, however, they have carefully analyzed the impact of following the directions and have decided that the directions are worthy of being followed as given, they are reacting on a higher, nonliteral, level.

When directions are not followed, it may mean that the student has been careless or unable to follow them, in which case the student has not reached the literal level of comprehension, which includes translation activities, i.e., carrying them out as given. Or, it may mean that the student reacted to the directions in a negative, or partly negative, way and, therefore, did not do explicitly as directed. Your job? To find out at what level the student was acting and what motivated the action. You might use introspective-retrospective techniques to find out at which level the student is thinking. See Table 7.1 to help you identify the level.

Table 7.1 Level of thinking used in following directions

Action	Reason	Level
Followed directions as given	It did not occur to student to do otherwise	Literal
	Interpreted and/or analyzed and/or evaluated directions and decided they were worth following explicitly	Interpretive (or higher)
Did not follow directions as given	Student was unable to do so; was too careless	Below literal
	Interpreted and/or analyzed and/or evaluated directions and decided they should not be followed or should be altered	Interpretive (or higher)

Consider the following directions. Would you follow the directions as given? Write *yes* in the blank if you would follow the directions as given, followed by a 1 for "literal level" or a 2 for "higher level." Write *no* in the blank if you would not follow the directions as given, followed by a 1 for "below literal level" or a 2 for "higher level."

1. Buy Chek-X cereal. Research proves it's the best for your health. ________
2. Buy Chek-X cereal. There's a toy in every box. ________
3. Work this nuclear physics problem successfully, and you'll win $5000. ________
4. With just ten dollars worth of material you can make this beautiful evening dress (or bookcase). Buy today. Make it when you have time. ________
5. The price of ice cream is 78¢ per half-gallon; milk is 25¢ a quart; bread is 58¢ a loaf. Add the prices to get the total cost. ________
6. Divide the compound word moonlight into syllables between the two morphemes. ________
7. Do this chemistry experiment exactly as directed in your textbook. ________
8. Do exercise 4 in your grammar book, and hand it in tomorrow. ________
9. "Set the table," your mother (father) tells you. ________
10. "Set the table," your wife (husband) tells you. ________
11. "You'll have to finish this project tonight," your boss tells you. ________
12. "Shoot those civilians in the ditch," your lieutenant in Vietnam tells you. ________

RECALLING SPECIFIC FACTS, DATES, AND DETAILS

Recalling details such as specific facts, names, and dates can be important for several reasons. First, there are certain details that every educated person should know, and not knowing them marks a person as uneducated. Knowing certain facts is necessary for a person to be able to carry on an intelligent conversation.

> Who is president of the United States? Vice-president? Who are your state senators? Who is prime minister of Canada? Of Britain? Who is president of France? Of Mexico? Who is the head of state in Italy, West Germany, Russia, China, etc?
>
> What are some plays that Shakespeare wrote? Who wrote *Don Quixote?* What characterizes Romantic poetry?
>
> Where is Tibet? Formosa? Baja California? Trieste? Cape Town? Bengal?
>
> When was America discovered? When was the Revolutionary War fought? The Civil War? When was the atomic bomb dropped on Hiroshima?

Batting averages, golf scores, and leading football teams are facts important to some groups of people.

Knowing how much air should be in an automobile tire is important to most drivers.

Knowing when school begins and ends is important to many people.

Knowing how much $2 + 2$ is, 4×4, $3 - 1$, etc., is important. And knowing what H_2O stands for is also important.

"Etcetra, etcetra, etcetra," said the king in *The King and I*. Many specific facts are important to know. But such details also serve as building blocks for forming concepts, and some facts are important principally as basic information from which it is possible to make inductions. Then, the generalization, or the principle, that was induced becomes the important idea, and the facts may not be important to remember any longer.

Details are best learned as they relate to the main idea they support. They may be remembered because they supply specific examples which make the principle or generalization more meaningful or because they supply supporting evidence for a conclusion.

The details may be the basic ideas that are used in formulating a generalization, as is true in inductive reasoning, and they may be remembered because they were the building blocks in recognizing a concept. On the other hand, a given generalization may be somewhat empty in meaning until concrete, supporting illustrations are recognized.

For example, a person might look at an orchestra and first notice details. He or she might group the following instruments together and then formulate a concept, or main idea, thus:

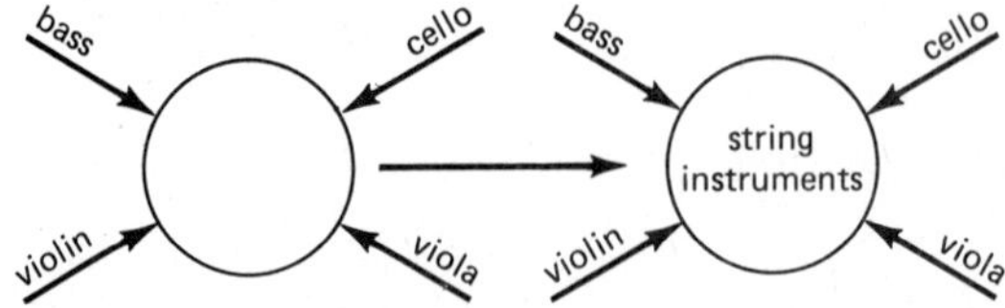

The above process illustrates *inductive* reasoning (moving from the specific to the concept, or main idea). A unifying concept is found and from this a main idea is formulated. The next step might be to look at the orchestra to see if there are any other strings present, e.g., a harp (deductive reasoning). After one identifies other strings present, the next step might be to think of other string instruments (e.g., lute, guitar, etc.) and question why they are not present (interpretive level). If one answers the question by logically understanding the reason they are not present, one is thinking on the critical-creative level.

One might, instead, begin with a general concept—e.g., woodwinds of a band—and later progress to identify each type. The following illustrates this:

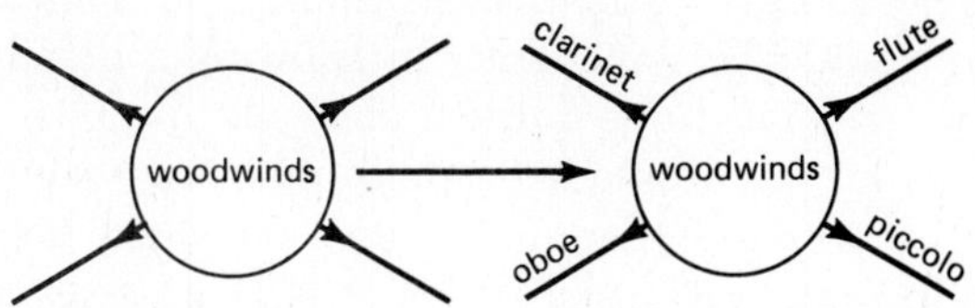

Such reasoning is termed *deductive.*

In both cases, details are related to the main idea. In *inductive* reasoning, details are identified and then related to formulate a main idea. In *deductive* reasoning, the main concept is first identified and from this supporting details are assumed or identified.

When it is important that details be remembered, they should be related to the main idea they support. When a main idea has been stated, students could be asked such questions as:

1. Give specific examples that support the given generalization—and any examples which do not. (expository: simple listing and contrast)
2. Give specific examples of factors the author said caused the effect. (chronological: effect → cause)
3. Give specific examples of factors the author suggests might follow if a certain action is taken. (chronological: cause → effect)
4. What specific visual images combined to give the general impression you observed? (spatial)
5. What details supplied by the author would you include in sketching a picture of plantation life? (spatial)
6. What planets would you have to include to sketch a map of our universe? (spatial)

Additional examples of these types of activities are given in the sections of this chapter on main idea and sequence. Questions of detail are at the literal level only if the student *recalls* or identifies details given. If the student culls from the background of information details that support or contradict a given generalization, he or she is thinking above the literal level (see Chapters 8 and 9).

Unfortunately, knowledge of details is frequently overstressed in our schools. Too many questions that are asked in the classroom deal with details.

It is easy to ask detail questions and easy to grade the response. But how important is it for students to know the details? What insights into human nature will details give them? Do details help them get a "feel" for history? Do details give them some perspective to help them think more logically, humanly, or spiritually? There should be some value in knowing a detail for it to be important enough for students to be quizzed about it.

A good strategy for you would be to think about your course. What specific facts, dates, and names are important? These you might help students learn. Which are there to round out main ideas but in themselves are relatively unnecessary to know? These could be discussed in relation to the main idea or to formulating a concept, but need not be stressed or remembered. For example, in studying this book, it is important for you to know that new words have entered our language in several ways, e.g., through a blending of the first part of one word with the final part of another. You might remember a few examples, but to remember them all is unnecessary. It is the principle that is important, especially if you are going to teach English. A more important principle of language growth for you to remember if you are a science teacher is that many new words have entered our language by combining morphemes, or even by direct borrowing. The social scientist might also find acronyms of vital interest and importance. But details, in themselves, are rarely as important as is indicated by the stress put on them in our schools. And time spent on them is time taken away from other kinds of intellectual activities.

RECOGNIZING AND RECALLING THE MAIN IDEA

Main idea is a term usually applied to the central thought of one or a few consecutive paragraphs—or of a unit composed of an integrated collection of sentences that form part of a complete work, such as a chapter, essay, or short story. The skill of recognizing and/or formulating a main idea is related to the skill of recognizing and/or formulating the central thought of a unit—such as the sentence, a collection of discrete but related items, or the theme of an essay, chapter, or story.

When readers *recognize* or *recall* a main idea *that is stated for them* or *that is a stereotyped concept* encompassing details that are supplied, they are reading or thinking at the literal level. However, when they must *formulate* a main idea by synthesizing details, possibly in a unique way, or by recognizing patterns of thought, or by reasoning inductively in any other way, they are thinking at a level higher than the literal. Sometimes it is difficult to know what level of thought was required of the readers for them to arrive at the main idea. Often, it may not be necessary to make such fine distinctions. We can work in a variety of ways to help students develop the ability of recognizing and recalling the main idea.

Family Names—Classifying

Teaching Strategies

We might, for example, begin finding or using family names for a series of discrete items.[2] In sequencing the development of this skill from easy to difficult, we might progress in this way:

1. Provide a list of family names. Also group like items (requires inductive *or* deductive *recall*), e.g.:

polygons	triangles	quadrilaterals	sets	fractions
angles	conics	mixed numbers	integers	whole numbers

   a) $\frac{1}{4}$, $\frac{1}{2}$, $\frac{1}{3}$ (fractions)
   b) $1\frac{1}{3}$, $12\frac{4}{9}$, $7\frac{10}{11}$ ____________
   c) square, parallelogram, rectangle, rhombus ____________
   d) 4, 8, 10, 47 ____________
   e) 3, —8, 27, 31, —14 ____________
   f) right, isosceles, equilateral ____________
   g) obtuse, right, acute ____________
   h) null, empty, universal, subset ____________
   i) circle, ellipse, parabola, hyperbola ____________
   j) octagon, hexagon, square, pentagon ____________

2. Combine family name with subpoints. Students circle family name (*requires inductive or deductive recall*), e.g.:
   a) diode, transistor, (semiconductor), integrated circuit rectifier
   b) diode, triode, tube, regulator, pentode
   c) impedance, resistor, capacitor, inductor, reactor
   d) resistance, impedance, inductive reactance, ohmage, capacitive reactance
   e) volts, amps, ohms, watts, measurement
   f) cathode ray tube, television, oscilloscope, computer input mirror, cardiac machine
   g) analog, digital, CPU, memory computer
   h) PNP, NPN, semiconductor device silicon amp. transistor
   i) flip-flop, A-stable, multivibrator, bi-stable, unstable
   j) ohmeter, multivibrator, amplifier, electron device, voltage regulator

3. Group like items, but do not supply family names (requires inductive *recall*), e.g.:
   a) and, or, but, yet (conjunctions)
   b) oh, gosh, hooray, hey ______
   c) mother, cat, house, chair ______
   d) he, she, they, I ______
   e) walk, jump, type, yell ______
   f) quietly, slowly, quickly, softly ______
   g) tall, skinny, red, beautiful ______
   h) big, high, tall, giant ______
   i) I'll, we'll, isn't, he's ______
   j) steak-stake; beat-beet; fair-fare ______

4. Supply family names. List items ungrouped (requires inductive *or* deductive *recall*), e.g.:

robin	man	trout	fly	dog	python
butterfly	lark	eagle	penguin	piranha	gila monster
whale	katydid				

Animals

I. *Birds*
   A.
   B.
   C.
   D.

II. *Fish*
   A.
   B.

III. *Insects*
   A.
   B.
   C.

IV. *Mammals*
   A.
   B.
   C.

V. *Reptiles*
   A.
   B.

5. Supply family names. List no items (requires deductive *recall*), e.g.:

I. *Bones*
   A.
   B.
   C.
   D.

II. *Muscles*
   A.
   B.
   C.
   D.

III. *Glands*
   A.
   B.
   C.
   D.

IV. *Organs*
   A.
   B.
   C.
   D.

6. Do not supply family names. List items ungrouped. Students form outline (requires inductive *recall* if stock response is given—planets, stars), e.g.:

chicken	seal	alligator	oriole
colt	bat	antelope	hamster
duckling	fish	raccoon	owl
cow	elephant	whale	mouse
kitten	salamander	squirrel	turtle
sheep	lobster	giraffe	cat
bear	zebra	skunk	puppy
dog	deer	kangaroo	calf

Syntactical Synthesis[3]

To teach students to recognize the central thought (kernel) of a sentence, proceed as follows.

Teaching Strategies

1. Teach them to recognize the subject (noun) of a sentence. Have them underline the noun (N) on each of a series of sentences.
   a) José threw the ball over the fence.
   b) The grass has turned brown.
   c) The mountain range runs for 250 miles.
   d) Gas is escaping from the furnace.
2. Teach them to recognize the verb (V) of a sentence. Have them underline the V with two underscorings.
   a) José threw the ball over the fence.
   b) The grass has turned brown.
   c) The mountain range runs for 250 miles.
   d) Gas is escaping from the furnace.
3. Give them experience with a variety of patterns to help students recognize common kernels (N = subject noun, N_2 = predicate noun, V = verb, Lv = linking verb, A = adjective, Av = adverb).
   a) Gregory is reading. (N V)
   b) Maria sang loudly. (N V Ad)
   c) Rick made a homerun. (N V N_2)

d) Nadia named her horse "Star." $(N\ V\ N_2\ N_3)$
e) The matador made the bull angry. $(N\ V\ N_2\ A)$
f) Charlotte is a cat. $(N\ Lv\ N_2)$
g) The bull is irate. $(N\ Lv\ A)$

4. Next, combine the two processes of underlining kernels of sentences and finding family names to literally induce the main idea of a paragraph:

   The factories of the South spin and weave cotton cloth and make it into clothing. They make iron, steel, and machinery from iron ore. They make fertilizer for farms from phosphate rock. They make furniture from their lumber. And they make rayon and paper from their cotton and wood pulp.

   Find the family names for the:

   N's: factories, they, they, they, they, = factories
   V's: spin, weave, make, make, make, make, make = make
   N_2's: cloth, clothing, iron, steel, machinery, fertilizer, furniture, rayon, paper = various products

   Main Idea: Factories (of the South) make various products.

5. When there are elaborations of sentence length or of several sentences, underscore kernels only in basic sentences:

   To some, a home is a haven (removed from the hectic pace of the outside world. It is the place where family members enjoy one another and also where each may pursue special interests, sometimes in solitude and at other times with one or more family members or friends). For other families, it is always "open house," (with visitors made welcome at any time without advance planning or preparation).

   Find the family names for the:

   N : home, it = home
   V : is, is = is
   N_2: haven, open house (contrast, no family name. We have a contrast paragraph.) = haven, open house

   Main Idea: Home for some is a haven; for others, an open house.

Placement of Main Idea Statement[4]

Teach students that when stated, the main idea, or central thought, of a paragraph can be found anywhere within the paragraph. The following symbols might be used to exemplify this. The horizontal line in each symbol indicates the place of the main idea.

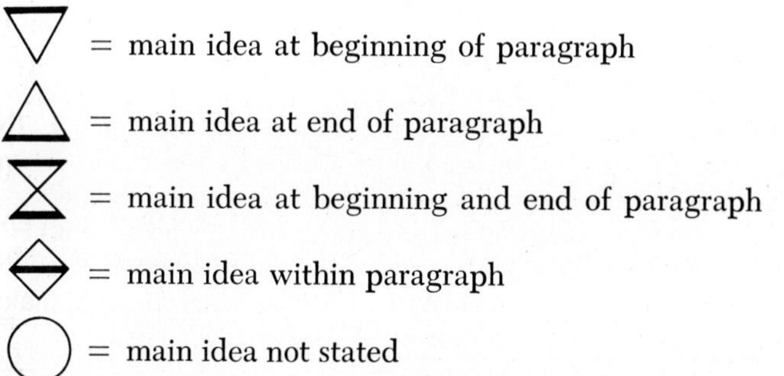

Give students experience with all of these types of paragraphs. Select paragraphs from reading materials available to your students. Ask students to underline the main idea and to draw the symbol that illustrates the location of the main idea. For example:

> Some words that formerly stood for a particular action or thing have gradually become more inclusive in meaning. Such a word is *companion* (Latin, *com,* together + *panis,* bread), literally "a bread-sharer." Closely related is *company,* a general term which today is not restricted to "a group that shares bread." A *lord,* literally "loaf-keeper," has vastly wider responsibilities than keeping loaves. *Companion, company,* and *lord* all go beyond the restricted association of bread; the meanings of these words have become generalized. The process is generalization.*

> The three general ways of speaking that you have been studying are called the casual, consultative, and deliberate keys. Each of us is most at ease in the casual key, enjoying a drifting conversation with friends and acquaintances. When we speak in the consultative key, we explore a problem with another person, asking for information, making explanations, and attempting to reach a fuller common understanding. We are consulting with others. Before using the deliberative key, we frequently deliberate, planning our ideas and putting them in a helpful order for our listeners. We frequently must say more in order to be understood by a large audience than we would need to say in speaking to just one or two people, for our listeners do not have the chance to interrupt us with questions or show us that they are following our thoughts.†

* T. C. Pollack, *et al. The Macmillan English Series—English 12.* New York: Macmillan, 1964, p. 176. Reprinted by permission.
† Bernard Tanner, *et al. English 9.* Menlo Park, Calif.: Addison-Wesley, 1968, p. 10. Reprinted by permission.

Before we take up thermodynamics itself, it is appropriate for us to look into the three different mechanisms by which heat may be transferred from one place to another. . . . When we place one end of an iron rod in a fire, the other end becomes warm as a result of the conduction of heat through the iron. Conduction is a very slow process in air; a stove warms a room chiefly through the actual movement of heated air, a process called convection. Neither conduction nor convection can take place appreciably in the virtual void of interplanetary space. Instead, the heat the earth receives from the sun arrives in the form of radiation. These mechanisms all illustrate a fundamental fact: the natural direction of heat flow is from hot bodies to cold ones.*

Grip the metal so the layout line is just below the vise jaws when shearing it to a line. This will leave sufficient metal to finish by filing or grinding. When cutting, it is best to hold the metal in the vise without using vise jaw caps. This provides a better shearing action between the vice jaw and the chisel. Advance the chisel after each blow so that the cutting is done by the center of the cutting edge.†

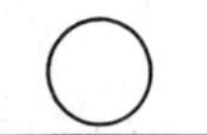

Even though we do not have a 20-cent coin, we often use the symbol $.20 to mean 20/100 of a dollar (or 20¢) just as we use the symbol $.25 to represent the value of our quarter. We use the mark $.45 to mean 45/100 of a dollar (or 45¢) because it is easy to write and to use in computation. When we deal with money, we use decimal symbols as abbreviations for fractions with 100 as denominator. For example, a symbol like $2.47 is an abbreviation for 2 dollars and 47/100 of a dollar. Since 2 + 47/100 is 247/100, we say that $2.47 is an abbreviation for 247/100 of a dollar. Explain why $23.51 is a symbol for 2351/100 of a dollar. Which of the symbols $23.51 and 2351/100 of one dollar is easier to understand and to use?‡

Ask students to follow this procedure throughout a chapter in a textbook. They may find that the author consistently places the main idea in a specific place, e.g., the first sentence in the paragraph.

---

* Arthur Beiser. *The Mainstream of Physics.* Reading, Mass.: Addison-Wesley, 1962, p. 200. Reprinted by permission.
† John R. Walker. *Modern Metal-Working.* South Holland, Ill.: Goodheart-Willcox, 1970, Unit 8, p. 1. Reprinted by permission.
‡ Charles Brumfiel, *et al. Arithmetic: Concepts and Skills.* Reading, Mass.: Addison-Wesley, 1963, p. 247. Reprinted by permission.

Other activities that help students recognize main ideas are:

1. selecting the best title from a list
2. matching a picture or illustration with a paragraph that describes it
3. selecting from a list of statements the one that best expresses the main idea
4. writing a series of headings for a series of paragraphs
5. matching titles of articles with titleless articles.

SEQUENCE

Sequence, as it relates to reading, refers to the order in which ideas are presented. "What ideas did the author relate first, second, third, etc.?" is a sequence-type question. Sequential patterns of discourse can be classified in one of the following three ways—chronological, spatial, or expository.

These are pure forms. In practice, however, almost all speech or writing is a combination of these patterns. We classify a passage according to the predominant pattern followed.

Chronological Order

Chronological order is time order. There are several time order patterns. The most obvious pattern progresses from beginning to end (first, second, third, fourth, fifth, etc.). Another chronological pattern is the reverse (fifth, fourth, third, second, first). Another common chronological pattern is known as the flashback pattern, in which either the end or the climax is given first, followed by a beginning-to-end sequence.

Much fiction is written in a forward-moving chronological pattern, although some, like *Rebecca* and *Good-bye Mr. Chips,* is written using the flashback technique. If you are asked to relate what you did during the past week, you might choose to go backwards: Friday, Thursday, Wednesday, Tuesday, etc.

History books are usually written in chronological order. So are biographies and autobiographies. Many literature anthologies are organized according to "periods" or "ages" of literature—the Elizabethan Age, the Romantic Age, the Victorian Age, etc.—and these "ages" are set in the book in chronological order.

The chronological order pattern can be related to the students' experiences in terms of their daily schedules (from the time they arise until they retire), and in terms of their weekly or yearly schedules. The progression of seasons is chronological, as is the progression of a lifetime. The steps of baking a cake, building a bookcase, performing a science experiment are in chronological order. Examples abound which we can use in clarifying this pattern to students.

Some paragraphs are written in chronological order, as is the following:

> Caesar now moved toward sole power. When Pompey and his followers fled to Greece, Caesar first made himself secure in Italy and Spain; then he defeated

> Pompey in Greece. He moved over into Africa, put Cleopatra on the throne of Egypt, and made Egypt an ally of Rome. In Asia Minor he drove out a dangerous tribe of barbarian invaders who had attacked Roman provinces. It was after this victory that he sent home his famous three-word message: Veni, Vidi, Vici—"I came, I saw, I conquered."*

When the chronological order pattern is important for students to recognize—for example, in understanding a chapter of a book—ask them to page through the chapter, noting main headings. Ask them if these headings, which represent main ideas, are given in chronological order. Ask them to jot down the main headings in the order of their presentation.

Translation level activities

After students have jotted down the main headings of a chapter, they can be taught to put these major ideas into another form, i.e., other than the simple recall-level listing form. Other common forms that could be used for the chronological pattern are: outline, flow chart, time line, and tree chart.

Outline

The outline is versatile and can be used for recording any organizational pattern. Roman numerals are usually used to indicate major headings; capital letters are used for first-order subheadings; and arabic numerals are used to indicate second-order subheadings. (A newer form utilizes arabic numerals throughout, with decimals to indicate subheadings.)

The outline is more than a simple listing. There never are fewer than two main points nor more than five main points. Similarly, there are never fewer than two nor more than five subpoints of any one order. Outlining means *dividing* and *classifying*. Nothing can be divided into fewer than two parts. And anything classified into more than five divisions becomes unruly and is lacking in organization.

A time order outline might look like the following:

Title: Specific steps are followed in a controlled experiment.

I. A question is asked.
II. A hypothesis is formulated.
III. A plan of attack is followed.
  A. First . . .
  B. Second . . .
  C. Third . . .

---

* Anatole Mazour and John M. Peoples. *Men and Nations: A World History*. New York: Harcourt, Brace and World, 1961, p. 115. Reprinted by permisson.

IV. Results are acted upon.
    A. Results are observed.
    B. Results are tabulated.
    C. Results are interpreted.

Using the newer form, our outline would look like this:

Title: Specific steps are followed in a controlled experiment.

1.0 A question is asked.
2.0 A hypothesis is formulated.
3.0 A plan of attack is followed.
    3.1 First . . .
    3.2 Second . . .
    3.3 Third . . .
4.0 Results are acted upon.
    4.1 Results are observed.
    4.2 Results are tabulated.
    4.3 Results are interpreted.

Which form do you prefer?

Flow Chart

Sometimes a flow chart will clarify and illustrate the chronological pattern better than will an outline. For example, instead of using the preceding outline, we might have drawn a flow chart like that in Fig. 7.1.

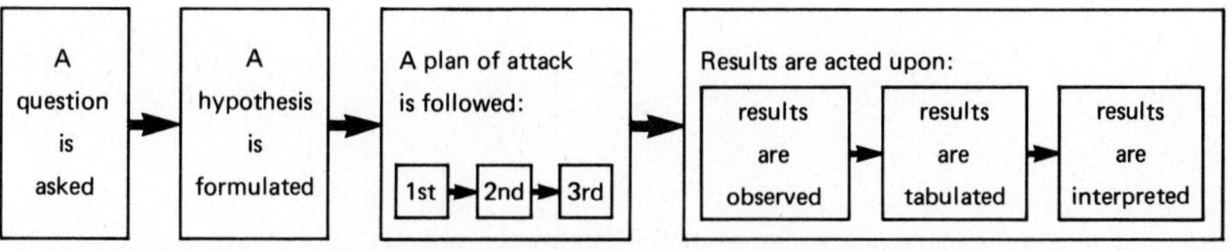
A question is asked
A hypothesis is formulated
A plan of attack is followed:
1st
2nd
3rd
Results are acted upon:
results are observed
results are tabulated
results are interpreted

Fig. 7.1 Specific steps are followed in a controlled experiment.

Figure 7.2, which shows another type of flow chart, is based on the paragraph that follows.

> The life history of the liver fluke is an interesting example of the dependence of parasites upon intermediate hosts. The eggs, which are produced in large numbers, are eliminated in the feces, or waste matter, of the sheep. Water is necessary for the survival and development of the fertilized eggs. In a swampy pasture they produce free-swimming larvae that infect certain snails. The snail

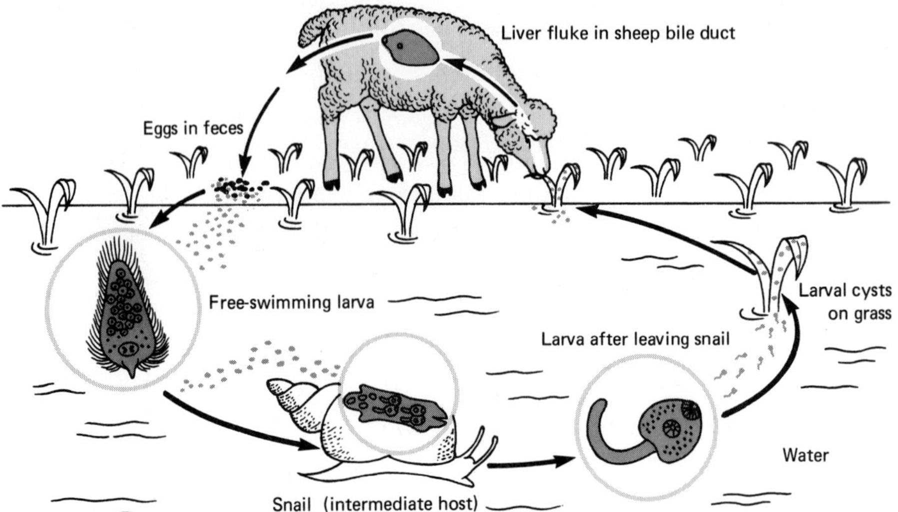

Fig. 7.2 Life history of a sheep liver fluke. (Reprinted by permission from William H. Gregory and Edward Goldman, *Biological Science for High School,* Boston: Ginn and Co., 1965, p. 270.)

is thus the intermediate host. In the snail's body changes occur in the fluke larvae that result in the production of other larvae. These escape from the snail and form cysts on blades of grass. When a sheep eats the infected grass, the cycle starts again.*

Other types of flow charts are illustrated in Figs. 7.3 and 7.4.

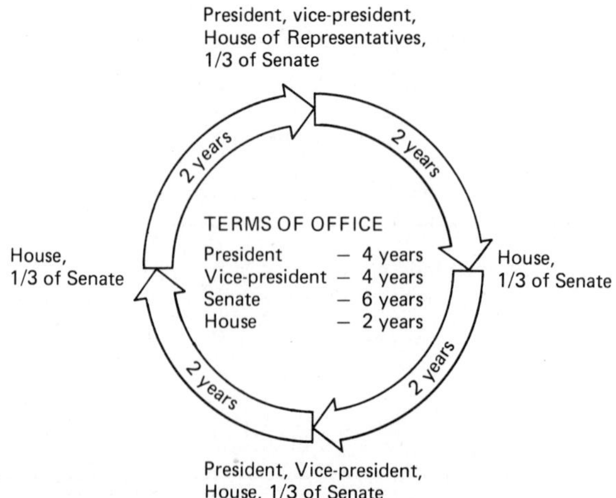

Fig. 7.3 Election cycle of United States politics.

* William H. Gregory and Edward Goldman. *Biological Science for High School.* Boston: Ginn, 1965, p. 270. Reprinted by permission.

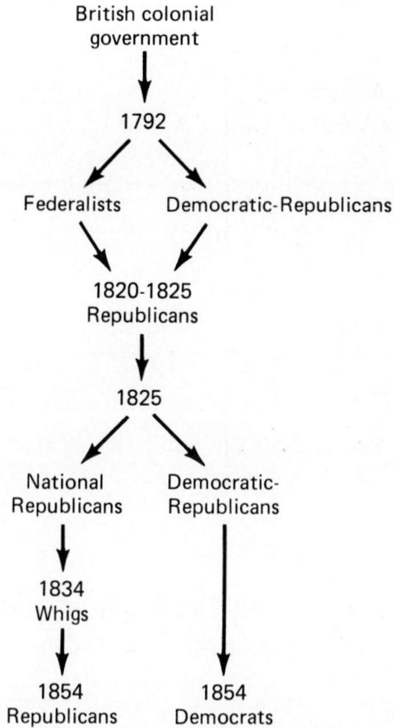

Fig. 7.4 The growth of United States political parties.

Time line

For recording other kinds of information, a time line might be useful. A typical time line is shown in Fig. 7.5.

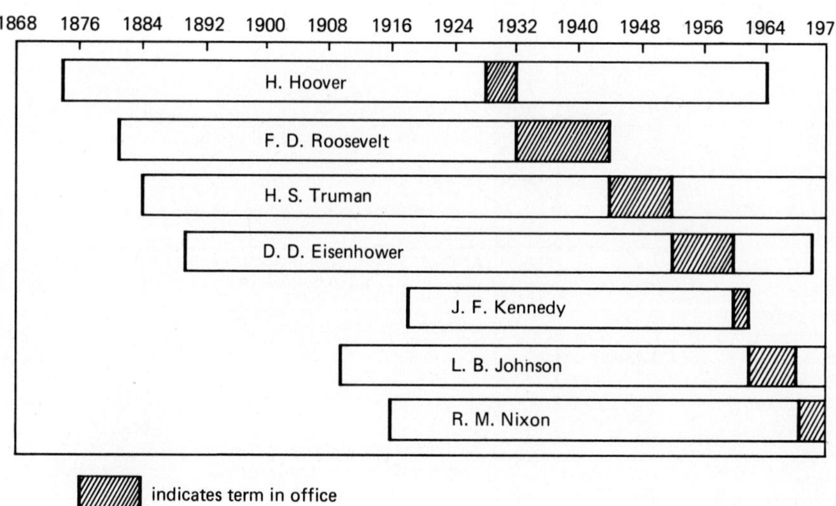

Fig. 7.5 Life spans of presidents of the United States with terms in office from 1928 to 1972.

Morning	6	
	7	breakfast
	8	
	9	
	10	
	11	
Afternoon	12	
	1	
	2	
	3	
	4	
	5	
Evening	6	
	7	
	8	
	9	
	10	
	11	
	12	

Fig. 7.6 Important events in my day (to be completed by student).

ANTEBELLUM PERIOD	1846	Wilmot Proviso
	1850	Compromise of 1850—admits California as free state, delays war
	1854	Kansas-Nebraska Act
	1857	Dred Scott Decision
	1860	Lincoln elected/Secession of South Carolina
CONFLICT	1861	Firing on Fort Sumter—Civil War begins
	1863	Emancipation Proclamation
	1865	End of War/Lincoln assassinated/Slavery abolished
RECOVERY	1867	Reconstruction imposes strict rule on South/U.S. purchases Alaska
	1869	White groups begin to regain power in South/Rise of Klu Klux Klan
	1876	Civil rights restored to Southern whites, ending Reconstruction

Fig. 7.7 American Civil War period.

A vertical time line format is also often useful. Figure 7.6 illustrates a very simple vertical time line. Younger students might be asked to list two to five events during each major time period that are important to them.

Then students might be shown how this same format could be used in relationship to a textbook or unit assignment, as shown in Fig. 7.7.

Tree chart

For recording genealogy, a tree chart is useful. Figure 7.8 on the following page shows the derivation of modern English in tree chart form.

Spatial Order

In spatial, or descriptive, order, the pattern of discussion is from area to area, or region to region. For example, a classroom can be described in relationship to its seating pattern, its pattern of windows, chalkboard space, bulletin board space, bookcases, etc. A garden can be described from its focal point, e.g., a birdbath, and then in concentric circles around it. Rainfall in the United States can be described starting at the West Coast and moving eastward. Similarly, the strengths and weaknesses of political parties are often described in relationship to regions of our country—the Deep South, the Midwest, the Far West, etc. All of these orders are spatial, since space, or area, is the unifying factor.

Students can easily give you examples of spatial order. Ask them what route they take in coming to school, or what route they followed on their last trip, or what route they would follow if they could go anywhere they wished. Ask them to describe the location of various animals in the zoo or products in a store.

Spatial order patterns are commonly found in most types of writing. Where did the American troops fight during World War II? requires a spatial-order answer, although it might also be organized chronologically. Where were American fighting men found in Vietnam in December 1971? must be answered spatially. Where would I look if I lost my golfball in an open field? must also be answered spatially—and by using a definite pattern, for example:

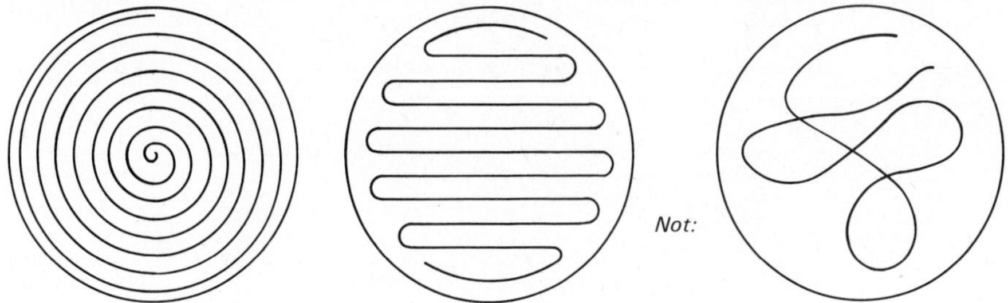

This item is similar to one found on a commonly used I.Q. test.

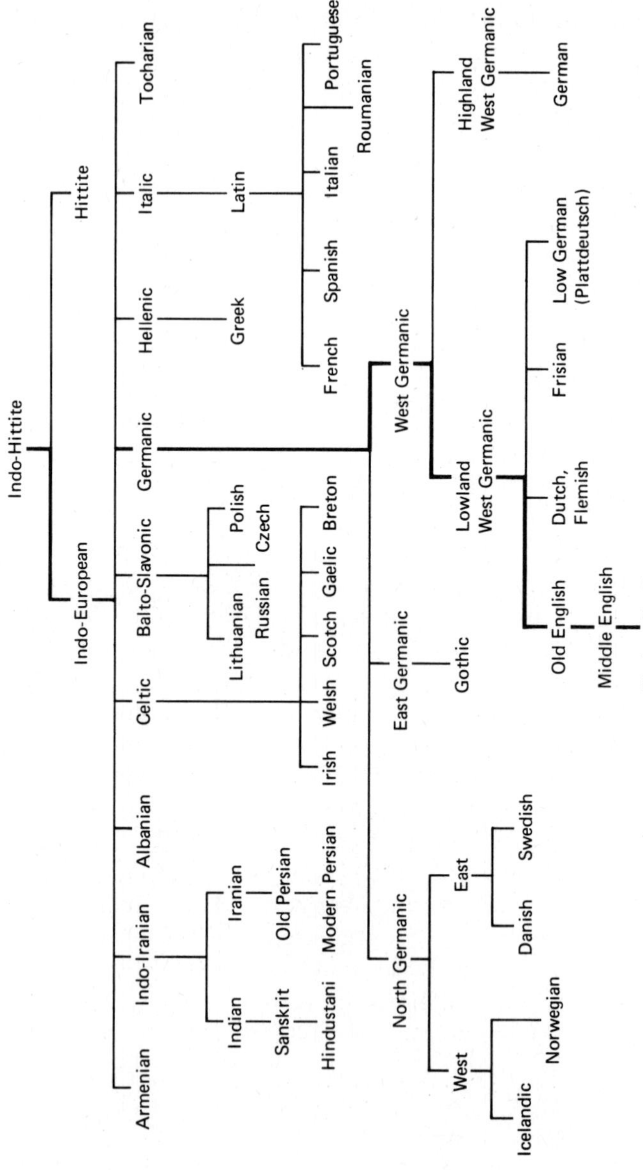

Fig. 7.8 The ancestry of modern English. (Reprinted by permission from *Teaching the English Language in Wisconsin*, Madison: Department of Public Instruction, 1967, p. 128.)

Translation level activities

To make sense out of a spatially oriented discourse, readers or listeners must recognize the pattern. To help them recognize and recall the pattern, several formats are useful. Among them are the outline, sketches, maps, floor plans, etc.

Outline

Any type of order can be recorded in outline form. The following outline demonstrates its use with spatially oriented ideas.

Title: The area surrounding the prisoner of war camp.

I. Between due east and due south was a vast swampland.
II. Between due south and north by west were soldiers stationed at close intervals.
III. Between north by west and north by east was a mountain range.
IV. Between north by east and due east was a river.

Sketch

Drawing a sketch—or studying one that is provided—often helps us to visualize a descriptive passage. Following are several examples.

> Closterium is a common desmid. Fission occurs along isthmus dividing plant into two semicells. Crystals in the vacuoles at each end of plant are continually agitated.*

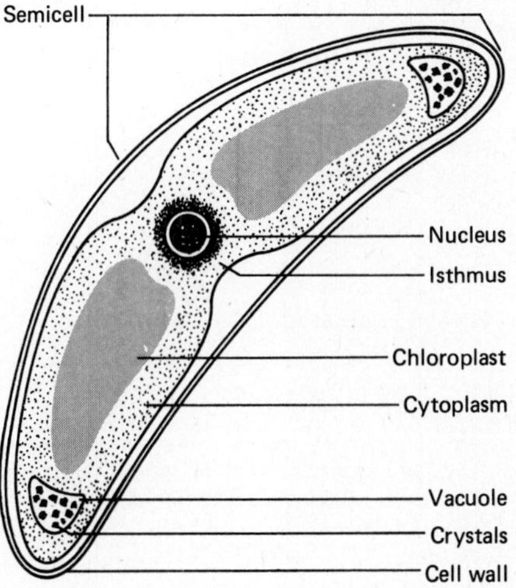

* Text and illustration from William H. Gregory and Edward H. Goldman. *Biological Science for High School.* Boston: Ginn and Co., 1965, p. 110, illustration 8–8. Reprinted by permission.

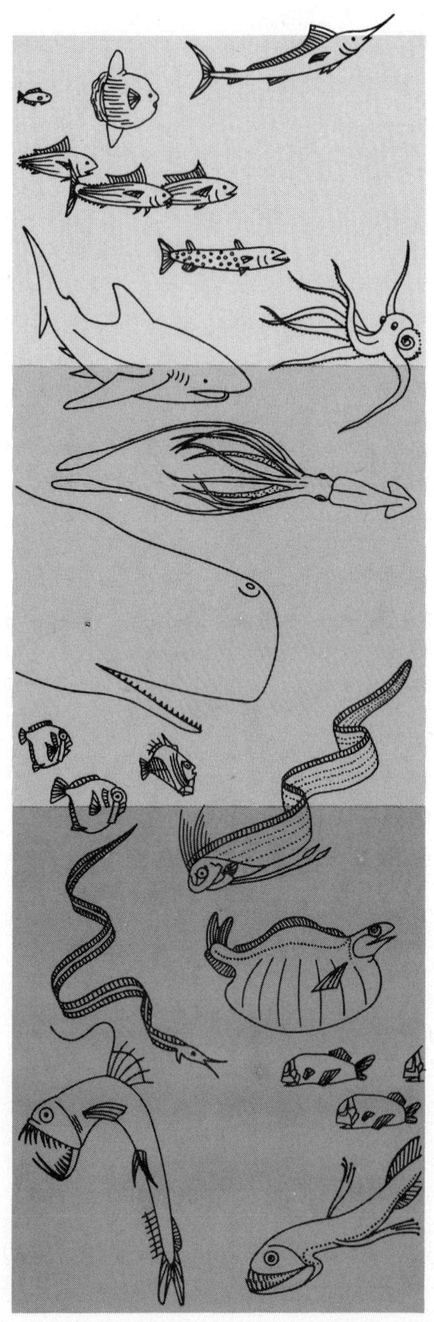

Living conditions such as temperature, pressure, amount of light, and kinds of food available are different at each level of depth in the ocean. The animals found at each level show a great variety of ways of adjusting to the different conditions.*

* Text and illustration from *Science Is Explaining* by Wilbur L. Beauchamp, *et al.*, p. 209. Copyright © 1963 by Scott, Foresman and Company. Reprinted by permission.

A figure is symmetrical or has symmetry if corresponding parts are alike in size, shape, and position. An isosceles triangle is symmetrical; a scaline triangle is not. Symmetry is one of the basic principles of design, because a harmonious balance between parts of a figure is an important element in beauty. Practically all living things exhibit symmetry. A leaf, like the one illustrated, has approximate *line symmetry*. That is, you can draw a line through the figure so that the designs on either side of the line are congruent. This line is called the *axis of symmetry*.*

Map

Maps can be used to translate a discourse into a visible pattern. We have maps of college campuses, cities, states, nations, and the world. It is possible to map almost any region. And a map usually clarifies a spatial organizational pattern better than can words. Figure 7.9 shows one example of how a map can be used to depict spatial organization.

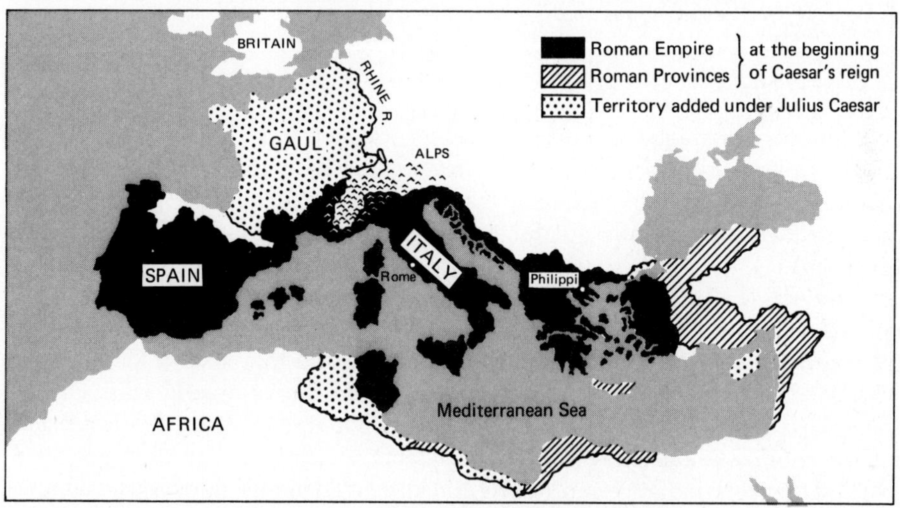

Fig. 7.9 The Roman Empire in 44 B.C., at the time of Julius Caesar. (From *Adventures in Appreciation,* Laureate Edition, by Walter Loban and Rosalind A. Olmstead, © 1963 by Harcourt Brace Jovanovich, Inc. and reproduced with their permission.)

* Text and illustration from Frank M. Morgan and Jane Tartman. *Geometry*. Boston: Houghton Mifflin, 1963, p. 200. Reprinted by permission.

Floor plan

Drawing a floor plan helps the reader visualize spatial organization. For example:

> The Aintree comes with a spacious loft, providing additional space for sleeping. The main level contains a basic living ell with a kitchen tucked in behind a free-standing bar. A large bedroom lies behind, with space for the luxury of a full bath across a narrow hall.*

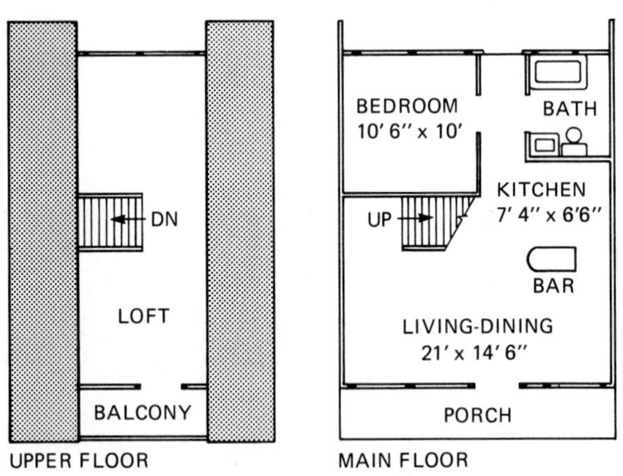

Expository Order

In expository writing the unifying factors are not time or space, but ideas and/or facts. Expository writing can be organized in the following kinds of patterns: cause to effect, effect to cause, question to answer, general statement to factors or details (deduction), details to general statement (induction), etc.

Students use these patterns regularly in their daily lives. For example, if you ask them why they chose the lunch they had, they might answer that it was nutritious, it did not have too many calories, and they like it. Or ask them what kind of a car they would buy—if they could buy one—and why. Or, ask them what the following adds up to: "I have not studied since the last exam. I have another exam today" (cause to effect). Ask them why they got an A (B, C, D, F) on the last exam (effect to cause). There are numerous examples that can be used to explain expository order.

The following is a typical expository passage of the deductive type (generalization stated first, followed by factors which compose it).

---

* Text and illustration from Lindal Homes, 10411 Empire Way South, Seattle, Washington. Reprinted by permission.

How can you assure a good credit rating? Specialists in consumer credit point to the "three C's" of a good credit rating—character, capacity, and collateral.

CHARACTER. How good is your reputation concerning payment of bills? When you are able to negotiate credit on your good name, you have established credit on the basis on your character. Among the personal traits that make you a good credit risk are your willingness, intention, and habit of meeting your financial obligations, plus the stability of your job and family and the continuance of your health.

CAPACITY. How prepared are you to meet financial obligations? Your ability to meet financial obligations is affected by your income. Is your income regular? Will it last over the length of time covered by your period of indebtedness? What other commitments might stop you from making regular payments?

COLLATERAL. What is your net worth? What assets do you have to guarantee financial responsibility? If you own property or other assets that may be transferred to the lender in the event you cannot pay your debts, you are securing your debt. Property used as security is called collateral. If you have the confidence of another person as to your character and your capacity to repay a loan, and he is willing to act as a co-signer on a note, he is offering his own character and capacity to you as collateral.*

Translation level activities

Such a pattern can be outlined easily. For the expository pattern, outlining is an exceptionally satisfactory translation activity. However, there are other visual patterns that are also highly useful. Among them are charts and various kinds of graphs.

Outline

The preceding passage can be outlined as follows:

Title: The "three C's" of good credit rating

I. Character	*or*	1.0 Character
II. Capacity		2.0 Capacity
III. Collateral		3.0 Collateral

Whole chapters in student textbooks should be surveyed by the students before they read them. After such a survey, when they note only main headings, students should be asked to formulate an outline—either mentally or on paper. This might be done as a class-wide or group activity if several texts are being used, and the outline written on the board. This survey step, either

---

* Dora S. Lewis, *et al. Housing and Home Management*. New York: Macmillan, 1969, p. 146. Reprinted by permission.

done by the students themselves or as a group activity, should be one of the initial steps in all reading assignments except those that are narrative.

After the headings are listed, students should be encouraged to anticipate what will be discussed under each heading. Students should be taught to ask questions about each heading. Then when they read silently, they should seek answers to these questions. After they have found the answers, they discuss them in class or recite them silently to themselves. They then review the complete chapter and possibly translate their knowledge, using an outline, another visible pattern, or a mental pattern. (In Chapter 5, SQ3R, a similar technique, was discussed in more detail.)

Graph

Graphs are very useful for recording expository information. Among the most common are spoke graphs, pie graphs, bar graphs, line graphs, and pictographs.

A *spoke graph* can be used to show basic relationships. The main idea, or theme, is stated in the center, and each major subdivision is written on an arm:

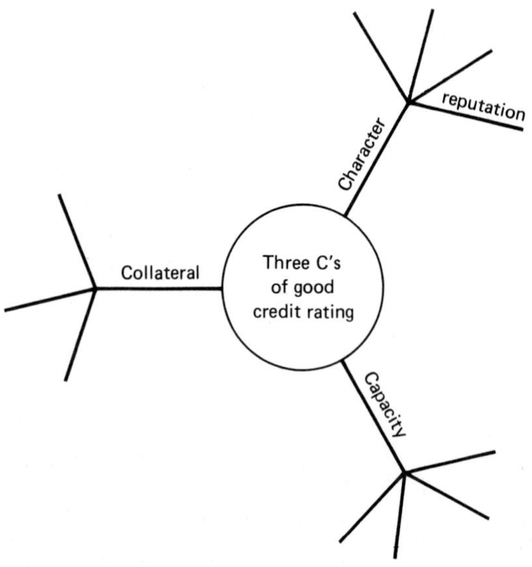

The *pie graph* can be used when the whole of something can be broken into weighted parts (Fig. 7.10). When sketching pie graphs, students should try to use no fewer than two or more than five major divisions whenever possible, as illustrated in Fig. 7.10(b). They should draw heavy lines to indicate

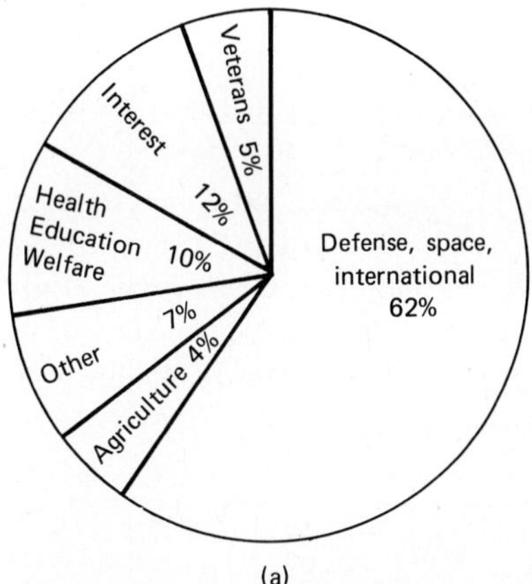

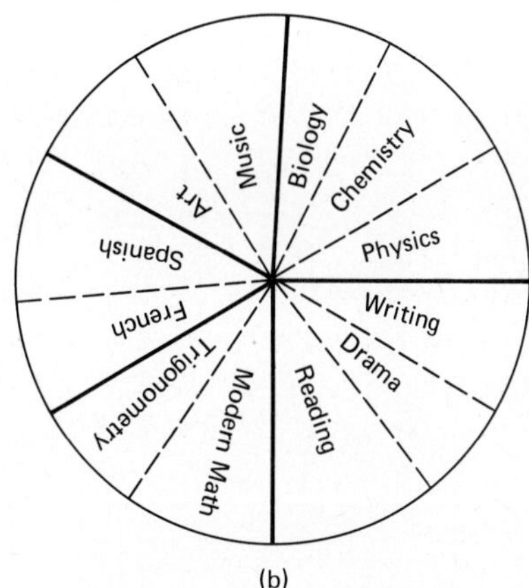

Fig. 7.10 Pie graphs: (a) expenditure of tax dollars; (b) factoring of students according to their electives.

major divisions. Subdivisions should be indicated with lighter lines or dashes. They should also make sure that the circle of a pie graph is always fullfaced, i.e., never askew. The visual image is distorted if the circle is not flat.

The *bar graph* is useful for recording quantities, e.g., inches of rainfall according to area or date, production of manufactured items, average temperatures, etc. (Fig. 7.11).

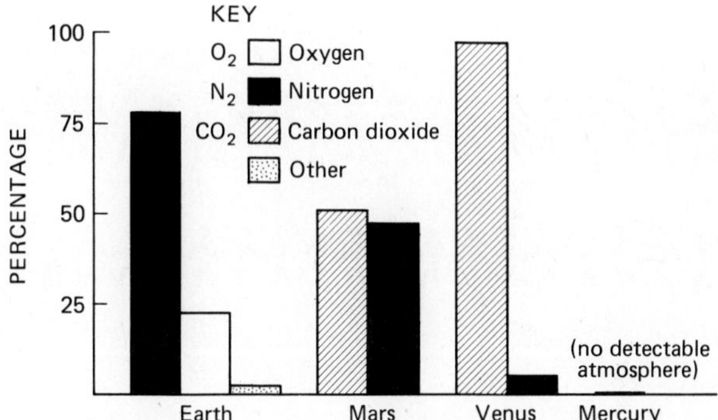

Fig. 7.11 Chemicals in the atmosphere of the inner (terrestrial) planets.

The *line graph*, a smoothed-out bar graph, is useful for many purposes, including comparisons, as in Fig. 7.12.

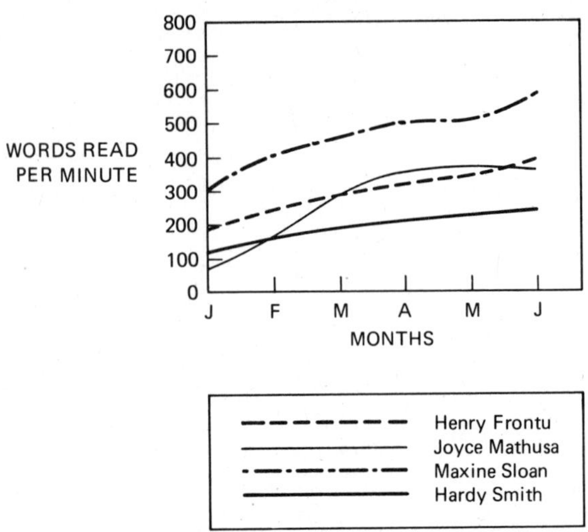

Fig. 7.12 Reading rate of four students in reading-improvement class, January to June 1972.

A *pictograph* is a type of bar graph in which illustrations are used instead of bars. They're usually more colorful and appealing than are bar graphs, but they serve the same purpose. Figure 7.13 is an example of a pictograph.

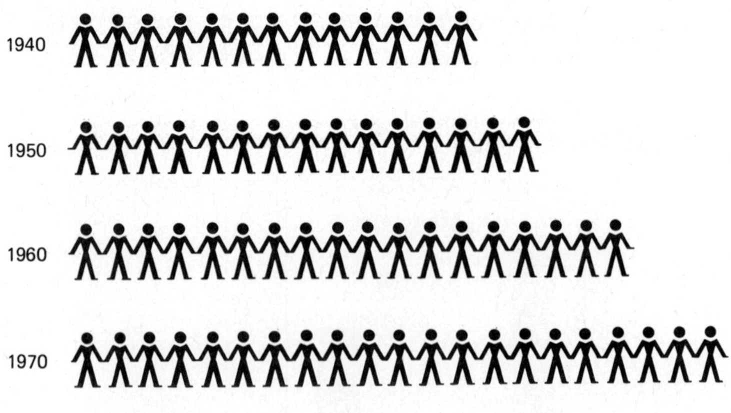

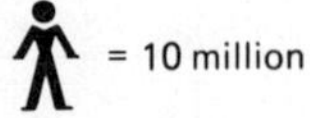

Fig. 7.13 Population of the United States from 1940 to 1970.

Chart

Charts are especially useful for making comparisons and are frequently seen in many types of readings materials. To reinforce your memory about this section of this chapter, fill in Table 7.2.

Table 7.2 Sequence at the literal level

Sequential patterns	Appropriate translation activities
chronological	time line,

Teaching Strategies

For translation level activities, such as those above, students normally survey a chapter or a part of a chapter or they carefully read a short section and illustrate it in one of the formats shown or, perhaps, in another more appropriate format suitable to the content.

Sometimes students have difficulty recognizing the type of sequential pattern being used. It will help them if they remember that there are just three basic types of cognitive organizational orders: chronological, spatial, and expository.

Below is a cartoon which exemplifies one possible effect of a divergent sequential answer to a question. The expected answer is "six," an expository answer. The given response, "cocktails," is chronological.

by Brant parker and Johnny hart

The Wizard of Id by permission of Johnny Hart and Field Enterprises, Inc.

Often authors use rhetorical signal words which give strong clues to the pattern. Students might be taught about the order which such words signal. For example, ask them what order the following words signal.

1. then, shortly after, finally	(chronological, forward)
2. on that account, hence, because	(expository, cause-effect)
3. furthermore, besides, also	(expository, simple listing)
4. however, on the contrary, the other	(expository, contrast)
5. ahead, behind, to the left	(spatial)
6. later, next, after an interval	(chronological, forward)
7. because of that, consequently	(expository, cause-effect)
8. to the north, the west, the east	(spatial)
9. in addition, also, another	(expository, simple listing)
10. at the coast, the shore, inland	(spatial)
11. this was most exciting, preceding it was, following it	(chronological, flashback)
12. finally, before that, even earlier	(chronological, backwards)
13. etc.	________

Additional activities for teaching sequence (literal level)

1. Use rhetorical signal words and the CLOZE technique for students to record events as explained in a reading selection, e.g.:

   There are three branches in our federal government. One is the ________ branch, composed of the President and Vice-President, and the Cabinet. Another branch is the ________, composed of the ________ Court and lower courts. The third branch is the ________ branch, composed of the ________ and the ________.

   Next, ask students to put this into chart form. This is organized in *expository order,* simple listing type. A spoke graph is excellent for illustrating this, e.g.:

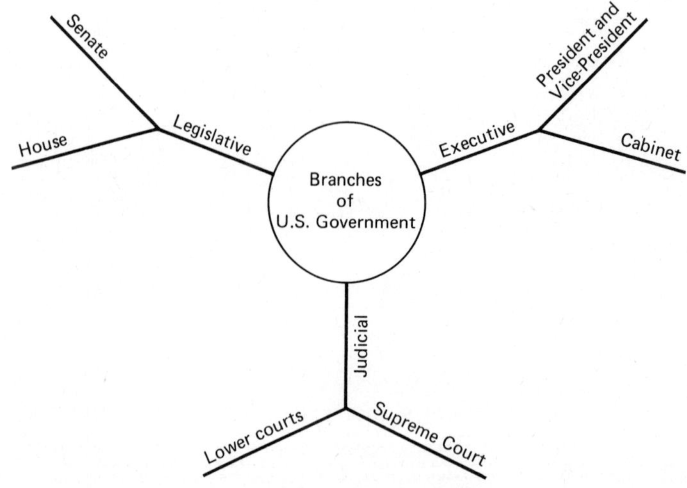

2. List major events in random order. Ask students to number them as they were given in the reading assignment, e.g.:

   Progress of action in a musical production

   ______ climax
   ______ encore
   ___1___ overture
   ______ opening scenes
   ______ finale

   Next, ask students to put this into a chart form. This is organized in *time* order, so a flow chart might be an appropriate format:

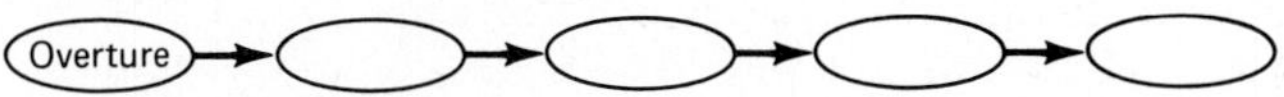

3. List major and minor headings from a reading assignment. Ask students to select major ideas first and put these into an outline using roman numerals (or arabics) for these points. Then have them place and indicate subpoints appropriately, e.g.:

   Planets within 150 million miles of the sun
   Planets more than a billion miles from the sun
   Planets between 400 and 900 million miles from the sun

Uranus	Pluto	Venus	Mars	Neptune
Jupiter	Earth	Saturn	Mercury	

   Their outline might look something like this:

   Order of Planets from the Sun

   I. Planets within 150 million miles of the sun
      A. Mercury
      B. Venus
      C. Earth
      D. Mars
   II. Planets between 400 and 900 million miles from the sun
      A. Jupiter
      B. Saturn
   III. Planets more than a billion miles from the sun
      A. Uranus
      B. Neptune
      C. Pluto

Since this organizational pattern is *spatial,* a sketch such as the following might be appropriate:

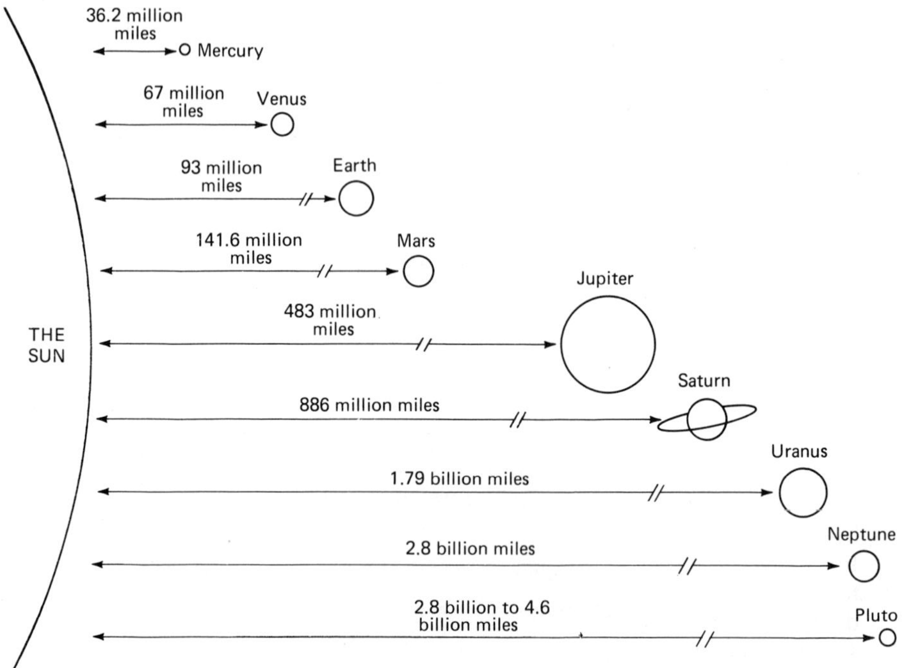

Fig. 7.14 Distances of the planets from the sun.

4. Select pictures or statements that illustrate parts of a reading assignment. Have students arrange them in order. (At higher cognitive levels, they might be asked to arrange them in as many different orders as are logically or aesthetically possible and to describe the implications of the different types of organizational patterns for the individual statements and the whole.)

5. Have students survey a chapter before reading it. You might allow them a fixed time in which to do this. Next ask them to outline, or otherwise illustrate, the structure. Teach them to ask questions about the main headings before they read the complete chapter.

6. At the beginning of the semester help students survey the whole book, including the Table of Contents. Help them to outline the main points of the Table of Contents or to illustrate it in some other way. Use no more than five main points. This may necessitate synthesizing ideas. For example, the Table of Contents of one book might look like this:

Texas History

1. The Indians of Texas
2. Europeans Explore and Settle in Texas
3. The Spanish People in Texas
4. Anglo-Americans in Texas
5. The Mexicans of Texas
6. The Texas Revolution
7. Rights and the Revolution
8. The Republic of Texas
9. A New State Takes Shape
10. The Civil War
11. Life During the Civil War
12. The Reconstruction
13. An Agricultural Empire
14. An Industrial Empire
15. The Urban Revolution

Notice that the author has simply listed the chapter titles. No attempt has been made to group them into units. Thus, the author's organizational pattern probably is not clear to the reader. The reader must classify in order to discover the overall pattern. Different readers, of course, might classify differently.

A possible classification pattern might include

Chapters 1, 2, 3, 4, 5 : Main Idea I. ____________________
Chapters 6, 7, 8, 9 : " " II. ____________________
Chapters 10, 11, 12 : " " III. ____________________
Chapters 13, 14, 15 : " " IV. ____________________

Next, this outline might be recast, using one of the illustrative formats suggested in the present chapter, perhaps a flow chart with chapters as subpoints under the main headings listed above.

SUMMARY

At the beginning of this chapter, the *cognitive domain*, as delineated by Sanders from the work of Benjamin Bloom and others, was briefly explained to serve as an introduction to this chapter and Chapters 8 and 9. The seven levels of the cognitive domain are: *memory, translation, interpretation, application, analysis, synthesis,* and *evaluation*. These levels are listed in hierarchical form, starting with the level which is least demanding intellectually.

Chapter 7 deals with the importance of, and ways of, teaching memory- and translation-type activities. Traditionalists consider these to be literal level activities. Four such reading comprehension skills have been discussed here. They are: (1) following directions as given, (2) recalling facts, dates, etc., (3) recognizing and recalling main ideas, and (4) recognizing and recalling sequence. Ways of teaching these skills at the memory and translation levels were explained.

Frequently, students find it difficult to *follow directions,* or they have learned to circumvent directions. Teachers must both give directions clearly and establish the practice of avoiding needless repetition. At times, teachers might make a game of following directions while keeping the content of the directions subject-centered. Students must be alert to the fact that some directions should be followed exactly as given, whereas others can be altered somewhat, and still others should not be followed at all.

Recalling facts, dates, and other details is another literal comprehension activity. Some facts are important for all educated people to know; others are needed to help the student generalize. Some facts are important as tools, e.g., mathematics tables, etc. However, many teachers overstress the importance of details.

Recognizing and recalling main ideas is a basic skill for higher level comprehension. Although this skill is usually at the literal level, a student lacking this skill cannot move up the ladder in cognition. Techniques for developing this skill are: *classifying* (finding family names), *finding kernels of sentences, finding kernels in paragraphs and synthesizing like parts of speech, locating the main idea* in a paragraph, and others.

Recognizing and recalling sequence is another basic skill. Three patterns were explained, as were translation level activities for recording each pattern. The *chronological pattern* lends itself to the following types of translation forms: *outline, flow chart, time line,* and *tree chart.* The *spatial pattern* can be recorded in *outline form* and in *sketches, maps,* and *floor plans.* The *expository pattern* also lends itself to *outline* form, plus *charts* and *graphs* of various types, such as *spoke graphs, pie graphs, bar graphs, line graphs,* and *pictographs.*

The teacher's job is to know both the content of the materials being studied and the cognitive skills necessary for understanding the content, as given here and in other chapters. In addition, of course, the teacher must know the students. Only then can the teacher decide which skills are essential to develop in order to help the students master the concepts. Usually, it is important to work not only at the literal level, but also at higher levels.

NOTES

1 J. P. Guilford. "Frontiers in Thinking that Teachers Should Know About," *The Reading Teacher* (February 1960): 176–182.

2 For a wealth of examples of such activities, see Rachel Salisbury. *Better Work Habits*. Glenview, Illinois: Scott, Foresman, 1966.

3 For the basic ideas included in this section, the author is indebted to Dr. Theodore L. Harris and associates in the Laboratory of Research in Basic Skills at the University of Wisconsin, 1966–1968.

4 See John L. Edwards and Nicholas J. Silvaroli. *Reading Improvement Program*. Dubuque, Iowa: Wm. C. Brown Co., 1969, pp. 29–35.

SUGGESTED ACTIVITIES

1. Name, in order, and briefly describe the seven levels of the cognitive domain as given by Sanders.
2. Name four literal level reading activities, and briefly describe each.
3. Design a microteach for following directions in your content area.
4. Describe three instances when it is necessary to follow directions as given and three instances when it might be wiser to alter directions or not follow them.
5. Design five different types of activities for teaching young people to recognize and recall main ideas in your content area.
6. Design a microteach for helping young people recognize and recall sequence in one of the following orders: chronological, spatial, or expository.
7. In a content area textbook, locate one graph, map, or chart for each organizational pattern (chronological, spatial, expository) and write four literal level questions about each. One of the four questions should be of each type: following directions, detail, main idea, and sequence.
8. Anticipate two ways in which the teaching of main idea and sequence can be done on a level higher than literal.

REFERENCES FOR FURTHER READING

Bloom, Benjamin, *et al. Taxonomy of Educational Objectives: Handbook I, Cognitive Domain*. New York: David McKay, 1956.

Bond, Guy L. and Miles Tinker. *Reading Difficulties: Their Diagnosis and Correction*. New York: Appleton-Century-Crofts, 1967, Chapter 11.

Carline, Donald E. *Teaching Children How to Learn*. Boulder, Colorado: University of Colorado Book Center, 1976.

Dawson, Mildred (ed.). *Developing Comprehension, Including Critical Reading*. Newark, Delaware: International Reading Association, 1968.

Dechant, Emerald V. *Improving the Teaching of Reading*, 2d ed. Englewood Cliffs, N.J.: Prentice-Hall, 1970, Chapter 13.

Duffy, Gerald G. (ed.). *Reading in the Middle School*. Newark, Delaware: International Reading Association, 1975.

Edwards, John L. and Nicholas J. Silvaroli. *Reading Improvement Program.* Dubuque, Iowa: Wm. C. Brown Co., 1969.

Guilford, J. P. "Frontiers in Thinking that Teachers Should Know About." *The Reading Teacher,* **23** (February 1960): 176–182.

Hafner, Lawrence (ed.). *Improving Reading in Middle and Secondary Schools, Selected Readings,* 2d ed. New York: Macmillan, 1974, Section 6.

Harris, Albert J. *How to Increase Reading Ability.* New York: David McKay, 1970, Chapter 6.

Herber, Harold (ed.). *Developing Study Skills in Secondary Schools* (Perspectives in Reading #4). Newark, Delaware: International Reading Association, 1965, Chapters 5, 6, 7.

Herber, Harold. *Teaching Reading in Content Areas.* Englewood Cliffs, N.J.: Prentice-Hall, 1970, Chapters 5, 6, 7.

Karlin, Robert. *Teaching Reading in High School.* Indianapolis: Bobbs-Merrill, 1964, Chapters 6 and 7.

Karlin, Robert (ed.). *Teaching Reading in High School—Selected Articles.* Indianapolis: Bobbs-Merrill, 1969, Chapter 6.

Laffey, James L. (ed.). *Reading in the Content Areas.* Newark, Delaware: International Reading Association, 1972.

Marksheffel, Ned D. *Better Reading in the Secondary School.* New York: The Ronald Press, 1966, Chapter 11.

Robinson, H. Alan and Ellen Lamar Thomas. *Fusing Reading Skills and Content.* Newark, Delaware: International Reading Association, 1969.

Salisbury, Rachel. *Better Work Habits.* Glenview, Illinois: Scott, Foresman, 1966.

Sanders, Norris. *Classroom Questions—What Kinds?* New York: Harper & Row, 1966.

Smith, Richard J. and Thomas C. Barrett. *Teaching Reading in the Middle Grades.* Reading, Mass.: Addison-Wesley, 1974, Chapter 3.

Weiss, M. Jerry. *Reading in the Secondary Schools.* New York: Odyssey Press, 1961, Section 5.

Chapter 8

INTERPRETING AND APPLYING IDEAS IN READING

What interpretive level skills are important in content area subjects? How can these skills be taught?

What are application level activities?

Can we help students see opportunities that may arise in the future to use what they have learned in our classes?

INTRODUCTION

The purpose of this chapter is to explore and suggest ways of helping students *interpret* printed materials and *apply* ideas they have gained through reading. Chapter 9 deals with the development of the skills called *analysis, synthesis,* and *evaluation,* often referred to as critical-creative reading.

The major difference in thought process between functioning at the levels discussed in Chapter 8 and that discussed in Chapter 9 is this: to function at the analysis, synthesis, and evaluation levels requires the use of formal logic and/or a conscious knowledge of the thought processes being used. To function at the interpretation and application levels does not. Few students (or even teachers) are prepared to use logical argumentation of a formal type, yet most can be taught to think beyond the very obvious "common sense" level.

When the questioning technique is used for teaching, *it is important to note that the form of a question does not determine the level of thought required to answer it.* The same question, in fact, asked of various students might elicit simple recall from some, interpretive reasoning from others, and analytic, synthetic, and evaluative judgment from others. Yet their answers might be similar.

What appears to be a complex evaluation question, for example, might draw a memory level response from a student who listened to his or her parents discuss the matter the night before. Another student might answer it by fusing ideas and seeing relationships without consciously knowing how he or she did so. Still another student might have formulated standards against which he or she judged the worth of the ideas presented. The teacher who uses *introspective-retrospective techniques* could identify the level of thought used by a student. ("How did you arrive at that answer? What makes you think so? Who advocates that point of view?")[1]

Sometimes it is extremely difficult to identify the cognitive level used unless we control conditions, as can be done in research. Sometimes it is not too important to know the level of thought used.

Understanding, then, that we lack some precision in our classification system because we cannot control all variables, e.g., a student's past experience, let us proceed. In this chapter, we shall examine the levels of interpretation and application. In Chapter 9, analysis, synthesis, and evaluation will be discussed.

INTERPRETATION

For students to work at the interpretation level, they must be aware of *relationships* that exist between the ideas expressed in the materials at hand and something within their own bank of ideas—the ideas they have stored in their memories from past readings and experiences. Only part of the relationship exists in the immediate source; the other part comes from within them.

The idea external to the material at hand is what allows the student to go beyond literal comprehension of the ideas presented by the author. If we recognize this fact, we also recognize the importance—to the individual student—of using a variety of materials in the classroom. And we recognize the importance of helping the student relate ideas in the presently used materials with those in other materials and with past experiences in order to facilitate interpretation.

The following are types of activities which might be interpretive. (They will be at a lower level if the activity is simple recall from a previous experience. They will be at a higher level if formal logic or scientific evidence is used in the thinking process.)

1. *cause-effect relationships,* when only one is given
2. *anticipating* what is to follow or inferring what has come before
3. *inducing main idea or theme* when they are not stated
4. *classifying*—convergently or divergently—without prompts or stereotypes
5. *making comparisons*—likenesses and differences
6. *inferring time, place, mood*
7. *inferring motives* of characters or real people
8. *responding to imagery*—living vicariously, having mental pictures—being able to touch, smell, see, hear, taste through the imagination
9. *empathizing*—a deeper vicarious experience than achieving imagery.

If we analyze these nine discrete listings, we can see that the first four are closely related and the last four are closely related. In accordance with our principle of outlining as set forth in the previous chapter, we have three broad categories of interpretive level activities. The first and third categories happen to have *four* identifiable components, and the second has *two.* (Thus, we have *from two to five main points* and *from two to five* subpoints.)

We might call the general categories relations, comparisons, and insights. Thus, our outline would look like this:

Title: Interpretive Thinking Skills

1.0 Perceiving unstated relationships

  1.1 Anticipating and "retrospecting"

  1.2 Recognizing cause-effect relationships

  1.3 Classifying convergently and divergently

  1.4 Inducing main idea and theme

2.0 Making comparisons

  2.1 Seeing likenesses (analogies)

  2.2 Seeing differences (contrasts)

3.0 Achieving insights
- 3.1 Inferring time, place, mood
- 3.2 Inferring motives of characters and real people
- 3.3 Responding to imagery
- 3.4 Empathizing with characters and real people

Even the subpoints might be *paired.* Do you see similar types of thinking processes between activities related to points 1.1 and 1.2, between 1.3 and 1.4, between 2.1 and 2.2, between 3.1 and 3.2, and between 3.3 and 3.4?

Let us look at kinds of activities related to each of the pairs of subpoints.

Anticipating and "Retrospecting"/Cause-Effect

What will follow? or What will come next? are anticipation questions. What came before? or What preceded this action? are retrospective questions. If a cause-effect relationship is to be established, the following types of questions would be appropriate for seeking the cause: What caused the situation to exist? What factors led up to the necessary conclusion? When looking for effect, on the other hand, the following types of questions would be appropriate: What is likely to happen if the following conditions exist? What is likely to happen now that we have performed this action?

In anticipation and retrospective activities, a cause-effect relationship has not been established. Sequence is being considered: what follows, or will follow, a situation—or what normally precedes, or has preceded, a situation—are different questions from those that establish or assume (at the interpretive level) a cause-effect relationship.

For example, people can become drug addicts only if drugs are available to them. Yet the mere availability of drugs does not mean that people will become addicts. The availability of drugs is a necessary, but not a sufficient, condition to establish or even assume a cause-effect relationship. However, availability of drugs must *precede* addiction.

In content area subjects, the following kinds of questions can be used to encourage anticipation and retrospection or to help students observe factors that might be found "traveling together," which would give us leads to the possibility of the existence of a cause-effect relationship.

Teaching Strategies

In mathematics

1. *Biography:* What do you think preceded Einstein's success as a mathematician? Check his biography to see if you are correct. Were these conditions necessary and sufficient to cause his success? Could you, with the

same conditions available, be equally successful if you took advantage of them? Is an "X" factor operating? If you think so, attempt to define it. Is it available to you?

2. *Word problems:* Read a word problem such as the following:

   You and your friends are planning a picnic. Your job is to bring hot dogs, buns, and potato chips for the crowd. Sixteen people are expected, and you have five dollars to spend. At the grocery store you find that hot dogs are 89¢ a dozen, buns are 45¢ a dozen, and potato chips are 79¢ for a large bag. Do you have enough money to buy enough hot dogs and buns so that everyone will get at least two, and still have enough money for a bag of potato chips? What is the exact cost?

   Anticipate the approximate cost $(3 \times .90) + (3 \times .50) + .80 = 2.70 + 1.50 + .80 = 5.00$. Then figure the exact cost. Then compare the two. If there is a large discrepancy, it is possible that the "exact cost" answer is wrong, since the arithmetic in it was more difficult than the arithmetic in the approximate-cost computation.

3. *Visual problems:* Is the total area of circles A and B and of the triangle C greater than, equal to, or less than the area of square D?

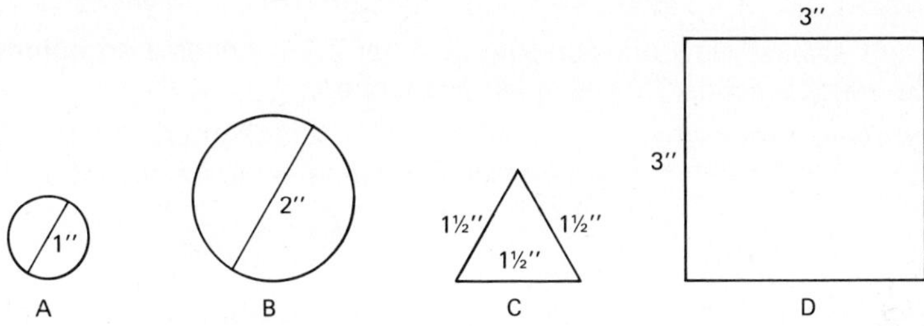

   Anticipate the answer before computations are made. After the computations are completed, compare the "exact" answer with the anticipated answer. If there is a sizable discrepancy, repeat the operations.

In science

1. *An experiment:* Look at this pineapple plant. Do you think it was given too much water before it died? Too much or too little sunlight? What else might have caused it to die? Can you suggest ways of setting up an experiment to see which of these factors or which combination of these factors may have caused the plant to die? (Such discussion might precede an actual experiment with pineapple plants and/or might be used in a preliminary discussion to help students relate to a botany experiment in their manuals.)
2. *An experiment:* What do you think would happen if you reversed the order of some of the steps in the following experiment, doing step 4 *before* step 3? What would happen if you used the wrong proportions? (This would be a

higher-level question *if* formal scientific reasoning was used. It would be at a lower level *if* it was recall.)

3. *Biography:* Having studied the discoveries made by the Curies, attempt to place the discoveries in chronological order. Check the biography to see if you are correct.
4. *Scientific discoveries:* Name several scientific discoveries which are important to you and/or list what you consider to be the twelve most important scientific discoveries of all time. Where were these discoveries made? Did the geographic areas of the countries make possible these discoveries? Did the climate of thought of the area or nation make possible the discoveries? Why were these discoveries made when and where they were?

In social studies

> "The reforms have worked just as well as we predicted—and even better than we expected," says one top American official here.
>
> —Peter R. Kann in the *Wall Street Journal.*
>
> *New Yorker:* One top and very *candid* American economic official.[2]

1. *Current events:* What do you think will happen if our population doubles by the year 2000? If we attain zero population growth by the year 2000?
2. *Current events:* How did our city (or other area) become so polluted? Give three major reasons. Discuss their interaction.
3. *Biography:* From what you know about the background of the President, discuss factors which may have caused him to make his recent decision.

In English

1. *Fiction:* Read to the climax of the story. Then close your book and write an ending. Compare your ending with the author's.
2. *Mystery:* Read the last chapter of the book. Write a beginning. Compare your beginning with the author's.
3. *Character analysis:* What do you think was Hamlet's fatal flaw? What were his greatest strengths?

Classifying/Inducing Main Idea and Theme (Concept Development)

Classifying, or grouping, items, sentences, paragraphs, or ideas into generally agreed upon categories is a convergent thinking activity. The same is usually true if the activity is selecting from several choices the main idea of a paragraph or the theme of a longer work. Certainly exceptions can be stated, but in general this is true. Further, such activities are usually at the literal level and were amply discussed in Chapter 6.

However, *formulating* a main idea and classifying items or ideas when such classification patterns are not simply recalled are interpretive level activities—at least.

Teaching Strategies

1. Compare the thought processes involved in selecting the main idea in a passage which contains the main idea with a like passage which does not, e.g.:

   First passage—main idea stated

   Once in power, Caesar showed himself a statesman as well as a politician and general. He made vast reforms and planned even more. His first attention went to the provinces. He granted citizenship to many provincials. As governors he chose trained men and paid them a fixed salary. Other officials were sent to check on the governors, removing those who did not rule well. Land which had been seized by wealthy men was regained and divided among landless farmers and veterans. This move established groups of Romans throughout the provinces, and thus spread Roman culture and influence. Caesar also gave membership in the Senate to many provincials.

   Caesar secured laws to relieve poor farmers and men who could not pay their debts. He improved the roads so that armies as well as traders could move quickly to all parts of the empire.*

   Second passage—main idea not stated

   . . . Caesar's first attention went to the provinces. He granted citizenship to many provincials. As governors he chose trained men and paid them a fixed salary. Other officials were sent to check on the governors, removing those who did not rule well. Land which had been seized by wealthy men was regained and divided among landless farmers and veterans. This move established groups of Romans throughout the provinces, and thus spread Roman culture and influence. Caesar also gave membership in the Senate to many provincials.

   Caesar secured laws to relieve poor farmers and men who could not pay their debts. He improved the roads so that armies as well as traders could move quickly to all parts of the empire.*

2. Ask students to put the following items into two groups.

   grapefruit cucumber banana onion

   The convergent—middle-class—way of grouping these is according to function:

Fruit	*Vegetable*
grapefruit	cucumber
banana	onion

* Anatole G. Mazour and John M. Peoples. *Men and Nations: A World History.* New York: Harcourt, Brace and World, 1961, p. 115. Reprinted by permission.

In fact, on a commonly used I.Q. test, such a grouping pattern is the only one for which the student is given credit. In what other ways could these four items be logically grouped? According to shape? Color? Sorry, no credit! Why not? Because that's not the way *middle-class* children think—another reason that commonly used I.Q. tests are unfair to culturally different children.

3. Ask students to group items in as many ways as possible: e.g., in how many ways can the following items be grouped?

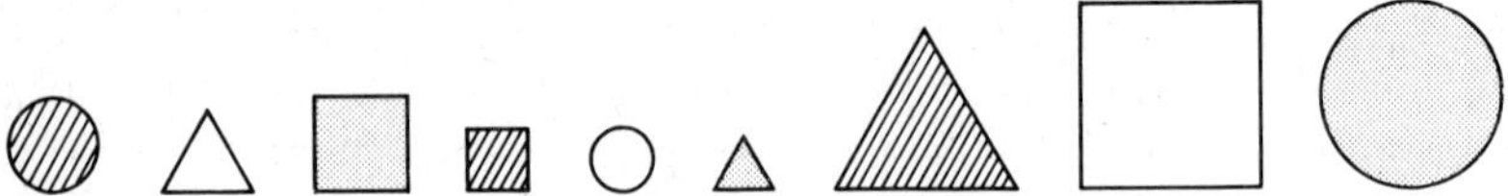

Or these?

a b c d e f g h i j k l m n o p q r s t u v w x y z

Or these?

monkey	cactus	grape	diamond
gold	dinosaur	lime	daisy
whale	mouse	ruby	rose

Might their classification system depend on whether they are studying phonics or science, whether they are playing "Twenty Questions," or the way their mind works?

4. Take the theme of several or many books, the main ideas from stories or sections of chapters, or simply terminology related to a topic. The topic might be related to a unit of study or just a chapter of a book.

For example, the topic might be "artificial satellites." The following might have been discussed in several magazines or newspaper articles or even in book chapters:

Vanguard	Echo	Aeros	Telstar
Relay	Early Bird	Tiros	Nimbus
Discoverer	Explorer	Courier	

Students might classify these in *chronological order:* when they were launched, how long they will last, how long it takes them to trace their routes, etc. Or they might classify them in *spatial order:* where they are now, their launching sites, how large they are, what they look like, etc. Or they might classify them in *expository order:* their purposes (scientific, communications, weather), their efficiency, their equipment, etc. Does each method of classification inspire us to look at the satellites and the satellite program differently?

5. Have students compile a list of terms related to a topic. You may have them freely list terms they know, or you may wish to ask them to list only those

terms used in certain books or articles. If you are using several books, you might ask students using different books to form separate lists, one for each book. (See activity 4, pp. 139–140 of this book.) Another technique is to list one word per card and have different colored cards keyed to different books.

Next, ask students to classify ideas within books and across books using different patterns: chronological, spatial, expository (cause-effect, effect-cause, similarities, differences, etc.). Then ask them to compare effects of classifying in different ways.

Instead of using terms, or in addition to doing so, you might use the same technique with main ideas.

6. Ask students to look at organizational patterns of chapters on the same general topic in textbooks or of organizational patterns of complete textbooks. For example, if they look at literature anthologies they might find the following types of organization of complete books:

   a) *historical* (chronological): progressing through periods of literature

   b) *genre* (expository): progressing from one literary form (e.g., poetry, short stories, drama, etc.) to another

   c) *comparative* (spatial): progressing from one country, or area, to another

   d) *thematic* (expository): progressing from one literary theme, or concept (e.g., courage, danger, romance, altruism, etc.), to another

   The major classification pattern may subsume under it all, or most, of the others. But the major emphasis remains with the major classification system. For example, if the classification system were thematic and the theme were *courage,* we could study under that theme literary works in which courage was displayed—from all countries (or selected countries and languages), of all literary forms (or selected literary forms), of all ages (or selected ages), etc.

   On the other hand, if the approach were one of literary genre, and we were studying *poetry,* we could study poetry (or a specific type of poetry) of all countries (or selected countries or languages), of all topics (or selected topics), of all ages (or selected ages).

   [Notice that the major organizational pattern influences point of view and much of what is learned—even the degree to which ideas may be appreciated.

   If you were teaching a unit by using several textbooks and also trade books, how might you approach the subject you were teaching? Suggest organizational patterns of each of the following types: chronological, spatial, expository.]

7. After items are grouped, and possibly put in outline form, ask students to induce a title, thesis statement, or theme telling what the whole is about. Possibly a summary statement should be composed.

Activities, then, that might be engaged in are:

a) inducing these statements, or themes
b) summary or précis writing
c) testing for card stacking (Is only one point of view presented?)
d) headline writing

Two examples of headline writing follow.

CONCORDE TEST FLIGHTS COULD
LAND IN SUPREME COURT
—Headline in the Pasco-Kennewick-Richland (Wash.) Tri-City Herald.

New Yorker: Not without some remodeling.[3]

KING FAISAL
LEAVES S.F.
—IN 3 PLANES

—Headline in the *San Francisco Chronicle.*

New Yorker: Kings do things right.[4]

Making Comparisons

Activities that help students focus on similarities and differences are important not only academically but also practically. How do students decide which suit or car they want to purchase? How do they decide where they will travel or what sport they will engage in or which book they will read?

Usually, such decisions are best made by comparing alternatives, not just by zeroing in on one item as though blindfolded.

> Fox, chief of the Police Department's juvenile aid division, told a workshop on gang control that policemen and gang members have many things in common. Among them he said were:
> Both usually come from families.
> —Dayton (Ohio) *Daily News*
>
> *New Yorker:* That's enough. We don't need to hear the others.[5]

Teaching Strategies

In mathematics

1. Compare the distances that a horse would have to run if he were always in the inner lane rather than the outer lane of the Derby racetrack? If they are different, what is the measured distance?

2. Which three of the following geometric figures are *most alike:* square, circle, oval, sphere? Why?
3. *Compare* the cost of a trip to Mexico City, Honolulu, and Jamaica in regard to air fare, hotel rooms in first-class hotels and second-class hotels, and food.

In science

1. Compare the hibernating habits of a black bear and a hamster.
2. Which four of the following animals have eating habits which are *most alike:* monkey, ape, lemur, orangutan, gibbon, chimpanzee?
3. *Compare* the use of helium with other gases used to inflate and provide lift for balloons in regard to cost and safety.

In social studies

1. Compare the arguments of environmentalists and harp seal hunters (tuna fishermen, etc.) in relation to the balance of nature and the ethics of killing certain species.
2. Which two of the following countries are *most alike* in the quality of their contribution to peace talks in the 1970–1972 Vietnam negotiations: France, England, West Germany?
3. *Compare* the Roman and Greek Empires' contributions to modern thought in theology and art.

In English

1. Compare the dramatic literature of France and England during the seventeenth century.
2. Which four of the following authors are *most alike* in philosophy: Wordsworth, Keats, Shelley, Byron, Coleridge? In form?
3. *Compare* Shakespeare and Cervantes in regard to quantity of writing which survives and their sense of humor as reflected in their major works.

Inferring Time, Place, Mood/Inferring Motives of Characters and Real People

Activities related to the identification of reasons for a thought occurring to a person or for a person (or fictional character) participating in a particular activity relate to inferring motives of characters and real people.

In literature and social studies

Inferential skills are especially important in reading literature and social studies, including current events, as well as in daily living. When only partial information is given and readers must place the ideas in time (or era) and/or area, they are making inferences. When they must assess the mood (or emotional feelings) or tone (general effect or atmosphere), they are dealing with this skill. For example, one might infer *time* and *mood* from the following episode:

> Mr. Anders, the schoolmaster, tried to comfort his pupils. He said that air-raid shelters were found in every country, but they were only a precaution. He was sure they would never be used.
>
> "Norway's safe from war," he said. "Our country's been at peace for over a hundred years. We've no quarrel with anyone and no one has a quarrel with us. Let's not worry about a thing as unlikely as war."
>
> There was a knock on the classroom door. Uncle Victor came in. He was a great favorite with all the children. When he visited the school he always told a sea story, and so today they settled back for one of his salty tales. But it was no sea story that brought Captain Lundstrom on this occasion. He whispered a few words to Mr. Anders and then spoke to the class.
>
> "Now that we're building bomb shelters, we ought to have an air-raid drill," he said. "We want to teach everyone to go in orderly fashion to the shelters and not to be crowding the doorways."
>
> "Just like a fire drill," Mr. Anders said."*

And from the following passage the reader can infer *time* and *place:*

> The exuberance of the age carried over into every field of human endeavor. The universities were full of intellectual vitality and disputation, fruitful in sifting truth. In this age schoolmen dared to apply the rationalism of Aristotle to the elucidation of articles of faith; in this age pagan philosophy and Christian theology came to terms, and eminent theologians established the principle that there is no quarrel between faith and reason. In this age intellectual giants fought with razorlike logic to subdue their adversaries before a university public numbering thousands. In this age every art flourished to an astounding degree. We have from this period a vast, vigorous, anonymous literature: the *Nibelungenlied, Aucassin and Nicolette, Reynard the Fox,* the *Fioretti*—to give only a sampling.†

From the following poem, we can interpretively read the *eternality of time* (unimportance of literal time) and the *universality of place* (unimportance of literal place):

---

* From the book *Snow Treasure* by Marie McSwigan. Copyright 1942 by E. P. Dutton & Co., Inc. Renewal © 1970 by Kathryn McSwigan Laughlin. Published by E. P. Dutton & Co., Inc. and used with their permission.

† Ruth Mary Fox. *Dante Lights the Way.* Milwaukee: Benziger Bruce & Glencoe, 1958, p. 4. Reprinted by permission.

OZYMANDIAS

I met a traveller from an antique land
Who said: Two vast and trunkless legs of stone
Stand in the desert. Near them, on the sand,
Half sunk, a shattered visage lies, whose frown,
And wrinkled lip, and sneer of cold command,
Tell that its sculptor well those passions read
Which yet survive, stamped on these lifeless things,
The hand that mocked them, and the heart that fed:
And on the pedestal these words appear:
"My name is Ozymandias, king of kings:
Look on my works, ye Mighty, and despair!"
Nothing beside remains. Round the decay
Of that colossal wreck, boundless and bare
The lone and level sands stretch far away.

Percy Bysshe Shelley

To demonstrate the eternality and universality of this poem, the reader might suggest other names for Ozymandias, e.g., Hitler, Joseph McCarthy. Who else? Personalities from literature might also be used.

Inferring motives of characters and real people is of utmost importance if we are to understand what is going on in literature and the real world. Sometimes a motive is not explained, and sometimes a motive is given, though it may not be the true one. Note, for example, the importance placed on motive in determining the penalty for a crime. Recall the debates and discussions related to Senator Edward Kennedy's delayed report to the police of the tragedy at Chappaquiddick.

Awareness of motive can be taught to the very young and can be developed more fully as students mature. For example, why did the stepmother in *Cinderella* treat her daughters and her stepdaughter differently? Why did Charlotte befriend the pig in *Charlotte's Web*? Why did Brutus assist in the slaying of Caesar? Why did Hamlet at one time treat Ophelia as if she were insane?

Motives can be related to authors and the themes of their works. What, basically, was William Golding trying to explain in *Lord of the Flies*? What was Huxley saying in *Brave New World*; Cervantes in *Don Quixote*? And, of course, motives can be related to acts of senators and representatives in Congress, to the President of the United States, and to deeds of your acquaintances, etc.

In science

Not to be forgotten, however, is the importance to scientists of inferring time and place of the development of such things as rock formations, the continental drift, various species of animal and plant life, etc., and also of inferring motives of scientists (including themselves) as they relate to the kinds of research they pursue and the value they give to the research of others.

In mathematics

Mathematicians are also concerned with inferring moods and motives of people when they design a bridge or a highway. They may be interested in ancient or comparative architecture because it suggests the possibility of improving the present, making a home or a community a more desirable place in which to live. They may see mathematical patterns in music and art and from these be able to infer the mood and/or the era of the creator.[6] Like scientists, they should also be concerned with inferring their own and others' motives in relation to specific areas of interest.

Responding to Imagery/Empathizing with Characters and Real People

When readers respond to the imagery of a passage, they mentally see, feel, hear, touch, or smell in accord with the description. They live vicariously—possibly in a different age or place.

Closely related to this is the ability to empathize. Empathy suggests the totality of experience. When we empathize, we become another person, or we are so much the other person that there is an intimacy of feelings, thoughts, and motives. Different from sympathy, which suggests a spontaneous emotion in time of misfortune, empathy suggests involvement with another person or fictional character to the extent of vicarious, or imaginative, identification. Such responses are probably best classified in both the cognitive and affective domains.

Some examples of passages replete with imagery are given below. To which physical sense, or senses, does each appeal or relate?

1. "The atmosphere churned. The dirt of years, tobacco of many growings, opium, betel nut, and moist flesh allied themselves in one grand assault against the nostrils."[7]

   smell
   ____

2. The anthropologist stared in amazement as he viewed before him the ruins of the ancient civilization of Zandu. He could not wait to walk among the ruins.

   ____

3. "Long ago a primitive hunter caught a large fish. It was so large that he wanted to be able to tell people about it after he had eaten it. He found a forked stick that fit his fish. . . . Then he ate the fish.

"Later this hunter's friend caught a fish and boasted that his fish was just as long as the hunter's. How could the hunter prove him wrong (or right)?"*

---

4. "To $1^1/_2$ cups papaya pulp add juice of 1 lemon, $^1/_2$ cup sugar, and beat into 2 stiffly whipped whites of eggs. Cook. Serve with whipped cream."[8]

It is impossible in a brief exposition to exemplify empathy. Yet surely you can recall a person who can read your thoughts—who can predict your actions and is on your side. You, no doubt, remember going to a movie and imagining yourself to be the hero, if you are a man, or the heroine, if you are a woman. You have probably felt the same way when you have read some books.

APPLICATION

To work at the application level, a level higher than interpretation, one must *without prompts* recognize a situation in which a previously learned principle applies and utilize the principle successfully. This is frequently called *transfer of learning*.

You are learning about the teaching of reading in this course. If you were in a classroom, could you recognize a situation that calls for the teaching of a particular reading skill or level of comprehension and also teach it with success? If so, you are functioning at the application level—at least. All content area subjects provide ample opportunity for working at the application level.

Perhaps one reason that most students find word problems in mathematics harder than simple process problems is that word problems are usually at the application level. Success in working a word problem is not determined simply by properly performing the arithmetic task, but rather by first properly identifying the task. Such identification requires the singling-out of that task from all others as the appropriate one to solve the problem. It also often requires recognition of the fact that some information is irrelevant. Cognitively, this is a high level activity.

Look at the following problems:

1. A cubic mile of sea water contains about 38 pounds of gold.
   a) How many cubic miles of water would be needed to have 1596 pounds of gold?
   b) One pound of gold will make a thin wire about 900 miles long.
      The distance around the earth is 24,902 miles. With the gold from

---

* Robert E. Eicholz, *et al. Modern General Mathematics.* Menlo Park, Calif.: Addison-Wesley, 1969, p. 135. Reprinted by permission. Copyright © 1969 by Addison-Wesley Publishing Co., Inc. All rights reserved.

1 cubic mile of sea water, how many feet of wire would you have left after you wrapped it around the earth once?*

2. How many stamps does David have in his collection if 16% of them are less than one year old and 25% of those that are older than one year, or 26 in number, are Japanese?

What thought processes are required of the students if they are to successfully work problems 1 and 2? Is there any irrelevant information included?

Similar types of activities are found in science materials.

In social studies, predicting how a segment of the population will vote is an application level activity. Similarly, predicting how individuals or groups will act in any circumstance is at the application level. What one must do in making such predictions is draw from past knowledge that which is appropriate to the solution of the problem and use it effectively in making realistic predictions. Such activities will be at higher cognitive levels if more than common sense reasoning is used. Can you think of other social studies activities that might be considered application level activities?

In English, students frequently study grammatical principles, possibly the Latin type or modern linguistic type. Many students do well on such activities. Yet, how many of them use these principles in their writing? Frequently, there is little transfer! Like the girl who stayed after school to write on the board "I have gone" 500 times and on completion of that task wrote a note to the teacher saying, "I have went home," many students fail to see the relevance of grammar to their own writing. Reaching the application level is a difficult task for many, and direct teaching is frequently necessary to effect transfer.

Do students sometimes read literature, and possibly even identify the theme, without pondering its relevance to life, or to their lives? If so, they have not reached the application level. So, too, of history and the arts, and of science and mathematics, and of all that is "learned." Sometimes information is compartmentalized and used only in specific situations—without being generalized. Such is the case when a student spells well in English class, but poorly in all other classes.

Teaching for transfer is essential. Expecting students to transfer—and helping them to do so—is also important. The teacher's task here is difficult. Too many prompts lower the level of the activity—possibly to the literal level. Too few prompts make the transfer impossible for some students. When a new principle is learned, the teacher might ask the class to suggest occasions when this principle might be used in the future. Thus, transfer when the occasion arises might be facilitated.

---

* Robert E. Eicholz, *et al. Modern General Mathematics.* Menlo Park, Calif.: Addison-Wesley, 1969, p. 109. Reprinted by permission.

Teachers might lead students in application level activities by asking questions such as

1. What is the most logical thing to do if . . . ?
2. What is the most interesting thing to do if . . . ?
3. What is the most altruistic or humanitarian thing to do if . . . ?
4. What is the fairest thing to do if . . . ?

Students must use their background of experience to answer these questions. Their experience includes their philosophy about people and fairness as well as their intellectual background.

Students might be asked if they know of anyone who has been in a situation such as any of those cited above and if they know how they reacted. They might be asked to evaluate the reaction.

Application level activities might also revolve around the use of appropriate reference materials. Questions might be asked which require students to use research techniques. At the application level, students would be required to decide which resources are most appropriate for answering a question, and they would be required to use these resources in finding the answer.

Such reference materials range from indexes of materials (the *Reader's Guide to Periodical Literature*, the *Art Index*, etc., the card catalog) to reference materials (encyclopedias, almanacs, dictionaries) to types of literature (textbooks, various genre of literature, e.g., biography, poetry, essays, novels, etc., newspaper articles, magazines and journals) to community, state, and national resources (community leaders and archives, etc.). More information about reference indexes and materials is given in Chapter 11.

SUMMARY

Reading comprehension abilities called *interpretation* and *application* have been explained in this chapter. Basically, the thought processes involved in *interpretive activities* require the reader to see a relationship when only part of the relationship is given. The other part is supplied from the reader's background of experience. This related experience may have been gained through reading, listening, or otherwise observing—either consciously or subconsciously. For the activity to be interpretive, the reader must grasp, or formulate, the relationship. Otherwise, the activity is at the memory or translation level.

The following types of interpretive activities were explained and exemplified: *perceiving unstated relationships* (anticipating and retrospecting, recognizing cause-effect relationships, classifying convergently and divergently, inducing main idea and theme), *making comparisons* (seeing likenesses and differences), *achieving insights* (inferring time, place, mood, motives of characters and real people, responding to imagery, empathizing with characters and real people).

Application level activities require the reader to both *recognize* a situation in which a previously learned principle applies and *use* the principle successfully. Commonly, this is called *transfer* of learning.

Word problems in mathematics are frequently more difficult than simple process problems because many of them require the students themselves to identify from all they have previously learned the process to be followed in solving a specific problem. In addition, the students must carry through the process successfully.

In all classes, students frequently compartmentalize their knowledge and use it only when directly guided to do so. Teachers must exert efforts to help students see when previously learned knowledge or principles might apply to a present situation and also to understand that what they are learning at the present time may be used in the future. Too much guidance, however, lowers the level of activity; too little makes it impossible. To strike a balance takes experience.

NOTES

1 See William S. Gray. "New Approaches to the Study of Interpretation in Reading." *Journal of Educational Research,* **LII** (October 1958): 65–67.

2 *The New Yorker,* March 13, 1971, p. 136.

3 *The New Yorker,* April 19, 1976, p. 100.

4 *The New Yorker,* June 26, 1971, p. 88.

5 *The New Yorker,* January 23, 1971, p. 65.

6 "Donald in Mathmagic Land." Glendale, California: Walt Disney Educational Material Co., 1960. Junior-Senior School Level, 26 minutes.

7 Thomas Burke. "The Chink and the Child," in *The Golden Argosy,* ed. Van H. Cartmell and Charles Grayson. New York: The Dial Press, 1955, p. 67.

8 Bertha Munks. *Florida's Favorite Foods.* Tallahassee: State of Florida Department of Agriculture, 1957, p. 129.

SUGGESTED ACTIVITIES

1. List three different types of interpretive level activities, and indicate subactivities which belong with each.
2. Name two characteristics of all application level activities.
3. Design a five-minute microteach showing how you might teach either anticipation or retrospection in your content area.

4. Design a ten-minute microteach showing a way in which you could teach divergent classification in your content area.
5. Using a chapter in your content area textbook, write six different types of interpretive level questions.
6. Using the same chapter, write two application level questions.
7. Compare the relative merits of literal level activities with those of the interpretive and application levels.

REFERENCES FOR FURTHER READING

Beery, Althea, Thomas C. Barrett, and William Powell (eds.). *Elementary Reading Instruction: Selected Materials.* Boston: Allyn and Bacon, 1969, Chapter 7.

Bond, Guy L. and Miles Tinker. *Reading Difficulties: Their Diagnosis and Correction.* New York: Appleton-Century-Crofts, 1967, Chapter 15.

Carline, Donald E. *Teaching Children How to Learn.* Boulder, Colorado: University of Colorado Book Center, 1976.

Dawson, Mildred (ed.). *Developing Comprehension, Including Critical Reading.* Newark, Delaware: International Reading Association, 1968.

DeBoer, John and Martha Dallman. *The Teaching of Reading.* New York: Henry Holt, 1970, Chapter 6.

Duffy, Gerald G. *Reading in the Middle School.* Newark, Delaware: International Reading Association, 1975.

Hafner, Lawrence E. (ed.). *Improving Reading in Middle and Secondary Schools, Selected Readings,* 2d ed. New York: Macmillan, 1974, Sections 4 and 10.

Harris, Albert J. and Edward R. Sipay. *How to Increase Reading Ability.* New York: David McKay, 1975. Chapter 17.

Herber, Harold (ed.). *Developing Study Skills in Secondary Schools* (Perspectives in Reading #4). Newark, Delaware: International Reading Association, 1965.

Herber, Harold. *Teaching Reading in Content Areas.* Englewood Cliffs, N.J.: Prentice-Hall, 1970, Chapters 5 and 6.

Karlin, Robert. *Teaching Reading in High School.* Indianapolis: Bobbs-Merrill, 1964, Chapters 6 and 7.

Karlin, Robert (ed.). *Teaching Reading in High School—Selected Articles.* Indianapolis: Bobbs-Merrill, 1969.

Laffey, James L. (ed.). *Reading in the Content Areas.* Newark, Delaware: International Reading Association, 1972.

Marksheffel, Ned D. *Better Reading in the Secondary School.* New York: The Ronald Press, 1966, Chapter 8.

Olson, Arthur V. and Wilber S. Ames (eds.). *Teaching Reading Skills in Secondary Schools.* Scranton, Pa.: International Textbook Co., 1970.

Otto, Wayne and Richard J. Smith. *Administering the School Reading Program.* Boston: Houghton Mifflin, 1970.

Robinson, H. Alan and Ellen Lamar Thomas. *Fusing Reading Skills and Content.* Newark, Delaware: International Reading Association, 1969.

Sanders, Norris M. *Classroom Questions—What Kinds?* New York: Harper & Row, 1966, Chapters 4 and 5.

Schubert, Delwyn G. and Theodore L. Torgerson (eds.). *Readings in Reading: Practice, Theory, Research.* New York: Thomas Y. Crowell Co., 1968.

Spache, George. *Toward Better Reading.* Champaign, Illinois: Garrard, 1963. Chapters 4, 16, and 18.

Chapter 9

ANALYZING, SYNTHESIZING, AND EVALUATING IDEAS THROUGH READING

What is the basic difference in thought processes between analysis-synthesis-evaluation activities and interpretive level activities?

What is analysis as a reading process? How can techniques of analysis be used in all classrooms?

What is synthesis as a reading process? How can we teach students to synthesize?

What is involved in evaluation? How can we help students evaluate ideas?

INTRODUCTION

Analysis, synthesis, and evaluation activities are frequently referred to as critical-creative thinking abilities. Much has been written and spoken about such abilities, yet the frequency of their use in many classrooms is appallingly scarce. There are several reasons for this.

For students to think at these higher levels, they must use a wide variety of materials. And it is necessary for the teacher to help them find the common core of such materials as well as relate their previous experiences to ideas gained in their present reading materials. Normally, not all students in the same classroom will have read the same things, nor will they have had the same experiences. A skillful teacher is, indeed, necessary. This is true even at the interpretive and application levels, but greater knowledge and skill on the part of the teacher are necessary to help students function on these higher levels.

Frequently, students attach a halo to the printed word, thinking that anything that is in print must be true. On the other hand, some of these same students find it extremely difficult to suspend judgment of ideas in materials long enough to know what the author is saying if the author's ideas and opinions differ from theirs. The reader becomes emotional, and does not even know what the author has said.

When controversial issues are being studied, the teacher's first questions should be at the literal level. When the teacher is satisfied that the students have grasped the author's ideas, then—and only then—should students be asked to react at higher levels. One important kind of activity here is to ask students to put themselves in the author's place—to recognize and think from the author's value system and to see if what the author has said makes sense in this value system. Then, the value system itself should be evaluated.

For example, making extensive trips into outer space and spending millions or billions of dollars on them makes sense to many middle- and upper-class citizens. They may have an insatiable curiosity about what lies beyond our planet. And, in addition, they may be able and willing to postpone immediate satisfaction with the hope that in time at least some of their questions will be answered. From their point of view, money spent on space travel is well spent.

On the other hand, those who are starving or who are living in the midst of race tumult and those who empathize with these people probably feel that immediate internal reform in our country is far more important. From their point of view, it would be far better to spend the tax dollar on urban renewal and on improving race relations and job opportunities.

Students in a class should be taught to examine various points of view, looking for the rationale behind each. They should attempt vicarious empathy with those who feel differently. Each of these points of view is perhaps legitimate—as it relates to a subculture.

Within a society such as ours the basic problem may be one of establishing priorities. The subcultures interact with and affect one another. Indeed, if the destitute decide to blow up NASA, our space program would be set back considerably. It is also possible, however, that our space program may, in time, immeasurably benefit the needy, and certainly it gives employement to many.

Other examples abound and may help clarify the growing realization that various value systems function within our society. Thirty years ago, many teen-agers listened to jazz only when their parents were out. It was the same with rock-and-roll not too long ago. And today and tomorrow it is sure to be something else.

Certain very traditional moral values within our society are widely questioned today, particularly values that relate to premarital sex. Parents may have one value system, but if they do not attempt to listen to their adolescent sons and daughters and attempt to see their point of view, communications will very likely cease. They may thus give up the chance of converting their children —or of being converted themselves.

The classroom atmosphere must allow for divergence in opinions. There must be freedom of expression. The teacher must learn to refrain from making judgments, e.g., praising one student for an opinion and rejecting others. Instead, students should be encouraged to test their ideas, to think further about them. They might, however, be evaluated on their logic, or lack of it.

Another important point must be made; that is, that critical reading (analysis of propaganda, of semantics, of authenticity of sources, etc.) should not be carried out in a predominantly negative way. Unfortunately, the word "critical" has pejorated in American usage, for "critical" suggests fault-finding. (Even the word "propaganda" has pejorated.) Persuasive language and techniques are not all bad. The word "critic" more nearly suggests the meaning intended when we talk about "critical" reading. Art critics, for example, are not fault-finders. They are judges. Part of their job is to identify and describe the best.

Analysis (plus synthesis and evaluation) is a good word for our idea at the present time. Sometimes, students might simply be asked to pick out the best characteristic of an article or advertisement, etc., or the most useful idea. If they are to create, these useful ideas or characteristics will come in handy. (For example, if a student is to become a commercial artist, which activity will help most: (1) picking out the ten most useful ideas or characteristics from a group of advertisements and combining them, or (2) picking out the ten most worthless ideas or characteristics and trying to avoid them?)

Although we are talking about three levels, or types, of activities in this chapter, activities classified at one of these levels by some people might be classified at another level by others. The boundaries are artificial, as critical-creative reading activities frequently require several levels of thought.

ANALYSIS

In analysis (one of the three highest levels in the cognitive domain), a complete statement is broken, or separated, into its component parts for individual study. In addition, a student thinking on the analysis level "must be conscious of the intellectual process he is performing and know the rules for reaching a valid and true conclusion."[1] Lower levels of thinking do not require the student to be aware of the precise thought process being used.

The area of *semantics*, as discussed in Chapter 6, belongs at the analysis level. If students are *aware of how words work*—for example, by being aware of multiple denotations, connotations, hyperbole, euphemism, etc.—they are consciously aware of some techniques used for persuasion. Similarly, being able to consciously distinguish between vague and precise use of language and to judge the effectiveness of language are analytical techniques.

Related to the area of persuasion are the following activities:

1. making judgments related to the authenticity of a source of information
2. distinguishing between fact and opinion
3. analyzing propaganda
4. detecting fallacies of reasoning

Each will be explained in the following sections.

Authenticity and/or Choice of a Source of Information

Who is the best person to make an accurate and unbiased statement about a subject? Such a question is a good starting point for judging the authenticity of a source of information. For example, multiple-choice items such as the following might be supplied. The student is to check the source that is *likely* to be the best one from the three supplied.

1. The poem "Grazing Grass" is a modern classic.

    _____a) Jon Robson, poetry editor of *The World in Review*
    _____b) Jim Jonski, gym teacher at Fordheights Secondary School
    _____c) Geraldine Sloan, glamorous actress

2. Switzerland has the highest per capita income of any country in Europe.

    _____a) Elaine Brooks, bank teller
    _____b) Jonathan DeLonge, star basketball player
    _____c) Dr. Alice Kline, professor of economics, Townheights University

3. The human body needs five main classes of nutrients: vitamins, fats, minerals, carbohydrates, proteins.
   _____a) James Greene, business manager of Taco House Restaurants
   _____b) Svelta Smith, director of Slymnastics Spa
   _____c) Ross Jones, high school general science teacher

4. Two negatives do not make a positive in English.
   _____a) Virginia Karbunki, mathematics teacher
   _____b) Marchance Hubbard, high school principal
   _____c) Juanita Duran, English teacher

5. Modern mathematics is on its way out.
   _____a) Jim Brown, high school student
   _____b) Henry Osborne, editor, *Mathematics for Today's Students,* 1945
   _____c) Jerome Slomowicz, chairman of research, USOE

6. This sundae contains only 250 calories.
   _____a) Roberta Fatma, only 15 and already 175 pounds
   _____b) Velma Hodges, home economist
   _____c) Walter Smithsona, soda jerk

Such activities should be used to spur class discussion—to get students *thinking about* the importance of selecting appropriate sources for specific kinds of information. Such an exercise is not meant to be graded, but rather to introduce discussion and possibly debate—to lay the foundations for an analytical task which is, indeed, difficult and, certainly, is not a simple multiple-choice activity.

Such an activity might be further extended by asking such questions as: (1) What makes the person think so? Which evidence seems to support the judgment best? and (2) Why does the person want me to think so? Which person would be least prejudiced by selfish motives? The following exercise exemplified this strategy.

In *part 1* of each question, check the person who is likely to be the best qualified to make the given statement. In *part 2,* check the person who is likely to be least biased by selfish motives. In *part 3,* check the evidence which best supports the judgment.

Astroturf is as safe to use on a football field as is grass.

1. *Who said so?* Which person is best qualified to make this statement?

   _____a) Hugh Jefferson, Patterson High's football coach

_____b) John Harwick, professor of health and physical education at State University

_____c) Gail Johnson, president of the school board

2. *Why does the person want me to believe this?* (From whom did the information come?) Which person seems least biased by selfish motives?

   _____a) Janice Eagleson, owner of Eagleson's Garden Shop

   _____b) Jim Smith, president of Smith's Carpet Store

   _____c) Oscar Henderson, chairman of research for the department of health and physical education at State University

3. *What makes the person think so?* What evidence best supports the judgment?

   _____a) "There were no serious accidents on the astroturf field at State University this year."

   _____b) "A survey of 20 universities—ten using astroturf and ten using grass—showed no significant differences in accident rate or seriousness over the past three years."

   _____c) "Astroturf is as thick as grass, and more regular. It should therefore be as safe as grass to use."

The student must recognize the fact that even so-called authorities often differ in their points of view and judgments. Two Ph.D.'s in reading might differ radically in their recommended approaches to beginning reading instruction, and a third might advocate a third approach. Several biographers might shed altogether different light on the same subject. Well-trained and prominent newscasters may differ in their interpretation of current events. Two textbooks on the same subject may differ radically. Even two medical doctors may recommend different treatments for the same malady.

Therefore, students must be encouraged to compare sources of information on the same subject. They should be encouraged to compare the backgrounds and biases of the authors and to make their own judgments or *withhold judgment* until they have more information.

Teaching Strategies

1. To help students choose the best source, or sources, of information have them *first* fill in from a list at the top of the page the best source to complete each statement. Together with them, check the answers to see with which sources they are unfamiliar. Then show them how to use these sources, e.g.:

almanac	dictionary	encyclopedia	ruler
thermometer	thesaurus	atlas	calendar

   a) To locate the famous ship canals of the world you would refer to a (an) ______________.

b) You would go to a (an) ____________ to find the former Miss America winners.

c) If you want to find when Abraham Lincoln's birthday is celebrated, you would look in a (an) ____________ or a (an) ____________.

d) To find out how the word *kindergarten* originated you would look in a (an) ____________.

e) You would use a (an) ____________ to find how many millimeters there are in a five-dollar bill.

f) To find six synonyms for the word *funny,* you would look in a (an) ____________.

g) If you would like to find out what dates Ash Wednesday and Easter Sunday fell on in 1933, you would refer to a (an) ____________.

h) The name of the largest desert in northern Africa might be located in a (an) ____________ or a (an) ____________.

i) You would use a (an) ____________ to make sure candy is at the right temperature to mold.

2. When studying a topic, ask students to describe people who might present the topic from varying perspectives. Then help them locate reading materials written by such people and compare the points of view. For example, in a book about the Civil War, would it matter who the author was? Would a Northerner present ideas differently from a Southerner? Would a French person's ideas differ? Would you expect a book written in 1865 to differ substantially from one written in 1975?

3. When studying a topic, make available a variety of literary genres. For example, compare the role of the American vice-president as portrayed in the play *Of Thee I Sing* by Cole Porter with news articles, editorials, biographies, and autobiographies about Spiro Agnew, Lyndon Johnson, Richard Nixon, Harry Truman, Nelson Rockefeller, and Walter Mondale as vice-presidents. Or, when studying about courage, compare the impact of certain poems with that of novels, short stories, biographies, etc.

4. Compare the same event as reported in two local newspapers and several school papers (e.g., the last football game played by your school's team). Also compare an event as reported in a local paper, the *New York Times,* the *Christian Science Monitor, Time, Newsweek,* etc.

5. Compare two or more biographies of the same person, or a biography with an autobiography.

6. Compare several advertisements for competing products.

7. Compare Chamber of Commerce materials from several geographical areas.

8. Compare campaign speeches with the carry-through.

9. Compare several editorials about our space program—one advocating the pro point of view, another the con.

10. Compare a textbook discussion of an event in history with a biographical and/or fictional account.
11. Compare television offerings in your community with those in New York City, London, Canadian cities, Mexican cities.

Fact versus Opinion

Students must learn to distinguish between a *statement of fact* and a *statement of opinion.* A statement of fact can be either verified or proved false. A statement of opinion, however, is an expression of personal feeling, and it cannot be objectively proved to be true or false. Opinions may be swayed by emotions or reason. Facts are based on actuality. (Of course, what is considered a fact today may not be considered as such tomorrow.)

The following exercise exemplifies how students might learn to distinguish between fact and opinion.

1. John H. Glenn was born in 1921.
2. John H. Glenn was the first American to orbit the earth in space.
3. John H. Glenn is the greatest of all American astronauts.

Can the date of John H. Glenn's birth be verified? Can it be proved that he was, or was not, the first American to orbit the earth in space? Can it be objectively determined that he is, or is not, the greatest American astronaut?

The first two statements can be proved true or false by consulting official records. However, the third is a matter of judgment, or opinion.

Which of the following are statements of fact (i.e., they can be proved true or false by using objective evidence)? Which are opinions?

__F__ 1. Richard Nixon was born in 1913.

_____ 2. Richard Nixon was the 37th president of the United States.

_____ 3. Richard Nixon promoted more reforms than any other president since F. D. Roosevelt.

_____ 4. Two plus two equals four.

_____ 5. Adding is easier than subtracting.

_____ 6. Seven minus four equals eight. [A statement of fact, though false]

_____ 7. Algebra is less enjoyable than geometry.

_____ 8. Geometry is more useful than algebra.
_____ 9. Trigonometry should be taught in college.
_____ 10. Everyone needs three years of high school mathematics.
_____ 11. Chaucer is the greatest English poet.
_____ 12. Cervantes is the greatest author Spain has ever produced.
_____ 13. *Hamlet* has been produced more often than any other Shakespearean play.
_____ 14. "It is me" is incorrect grammatically.
_____ 15. Water freezes at 32°F.
_____ 16. Water freezes at 32°C. [A statement of fact, though false.]
_____ 17. Babies develop coordination at different rates.
_____ 18. Science is fascinating.
_____ 19. The space an object occupies is known as its volume.
_____ 20. Einstein was the greatest of modern mathematicians.

Teaching Strategies

1. One way of working on fact-opinion is to take statements of one type and convert them to the other type, e.g.:

Opinion	*Fact*
a) It was warm today.	a) It was 85° today.
b) The car was expensive.	b) The car cost $4500.00.
c)	c) We had 10 inches of rain this year.
d) The air is heavily polluted.	d)
e)	e) She has an I.Q. of 125.
f) It'll cost a lot to have your TV repaired.	f)
g)	g) He's 35 years old.
h) He's been mayor for ages.	h)

2. Another technique to use when reading a textbook, magazine, or newspaper article is to underline facts and circle opinions. Then students can be taught where they can verify or prove false the statements of fact. And they can weigh the opinions against others—from their background of experience or additional reading materials. Materials such as the following might be used.

NEW SCARE OVER NEAR MISSES BY JETS*

Just how safe are the air routes over major U.S. cities? In the past year alone, two crashes—one outside Washington's Dulles International Airport, the other at New York's John F. Kennedy International Airport—have taken a toll of 206 lives, and the dangers of midair collisions at the nation's busiest airports become more evident daily.

Much depends upon the alertness and ability of the air-traffic controllers. Says Captain Duell:

"They are a fantastic group. We pilots put our faith in them—we have to. But we also know that this has to be a two-headed system. The pilot has to work and think right along with the controller."

The concept of the pilot as the final authority for the control of his aircraft is the axiom upon which aviation safety is based. The man in the left front seat must accept that responsibility and never look elsewhere for another party to make his decisions.

Absolute command authority is not some chauvinistic notion that finds its roots more in emotional egoism than sound logic.

Shifting control to someone who is not in the left front seat is like asking a manager of a branch switching office to establish corporate policy for AT&T. He doesn't have all the facts in their proper perspective, and his decisions would reflect that.

One controller put it rather bluntly: "Only the controller knows what is going on all over the airport, and you could be holding for any number of reasons, reasons that we do not have to tell you about. Do what you are told and stay off our backs, and you will enjoy flying much more."

* Excerpts, in clockwise order starting from top left, are from *Newsweek*, December 22, 1975, p. 90; *U.S. News and World Report*, December 22, 1975, p. 36; "The Union: Benign and Protective," in *Flying*, October 1975, p. 43; "The Controller," by Richard L. Collins in *Flying*, October 1975, p. 40. "The Issue," by John W. Olcott in *Flying*, October 1975, p. 41.

HARRY TRUMAN— NEW FOLK HERO?*

So turn to a happier figure, Harry Truman. Can anybody doubt that his sudden revival is a deep-seated folk yearning for courage, honesty and direction? Harry Truman was a spunky little cuss, a fox-terrier of a man, who deserves to be remembered with affection and who might well inspire a great nation in time of gloom.

INDEPENDENCE, Mo.

History is smiling on America's 33rd President, Harry S. Truman.

When the late Chief Executive left office in 1953, he was reviled in some quarters. This was the man who fired General of the Army Douglas MacArthur during the height of the Korean War. The President also was attacked in the press for supposedly associating with corrupt politicians.

Everyone's Wild About Harry

Still the Truman mania—like so many aspects of the 1970s—must finally be traced to Watergate. After the fall of Richard Nixon, the memory of a plain-spoken, no-nonsense President was all but irresistible. "In our day," says his daughter, "honesty was taken for granted." These days, Truman's appeal appears strongest among young people who have no personal memory of him.

And yet, some 25 years after leaving office and 2½ years after his death. Harry Truman has assumed the dimensions of a folk hero. Truman buttons bring up to $150 at antique stores. The Truman Library in Independence, Mo., is thronged with visitors. *Plain Speaking,* Merle Miller's account of some salty talk with the 33rd President, has sold 2½ million copies.

Trumania in the '70s

* Excerpts, in clockwise order starting at top left, are from *The New Republic,* October 11, 1975; *U.S. News and World Report,* September 29, 1975; *Time,* June 9, 1975; and *Newsweek,* March 24, 1975.

3. Relate *fact versus opinion* decisions to content area reading; e.g., write F for a statement of fact, O for a statement of opinion:

In English

____*Beowulf* is an example of Anglo-Saxon literature.

____*Beowulf* is the best Anglo-Saxon epic written.

____Most students who are required to turn in outlines of papers they have written write the outlines after they write the papers.

____The authors of the four English composition books used in our school recommend that the outline for a paper should be written before the paper is written.

In social studies

____On the night of December 16, 1773, a band of American colonists dressed as Indians climbed on board Captain Hall's ship and emptied chests of tea overboard.

____What they did there changed the course of history for the good.

____Ben Franklin was better known in his time than both King Frederick the Great of Prussia and Voltaire, the famous French philosopher.

____In 1752, Ben Franklin proved lightning was a kind of electricity.

____The best nation is one formed from people of many nationalities.

____*E pluribus unum* means "from the many, one."

____Jackie Robinson was the first black to play professional baseball.

____If Jackie Robinson had failed to stick it out, probably there would be very few black athletes in America today.

In science

____Light is a form of energy.

____Light is a better form of energy than is sound.

____Neil Armstrong was the first man to walk on the moon.

____Armstrong and Aldrin made the most important discoveries about the moon.

____You can get away from air pollution by leaving the city.

____Harmful ingredients in the air cause pollution.

In mathematics

____Base 10 is the most accurate and easily used numerical system.

____The number 10 became the base of our numerical system because early humans counted on their fingers.

____Multiplication is learned after the addition process.

____The short form of multiplication is easier than the long form.

____The sign $\geq$ means the same as the sign $=$.

____There are three signs used to designate inequality.

4. Take complete paragraphs from books or articles students are reading and have students underline the sentences (or parts of sentences) that are statements of fact and circle those that are statements of opinion, e.g.:

In English

About 250 million people in the world speak English. It is the native tongue of most citizens of the United States, Britain, Canada, Ireland, New Zealand, and Australia. In many other nations, people speak English as a second language, and they speak it almost as well as their native tongue. In the future it is quite likely that most people throughout the world will be able to converse in English.

In social studies

In 1914, World War I broke out in Europe. France, Russia, and Great Britain fought against the "Central Powers" of Europe—Austria, Germany, and Hungary. It was the bloodiest war in all history. Both civilians and soldiers fell like flies before the weapons of modern warfare, including poison gas, land mines, tanks, and machine guns. Most people hoped there would never again be another war and this was termed "the war to end all wars."

In science

Now you can see that it is important to eat the right foods to grow well, feel well, and look well and that no one food will make you a beauty contest winner or a champion athlete. But eating the proper foods each day will help give you good health. To be sure that your diet takes care of your body needs, scientists recommend that you eat foods from each of four groups daily.

In mathematics

The word *geometry* is derived from the Latin *geo* and *metria,* meaning "earth measure." It is surely one of the most interesting and useful fields of mathematics. In its beginning stages in Egypt and Babylonia, geometry was the basic mathematics associated with such practical problems as measuring fields, dikes, and pyramids. Geometry's most important theorem, the Pythagorean, was used by the Babylonians in their land measurements before the Golden Age of Greece.

Propaganda Techniques

Some propaganda techniques can be classified legitimately in the area of figurative, or connotative, language. True, most propaganda techniques involve more than a word—they utilize phrases, sentences, paragraphs, and also illustrations. However, basically the *language* (or illustration) of propaganda is designed to sway, to influence people.

Propaganda can be good or bad. It can serve useful purposes in persuasion. But it can also be tricky: it can fool the naive. Students should be made aware of propaganda techniques so that they are able to evaluate persuasive arguments logically. The following types of propaganda techniques will be explained briefly: bad names, glad names, testimonial, transfer, plain folks, card stacking, and band wagon.

Bad names

Bad names are those expressions whose connotations are unpleasant. The terms are employed to incite hate, and to cause fear, dislike, or distress. It is not difficult to think of many bad name (sad name) expressions. Here are a few:

communist	itchy
lemon	cheap
yellow	skinny
un-American	fat

Glad names

Glad names, on the other hand, are expressions with pleasant connotations. Sometimes called "glittering generalities" or "purr words," glad names are used by advertisers to describe *their* products, though they may use sad names to describe the products of their competitors. Glad names are used by all of us to convince others of our opinions or to sway them to our point of view. Some glad names are:

marvelous	smooth
supercalifragilisticexpealidocious	economical
All-American	slim
glamorous	pleasantly plump
healthful	

Testimonial

A testimonial is a tribute; at its best, an affirmation or declaration of gratitude honestly recommending a person, theory, or thing. Testimonies are given by people who are grateful for their religion, their government, their university, or their favorite sports hero. Our progress in space is a testimony to our society. On the other hand, our racial problems testify to apathy or to negativism in our society, as does pollution.

In advertising, a testimonial is often rendered by a glamorous movie star, a famous athlete, a zesty barking dog or a purring cat, or possibly by a plain folk. In most cases, the testimony is well paid for.

Transfer

In the transfer technique, a highly regarded person, symbol, or concept is somehow related to the idea or product that is "being pushed." Many students "buy" professor's ideas if attached to the idea are the words "research proves . . . ." Or, we buy toothpaste because "dentists endorse it" or because it contains some ingredients that sound very scientific. The eagle or the American flag may be pictured on a dictionary to help increase sales. Or, a picture of a baby or a movie star may attract us to a magazine.

Careful now—not all propaganda is bad! Much is good.

Plain folks

We are all familiar with politicians who kiss babies and parade their families in front of the public. And we have all seen pictures of candidates with holes in the soles of their shoes—a technique that may, however, backfire in time of prosperity. The affluent Stevenson was thus pictured—to play down his intellectual image. A friend of mine, a staunch Democrat, clipped this picture and pasted it to her door with the inscription: "Don't let this happen to you—vote for Ike."

The plain folks technique is gaining popularity in advertising today. Note the increasing number of ads in magazines, newspapers, and on T.V. in which average looking people, rather than the ultraglamorous, appear.

Card stacking

Card stacking is a technique we all use—not just advertisers, politicians, governments, etc. Not at all! What does the child who comes home with a poor report card tell the family? Does the child present both sides fairly? What about the local Chamber of Commerce? And the woman whose favorite plant lost—or won—at the local floral show? What about you when you did not get that raise or that "A"?

The old art of debate forced sides to deliberately card stack. Each side presented only the best of one point of view and the worst of the other point of view. And what do lawyers do in presenting their cases? Card stacking is probably as old as humanity and is with us to stay. But we should be alert to it.

Band wagon

It is the rare person who is not anxious to "be with it," to join the crowd. Nowadays, almost everyone wants to go to college, even those who would benefit more from doing something else. We all pick up the latest slang, use it until we tire of it, and then discard it, as does the rest of our crowd—for the newer slang or jargon.

The constant plea, *everybody's doing it,* should trigger us to serious thought and careful analysis and evaluation. *Is everybody doing it? And do we wish to be one of these anonymous everybodies? Perhaps we should dare to be different.*

Teaching Strategies

1. The most obvious, and perhaps overused, way of analyzing propaganda is to examine *advertisements.* Naturally, they are full of "selling techniques." Certainly, students—even young children—should learn to examine sales pitches on T.V., on billboards, in newspapers, and in magazines. Look for "truth in advertising." Contrast truthful ads with those that abound with "tricks." The following questions should be asked:
   a) Who are the propagandists?
   b) Whom are they serving?
   c) What is their aim in writing on (speaking about) this subject?
   d) To what human interests, desires, emotions do they appeal?
   e) What techniques do they use?
2. Examine *editorials* or *features* in newspapers and *essays.* Can you find evidence of card stacking or of a balance in presenting and weighing all sides of the issue? Are other propaganda techniques used or avoided?

   In science the topics might relate to space travel, ecology, recent discoveries, etc.; *in mathematics,* to the "floating dollar," comparative prices, rise in the cost of living, etc.; *in social studies,* candidates for office, evaluations of the performances of those who hold office, the race problem, etc.; *in English,* to drama critiques, school language programs, book reviews, etc.
3. Compare the reports of the *same sports event* in several newspapers and/or news magazines, especially in the newspapers of two home towns or the two local schools. Is there card stacking? What about bad names, glad names, etc.?
4. Ask students to collect several sets of advertisements and/or articles or excerpts in which propaganda techniques have been used. (Advertisements might be used first, followed by excerpts from discussions related to an issue important in your class.)

Ask students to circle one technique in each ad or excerpt, name it, and then file the clipping in a box with the propaganda technique listed on it. Or, use a bulletin board display, perhaps like the following, with pockets prepared for each technique. They then file their clippings in the appropriate pockets:

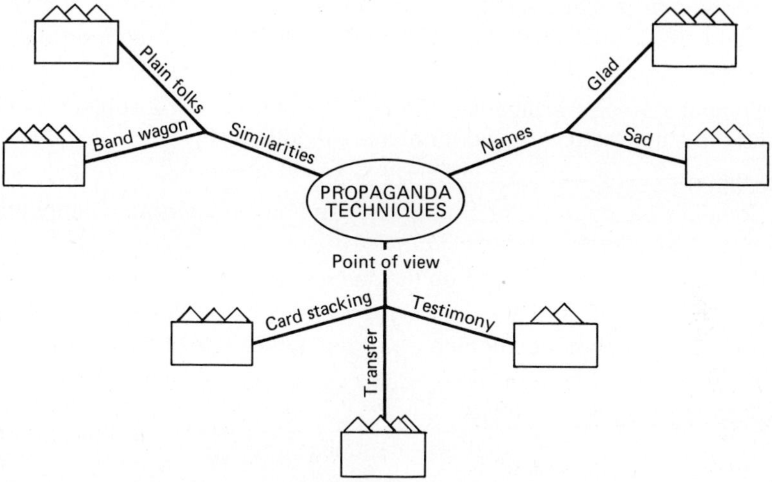

Then, different pockets can be emptied, one at a time, and the circled technique can be read to the whole class. For example, from the *plain folks* pocket might come:

"They liked his image as a 'rags-to-riches' guy. . . ."
"He comes from humble beginnings. . . ."
"I behaved thoughtlessly and stupidly, I'll admit, but I'll make it up. . . ."
"Gerald Ford toasts his own English muffins, enjoys family life, walks the dog. . . ."
"Jimmy Carter carries his own suitcase on the plane. . . ."

From the *band wagon* pocket might come:

"The new picture everyone's rushing to see. . . ."
"The palpable tingle of victory brought the party willingly under Carter's yoke. . . ."
"There was a contagion to the numbers. . . ."
"Everyone is wearing it. . . ."
"More hospitals use ______________ than any other diaper."
"Fifty million Frenchmen can't be wrong. . . ."

From the *card stacking* pocket might come:

"Now the battle of the 'tummy bulge' can be won—with our Waistline Trimmer."

"Vote for ________________. You'll get more and more services from the government."
"Buy ________________ Spray. It eliminates cat odors." (Nothing is said about the fact that it is toxic to cats!)
"Now . . . get real smoking satisfaction. The taste is mild and pleasant."
"Come visit ________________. The water is warm, the waves are vigorous. . . ." (Nothing is said about the polluted water.)
"Enjoy legal grass. Legal grass is legal to smoke."
Etc.

5. Compare a *news* article with an *editorial* on the same subject. Is the news article more factual, the editorial more emotional?
6. Compare a *poem* and a *short story* on the same theme.
7. Compare *biographies* (or a biography and an *autobiography*) about the same person by different authors.
8. Compare several *textbooks* on the same subject.
9. Compare *people* in the public eye. Which use emotional language? Which are more literal in their choice of words? Which card stack?
10. Which of the following expressions would you choose to use if you were describing a friend? an enemy?

    yellow—cautious
    curious—busybody
    colorful—gaudy—flashy
    lies—white lies—fibs
    patriotic—chauvinistic
    janitor—engineer

    Have the class form in random groups and play the "run" game (Chapter 6, p. 102). This time, each group in turn must suggest pairs of words, like the above, and tell which they would use in describing a friend and which they would use in describing an enemy.
11. Write two paragraphs describing the same person, place, product, or event. One paragraph should be slanted favorably; the other, unfavorably. Then write another as factually as possible, presenting both points of view.
12. Compare the impact of the following philosophy with that of modern linguists, especially as it would affect children in a classroom: Henry Higgins (from *My Fair Lady,* i.e., *Pygmalion* by G. B. Shaw): "Why can't the English teach their children how to speak:/ Norwegians learn Norwegian; the Greeks are taught their Greek./ . . . Why can't the English teach their children how to speak?/ This verbal class distinction by now should be antique."

Fallacies of Reasoning

There are eight fallacies of reasoning students should understand. Each will be explained briefly here, and examples will be given.

Mistaken causal relationship

A mistaken causal relationship is the error of assuming that something is the cause of an effect when it is not. Frequently, such a fallacy occurs in relationship to correlation: two factors are found to correlate to a high degree and, therefore, it is assumed that one causes the other. For example:

1. It is well known that most successful people have large vocabularies (success and size of vocabulary correlate). Therefore, many people assume that the large vocabulary caused the success. And, therefore, many schools spend an abundance of time on vocabulary, *per se,* working on vocabulary exercises divorced from the content of the course (vocabulary workbooks, etc.).

   The fact may be that the two factors interact—the more successful people are, the more experiences they have, and the larger their vocabularies are likely to be. Moreover, both success and a large vocabulary may be caused by high intelligence, insatiable curiosity, and drive. These may be the real causes of *both* the success *and* the large vocabulary.
2. Children who know the alphabet before they enter school are likely to be better readers than are children who do not know the alphabet when they enter school (knowledge of the alphabet upon entering school correlates with success in reading). Many school systems assume this means that knowledge of the alphabet, *per se,* causes the success in reading. Their first efforts with children are to teach the alphabet. This is an oversimplification.

   The basic question is *why* did the children know the alphabet. This gives the basic cause for their success in reading. They were both *interested* enough and *intelligent* enough to learn the alphabet. They had good *visual discrimination, auditory discrimination, sequential sense,* and possibly *motor skills.* Finally, *somebody cared* enough to teach them the alphabet. These are the factors that the school should develop, for they are the real causes of success in reading. Knowledge of the alphabet, of course, is one of the basic skills, though not the cause, of success.
3. Chanticleer, the rooster in an old folk tale, got to thinking he was a very important individual because early every morning he crowed—and, behold, the sun came up.

Statistical fallacy

A statistical fallacy is a result of the error of applying the wrong statistics to a situation or of misinterpreting the statistical finding. For example:

1. Graduates of Harvard University earn an average of $30,000 per year, whereas graduates of Wisconsin earn $20,000 per year. True? Possibly! But what *average* was used? Was it the mean, median, or mode?

If several graduates of Harvard are millionaires, possibly because of family background rather than education, and the *mean* average was used, the result is misleading. The *mean,* or arithmetic, average emphasizes extremes, which may be irrelevant for our consideration. The *median* average is the one to use here. Another consideration is that the ratio of men to women is far greater at Harvard than at Wisconsin.

2. A teacher reported that students in his class earned the following grades: 60, 61, 62, 65, 65, 66, 67, 68, 70, 98. The average of these grades is 68.2. He reported that it was discouraging to find that 8 out of 10 students made below-average grades.

   His next-door neighbor reported his pleasure with his students, for 8 out of 10 of his students made above-average grades! The grades in his classroom were: 20, 60, 61, 62, 65, 65, 66, 68, 70. His average was 60.4.

3. Salaries of beginning teachers have skyrocketed. Whereas in 1950, beginning teachers could expect to earn \$2200, and in 1960 they could expect \$4500, today they are likely to receive \$9500. (What about comparative costs of living?)

4. Graphs are frequently used for recording statistical findings. It is possible to construct such graphs in misleading ways. For example:

   a) I am a teacher of a speed-reading course and wish to demonstrate the success of the course. I might use a graph such as this (Fig. 9.1):

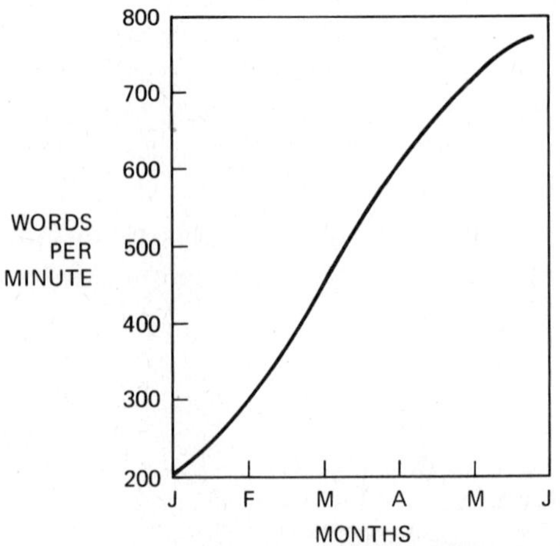

Fig. 9.1 Gain in rate of reading from January to June.

b) I may be the speed-reading teacher's worst enemy (Fig. 9.2):

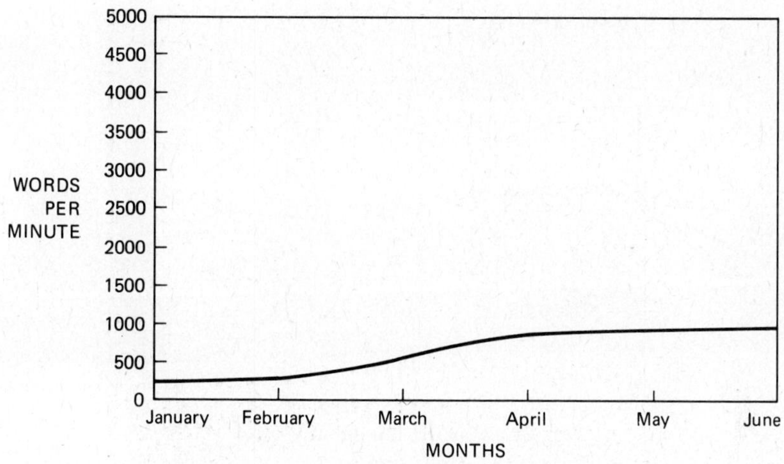

Fig. 9.2 Gain in rate of reading from January to June.

c) Somewhere in between may lie the truth (Fig. 9.3):

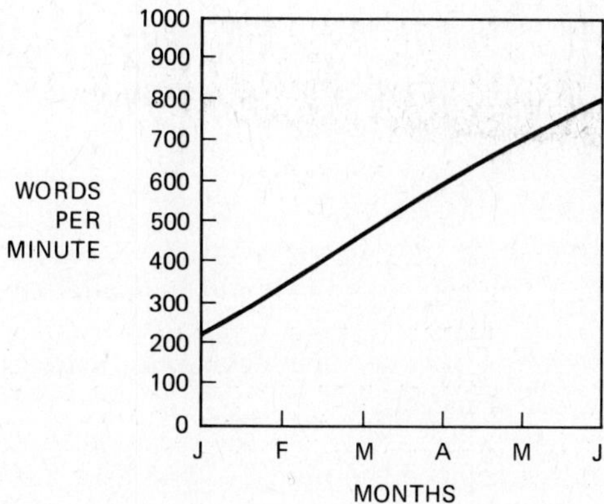

Fig. 9.3 Gain in rate of reading from January to June.

5. Pie graphs must be drawn full-circle to avoid distorted impressions. Note the false visual impression given in Fig. 9.4(a).

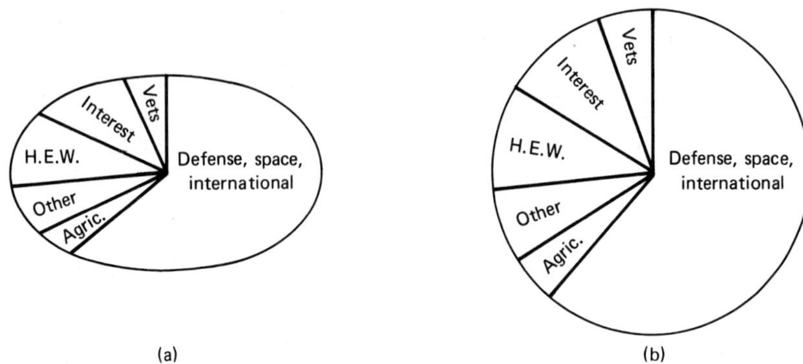

Fig. 9.4 How the tax dollar is spent.

False analogy

An analogy is false when the two things being compared are different in an area essential to the purpose of the analogy. For example:

1. Q: Do two negatives make a positive in English?
   A: Yes! In mathematics, so too in English, two negatives make a positive. Multiply -2×-4, and the result is $+8$, a positive number. It's true in mathematics and true in English. Two negatives make a positive.

   Q: When I say, "I don't have no money," what do you think I mean?
   A: You're loaded!

   Q: And what do I mean when I say, "I'm not unhappy?"
   A: You're blissful.

2. Q: Is motorcycle riding dangerous?
   A: No—the death rate of motorcycle riders is slightly below that of the general public. (The comparison should be made between age-mates.)

3. Since individuals cannot relieve their economic distress by increased expenditure, neither can a nation.

4. "A majority can never replace the man. . . . Just as a hundred fools do not make a wise man, an heroic decision is not likely to come from a hundred cowards." (Adolf Hitler)

Oversimplification

An oversimplification results from failure to examine all possibilities. There frequently is some truth in an oversimplification, but not enough. For example:

1. Maria argued that she was a poor reader because all of her family was poor in reading.
2. "Germany will be either a world power or will not be at all." (Adolf Hitler) (The "either-or" fallacy. Are there just two possibilities?)
3. "Either the husband is boss or the wife is." (The "either-or" fallacy.)
4. "Nothing can have value without being an object of utility. If it be useless, the labor contained in it is useless, cannot be reckoned as labor, and cannot therefore create value." (Karl Marx)

Stereotyping

Stereotyping is the process of overemphasizing characteristics that groups of people or objects are thought to have in common and underemphasizing the uniqueness of individuals. Redheads are ill-tempered; mothers-in-law are bossy; professors are absent-minded; Mexicans are lazy.

Stereotyping includes giving stock, or conventional, responses: the *only* valid way to group grapefruit, bananas, onions, and cucumbers is according to function, i.e., fruits versus vegetables. Nonsense!

The importance of *breaking the stereotype* cannot be overemphasized if we are to progress in our democratic society and if we are to foster creativity. We must value the uniqueness of the individual and see people as multi-faceted. Since creativity is a form of synthesis, dependent on analysis (analysis is breaking apart, synthesis is putting together), if what students see as parts of a whole are stereotypes, nothing unusual will emerge as the parts are put together.

1. What is the most obvious way to group the following people? How many other ways can they be grouped? Do you have to know a great deal about them as individuals to group them in a variety of ways?

Jackie Robinson	Charles Percy	Barbra Streisand
Ethel Waters	Langston Hughes	George Wallace
Rod McKuen	Lee Trevino	Spiro Agnew
Sandy Koufax	Pearl Bailey	Ted Kennedy
James Baldwin	John Connally	Edward Brooke

2. Are women stereotyped professionally in the United States? Figure 9.5 shows the percentage of doctors who are women in various countries.

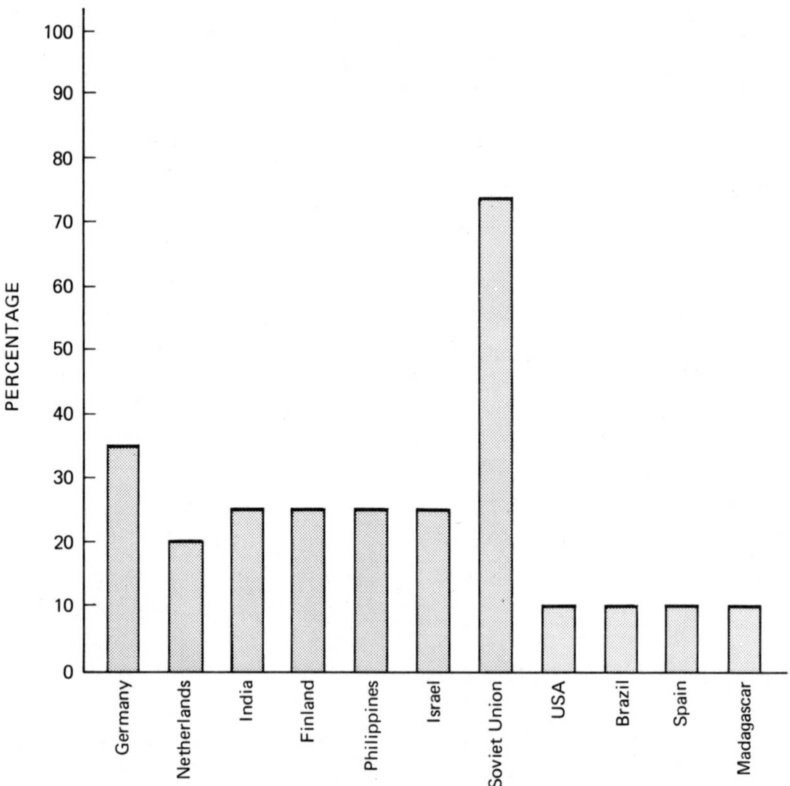

Fig. 9.5 Percentage of doctors who are women in various countries.

3. Select a section of a book or an article which praises the accomplishments of a man. Substitute a feminine name for the man's name and use feminine pronouns instead of masculine. What is the effect? Do the same with an article about a woman by substituting a male name and masculine pronouns for the feminine.

Ignoring the question

Ignoring the question is the act of digressing into an irrelevant argument to make a point. All students and teachers are familiar with this technique. When students do not know the answer to the question asked, they write the answer to another, with the hope of getting some credit. Not only students use the technique, however. For example,

> Q. How can inflation continue while unemployment keeps rising?
> A. The course of inflation is like that of a ship entering a strange harbor, the momentum carries it forward even after the captain has signaled "slow" to the

engine room. Key business indicators alert economists to the changing course of inflation, but like the myriad signal flags on a ship, the general public is not aware of their meaning. The unemployed dock workers are on the pier eagerly waiting to unload the cargo, but the tidal currents make the ship's progress toward port seem painfully slow. The experienced harbormaster knows the ship is coming in, but he is unable to communicate the certainty to those waiting to serve. Mid-course corrections by the captain only cause the uninformed to doubt his ability to bring the ship in successfully.

—*United States Investor*

New Yorker: Next question.[2]

Begging the question

Begging the question relates to *deductive reasoning* and, more formally, to syllogistic reasoning. It is the process of assuming that a generalization, or premise, is true when it has not been proved to be, and when it may, indeed, be false. Any deduction from such a generalization is faulty. For example,

1. Major Premise: I dislike boring subjects.
   *minor premise: Philosophy is boring.
   Conclusion: I dislike philosophy.
2. *MP: I get D's only when I have a lousy teacher.
   mp: I got a D.
   C: I had a lousy teacher.
3. Of course he voted for Nixon. He's a Republican, isn't he?
   *MP: All Republicans voted for Nixon.
   mp: He's a Republican.
   C: He voted for Nixon.
4. Of course she's selfish. She's a woman, isn't she?
   *MP: ________________
   mp: ________________
   C: ________________
5. Evidence was produced that a certain statesman, although he denied that he had done so, had read a certain secret document. The evidence was met with a rebuttal: "How could a man of his character have told an untruth?"
   MP: ________________
   mp: ________________
   C: ________________

---

* true?

6. "Oh . . . ," said the Cat: "We're all mad here. I'm mad. You're mad." "How do you know I'm mad?" said Alice.
   "You must be," said the Cat, "or you wouldn't have come here."
   (*Alice in Wonderland*)

   MP: ____________________

   mp: ____________________

   C: ____________________

7. We have assumed that he is a Communist because he said he is not. We know that Communists are taught to deny party membership.

   MP: ____________________

   mp: ____________________

   C: ____________________

Sometimes both the major premise and the minor premise are true, but a valid conclusion cannot be drawn because the premises lack a balanced relationship or do not supply enough information. For example:

1. MP: All dogs have tails.
   mp: My monkey has a tail.
   C: No conclusion.

2. MP: Everyone in the assembly voted for Costanga.
   mp: My father voted for Costanga.
   C: ____________________

3. MP: If I get an A in this course, I'll be off probation.
   mp: I got a B in the course.
   C: ____________________ (No conclusion. The MP isn't "Only if I get an A"—I may be off probation if I simply pass the course.)

Circular arguments are also related. For example:

1. Capital punishment for murder is justified because it is right to put to death those who have committed murder.
2. In a debate Jerome asserted that some of his opponent's facts are not true, and he challenged him to prove them. The opponent, Marcus, replied that facts are facts and cannot be false and that since Jerome himself has called them facts, it is absurd to question their truth.
3. "Analogue . . . is something having analogy to something else."

Hasty generalization

An error in *inductive reasoning*, a hasty generalization is a conclusion drawn with insufficient evidence. It is difficult to conclude that a small sample is typical. At best, it is chancy to generalize from limited evidence. Limited evidence, instead, might lead to a hypothesis which could be further tested. For example:

1. I've been in El Paso for a week, and it has rained every day. There is some reason other than shortage of rain that makes it a desert.
2. Huberto, Walter, and Jim got A's in physics. This indicates that boys are smarter than girls.
3. Seventy percent of our homeroom voted for Nancy for senior president. She'll win!
4. Harry S. Truman, with a broad smile, was pictured in 1948 holding a morning paper whose headlines shouted, "Thomas E. Dewey Elected President."

SYNTHESIS

Synthesis is the act of combining, or unifying, separate elements into a coherent whole. At the simplest level, synthesis is the act of compounding: two items may be put together to form one. For example, we have looked at morphological synthesis:

air + port = airport

car + port = carport

ex + port = export

im + port = import

able + port = portable

Other examples abound. Flour and water can be synthesized to make paste, but the right proportions must be used. In how many ways can two flowerpots be used together? In how many ways can sterling silver and turquoise be used together? One way might be in the making of jewelry, and how many designs are possible? The answer, of course, is that there are sometimes an infinite number of ways of combining just two items!

Inventive chefs use common, ordinary ingredients to synthesize gourmet delights, whereas an uninventive cook, using the same variety of ingredients, may repeat the same menu week after week. Knowledge and availability of an unusual spice or other ingredient may add sparkle to an otherwise mundane menu. And unusual combinations of ingredients found in every kitchen can add glamor. Baked Alaska, for example, is made from ice cream, egg whites, sugar, and a few other ingredients everyone has at home.

Look at the varieties of architecture used in the world today. Each springs from the synthesis of a variety of materials. Frequently, the same materials are used, but in different proportions and combinations.

You might even try to recall the many different kinds of very simple objects you have seen. How many clock designs have you noticed? How many watches? How many chairs? Bookcases? Pillows? Dresses? Each results from a unique synthesis.

But we have been talking about material things. Actually, material objects, except those that are supplied by nature, are the result of human thought objectified. And the thought is a synthesis—the unification of ideas culled from various sources.

Subjective thought, however, is also a synthesis. Conversation, unless it is simple recall from a single source, is based on the synthesis of ideas. Research papers, classroom discussions, examinations, etc., offer an opportunity for encouraging synthesis, though too often they result in simple recall because we as teachers ask for such responses. *The kinds of questions asked, or the kinds of activities engaged in, determine the thought processes that will be used.*

Why not encourage activities requiring synthesis? We cannot do so if we use a single source, however, and if we do not relate to the student and his or her background of experience. We cannot do so if we have decided what the answers are and if unusual responses are not welcome in our classrooms. We cannot do so if we do not allow students to go off on tangents and if we do not allow individualized study and informal sharing of ideas. We cannot do so if we praise responses that agree with ours or if we look with approval on those who "choose" to read what we think they should choose to read. Encouraging synthesis is, indeed, a formidable task. Many of us must reorganize ourselves in order to do it.

A very important point must be made here. If we wish to encourage the objectification of thoughts or objects that are useful in a positive way, we must be alert to discourage an excessive amount of fault-finding at the analysis level and to encourage the search for facets or ideas of a positive nature. Instead of asking only what is wrong, we must also learn to ask *what is right.*

We all know people who get along with a wide variety of individuals because they can see something to admire in each. And we know others who have a limited circle of friends, all of whom fairly well agree with them. We all know people who can read a book or go to a lecture and be happy they did so because they got *one useful idea from it.* And we know those who cannot find the useful idea because they dwell on all the others. Too often, of course, we may fall asleep waiting for that one usable idea. Creative people are possibly those who persist until they find it.

The purpose of this discussion is not to argue that we need not be alert to dangers—fallacies of reasoning, ineptitude, etc. Rather, we must, in addition, look for the positive. Critical reading need not be predominantly negative. If we are to create (synthesize), we must create with something or with some ideas. If we stress fault-finding in analysis, what will our creations be?

There are, of course, two basic kinds of synthesis. From J. P. Guilford we get the terms *convergent production* and *divergent production.*[3] Convergent production results from synthesizing ideas or materials in a typical way. Certain ideas add up to a best answer or generalization, or at least a conventional one. However, these same ideas, possibly plus or minus others, might add up to something quite unusual or unique. This is divergent production.

Some authors consider both convergent and divergent production to be creative acts. Margaret Mead argues that children who synthesize in a way that results in a convergent response have performed a creative (for them) act, though their response does not add to the world's wealth of ideas. Others argue that only divergent production is truly creative, for only divergent production adds variety of concepts, ideas, and/or products.

What kinds of activities encourage synthetic thinking in content area classrooms? Among them are the following:

1. "production of a unique communication"
2. "production of a plan, or proposed set of operations"
3. "derivation of a set of abstract relations."[4]

Let us look at each of these in more detail.

Production of a Unique Communication

A unique communication can be a message on a postcard, an essay, a short story, a poem, a book, etc. As it relates to the teaching of reading, this communication should evolve at least partially from ideas gained through reading. In addition, or instead, the communication itself could serve as reading material for students and/or their classmates.

For the communication to be on the synthesis level for students, it must be the result of their original thought, not simply a form of recall or translation. In addition, students must be able to logically or artistically justify the process and/or the product of their thought.

Some characters in literature are like real people. The author has put them together so that they are believable. After reading a book, we feel we know such personalities. Others are stereotypes—like cardboard. If we know the type, we know what the character will do. Such stereotypes may serve a purpose, even in the best literature, for there can be too many multifaceted (real) people in a story. Yet, the evolution of a "real person" requires synthesis on the part of an author. The description of a stereotype, or cardboard, personality requires recall of obvious dimensions.

Teaching Strategies

In social studies

In a social studies class, a panel discussion could be held with each participant representing a real individual. The participant would have to study this person well—to know the person's philosophy and way of reacting. The participant would have to recall the person's activities and analyze the person's reasons for acting as he or she did. In addition, the participant would have to be able to predict logically how the person might react to a timely issue.

1. Individual writers of the American Constitution might discuss their feelings about the Civil War.
2. Writers of the Monroe Doctrine might discuss their judgment of our involvement in the World Wars, Korea, and/or Vietnam.
3. Several senators, representatives, governors, the president, and/or vice-president might discuss a current issue.
4. A hippie or a drug addict might be impersonated and tell how he or she feels about a particular issue or living condition. Several might interact—a hippie and a nonhippie, for example.
5. A black might be impersonated by a white and a white by a black. They might converse about civil rights, etc.
6. A boy might pretend he is a woman looking for a high-level job. And a girl might be the male employer.

In English

Similar panels, or dialogues, could be held in other classes. In literature, several authors might discuss modern poetry. Cervantes might talk with his contemporary, Shakespeare. Or, characters from different plays or stories might interact. This need not be stern stuff; it might be entertaining.

> The other night she was seen on television as plain—if that is possible—Jane Eyre opposite George C. Scott's Heathcliff.
>
> —Kevin Thomas in the *Los Angles Times.*
>
> *New Yorker:* It's possible, but it's sort of complicated.[5]

In science

Madame Curie might tell what she thinks of the atom bomb. And the geographer, Columbus, might talk to Balboa. Two modern biologists or chemists might debate an issue. An executive of a detergent firm might talk with the president of National Wildlife or with Albert Schweitzer.

In mathematics

Einstein might talk with Frank Lloyd Wright about triangles or arches. A modern mathematician might carry on a dialogue with an old-fashioned arithmetic teacher. A topologist might demonstrate figures in space and talk with Euclid about the beginnings of geometry.

In all subjects, students might write short research papers debating an issue, answering a question, or predicting what will happen in the future. The important thing is that the answer should not be copied.

Teachers must be skilled in assigning topics that require original thought. This may mean that they relate the topic to a local or a hypothetical situation. Or, it may mean that they limit the input; for example, they may briefly present several positions or ideas and require the synthesis within the hour. There are, of course, obvious advantages and disadvantages to such an assignment.

Production of a Plan of Operation

Can a student plan the steps that should have been followed (post-mortem) or that might be followed in carrying out an activity? Post-mortems are sometimes simple, as in playing bridge. After the cards have been played, it is easy to say what should have been done and to find logical arguments for such action. While one is playing, it is not as simple.

Answering the question "How should we have proceeded?" in a situation in which we did poorly may help us act more intelligently in the future. Teachers ask themselves this question when a student does not work up to capacity level. Even though the student may no longer be in the teacher's class, answering such a question may help the teacher when working with other students.

Students who fail a course might be encouraged to design a plan of action for passing it the next time. And they might follow their plan!

Representatives in the student council might draw up a plan for a schoolwide election. Or, they might design a course of action to follow in requesting more "student power."

Students can be involved in proposing courses to be offered by the school. And they can be involved in choosing topics to be covered in old and new courses. Students, individually or in groups, might design their own reading lists and be allowed to alter them as they progress.

Students might formulate hypotheses and test them in the school and community. Some students work on projects to raise money for scholarships or for camperships or for band trips, etc. Students might suggest plans that they think would be successful. Girl Scouts sell cookies, some groups wash cars, others clean up neighborhoods. Surely other plans might work—and possibly better. The ideas may come from the youngsters.

Plans should also be related to course work. Students plan how they will solve mathematics problems. It should not all be done for them. They plan how they will find information they need to answer different kinds of questions. They hypothesize whether or not an act of the president will work.

Derivation of a Set of Abstract Relations

The derivation of the Pythagorean theorem—that the square of the hypotenuse is equal to the sum of the squares of the legs—is an example of what is meant by the derivation of a set of abstract relations in mathematics. Here, the thought process is inductive.

On the other hand, a set of abstract relations may also be deduced. Such is the case when a student, without prompts, proves a geometric theorem. Usually, the thought process in such a case will be *convergent* production; i.e., the student will follow a conventional path in proving the theorem.

It is important to note here that the *set of relationships* may be arrived at inductively or deductively. If they are arrived at *inductively*, individual items or subpoints are used in formulating a generalization. Many items may be observed, and where similarities are found, the items are grouped together. Unlike items are in another group. In divergent production, items will be grouped in unique, but in logically or artistically justifiable, ways.

In *deductive* reasoning, the generalization, or principle, is given, and the set of items, or subpoints, must be derived. At the synthesis level, this means that the subpoints must be related to one another. In divergent production, a unique item may be identified or a unique relationship may be found to exist.

Teaching Strategies

The following kinds of activities are appropriate.

In science

1. Derive a set of scientific principles that will tell us what the best date is for our next trip to the moon or for a class fieldtrip.
2. Derive a set of scientific principles that will tell us in our hometown how deep each of a variety of seeds should be planted.
3. Derive a set of scientific principles that will tell us the best place in a given region to build a paper mill (etc.).
4. Describe at least ten different scientific characteristics by which a diverse group of people might be grouped, e.g., race, blood type, etc.
5. Describe at least ten different scientific characteristics by which a diverse group of animals might be grouped, e.g., nutrition, locomotion, reproduction, locale, etc.

In mathematics

1. Derive a set of mathematical principles that will tell us how to compute the cost of living in a specific geographical area.
2. Derive a set of mathematical principles that will tell us how much it costs the average student to attend your school.
3. Derive a set of mathematical principles that will tell us how to compute the comparative cost of driving a new Cadillac and a new Volkswagen to the second nearest city in the closest state to you.
4. Describe at least ten different mathematical characteristics by which diverse geometric objects can be classified, e.g., plane, solid, angular, curved.
5. Describe at least ten different mathematical characteristics by which numbers can be classified, e.g., odd, even, negative, positive, whole, fractions, etc.

In English

1. Derive a set of linguistic principles that will tell us how to formulate phonics generalizations or what appropriate English is in a specific situation.
2. Derive a set of literary principles that will tell us if a new book is likely to become a classic.
3. Derive a set of literary principles that will tell us if the author of an article uses the card-stacking technique and if so, if it is a legitimate use of the technique.
4. Describe at least ten different linguistic characteristics by which a diverse group of words can be classified, e.g., parts of speech, signal words, two syllables, one syllable, containing vowel pairs, words with connotations, etc.
5. Describe at least ten different literary characteristics by which a diverse group of literary pieces can be classified, e.g., American, British, French, poetry, prose, modern, about people, about nature, etc.

In social studies

1. Derive a set of economic principles that will tell us where people with certain jobs or professions are likely to live in your community.
2. Derive a set of ethnic principles that will tell us where certain groups of people are likely to live in your community.
3. Derive a set of principles that will tell what new products should be produced in your community.
4. Describe at least ten different sociological characteristics by which a racially diverse group of people may be classified, e.g., education, language, religion, sports, hobbies, homes, etc.
5. Describe at least ten different cultural characteristics by which we can classify ancient civilizations, e.g., language, tools, artifacts, clothing, dwellings, religion, etc.

EVALUATION

The highest level of the cognitive domain is evaluation. The common meaning of the term "evaluation" differs from its use in this chapter. Students who "evaluate" frequently do so by recalling what someone else has said. They know a book is a classic because it is on all the lists. They know a Broadway play is mediocre because they read the review in *Time* or *Newsweek*. They know the President's new policy will not work because the newscaster said so, and they can parrot the reasons. This is not what we mean here by evaluation.

Our definition of evaluation includes two steps, both of which must be performed by the students themselves. First, *they must set up standards* against which they will judge the value of an idea, or complex of ideas, or an object. Second, *they must judge the "goodness of fit"* between the standards and whatever it is that is being evaluated.

Sometimes, there is a gradation in the evaluation system. Teachers, for example, set up standards against which they judge the quality of a student's work. These standards are frequently complex and include such factors as objective cognitive judgments (from tests, etc.), subjective cognitive judgments (from essays, class discussions, etc.), affective involvement of the student (from class observations, etc.), effort, and improvement, etc. Students are judged against such criteria and a grade results: A, B, C, D, or F, and possibly a summary comment is made.

Those charged with hiring personnel in a large company also set up standards against which they judge candidates for positions. Some people are hired, and others are not. Some start at excellent salaries, whereas others get the minimum. So, too, candidates for a position decide what the job must offer for them to accept it. The consideration frequently includes location, salary, working conditions, possibility for promotion, etc. Candidates, then, compare the job description with the criteria they have set up and take the job that offers the "best fit."

So, too, some students enter college as "honors" students. Others enter in the regular program. Others enter on probation. Some can enter one university, college, or school but not another. The "goodness of fit" factor is operating in all of these situations.

What is required of students if they are to think evaluatively is that *they* set up the criterion and then judge against it for goodness of fit. Although discussed here as the highest level of the cognitive domain, such evaluation activities also occur at the analysis and synthesis levels.

In setting up such criteria, students must recognize certain principles. One is that there are some *universal truths* against which ideas may be evaluated. That is, there are some factors that every thinking person accepts as true or valuable. It is difficult to give an example of such truths. They might be facts that are observable, e.g., the earth spins on an axis, in some climates certain vegetation flourishes and others do not, the air gets thinner as we ascend a mountain, etc.

Few, if any, values are universal. *Values relate to particular cultures* and subcultures. Certain mores, strange to us, make sense to others. Shirley MacLaine, for example, explains in *Don't Fall Off The Mountain* that in some countries tact is more important than truth, and the worst sin one can commit is to cause a person to lose face. Margaret Mead explains that in some cultures a woman must bear a child to be considered marriageable. Even in our society, the value of an object or idea frequently relates to an age group or to a socio-economic stratum.

Another consideration relates to *individual taste*. Some objects or ideas are of value to one person but not to another. My house might be great for me, but if I had ten children it might be too small, in the wrong location, and too fancy. A Rolls-Royce might be the only car for the Queen of England, but for her husband, a snappy Porsche is better. For some students, direct instruction in improving their rate of reading may be extremely valuable. For others, it would be the worst thing. One book might be the ideal one for one child, but dull for another.

Thus, when standards are being formulated, students must keep in mind the *purpose* of their evaluation. Is it to judge against universal truths? Is it to judge according to a special culture or subculture? Is it to judge according to an individual's tastes or needs?[6] Each will require a different set of standards.

Following is an edict which came from the office of General Douglas MacArthur at the end of World War II. It contains criteria set up by the Allies against which all newscasting and newspaper reports originating in Japan would be judged during the initial period of the Allied occupation. If there was the slightest deviation, the right of the offending station or paper to broadcast or publish was suspended. This memorandum exemplifies a real-life situation in which standards were carefully formulated for the purpose of evaluation in order to protect the Allies.

OFFICE OF THE SUPREME COMMANDER FOR
THE ALLIED POWERS

19 September 1945

AG 000.73 (18 Sept. 45) CI
Memorandum for: Imperial Japanese Government
Through: Central Liaison Office, Tokyo
Subject: Press Code for Japan

1. News must adhere strictly to the truth.
2. Nothing shall be printed which might, directly or by inference, disturb the public tranquillity.
3. There shall be no false or destructive criticism of the Allied Powers.

4. There shall be no destructive criticism of the Allied Forces of Occupation and nothing which might invite mistrust or resentment of those troops.

5. There shall be no mention or discussion of Allied troop movements unless such movements have been officially released.

6. News stories must be factually written and completely devoid of editorial opinion.

7. News stories shall not be colored to conform with any propaganda line.

8. Minor details of a news story must not be overemphasized to stress or develop any propaganda line.

9. No news story shall be distorted by the omission of pertinent facts or details.

10. In the make-up of the newspaper no news story shall be given undue prominence for the purpose of establishing or developing any propaganda line.

For the Supreme Commander

HAROLD FAIR,
Lt. Colonel, A.G.D.
Assist. Adjutant General*

Teaching Strategies

Following are some examples of evaluation activities that might be used in content area subjects:

In science

1. Assume that you are an industrialist in your community and have been accused of allowing your industry to pollute the air or water, etc. Prepare a set of criteria by which you could attempt to justify your action.
2. Assume that you are a private citizen suffering from industrial pollution. Determine a set of criteria by which you could attempt to justify the suspension of the industry's permit to carry on business.
3. Set up three important criteria against which you might evaluate the relative worth to you of each experiment in the laboratory manual. Judge against the criteria, and number in order of importance the ten most valuable experiments.
4. Set up five criteria that could be used in evaluating the importance of specific vitamins to the health of the human body. Judge the importance of each vitamin in relationship to the criteria, and tell which are necessary for human consumption and the quantity that is necessary.
5. Imagine that you are in charge of the scientific branch of the U.S. space program. If the astronauts could bring back only 80 pounds of materials from their first trip to Mars, tell what would get first, second, third, fourth, and fifth priority—and why.

* William J. Coughlin. *Conquered Press: The MacArthur Era in Japanese Journalism.* Palo Alto, Calif.: Pacific Books, 1952, pp. 149–150. Reprinted by permission.

In mathematics

1. You are in charge of awarding a Pulitzer Peace Prize to the most outstanding mathematician in the world during the past decade. Set up criteria against which you would judge contributions of all candidates. Name five candidates, and list them in order according to their worthiness to receive the prize.
2. You have decided to author a book on biographies of great mathematicians of all times. You can include only 12, however. Tell what criteria you would use to judge whether or not a mathematician should be included. Name, in order of importance, the 12 you would select.
3. Set up criteria—including cognitive and affective—against which you would judge the comparative worth of modern mathematics and traditional mathematics programs.
4. Set up criteria against which you could judge the relative worth of the metric and other systems. Tell which system the U.S. should officially adopt for the future.

In social studies

1. Set up five criteria against which you can judge whether or not the ecology program in your community is making satisfactory progress. State the relative strengths and weaknesses of your community's program, and make three recommendations for immediate action, and three for near-future action.
2. Set up four criteria that could be used to justify polygamy (either polyandry or polygyny). Set up four that could be used to justify marriage for life. Set up four that could be used to justify serial monogamy.
3. Set up criteria that could be used to justify capital punishment. Set up criteria that could be used to invalidate capital punishment. Weigh them. Which do you favor? Why?
4. Set up criteria to help you determine when you should and should not obey orders. Are yours the same as those of your classmates? Why might they be different?

In English

1. Set up eight criteria against which you could judge which one of five plays should be next year's senior class play at your school. List in order the best three to present. Compare these with your classmates' choices.
2. You can select 100 paperback books for your classroom library. Set up criteria that will enable you to judge the 100 best books to buy. Write the list.
3. A local radio station has offered to give your class 20 minutes of time once a month for four months. Your students are to read poems during this time. Have students set up criteria to enable them to select the poems for each program. List the poems that would be read on each program.

4. A new Broadway play is to premier in your town, and one of your students is to serve as the critic for your local paper. He or she is to be selected in competition with other students in your class. Tell how the choice will be made.
5. Along with your class, set up criteria for assigning a grade to a composition. After the students have written their next theme, have each paper graded by three different students. Compare grades.

SUMMARY

Critical-creative reading and thinking are defined in this chapter as requiring the skills of *analysis, synthesis,* and *evaluation.* Such cognitive abilities require readers or thinkers to reason using techniques of formal logic or at least to be consciously aware of the thought processes they are using.

Analysis requires the examination of parts of the whole. Common analytical procedures in reading involve knowledge of semantics and persuasive techniques, including propaganda, judging the authenticity of a source of information, differentiating among facts, opinions, and values, and recognizing fallacies of reasoning. Although it is important to be aware of both ineptitude and danger, analytical activities should often stress the positive.

Synthesis is the act of combining, or unifying, elements into a coherent whole. Compounding is a simple form of synthesis. Useful synthetic activities involve the production of a unique communication, production of a plan of operation, and derivation of a set of abstract relations—inductively or deductively. Synthesis at times involves *convergent production*; at other times, *divergent production.*

Evaluation requires the *establishment of standards* and also a judgment as to the *goodness of fit* of the idea or object being evaluated in relationship to the standards. It is necessary for the evaluator to keep in mind the fact that there are three principles governing evaluation: (1) some ideas may be judged against *universal truths,* (2) some must be judged as they relate to *values of a particular culture or subculture,* and (3) some are judged as they relate to *individual taste.* Each requires the recognition of different types of criteria against which the goodness-of-fit test is made.

NOTES

1 Norris M. Sanders. *Classroom Questions—What Kinds?* New York: Harper and Row, 1966, p. 98.

2 *The New Yorker,* March 6, 1971, p. 69.

3 J. P. Guilford. "Frontiers in Thinking That Teachers Should Know About." *The Reading Teacher,* **23** (February 1960): 176.

4 Benjamin Bloom, *et al. Taxonomy of Educational Objectives—Handbook I: The Cognitive Domain.* New York: David McKay, 1956, pp. 168–172.

5 *The New Yorker,* June 12, 1971, p. 95.

6 Norris M. Sanders, *op. cit.,* pp. 144–146.

SUGGESTED ACTIVITIES

1. Name five different types of analysis level activities.
2. Pick two different types of analytic activities and design an exercise or activity for each in your content area.
3. Describe two instances when convergent synthesis is preferable to divergent synthesis, and two instances when divergent synthesis is more desirable.
4. Design a five- to ten-minute microteach to introduce one aspect of synthesis in your content area. Video-tape it for self-evaluation.
5. Name two necessary characteristics of evaluation level activities.
6. Give two examples of each of the following: (a) a universal truth, (b) a value that relates to a particular culture or subculture, (c) a consideration that relates to individual taste.
7. Design a set of criteria against which you could evaluate the worth of an idea, article, or book in your content area.
8. Design a microteach in which you would explain to students how they might: (a) select ideas from a variety of sources, (b) synthesize these ideas into a meaningful whole, and (c) evaluate the worth of the synthesis.
9. Compare the relative value of the seven levels of activities in the cognitive domain in your content area. Which level is most important, least important? Are all important? Why?
10. Discuss with your classmates the relative amounts of affective involvement students are likely to expend when they are working on literal level activities with the amounts of affective involvement expended when they are working on higher level cognitive activities. Which activities do you prefer? Why?

REFERENCES FOR FURTHER READING

Altick, Richard. *Preface to Critical Reading.* New York: Holt, Rinehart and Winston, 1969.

Bartley, W. W. III. "Lewis Carroll's Lost Book on Logic." *Scientific American.* **227,** No. 1 (July 1972): 39–46.

Beery, Althea, Thomas C. Barrett, and William Powell (eds.). *Elementary Reading Instruction: Selected Materials.* Boston: Allyn and Bacon, 1969, Chapter 7.

Cheney, Arnold B. *Teaching Reading Skills through the Newspaper.* Newark, Delaware: International Reading Association, 1971.

Degler, Lois Sauer. "Using the Newspaper to Develop Reading Comprehension Skills," *Journal of Reading,* **21,** No. 4 (1978): 339–342.

Dieterich, Daniel. *Teaching about Doublespeak.* Urbana, Illinois: National Council of Teachers of English, 1976.

Eller, William and Judith G. Wolf. *Critical Reading: a Broader View* (an annotated bibliography). Newark, Delaware: International Reading Association, 1969.

Hafner, Lawrence E. (ed.). *Improving Reading in Middle and Secondary Schools, Selected Readings,* 2d ed. New York: Macmillan, 1974, Sections 4 and 10.

Henry, George H. *Teaching Reading as Concept Development.* Newark, Delaware: International Reading Association, 1974.

Karlin, Robert. *Teaching Reading in High School.* Indianapolis: Bobbs-Merrill, 1964, Chapter 6.

Karlin, Robert (ed.). *Teaching Reading in High School—Selected Articles.* Indianapolis: Bobbs-Merrill, 1969.

King, Martha, Bernice Ellinger, and Willavene Wolf (eds.). *Critical Reading.* Philadelphia: Lippincott, 1967.

Massialas, Byron and Jack Zevin. *Creative Encounters in the Classroom.* New York: John Wiley, 1967.

Olson, Arthur V. and Wilber S. Ames (eds.). *Teaching Reading Skills in Secondary Schools.* Scranton, Pa.: International Textbook Co., 1970.

Sanders, Norris M. *Classroom Questions—What Kinds?* New York: Harper & Row, 1966, Chapters 6, 7, 8, 9.

Spache, George. *Toward Better Reading.* Champaign, Ill.: Garrard, 1963, Chapters 5 and 16.

Torrance, E. Paul and R. E. Myers. *Creative Learning and Teaching.* New York: Dodd, Mead, 1970.

Zimet, Sara Goodman. *Print and Prejudice.* London, England: Hodder and Stoughton Educational, 1976.

Chapter 10

IMPROVING SPEED OF COMPRE-HENSION IN READING

What is the fastest rate at which anyone can read?

How can we teach students to skim effectively?

How important is flexibility of reading rate? How can we help students improve their speed of comprehension?

What mechanical devices can be used to improve a student's rate of reading? How useful are they?

INTRODUCTION

Most young people and adults wish they could read more rapidly than they do—and most could with the proper training. The *average* high school senior reads about 250 words per minute. With training, he or she could probably read about 500 words per minute. The question is, *should* this student read 500 words per minute. And if so, when?

A favorite joke of mine is, I am sure, pure fiction. During one of the famous Nixon-Kennedy debates, Nixon purportedly asked Kennedy if he had read a certain book. Kennedy, known for his ability to read rapidly, responded, "Of course I've read it, but at 1200 words per minute. . . . So you'll have to tell me what it's about."

Phenomenal reading rates have been reported, and sometimes it seems that a major restricting factor in speed reading is the inability to turn the pages fast enough.

VARIOUS RATES

Scanning and Skimming

It is, of course, possible to *skim* at rapid rates, and we can *scan* even more rapidly. *Scanning* is used when we wish to quickly locate a word, fact, date, name, etc. Our eyes glance rapidly over a page, or pages, to pick out the one detail we are seeking. We may scan an index, table of contents, page of a telephone book, or dictionary. We may quickly scan to find a section or idea we wish to read more carefully. To be able to scan is very useful, and students should be taught this skill.

Skimming is more thorough than scanning, for in skimming, we quickly view an entire section of printed material. We skim to get an overall view of the material—to summarize it, to grasp the sequence of events, to write an outline, to get the author's point of view, to see if the topics included suggest complete coverage or card stacking, and to see if we wish to read the material more thoroughly.

We may skim material in order to *preview* it so that we begin our reading with a framework, an "advanced organizer." Or we may skim in *review*, as an aid toward reconstructing what we have read.

Teaching Strategies

When textbook or other expository reading is done, the teacher should encourage students to skim both in preview and review. Students can be taught to skim and to see the value of skimming in a variety of ways. For example:

1. Have students open their textbooks to the beginning of a chapter. Together, read the title. Ask them to formulate a purpose or purposes for reading. Together, read the main headings of the chapter and the summary. Ask them to help you write an outline of the chapter on the board.
2. Have students open their textbooks to the beginning of a chapter. Tell them they will have three (or five) minutes to preview the title, formulate a purpose or purposes for reading, and grasp the main ideas so that they will be able to write an outline or summary. When time is up, have them close their books and then write the title, purposes for reading, and the outline or summary. Either discuss the result or collect the papers and grade them. Repeat this activity often.
3. After students have read a chapter, ask them to review it in a survey fashion, as suggested above. Ask them to write a summary or outline. If they previewed the chapter before reading it, ask them to compare their initial summary or outline with their final one.
4. Have the students preview, as suggested in items 1 and 2. Ask them if there appears to be card stacking. Ask what the author's point of view appears to be.
5. Ask individual students to preview an article they are considering reading. After doing this, and before they read the article, ask them if they think it will suit their purposes.
6. Ask students to preview two sets of similar materials—two articles, two essays, two chapters, two books. Ask them to explain the ways in which the materials appear to be alike (which topics do they include in common, what is the point of view, etc.), and in which ways they are different (which topics does only one include, etc.). Ask them which they would prefer to read if they could read only one, and why.
7. Ask students to preview two sets of related but dissimilar materials. Ask them if they know anything about the authors or if they can conclude anything about the authors from the main ideas or the sequence of the ideas that have been presented.

Rates Used for Complete Coverage of Material

How fast is it possible to *read?* When is it desirable to read at a very rapid rate? Is it ever preferable to read at slower rates? If so, when? These are important questions to consider. Let us begin with the first question. How fast is it possible to *read?* To answer this question, it is necessary to consider two basic concepts. One relates to the mechanics of reading; the other, to the ability of the reader to assimilate ideas.

The mechanics of reading

How do people's eyes move when they are reading? Do they move smoothly, as when they watch a bird in flight or an airplane come in for a landing? Or do they start, stop, start, stop, start, stop, etc?

Ask a friend to face you while reading a book. Watch how the eyes move. Then have the friend watch your eyes. Or, try the peep-hole test: cut a hole in the middle of a sheet of paper on which there is writing, and peep through the hole as the friend reads. Another possibility is that you use a mirror to watch the eyes.

Do the eyes move smoothly? If they do, your friend is not reading! As a matter of fact, words are being read only when the eyes are stopped. When the eyes are stopped, or fixed, on a word, a part of a word, or a phrase, then, and only then, is the reader taking in the visual image. Then the eyes move on to another word or phrase, and there is another fixation, during which time the reader again takes in the visual image. And then the eyes move on again to another word or phrase.

In continuous reading, *the fixation may last as briefly as one-sixth of a second,* and probably much longer. The reader's *eye-span* includes the number of letters or words that can be read during one fixation. George Spache states that an eye-span in continuous reading can be no wider than the length of *three words.* Thus, in one-sixth of a second, the fastest reader can read three words. After reading the three words, the reader's eyes must move on to the next phrase. This eye movement, called a *saccadic sweep,* takes the best reader about 1/30 of a second. Then the reader is ready to read another three words, etc.

So the total amount of time it takes to read three words and move on to the next phrase is $1/6 + 1/30$ second, or 6/30 (1/5) of a second. Therefore, in one second, speedy readers can read 15 words, and in one minute they can read 900 words.[1] They will read fewer words if lines are not composed of a number of words exactly divisible by three, for they then must make another fixation for the extra word or two.

Figure 10.1 shows this pattern of eye movements. At the present time, at least, there appears to be an upper limit in reading speed of about 800–900 words per minute, dictated by the mechanics of reading.

The student's assimilative ability

However, yet unanswered is the question of the upper limit which is set by an individual's ability (or desire) to assimilate ideas. Too many people neglect to seriously consider this factor when discussing speed of reading or attempting to help students increase their speed of reading. Frequently, these people are unaware of, or ignore, the fact that *eye movements are symptoms* of the mental processes that the reader uses while reading. That is, poor eye movements

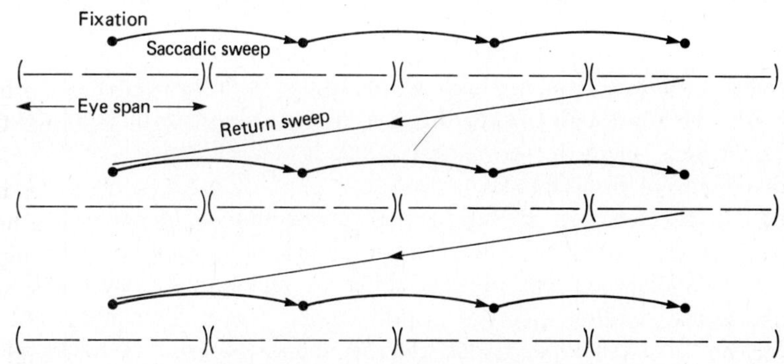

Fig. 10.1 Eye movements in reading.

usually are not the *cause* of slow reading but, instead, they are the *effect,* or *symptom,* of some malady, restricting force, or even mental set.

> Jane was an excellent student in high school—a math major who studied everything thoroughly. She enjoyed poetry, essays, the classics. Everything she read she pondered. She could tell you everything the author of the history book said, and she could (and would) react to it and critically analyze it. But there was one thing she never did unless forced to, and that was read fiction and biography. She was moved to tears if asked to give a book report on such a book because she *hated* reading such books.
>
> Have you ever heard this story before? I can't believe it's that rare. It is a real story. And it wasn't until Jane took her first Education course in reading in graduate school that she learned about how to teach students to vary their rates of reading, and she taught herself. One thing she had to learn was that it is sometimes unnecessary, or even undesirable, to remember *everything* in a book. In a month and a half, she taught herself to read fiction at a rate at which she could enjoy it. And she began devouring the books she had missed—about one a day.
>
> Some students have the opposite problem. They read *everything* rapidly. They must learn to slow down when reading math and science.

It does not make sense to assume that all ideas can, or should, be assimilated at the same rate. Some ideas are more difficult to understand than are others. Some must be understood thoroughly, whereas others need be understood only in general ways. This suggests that students should use different rates of reading for various types of materials and/or when reading for different purposes. Despite the fact that we have for years given lip-service to this idea, the accumulated evidence suggests that most students, in fact, do not vary their rates of reading. Moreover, there is some evidence that suggests that they can be taught to use flexible rates.[2]

The presence of some factors might inhibit a student from reading as rapidly as desirable. Among them are: poor near-point visual acuity, poor visual fusion, poor vocabulary and word attack skills, excessive attention to details, lack of interest in the reading material, inadequate background of information which relates to the material, and low intelligence. (See Chapter 1 for a discussion of these factors.)

There is little point in stressing rate if one or more of the inhibiting factors is present. If the student's vision is poor, a correction can be made in most cases. If vocabulary or word attack skills are inadequate, these skills must be built. If the reading material is dull to the reader, in some cases other material can be substituted. If not, interest should be built. A background of information also can be built. Perhaps nothing can be done about intelligence. It would, of course, be folly to expect a student with a low I.Q. to read as rapidly as one with a high I.Q—all else being equal.

Flexibility of rate

Flexibility of rate is the keynote to reading success. Some things should be read slowly, others rapidly, and others at a moderate rate. There is no point in reading something too rapidly for proper ingestion and digestion of the ideas. Nor is there good reason for reading anything so slowly that the train of thought is lost.

The *difficulty of the material* (for the reader) and the reader's *purpose for reading* it should determine the rate used. Speed in itself is neither a virtue nor detriment; neither is a slow rate, in itself, a virtue or detriment.

Worthy of consideration is evidence from empirical data that individuals usually read at a constant rate from one grade level to another grade level of material if rate is computed by using either a syllable or letter count, rather than a word count. People read a greater number of words per minute in easy materials than in difficult materials, but word *length* in easy material is shorter than is word length in more difficult material. For a more thorough discussion of this idea and others related to "rauding," see sources listed in note three at the end of this chapter.[3]

The rate must be appropriate to the reader, the material, and the reader's purpose. Poetry might be read over and over. It might be read orally. To compute the words per minute makes little sense. Poetry should be pondered. It has its own rate. Rushing through it makes as much sense as rushing through a symphony.

But when we lose ourselves in a novel or textbook, rate might be a virtue. When we live vicariously, we forget we are reading words or phrases. Ideas come through "loud and clear" as we flash through (at less than 900 w.p.m.). We are in orbit, and our fastest rate comes in handy when we are reading for escape or when we are reading something we already know quite a lot about. No point in dawdling!

Other rates come in handy, too. Sometimes a sentence must be read over and over before it makes sense to the reader. It is not always bad to regress. At other times, a steady moderate rate is best.

When should a student read at fast, medium, and slow rates? Table 10.1 might serve as a guideline.

Table 10.1 Guide to determining proper reading rate

Rate	Difficulty of material	Purpose for reading
fast	independent level	to get general idea, main points, for pure enjoyment, especially of plot, escape
	instructional level	to thoroughly preview, get main headings, main ideas, sequence, to review
medium	independent level	to read to remember sequence for later recall, to appreciate style of writing, for greater depth of understanding than would be possible at a faster rate
	instructional level	to note important details, to formulate main ideas, to interpret, to classify
slow	independent level	to mull over ideas, to absorb and analyze thoughts, to anticipate uses for ideas, to promote tangential thinking
	instructional level	to examine thoroughly, to analyze, criticize, react to ideas, evaluate ideas, to solve problems, to follow directions

CLASSROOM ACTIVITIES THAT HELP BUILD SPEED OF COMPREHENSION

In many cases, a teacher can help students improve their speed of comprehension. First, students must be made aware of the fact that fast reading is not necessarily poor reading. The teacher might explain that --- we --- do --- not --- think --- in --- single --- words. We think --- in phrases --- or in sentences. Why not read in phrases?

Students who read one word at a time will have read 27 different ideas by the time they finish a 27-word sentence. They may forget what the beginning is about by the time they reach the end. If they read in three-word phrases, they will read only nine ideas. (This is an oversimplification, of course, but the point is nonetheless valid.)

Also, if they read too slowly for their ability, their minds will wander. They will think about next weekend, or last weekend, while their eyes pass over the words. They will not get much out of their reading. If they read at the optimal rate, they will be challenged, and their minds will not wander. *After* they finish their reading, they can think about next weekend.

Teaching Strategies

The following techniques should prove helpful in improving speed of comprehension:

1. When easy and interesting materials are being used, students should be timed periodically when reading them. Questions to be answered should be of a general nature—main idea, sequence, summary, etc.

   Students should compute their rates of reading. To find the words per minute, students are instructed to divide the time it took them to read the passage (time is expressed in minutes and fractions thereof) into the total number of words in the passage. For example, a student who reads a 1000-word passage in 3 minutes 30 seconds would divide 3.5 into 1000 to get the words-per-minute count:

   $$\begin{array}{r} 286 \text{ words/minute} \\ 3.5\overline{)\;1000.0} \end{array}$$

   Students should chart their rates in a graph. Emphasizing improvement is important.

2. *The content area teacher* should teach students to *survey a chapter* before they read it. Thus, they have the framework in mind before they begin to read the complete chapter. Having such an "advanced organizer" facilitates efficient reading.

3. *The content area teacher* should state purposes for reading to direct the students' thoughts. Teachers should teach students to formulate their own purposes also.

4. Exercises designed specifically for improving rate of reading can be used. *Content area passages can be altered slightly* by inserting an irrelevant remark. Below is an example of a type of exercise any imaginative teacher could design. Such an exercise could be given to students about once a week, using ideas from that week's assignments. Probably two or three pages should be used at a time, each one timed individually.

   Directions: Read as rapidly as you can. In each numbered item there is an irrelevant word or phrase. Underline it. When you finish each four-item page, record the last time that was written on the board.*

   1. (English)

   Artistic unity is essential to a good plot. Best writers exercise a rigorous selection: they include nothing that does not advance the central intention of the story nor anything the cat from next door said.

* Most of these examples were written by Iris Morgenstern, graduate student, The University of Texas at El Paso.

2. (Science)

Blood-vessel space is controlled by the changing size of the vascular system. This is accomplished by the contractions, relaxations, and night driving phobias of the smooth muscles in the walls of the arteries and veins.

3. (Art)

The distrust between artist and the public was mutual. To the businessman, an artist was little better than an impostor who demanded ridiculous prices for something that could hardly be called honest work. Among the artists it became a pastime to shock the burghers out of their complacency and butane electrical outlets and to leave them bewildered and bemused.

4. (History)

Turn back the clock of time to the year 1387. Approaching Tabard Inn in the town of Southwark across the river from London is a band of pilgrims. Traveling on eagleback, they will have a long, slow journey to Canterbury, about 65 miles to the southeast.

Time ________

1. (Mathematics)

According to the Pythagorean theorem the square on the hypotenuse is equal to the sum of the squares of the legs. When using this theorem, one must be sure to have a right triangle with shapely legs.

2. (Science)

Starches and sugars are the chief sources of energy for herbivorous and omnivorous animals. Carnivores, however, do not rely on these foods for their primary energy source, but on protein, fats, and iced cannons.

3. (Home Economics)

Cabbage held in cold storage shows no appreciable loss of ascorbic acid for one or two months. Some loss occurs by the third month, however. Cabbages taken from the middle of the clock may be held in the refrigerator for a week without appreciable loss of ascorbic acid.

4. (Home Economics)

Jelly is a product made from fruit juice. An ideal jelly is stiff enough to hold its form when removed from the mold yet sufficiently delicate in texture to quiver and decode a cryptogram. It is transparent and has the characteristic color and flavor of the fruit from which it is made.

Time ________

5. Time students as they underline the words that are the same as the key word. Use content area words.

1) cabinet:	oracle	domain	local	cabinet
2) colony:	tariff	colony	budget	veto
3) repeal:	revenue	ratify	repeal	statute
4) treasury:	treasury	revision	decree	concede
5) impeach:	secede	writ	local	impeach
6) appoint:	regulate	appoint	quorum	senator
.				
.				
.				
20) tariff:	annul	anarchy	budget	tariff

Time ________

6. Time students as they underline a synonym for each key word.

1) adjacent:	bordering	intercepting	equivalent	bisecting
2) symmetry:	secant	balance	common	locus
3) altitude:	radius	degree	height	similar
4) theorem:	tangent	base	coincide	postulate
5) converse:	diagonal	opposite	proof	geometric
6) external:	axiom	outer	polygon	altitude
.				
.				
.				
20) midpoint:	center	degree	radius	perimeter

Time ________

7. Time students as they underline an antonym for each key word.

1) consonant:	vowel	phoneme	morpheme	grapheme
2) debate:	argue	speak	agree	read
3) résumé:	partial statement	complete statement	axiom	synopsis

4) predicate:	adjective	verb	noun	subject
5) prefix:	root	suffix	vowel	noun
.				
.				
.				
20) salutation:	closing	beginning	middle	letter

Time ________

8. Students can use cards or envelopes to cover successive lines of print. They read the lines just before they are covered. The students move their own cards down the page as rapidly as they can force themselves to read.

9. Teachers give the students class time for free reading of interesting material. Students are encouraged to read rapidly.

10. Timed exercises, such as the SRA *Rate Builders* and the McCall-Crabbs *Standard Test Lessons in Reading,* are useful in English and reading classes.[4] For good results, about four or five of these exercises should be used at least once every week.

MECHANICAL DEVICES, OR THE MYSTERIES OF SOME READING CENTERS

There are a number of mechanical devices that have been designed to help students improve their speed of reading. In general, this equipment is expensive, and after summarizing research, Robert Karlin concluded that "It appears that gains in rate of reading can be achieved through programs which include mechanical instruments. . . . It is apparent that instruction which does not favor machines not only can bring about these same gains but also . . . surpass them. Dependence upon expensive equipment to achieve suitable outcomes in reading rates cannot be recommended in view of present knowledge."[5] However, because of their popularity among teachers, some of these devices and their uses will be described here.

There are three types of machines: tachistoscopes, pacers, and film or filmstrip machines. (See references at the end of this chapter for trade names and companies.)

Tachistoscopes

Tachistoscopes, also called flashmeters, are designed to flash a single exposure on a screen at a rapid rate—usually between one second and 1/100 of a second (see Figs. 10.2 and 10.3).

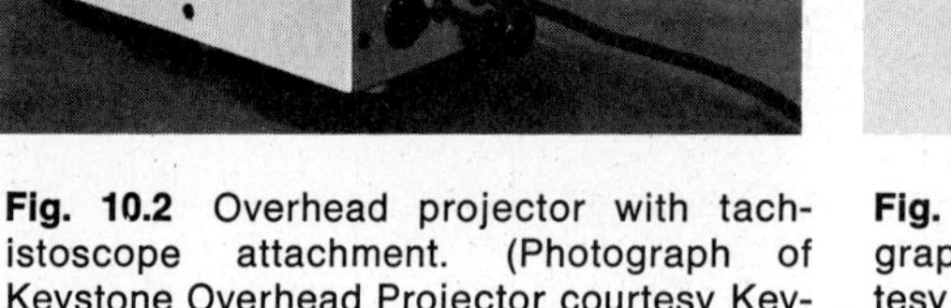

Fig. 10.2 Overhead projector with tachistoscope attachment. (Photograph of Keystone Overhead Projector courtesy Keystone View Company, Meadville, Pa.)

Fig. 10.3 Tach-X Tachistoscope. (Photograph of EDL Tach-X Tachistoscope courtesy Educational Developmental Labs, Huntington, New York.)

Anything might be included in this exposure—from pictures used in visual discrimination for reading readiness to digits to words or phrases. The exposure might look like any of these:

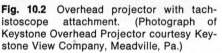

○ △ □ △ ○ ○ ⧖ □

6

7 2 1 5 9 6 4 3 2 7

is

to the zoo

The flowers are wilting.

Groups of students can work together for short periods of time using this machine. The teacher usually flashes the exposures using the 1/100-second setting, and the students record what they have seen. After about eight or ten exposures, students check their papers. Then the teacher flashes another series. About 20 or 30 exposures are seen at one sitting.

The object is to increase the eye span and to minimize the time for each exposure, or fixation. Single words and then two-, three-, or four-word phrases can be flashed. Accompanying these, at the same setting, can be digits—three- or four- or five-digit numbers. Sometimes the teacher starts flashing the tachistoscope at 1/25 of a second and works up to 1/100 of a second.

Hand Tachistoscopes

One application of linguistic theory appropriate to the improvement of phrasing and, therefore, to speed of comprehension is related to the use of signal words, or markers. Markers are of various types: noun markers (a, an, the; one, two, three; these, those, etc.), verb markers (is, am, was, were, has been, etc.), phrase markers (of, to, with, from, etc.), clause markers (since, however, nevertheless, etc.), question markers (who, what, where, when, why, which, *even*?). Such markers can be used as cues that a phrase or clause is beginning. Recognizing such markers will help students read in natural English phrases. This is especially appropriate for use in English or special reading classes.

Chalk-board exercises, flash cards, hand tachistoscopes, or mechanical tachistoscopes can be used in teaching this concept.

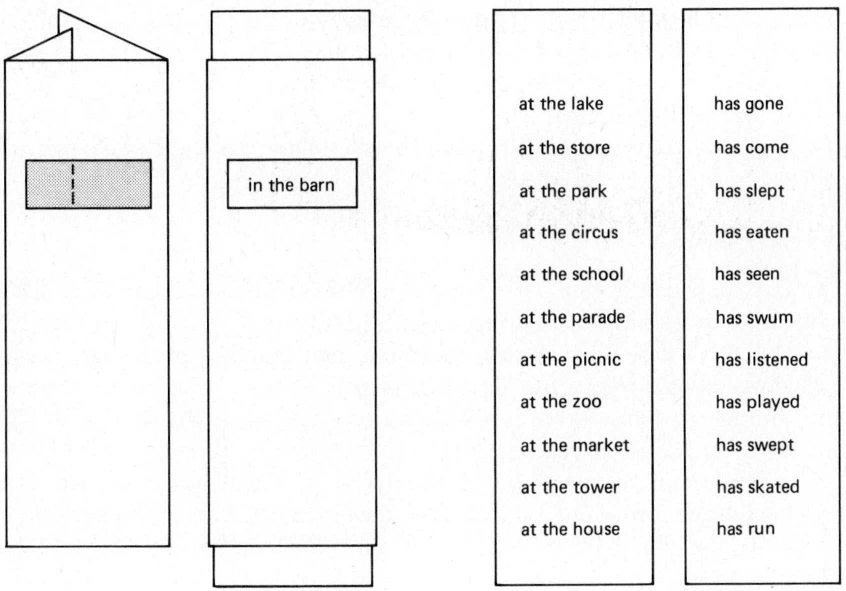

Fig. 10.4 Shadowscope, a pacer. (Photograph courtesy Psychotechnics, Inc., Glenview, Ill.)

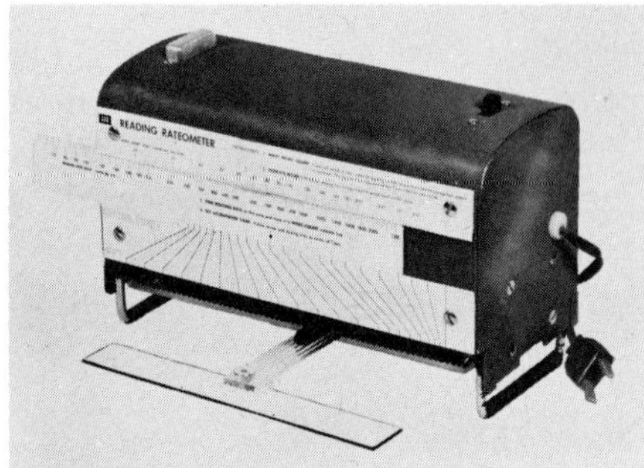

Fig. 10.5 Rateometer, a pacer. (Photograph of AVR Reading Rateometer courtesy Audio-Visual Research, Waseca, Minn.)

Pacers

Pacer devices incorporate a shade, metal bar, or light beam that moves down a page to cover successive lines of print at a rate set by the reader (see Figs. 10.4 and 10.5). The student reads *below* the shade or bar or within the light beam. Almost any type of reading material can be used, including workbooks, textbooks, and paperbacks.

Students are instructed to set the device so that it is comfortable for them, and then to set it slightly faster to push themselves just a bit. As soon as that rate becomes comfortable, they set the machine to go faster, etc. Some reading experts recommend that students alternate pages, reading one page on the machine, the next without it, etc. Or, students might read one on the machine and two or three without it. This might help to eliminate their dependence on the machine for increased rate.

Films and Filmstrips

Films that are paced so that one phrase at a time is exposed (about three flashes per line) are available with reading material at the high school level (see Figs. 10.6 and 10.7). These films can be used on a regular movie projector.

Machines designed to use filmstrips—with phrases exposed in sequence, with a sliding exposure, or with a full-line exposure—are also available. Filmstrips are available at all reading levels, from readiness through college levels. Workbooks accompanying some of these are very well planned and use a survey technique, programed vocabulary development, and statements of purpose before the film is read. In general, the films contain very high-interest reading materials.

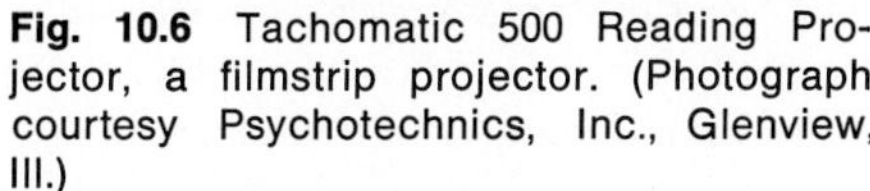

Fig. 10.6 Tachomatic 500 Reading Projector, a filmstrip projector. (Photograph courtesy Psychotechnics, Inc., Glenview, Ill.)

Fig. 10.7 Controlled Reader, a filmstrip projector. (Photograph courtesy Educational Developmental Labs, Huntington, New York)

The purpose of these machines is to increase students' reading rates by improving their left-to-right eye movements and by increasing the eye span. Such films and machines are frequently misused, however. Often, it is the advertising that leads to such misuse. Teachers who have such materials at their disposal should look carefully at their students to decide who might benefit from their use. How many students read at the same rate? And of these, how many will be likely to progress at the same rate? Instead of using such a device in a group situation, it is probably best to have students work individually, possibly in a small booth.

Such machines, if used properly, may be helpful in a reading program. But their purchase should be low on the priority list. Paperbacks and a variety of workbooks are essential to a successful program. The machines are accessories and may add some variety to an already good program. But they are not essential.

Extreme caution should be taken when working on the improvement of reading rate, especially when using mechanical devices. Frequently, use of these machines leads to the treatment of the symptoms rather than the cause of slow reading.

It is true that occasional students may read slowly just because they have not been trained to use a variety of rates. They may be science or mathematics majors and may not have learned to read other materials more rapidly. If they have no comprehension problems except those caused by a plodding rate, machines may help them a great deal. But most students read slowly because of poor word attack skills, inadequate vocabulary, poor comprehension, mind set, etc. Training their eyes to move more rapidly compounds their problem. The cause must be treated before, or along with, the rate improvement program.

SUMMARY

Most students have the potential to read more rapidly without decreasing their comprehension. However, rate in itself is no virtue. The *mechanics of reading* dictate that the fastest rate of reading that anyone can hope to attain is about 800–900 words per minute. However, the *ability of a person to assimilate ideas* often suggests that rates slower than the absolute maximum be used for greater thoroughness of understanding.

Students should be taught to read at various rates—at a slow rate for difficult material they are studying carefully, at a medium rate for material of moderate difficulty, and at a faster rate for easy material or when reading for escape. *The difficulty of the material and the purpose for reading it should determine the rate used at any specific time.* Students should also be taught to skim and scan. Techniques that any classroom teacher can use to help students improve their ability to skim and scan and to read at appropriate rates were suggested.

Mechanical devices—tachistoscopes, pacers, films, and filmstrips—that might be used in special reading classes were also explained. Such machines should be considered as accessories, to be purchased only if a wide variety of paperbacks, workbooks, kits, and other materials is already available in the classroom. On occasion, such machines can be helpful, but there is a real danger of misuse—or using them to treat the symptom rather than the cause of slowness in reading. Of course, whenever we work directly on improving rate, such a possibility exists. When we carefully check comprehension, there is a lesser likelihood of this.

NOTES

1 George D. Spache. "Is This a Breakthrough in Reading?" *The Reading Teacher,* **25** (January 1962): 258–263.

2 Leonard Braam. "Developing and Measuring Flexibility in Reading." *The Reading Teacher,* **26** (January 1963): 247–254.

3 See Ronald P. Carver. "Toward a Theory of Reading Comprehension and Rauding." *Reading Research Quarterly,* **13,** No. 1 (1977–1978): 8–63. Almost the entire issue of this *Reading Research Quarterly* is devoted to Carver's theory and reactions to it.

4 SRA *Rate Builders* from Science Research Associates, Inc., Chicago; McCall-Crabbs *Standard Test Lessons in Reading* from Teachers College Press, Columbia University, New York, 1961.

5 Robert Karlin. "Research in Reading." *Elementary English,* **37** (March 1960): p. 183.

SUGGESTED ACTIVITIES

1. Explain why Spache contends that 900 words per minute is a maximum rate for reading. Compare this rate with claims made by some "speed reading" schools. Explain how you would react to a principal or school board member who was anxious to establish a speed-reading class in your school.
2. Define eye-span, fixation, and saccadic sweep.
3. Design three different exercises or techniques to help students read more efficiently in your content area.
4. Design three exercises for teaching students to skim.
5. Describe the following types of mechanical devices in relation to their uses in a reading program: tachistoscope, pacer, and film and filmstrips. Review the professional literature. Is the purchase of such equipment justifiable? If so, when? If not, why?
6. Give specific examples of instances when each of the various rates (fast, medium, slow, skimming, scanning) is desirable when reading in your content area.
7. Assume that you will have a group of students for a period of one school year. Design a plan for integrating the teaching of the use of efficient rates of reading with the teaching of the content of your course. Precisely when and how will you teach students to scan? Skim? Read rapidly? Read at a medium rate? Read slowly? Make a hypothetical plan, plotting the integration of these skills with the teaching of content over a period of one year.

SUGGESTED ACTIVITY FOR UNIT THREE: DIRECTED READING ACTIVITY

Select a chapter or part of a chapter, a poem, essay, etc., appropriate to your content area. Design a Directed Reading Activity for this section.

1. First and second steps
   a) Show how you would do the first and second steps of the DRA. Give explicit questions and activities.

   b) Share these with your class or with a subgroup in your class. Discuss your ideas (and theirs). Revise your plan if you have gained new insights.

2. Fourth step (third step is silent reading)
   a) Show how you would proceed with step four if you were a classroom teacher. Choose one or the other approach suggested, or a combination. Be sure you can justify your approach in relationship to your reading assignment.
   b) Share your "discussion procedure" with your class or subgroup in the class. Revise your plan if you have gained new insights.

3. Fifth step
   a) Show how the reading activity can be extended. Suggest a variety of reading and/or other possible related activities. Give explicit examples. You may wish to design an Interest Inventory, similar to those given in Chapter 4.
   b) Share your extension activities with your class or subgroup in the class. Ask for further suggestions. Revise your plan if you have gained new insights.

REFERENCES FOR FURTHER READING

Berger, Allen and James D. Peebles (ed.). *Rates of Comprehension* (an annotated bibliography). Newark, Delaware: International Reading Association, 1976.

Bond, Guy L. and Miles Tinker. *Reading Difficulties: Their Diagnosis and Correction.* New York: Appleton-Century-Crofts, 1967, Chapter 15.

Carver, Ronald P. "Toward a Theory of Reading Comprehension and Rauding." *Reading Research Quarterly,* **13,** No. 1 (1977–1978): 8–63.

Ehrlich, Eugene. "Speed Reading Is the Bunk." *The Saturday Evening Post,* June 9, 1962.

Grob, James A. "Reading Rate and Study-Time Demands on Secondary Students." *Journal of Reading,* **14** (January 1970): 285–288, 316.

Hafner, Lawrence E. (ed.). *Improving Reading in Middle and Secondary Schools—Selected Readings,* 2d ed. New York: Macmillan, 1974, Section 9.

Harris, Albert J. and Edward R. Sipay. *How to Increase Reading Ability.* New York: David McKay, 1975, Chapter 19.

Karlin, Robert. "Machines and Reading: A Review of Research." *The Clearing House* (February 1958): 349–352.

Karlin, Robert (ed.). *Teaching Reading in High School—Selected Articles.* Indianapolis: Bobbs-Merrill, 1969, Section 9.

Owsley, Clifford D. "Confessions of the World's Fastest Reader." *Saturday Review,* June 9, 1960.

Schubert, Delwyn and Theodore L. Torgerson (eds.). *Readings in Reading—Practice, Theory, Research.* New York: Thomas Y. Crowell, 1968, Section 5.

Spache, George. *Toward Better Reading.* Champaign, Illinois: Garrard, 1963, Chapters 14 and 15.

Witty, Paul. "Rate of Reading—A Crucial Issue." *Journal of Reading,* **4** (November 1960): 102–106, 154–163.

MECHANICAL DEVICES

Tachistoscopes

1. *EDL Tach-X Tachistoscope*
   Educational Developmental Laboratories, Huntington, New York
   Shutter Speed: 1/100 to 1½ second
   Levels: k–adult

2. *Keystone Standard Tachistoscope*
   Keystone View Company, Meadville, Pennsylvania
   Shutter Speed: 1/100, 1/50, 1/25, 1/10, 1/5, 1/2, 1 second
   Levels: k–adult

3. *Rheem-Califone Percepta-matic Tachistoscope*
   Carlton Films, Beloit, Wisconsin
   Shutter Speed: 1/100 to 1/10 second
   Levels: 1–8 grades

4. *T-ap All-Purpose Tachistoscope Attachment*
   Lafayette Instrument Co., Lafayette, Indiana
   Shutter Speed: 1/100, 1/50, 1/25, 1/10, 1/5, 1/2, 1 second
   Comments: converts any brand of projector to a tachistoscope

5. *SVE Speed-I-O-Scope*
   Society for Visual Education, Inc., Chicago, Illinois
   Shutter Speed: 1/100 to 1 second
   Levels: 1–6 grades

6. *Electro-Tach*
   Lafayette Instrument Co., Lafayette, Indiana
   Shutter Speed: 1/100, 1/50, 1/25, 1/10, 1 second
   Levels: 1–college
   Comments: near-point for individual use

7. *Tachist-O-Viewer, Tachist-O-Flasher*
   Learning Through Seeing, Inc., Sunland, California
   Shutter Speed: 1/40, 1/20, 1/10, 1/5 second
   Levels: 1–12 grades

Comments: near-point for individual use; programs mainly phonics and vocabulary; series available for remedial classes

8. *AVR Eye-Span Trainer*
   Audio-Visual Research, Waseca, Minnesota
   Levels: 4–13 grades
   Comments: manually operated

9. *Phrase Flasher*
   The Reading Laboratories, Inc., New York
   Comments: manually operated; designed for individual use

Pacers

1. *Shadowscope*
   Psychotechnics, Inc., Glenview, Illinois
   Comments: uses a light beam

2. *Prep-Pacer*
   The Reading Laboratories, Inc., New York
   Comments: electrical pacer using disk

3. *AVR Reading Rateometer*
   Audio-Visual Research, Waseca, Minnesota
   Comments: three models: (a) above fourth grade level, (b) elementary and remedial, (c) advanced

4. *SRA Reading Accelerator*
   Science Research Associates, Chicago, Illinois

5. *Reading Pacer*
   Genco Educational Aids, Chicago, Illinois
   Comments: lesson rolls inserted like film in a box camera

Films or Filmstrips

1. *Controlled Reader, Controlled Reader, jr.*
   Educational Developmental Laboratories, Huntington, New York
   Level: k–adult

2. *Tachomatic 500 Reading Projector*
   Psychotechnics, Inc., Glenview, Illinois
   Levels: k–adult

3. *Craig Reader*
   Craig Research Inc., Los Angeles, California

UNIT FOUR

UTILIZING SCHOOL-WIDE RESOURCES AND STAFF

Unit Four focuses on a broader area than the classroom, for it deals with the use of a school library and its resources, and the designing of a school-wide reading program in which all school personnel can participate.

Chapter 11

USING LIBRARY RESOURCES

Co-authored by
I. Jean Stevens

How are most school libraries organized? What are the main divisions of the Dewey decimal system? What kinds of materials are classified in the card catalog? How are these materials listed in the card catalog?

What reference aids are useful for locating periodical literature? books that might be used in content-related reading? audio-visual materials? free or inexpensive materials useful in the classroom?

INTRODUCTION

Although every classroom should contain some supplementary resources, including a book collection, the school library—sometimes known as the instructional materials center, the multimedia center, or the learning resource center, etc.—remains the hub of research activity, the center in which most reference works are located, and the home of most of the school's resource materials. Students must be taught how to use such a resource center effectively, lest they waste invaluable time and effort in attempts to locate materials and ideas—and possibly fail to fully utilize the available materials. In addition, the use of some reference aids may guide them to request the purchase of materials they would like the library to own.

This chapter has been written to help you understand some of the basics of school libraries. The chapter is divided into two major sections. First, some of the basics of school library organization are explained—the Dewey decimal system and the card catalog. Second, basic reference aids frequently found in school libraries are listed and briefly described. Such reference aids include: reference guides to periodical literature (including general and specialized indexes), reference guides for book selection (according to both student interests and content area categories), desk dictionaries, biographical encyclopedias, general encyclopedias, almanacs, atlases, reference guides to periodicals which review audio-visual materials, and guides to free or inexpensive materials. Concluding the chapter is a list of sources which the teacher may wish to consider for use in teaching students how to use a school library.

If students are going to use multiple materials in the courses they study, it is important that such materials be available to them. And it is important that they know where to locate them.

LIBRARY ORGANIZATION

The Dewey Decimal System

Most school libraries in the United States use the Dewey decimal system to classify all of their nonfiction books. The system is simple for children and young people to understand and should be explained, as needed, to students of all ages.

Libraries that use this system normally shelve their books consecutively, beginning with the series numbered 100–199, followed by the 200s, the 300s, and so on. The only books generally omitted from this sequence are the 000–099 books (Generalities, or Reference Works), partly because many of them

---

Co-author of this chapter is Mrs. I. Jean Stevens, Assistant Professor of Curriculum and Instruction, College of Education, The University of Texas at El Paso.

are oversize, and fiction, which is usually located in the most accessible spot in the library.

The major divisions of the new Dewey decimal system are as follows:[1]

000–099: Generalities
100–199: Philosophy and Psychology
200–299: Religion
300–399: The Social Sciences
400–499: Language
500–599: Pure Sciences
600–699: Technology (Applied Sciences)
700–799: The Arts
800–899: Literature
900–999: General History and Geography

Some of the more useful and interesting subdivisions within these major divisions are:

- 000–099: Generalities
  - 010: Bibliographies
  - 020: Library Science
    - 028: Reading Aids
  - 030: Encyclopedias
  - 050: Periodicals and Their Indexes
  - 070: Journalism, Publishing, Newspapers
- 100–199: Philosophy and Psychology
- 200–299: Religion
  - 220: Bible
  - 290: Religions other than Christian
    - 291: Comparative Religion
    - 292: Classical Mythology
    - 293: Germanic Mythology
- 300–399: The Social Sciences
  - 310: Statistics
  - 320: Political Science
  - 330: Economics
  - 340: Law
  - 350: Public Administration
  - 360: Social Pathology and Services
  - 370: Education
  - 380: Commerce
  - 390: Customs
    - 398: Folklore
- 400–499: Language
  - 410: Linguistics
  - 420: English Languages
    - 421: Written and Spoken English
    - 422: English Etymology
    - 423: English Dictionaries
    - 425: English Grammar
    - 426: English Prosody
    - 427: Nonstandard English
    - 428: Standard English Usage
  - 430: Germanic Languages (with the same subdivisions as given under English above)
  - 440: French Languages
  - 450: Italian Languages
  - 460: Spanish Languages
  - 470: Latin Languages
  - 480: Classical Greek
  - 490: Other Languages
- 500–599: Pure Sciences
  - 510: Mathematics
  - 520: Astronomy
  - 530: Physics
  - 540: Chemistry
  - 550: Geology (Earth Sciences)
  - 560: Paleontology
  - 570: Life Sciences (Anthropology, Biology)
  - 580: Botany
  - 590: Zoology
- 600–699 Technology (Applied Sciences)
  - 620: Engineering
  - 630: Agriculture
  - 640: Home Economics
    - 641: Foods
    - 643: Home
    - 646: Sewing

649: Child Care and Home Nursing
650: Business
660: Chemical Technology

700–799: The Arts
- 710: Civil and Landscape Art
- 720: Architecture
- 730: Sculpture
- 740: Drawing and Decorative Arts
- 750: Painting
- 760: Graphic Arts (Prints)
- 770: Photography
- 780: Music
- 790: Recreation and Performing Arts
  - 792: Theater (Stage Presentations)
  - 793: Indoor Games and Parties
  - 796: Outdoor Sports and Games

800–899: Literature
- 810: American Literature in English
  - 811: American Poetry
  - 812: American Drama
  - 813: American Fiction (Classical)
  - 814: American Essays
  - 815: American Speeches
  - 816: American Letters
  - 817: American Satire and Humor
  - 818: American Miscellaneous Writings
- 820: English Literature
  - 821: English Poetry
  - 822: English Drama etc. (as under American Literature)
- 830: German Literature
- 840: French Literature etc. (as under Language 450–490)

900–999: General History and Geography
- 910: General Geography and Travel
  - 912: Atlases
- 920: General Biography and Genealogy
- 930: History of the Ancient World
- 940: History of Europe
  - 942: England
  - 943: Germany
  - 944: France
  - etc.
- 950: History of Asia
- 960: History of Africa
- 970: History of North America
  - 971: Canada
  - 972: Mexico and Middle America
  - 973: United States
- 980: History of South America
- 990: History of Other Areas
  - 999: Extraterrestrial Worlds (New to this edition of Dewey)

Variations:

B, 92, or 921: Biography (Individual)
F . . . . : Fiction
SC . . . . . . : Story Collection

The teacher who knows this system, or who has it accessible for reference, can easily guide students to sections in the library which will be most helpful to them for certain assignments. Certain relationships should become apparent. For example:

in English class:

420: English Languages
820: English Literature
942: English History

in Spanish class:

460: Spanish Languages
860: Spanish Literature
946: Spanish History

in Drama class:		in History (900–999):	
812:	American Drama	942:	English History
822:	English Drama	943:	German History
832:	Germanic Drama	944:	French History
842:	French Drama	Even 510.09	History of Mathematics
852:	Italian Drama	520.9	History of Astronomy
862:	Spanish Drama	530.09	History of Physics

If Sarah, for example, wishes to find books on English drama, she should be told to go to books numbered 822. And Michael, who has an insatiable interest in English history, should be led to look in the 942s. Alyce, who has a budding interest in sculpture, should look for her books in the 730s. And Alberto, a lover of botany, will find his favorite books numbered 580.

More detailed information about the Dewey decimal classification is available through many sources. Most common is the abridged edition of the current *Dewey Decimal Classification and Relative Index* (see note 1 at the end of the chapter). The subject cards found in a card catalog and the subject index in a book catalog also lead the user to the classification number.

The Card Catalog

The card catalog of a school library is an index to the entire collection of resources housed in the library. Besides containing the usual subject, author, and title cards for books in the library, the catalog also contains cards for the school's filmstrips, films, records, tapes, pictures, and information found in vertical and picture files. These cards guide the user to the desired sources of information.

Since there are so many ways of classifying nonprint materials, no attempt is made here to explain any one scheme. However, catalog cards for printed materials all follow a general pattern, as shown in Fig. 11.1. An explanation of the various items is given in Fig. 11.2. For example, variations of the author card are indicated in the "tracings." They are *subject cards* and *title cards*—and possibly joint-author cards and illustrator cards.

Frequently, the librarian types his or her own cards, using an abbreviated form, such as that shown in Fig. 11.3. Abbreviated subject and title cards are shown in Figs. 11.4 and 11.5, respectively.

All such cards are filed alphabetically in the card catalog by the first line. The Dewey decimal system classification number indicates the section of the library in which the book is located. For the book shown in Fig. 11.2, for example, that section is 973—United States history. Within this section, all

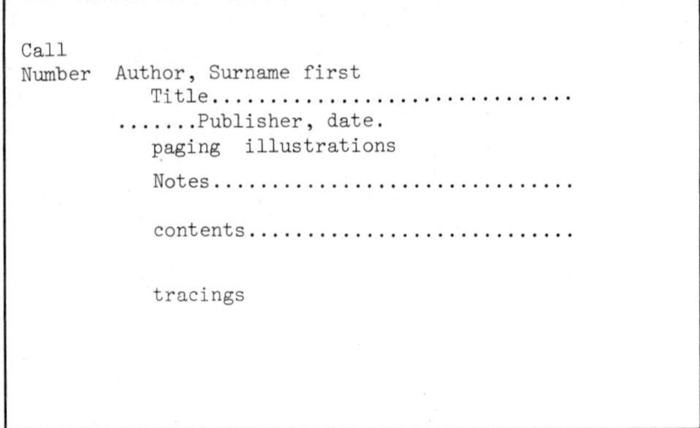

Call
Number Author, Surname first
Title.............................
.......Publisher, date.
paging illustrations
Notes..............................
contents...........................
tracings

Fig. 11.1 Skeleton author card, showing location of items.

books are classified according to the authors' last names. Thus, a book by Borrowman would be found before this book by Clark, and a book by Curti would be found after it. Alphabetizing by author within a Dewey number is the rule, except for individual biography (combined with autobiography), where the subclassification is by subject (the person written about).

Media cards usually are similar to book cards. They are often color-banded, a different color being used for each media: filmstrips, records, tapes, etc.

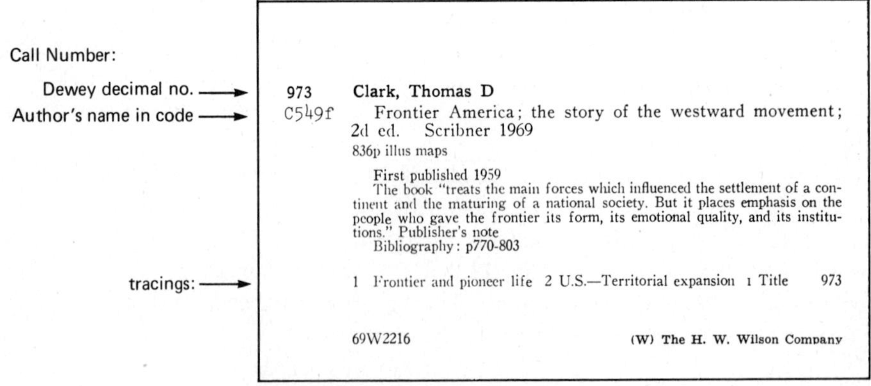

Call Number:
Dewey decimal no.
Author's name in code
tracings:
973 Clark, Thomas D
C549f Frontier America; the story of the westward movement; 2d ed. Scribner 1969
836p illus maps
First published 1959
The book "treats the main forces which influenced the settlement of a continent and the maturing of a national society. But it places emphasis on the people who gave the frontier its form, its emotional quality, and its institutions." Publisher's note
Bibliography: p770-803
1 Frontier and pioneer life 2 U.S.—Territorial expansion I Title 973
69W2216
(W) The H. W. Wilson Company
Arabic numerals indicate subject cards;
Roman numerals indicate title card and
all cards other than subject cards, e.g.,
joint author card, illustrator card, etc.

Fig. 11.2 Completed author card, with explanation of items.

```
973
C549f   Clark, Thomas D
            Frontier America; the story of the
        westward movement.  2d ed.   Scribner,
        1969.
            836p.  illus. maps.


            1. Frontier and pioneer life. 2.
        U.S.-Territorial expansion.  I. Title.
```

Fig. 11.3 Librarian's abbreviated author card.

```
973          FRONTIER AND PIONEER LIFE
C549f   Clark, Thomas D
            Frontier America; the story of the
        westward movement.  2d ed.   Scribner,
        1969.
            836p.  illus. maps.
```

```
973          U.S.-TERRITORIAL EXPANSION
C549f   Clark, Thomas D
            Frontier America; the story of the
        westward movement.  2d ed.   Scribner,
        1969.
            836p.  illus. maps.
```

Fig. 11.4 In abbreviated subject cards, the subject may be typed in either color or capital letters, to distinguish it from a title card.

```
973          Frontier America
C549f    Clark, Thomas D
            Frontier America; the story of the
         westward movement.  2d ed.   Scribner,
         1969.
            836p.  illus. maps.
```

Fig. 11.5 Librarian's abbreviated title card.

REFERENCE AIDS

Reference Guides to Periodical Literature

Although there is a Dewey number for periodicals and their indexes (050) and for newspapers (070), these numbers merely help the reader locate periodicals, newspapers, and indexes, not desired articles within these. The indexes, themselves, must be used for the location of articles.

There are several indexes, or reference guides, to periodical literature which are sometimes found in school libraries. *The Readers' Guide to Periodical Literature* and the *Abridged Readers' Guide* are the most common of such indexes. Others, listed below, may be found in some school libraries and are commonly found in local libraries.

Indexes to general and nontechnical magazines

1. *The Readers' Guide to Periodical Literature,* 1900–. New York: H. W. Wilson.

   An index to the contents of about 160 popular magazines, published twice monthly, September to June, and monthly in July and August. Cumulated volumes, which include all information from a number of issues combined into one alphabet, are available periodically.

   Each magazine article in the 160 magazines indexed is entered under both the author's name and the subject, and sometimes also under the title.

   For teaching the use of *The Readers' Guide to Periodical Literature* (or the *Abridged Readers' Guide*): *How to Use the Reader's Guide to Periodical Literature.* New York: H. W. Wilson, revised edition, 16 pages, 1973. This pamphlet is designed for teaching the use of the *Reader's Guide* to secondary and elementary school students. Class-size sets are free.

2. *The Abridged Readers' Guide to Periodical Literature,* permanent volumes available from 1948–. New York: H. W. Wilson.

   An index to the contents of about 44 magazines of general interest, especially suitable for use in elementary and junior high schools and other small libraries. It uses the same format as the *Reader's Guide* and is published monthly except in June, July, and August. The September issue includes indexing for these summer months. Cumulated volumes are available yearly.

Specialized indexes

1. *Applied Science and Technology Index,* 1958–. New York: H. W. Wilson.

   A subject index to about 225 periodicals in such fields as aeronautics and space science, chemistry, construction, earth science, electricity, engineering, industrial arts, machinery, mathematics, physics, transportation, etc. Published monthly, except July, and with annual cumulations.

2. *Art Index,* 1929–. New York: H. W. Wilson.

   An author and subject index to about 185 periodicals and museum bulletins, domestic and foreign. Includes such subjects as: archaeology, architecture, art history, crafts, fine arts, industrial design, interior decoration, photography and films, landscaping, etc. Published quarterly, with annual cumulations.

3. *Biological and Agricultural Index,* 1964–. New York: H. W. Wilson.

   An index to about 190 periodicals in such fields as: agricultural chemicals, economics, engineering, research, bacteriology, biochemistry, botany, conservation, ecology, forestry, marine biology, nutrition, veterinary medicine, etc. Published monthly, except August, with annual cumulations.

4. *Business Periodicals Index,* 1958–. New York: H. W. Wilson.

   A subject index to about 170 periodicals in such fields as accounting, advertising, automation, banking, communications, finance, investments, insurance, labor, management, taxation, specific businesses, etc. Published monthly, except August, with annual cumulations.

5. *Education Index,* 1929–. New York: H. W. Wilson.

   A subject index to about 240 educational periodicals, yearbooks, monographs, books, proceedings, etc. Published monthly, except July and August, with annual cumulations.

6. *Humanities Index,* 1974–. New York: H. W. Wilson.

   Formerly part of *Social Sciences and Humanities Index,* this is an author and subject index to 260 periodicals in fields of archaeology, dance, drama, folklore, history, music, religion, etc. Published quarterly, with annual cumulations.

7. *Social Sciences Index,* 1974–. New York: H. W. Wilson.

   Formerly part of *Social Sciences and Humanities Index,* this is an author and subject index to 263 periodicals covering information in fields of anthropology, economics, environmental science, geography, law and criminology, medical sciences, political science, psychology, public health, sociology, etc. Published quarterly, with annual cumulations.

Indexes to newspapers

1. *The New York Times Index,* September 1851–. New York: New York Times.

   A subject index to articles that have appeared in the *New York Times.* The brief summaries of these articles and dates of events may help students locate similar articles in local newspapers. It is published semimonthly, with annual cumulations.

2. *The Christian Science Monitor Index,* January 1960–. Boston: Christian Science Publishing Society.

   A subject index to articles that have appeared in the *Christian Science Monitor* issued monthly, with semiannual and annual cumulations. (Although students may not wish to locate an article in *The New York Times* or *The Christian Science Monitor,* finding a reference in one of the above indexes will help place the date for location of an article in a local or other newspaper.)

Selection aids for periodical literature

In addition, there are several sources designed to help an individual or a library select periodicals to be purchased for school use.

1. Dobler, Lavinia and Muriel Fuller. *World Dictionary of Youth Periodicals* (Third Enlarged Edition). New York: Citation Press, 1970.

   A graded and annotated index to periodicals from around the world of interest to young people. American periodicals are classified by subject. Others are classified according to the country that publishes the periodical.

2. Katz, Bill. *Magazines for Libraries,* 2d ed. New York: R. R. Bowker Co., 1972.

   A subject and annotated index to periodicals for school libraries of all levels, including college level. A *Second Edition Supplement,* 1974, lists additional periodicals and includes an *Index* to the 1972 edition.

3. Scott, Marian H. *Periodicals for School Libraries,* rev. ed. Chicago: American Library Association, 1973.

   An alphabetical and annotated index principally to American periodicals suitable for school libraries. It includes a subject index.

Reference Guides for Book Selection

Most school libraries contain reference guides to help in the selection of books according to student interests and content area categories. The use of such reference aids by teachers and students should lead to desired reading materials. In many cases, the use of such guides may lead to the purchase of certain books by the library. Among the most useful of such guides are:

Bibliographies for book selection—classifications by student interests[2]

1. National Council of Teachers of English. *Books for You: A Reading List for Senior High School Students,* rev. ed. New York: Washington Square Press, 1971.

   More than 2000 titles are included, each annotated. The book is divided into broad subject areas of interest to high school students.

2. National Council of Teachers of English. *High Interest—Easy Reading for Junior and Senior High School Reluctant Readers,* 2d ed., New York: Citation Press, 1972.

   Book titles are listed by subject, e.g., adventure (science, sea, historical, mystery, sports, western, etc.), animals (dogs, horses, etc.), family life, teenage adjustment, folk tales, vocational, etc. Each listing is briefly annotated.

3. National Council of Teachers of English. *Your Reading: A Booklist for Junior High Students,* 5th ed. Urbana, Illinois: National Council of Teachers of English, 1975.

   Written to be read and used by young people, this paperback lists over 1500 titles under interest areas such as: On being in love, On being friends, On being free, Of all time, On magic and the supernatural, and many others.

4. New York Public Library. *Books for the Teen Age.* New York: The New York Public Library, annually.

   Books are arranged by subject, with brief annotations on newer titles. It covers a wide range of interest and readability levels.

5. Nicholsen, Margaret. *People in Books.* New York: H. W. Wilson, 1969.

   Individual and collective biographies for all ages are indexed by subject. In many cases, grade-level ranges are suggested.

6. Owen, Betty M. *A Smorgasbord of Books: Titles Junior High Readers Relish.* New York: Citation Press, 1974.

   This is an alphabetical, annotated list of books of "demonstrated appeal" for seventh to ninth graders. It is divided into Teen Fiction, Teen nonfiction, Anthologies and collections, and Adult books.

7. Reid, Virginia M., ed. *Reading Ladders for Human Relations,* 5th ed. Washington, D.C.: American Council on Education, 1972.

   Book titles are listed in four sections, each related to extending sensitivity toward people, their values, and their ways of living: creating a positive self-image, living with others, appreciating different cultures, and coping with change. Each listing is annotated, and books are listed within a section in order of maturity and reading difficulty.

8. Root, Sheldon L., compiler. *Adventuring with Books: 2,400 Titles from PreK–Grade 8,* 2d ed. New York: Citation Press, 1973.

   This is an annotated listing of books, principally published since 1967, of special interest to kindergarteners through eighth graders. The books are listed under 14 broad subject groupings.

9. Spache, George. *Good Reading for Poor Readers,* 9th ed. rev. Champaign, Illinois: Garrard, 1974.

   Books of high interest and low reading level are listed by title according to subject. Each listing is annotated. Subjects such as the following are included: adventure, Africa, animals, aviation, China, folk tales, humorous tales, Mexico, music, mystery, Revolutionary period, etc. A listing of adapted and simplified materials is also included, as well as textbooks, workbooks, games, series books, magazines, newspapers, and book clubs.

10. *The Reader's Adviser,* 12th ed., 3 vols. Winifred F. Courtney, ed. New York: R. R. Bowker Co., 1974, 1977.

    The best books from around the world in almost every field of human knowledge are indexed by subject and annotated. Now available in three volumes:

    Volume 1—The best in American and British fiction, poetry, essays, literary biography, bibliography, and reference (1974).

    Volume 2—The best in American and British drama and world literature in translation (1977).

    Volume 3—The best in the reference literature of the world (1977).

11. Withrow, Dorothy E., Helen B. Carey, Bertha M. Hirzel. *Gateways to Readable Books,* 5th ed. New York: H. W. Wilson, 1975.

    Books for adolescents with reading problems (high interest, low reading level) are arranged by subject. The estimated grade level of difficulty is included, as are annotations. Some of the subject categories are: adventure, animal life, aeronautics and outer space, biography, careers, folk tales and myths, health and safety, history and geography, hobbies, humor, minorities, music and art, poetry and drama, science (various fields), science fiction, sports, transportation and communication, young people here and abroad, etc.

Bibliographies for book selection—classifications by content areas

Mathematics

1. National Council of Teachers of Mathematics. *The Elementary and Junior High School Mathematics Library,* 3d ed. Washington, D.C.: National Council of Teachers of Mathematics, 1973.

   Brief annotations of about 400 titles are organized on three levels: primary grades, intermediate grades, junior high school grades.

2. National Council of Teachers of Mathematics. *The High School Mathematics Library,* 5th ed. Washington, D.C.: National Council of Teachers of Mathematics, 1973.

   Materials are arranged by subject according to mathematical categories. Brief annotations are included.

3. Schaaf, William L., compiler. *A Bibliography of Recreational Mathematics.* Washington, D.C.: National Council of Teachers of Mathematics, 1973.

   Volume 3 updates previous volumes which were published in 1970 and are still available. It includes sources of individual and classroom games, puzzles, etc., arranged by mathematical subjects.

Science

1. American Association for the Advancement of Science. *The AAAS Science Book List,* 3d ed. Washington, D.C.: American Association for the Advancement of Science, 1970.

   Materials are arranged by subject according to the Dewey decimal system. The range of difficulty and interest is from grade 7 to young adult.

2. American Association for the Advancement of Science. *The AAAS Science Book List for Children,* 3d ed. Washington D.C.: AAAS, 1972.

   This contains annotated listings of over 1500 science and mathematics titles for children in grades kindergarten through 6, arranged by subject according to the Dewey decimal system.

Social studies

1. National Council for the Social Studies. *American History Booklist for High*

Schools: A Selection for Supplementary Reading. Washington, D.C.: National Council for the Social Studies, 1969.

Materials are arranged chronologically and are briefly annotated.

2. National Council for the Social Studies. *Reading Guide in Politics and Government* (Bulletin #38). Washington, D.C.: National Council for the Social Studies, 1966.

   Materials about American government are indexed by subject; those about foreign governments are indexed by country. Lengthy annotations are included.

3. National Council for the Social Studies. *World Civilization Booklist: Supplementary Reading for Secondary Schools*. Washington, D.C.: National Council for the Social Studies, 1968.

   Materials are arranged by time periods, and within that, by topics and geographic areas. In the second part of the volume, books are listed alphabetically by author and are annotated. A general estimate of age/maturity level for the materials is given.

4. U.S. Office of Education. *Books Related to the Social Studies in Elementary and Secondary Schools*. Washington, D.C.: U.S. Government Printing Office, 1969.

   Materials are indexed according to geographic areas and are briefly annotated. This is one of a series from the Educational Materials Center. Inexpensive and interesting.

Books and reading—about the adolescent reader

The books listed in this section, in contrast to those listed in the preceding sections, contain more conversation about why certain books are useful, about how to use books with young people, and which books should be given to young people.

1. Burton, Dwight L. *Literature Study in the High School*, 3d ed. New York: Holt, Rinehart and Winston, 1970.

   Designed for English teachers, this book explains how to teach the literature that appeals to young people. Representative books are listed according to genre and are briefly annotated.

2. Carlsen, G. Robert. *Books and the Teen-Age Reader: A Guide for Teachers, Librarians, and Parents*, 2d ed. New York: Harper & Row, 1972. Also in paperback. (Regularly up-dated.)

   A solid source, this book explains the stages of reading development and gives an ample number of examples (classified by genre), each annotated, of books that appeal to teenagers and young adults.

3. Cleary, Florence Damon. *Blueprints for Better Reading: School Programs for Promoting Skill and Interest in Reading,* 2d ed. New York: H. W. Wilson, 1972.

   Designed for both experienced teachers and librarians and those preparing to teach children in classrooms and libraries, this is divided into three parts: Reading Guidance: Foundations and Perspectives; Approaches to Reading Guidance Programs; and Programs for Reading Guidance.

4. Fader, Daniel and Elton McNeil. *Hooked on Books: Program and Proof.* New York: Putnam, 1968. Also in paperback, Berkeley S1508.

   A teaching method that worked with delinquent boys who could read but would not is explained. Illustrative lesson plans are given, and a reading list of 1000 paperbacks of appeal to young people is included.

5. Fader, Daniel, *The Naked Children.* New York: Macmillan, 1971.

   The author tried his program (as explained in *Hooked on Books*) at Garnet-Patterson Junior High School in Washington, D.C., with mixed success. He presents a good case for teaching English in every classroom.

6. Edwards, Margaret. *The Fair Garden and the Swarm of Beasts,* revised and expanded ed. New York: Hawthorne Books, 1974.

   The author describes how librarians can be trained to help young people get the most out of the library. Of special value is "The Tool Shed: A Practical Appendix," which covers principles of book selection, how to give book talks, and a brief reading list for younger adults to mature adult readers.

7. Pilgrim, Geneva Hanna and Mariana McAllister. *Books, Young People and Reading Guidance,* 2d ed. New York: Harper & Row, 1968.

   A strong part of this book is a lengthy section on adolescent needs in which the authors stress the importance of guidance in reading for growth toward maturity and include discussions of books which can be used toward this end.

Desk Dictionaries

Every library and classroom should contain a variety of dictionaries. Usually, the library also will have at least one unabridged dictionary. Among the better abridged dictionaries are the following:

College level

1. *The American Dictionary,* New Revised Edition. New York: Random House, 1968.
2. *The American Heritage Dictionary of the English Language.* Boston: Houghton Mifflin, 1976.
3. *Funk and Wagnalls Standard College Dictionary,* rev. ed. New York: Funk and Wagnalls, 1969.
4. *Random House Dictionary of the English Language.* New York: Random House, 1968.
5. *The Shorter Oxford English Dictionary on Historical Principles.* New York: Oxford University Press, 1973. (2 vols.)
6. *Webster's New Collegiate Dictionary,* 8th ed. Springfield, Massachusetts: G. & C. Merriam Co., 1975.
7. *Webster's New World Dictionary of the American Language.* Cleveland: The World Publishing Co., 1974.

Middle grade and secondary level

1. *Thorndike-Barnhart Advanced Junior Dictionary.* Chicago: Scott, Foresman, 1968.
2. *Thorndike-Barnhart High School Dictionary.* Chicago: Scott, Foresman, 1968.
3. *Thorndike-Barnhart Intermediate Dictionary.* Chicago: Scott, Foresman, 1974. (grades 5-8)
4. *The World Book Dictionary* (2 vols.). Chicago: Field Enterprises Educational Corporation, 1978.

General Reference Materials—Biographies, Encyclopedias, Almanacs, Atlases

Other very important reference materials available in most libraries are volumes containing biographies or references to biographical information; encyclopedias, which contain summary statements about a multitude of topics; almanacs, which contain weather forecasts, tide tables, astronomical information, lists, charts, and tables of various types; and atlases, which are bound collections of maps. A selected listing of such sources of information follows.

Biographies

1. *The Authors Series.* New York: H. W. Wilson Co.

   A series of volumes titled: *American Authors: 1600–1900, British Authors Before 1800, British Authors of the Nineteenth Century, European Authors: 1000–1900, The Junior Book of Authors* (about authors and illustrators of books for children and young people), *More Junior Authors, Third Book of*

Junior Authors, Twentieth Century Authors, First Supplement of Twentieth Century Authors, World Authors: 1950–1970.

Each volume contains biographies of authors (including pictures), a list of each author's principal works, and brief reference lists to critical sources. *The American Authors: 1600–1900* volume also contains sketches of many statesmen, religious leaders, and educators, in addition to authors.

2. *Concise Dictionary of American Biography.* New York: Charles Scribner's Sons, 1964.

   An abridgement of *The Dictionary of American Biography.* It is a ready reference to outstanding Americans no longer living.

3. *Current Biography* (monthly, with annual cumulations). New York: H. W. Wilson.

   Contains biographical sketches on important contemporary people in all fields. Sources of the information included are newspaper and magazine articles, books, and possibly the biographee himself or herself. References cited are included.

4. Nicholsen, Margaret. *People in Books.* New York: H. W. Wilson, 1969. A subject index to individual and collective biographies for all ages. In many cases, grade-level ranges are suggested.

5. *Webster's Biographical Dictionary.* Springfield, Mass.: G. & C. Merriam Co., 1974.

   Contains very brief biographical data about more than 40,000 prominent people in the world, with emphasis given to British and Americans. Pronunciation of names is included.

Encyclopedias

1. *Collier's Encyclopedia* (24 vols.). New York: Crowell-Collier, 1978. *Collier's Encyclopedia Yearbook* is available annually.

   A popular set, with large print.

2. *Compton's Encyclopedia* (26 vols.). Chicago: F. E. Compton, 1978. *Compton Yearbook* and *Yearbook of Science and the Future* are available annually.

   A curriculum-oriented set, with a fact index in each volume.

3. *Encyclopedia Americana* (30 vols.). New York: Encyclopedia Americana Corp., 1978. *Americana Annual* available. A set with many articles on America. It has an Index volume.

4. *Encyclopedia Britannica,* 15th ed. (30 vols.). Chicago: Encyclopedia Bri-

tannica. Inc., 1978. *Britannica Book of the Year* and *Yearbook of Science and the Future* are available annually.

A scholarly set, commonly called "Britannica 3."

5. *Encyclopedia International* (20 vols.). New York: Grolier, 1978. *Yearbook* available.

   An especially good set for junior high school. It is tested for readability.

6. *Merit Students Encyclopedia* (20 vols.). New York: Crowell-Collier Educational Corp., 1978. *Merit Students Yearbook* available.

   A junior and senior high school set which is curriculum oriented.

7. *New Book of Knowledge* (20 vols.). New York: Grolier, 1978. *Book of Knowledge Annual* available.

   A useful set for slow learners in junior and senior high school. Very colorful.

8. *World Book Encyclopedia* (22 vols.). Chicago: Field Enterprises, 1978.

   An accurate children's encyclopedia which can be used by all ages. It has an Index volume.

Almanacs

1. *World Almanac and Book of Facts.* New York: World-Telegram, annually.

   Found in most school libraries—paperback.

2. *Information Please Almanac.* New York: Simon and Schuster, annually.

   Contains information not found in *World Almanac.*

3. *Statesman's Yearbook.* New York: St. Martin's Press, annually.

   Contains information about governments of the world.

Atlases

1. *Britannica Atlas.* Chicago: Encyclopedia Britannica, 1976.

2. *National Geographic Atlas of the World,* 4th ed. Washington, D.C.: National Geographic Society, 1975.

Periodicals with Reviews of Audio-Visual Materials

Among the periodicals containing reviews, discussions, and critiques of audio-visual materials are those listed below. Reading appropriate reviews will help to keep teachers up to date and may guide their recommendations for the purchase of current materials. Students, too, may read such reviews and may use them to decide which of the available materials merit their attention.

1. *Audiovisual Instruction.* (Sept.–June). Anna L. Hyer. National Education Association, Dept. of Audio-visual Instruction, 1201–16th Street N.W., Washington, D.C.

   Educational technology for teachers and media specialists. Includes an index to audiovisual reviews in other publications. Reviews films, records, and new equipment.

2. *The Booklist* (twice monthly, September to July, one issue in August). Chicago: American Library Association.

   Reviews of print and nonprint (16-mm films, filmstrips, recordings, etc.) materials recommended for purchase. For all ages.

3. *Education Screen and Audio-Visual Guide* (monthly). Chicago: Trade Periodicals, Inc.

   Discusses and reviews media in sections on AV in religion, filmstrips, film evaluations, audio, and local production. A "New Materials" section evaluates films and lists them by subject, giving complete information for purchase.

4. *Media and Methods* (September–May). Philadelphia: Media and Methods Institute, North American Publishing Co.

   Emphasizes creative and practical methods to use with media, including paperbacks, in the secondary school classroom.

5. *Previews* (September–May). New York: R. R. Bowker Co. Selection aid for nonprint materials as well as media equipment, including tapes, filmstrips, films, slides, records, prints, kits, games, etc. There are critical reviews under broad subject areas.

6. *School Media Quarterly* (Fall, Winter, Spring, Summer). Chicago: American Library Association.

   This official journal of the American Association of School Librarians includes reviews of book and nonbook media, and bibliographies.

7. *Science Books and Films* (Quarterly: May, September, December, March). Washington, D.C.: American Association for the Advancement of Science.

   Includes critical reviews of films, textbooks, trade books, reference books for preschool through first two years of college in social sciences, pure sciences, mathematics, applied sciences, biographies, etc.

Reference Guides to Free or Inexpensive Materials

Free or inexpensive materials of quality can be used in various ways in the classroom. Such materials can be used to supplement textbooks and library reading, to give wider scope to a program and thus help develop critical-creative-evaluative reading skills, to illustrate reports and projects, and to brighten bulletin boards.

Among the guides to such materials are:

1. *Educators Guide to Free....* Randolph, Wisconsin: Educators Progress Service.

   Individual guides to such media as free films, filmstrips, guidance materials, health and physical education materials, science materials, social studies materials, tapes, curriculum materials, etc.

2. *Free and Inexpensive Learning Materials* (biennially). Nashville, Tennessee: George Peabody College for Teachers.

   A subject index (paralleling units frequently taught in elementary and secondary schools) to maps, posters, pictures, charts, pamphlets, and other free or inexpensive educational aids.

3. *Selected Free Materials for Classroom Teachers.* Belmont, California: Fearon, periodically revised.

   A subject index organized by nationally recognized curriculum topics to free materials useful in the classroom.

4. *Vertical File Index* (September–July). New York: Wilson Publications.

   A subject and title index to selected pamphlets, booklets, leaflets, and mimeographed materials of interest to general libraries.

SUMMARY

This chapter was written in two major divisions. One part was concerned with the organization of a school library; the other part, with various types of reference aids found in many school libraries and some classrooms.

First, the Dewey decimal system was delineated, with main divisions and some major subdivisions given. It is important that the reader note the pattern of this system, for such recognition will make it easily usable. Then, the card catalog was briefly explained, and several kinds of cards—author, subject, and title—were illustrated. The card catalog contains an index of not only all books in the library, but also such other school resources as filmstrips, films, records, tapes, pictures, and information found in vertical files and picture files. The latter types of cards are often color-banded to indicate the specific type of material.

Next, reference aids that many school libraries own were listed and annotated. Guides to periodical literature were given first. The most common of such guides is *The Readers' Guide*, an index to popular magazines, and *The Abridged Readers' Guide*. Specialized indexes, however, are often more valuable if the student is engaged in content area research. Six specialized indexes were mentioned: *Applied Science and Technology Index, Art Index, Biological and Agricultural Index, Business Periodicals Index, Education Index, Social Sciences Index,* and *The Humanities Index.* Although some of these may not be found in a school library, most are found in local libraries, and students should be aware of their existence. Two indexes to newspapers were also included.

Basic reference guides for book selection were also included. Three specific types were mentioned: guides in which classifications are related principally to student interests (probably English and/or humanities), guides in which classifications are related to content area subjects, and guides that discuss the adolescent reader and how to use books with young people. There is a great deal of overlapping among these categories, and most teachers will find all of these guides useful.

Next, popular desk dictionaries and general reference materials (encyclopedic biographies, encyclopedias, almanacs, and atlases) were noted. The concluding sections dealt with periodicals containing reviews of audiovisual materials and guides to free or inexpensive materials.

It is hoped that the classroom teacher will use a variety of materials—multilevel, multiinterest, and multimedia—and that these references will serve as guides to the selection of such materials. Also, it is hoped that students will be made aware of these guides and will use them to find important information.

NOTES

1 Melvil Dewey. *Dewey Decimal Classification and Relative Index.* Lake Placid Club, New York: Forest Press, 1971.

2 See "What Every Professional Reference Library Should Include," a brochure listing timely resources for the location of supplementary reading and audio-visual materials for secondary schools. Urbana, Illinois: National Council of Teachers of English.

SUGGESTED ACTIVITIES

1. List from memory the major divisions of the Dewey decimal system. Give exact numbers of important materials in your content area.
2. Name three types of cards for books commonly found in a card catalog.
3. Using a timely topic in your content area, indicate which *periodical* guide, or guides, would be useful in locating appropriate materials. Using the guides, write a list of at least 12 current articles that relate to the topic.
4. Select a content area topic, or theme, that might interest your students or prospective students. Tell which guides to *book selection* would be appro-

priate for students to use in making book choices. Use these guides to write a list of 12 appropriate books. If readability levels for the books are given, include them.

5. Design a content area assignment in which students are required to use periodical literature, books, general reference works (almanacs, encyclopedias, encyclopedic biographies, atlases, dictionaries), and audiovisual aids. Indicate which aids you and they should use to locate such materials and which general reference works might be used. Finally, include an annotated list of appropriate materials for their use.

REFERENCES ON THE USE OF THE LIBRARY AND REFERENCE MATERIALS

Advanced Library Reference Skills—grades 7–12 (and *Library Reference Skills*—grades 3–6). Chicago: Reference Divisions, Encyclopaedia Britannica Educational Corp. (An example of a program designed for teaching students how to use various reference materials. Overhead transparencies are included, as well as a teacher guide. Student resource books, for the elementary level only.)

Berner, Elsa. *Integrating Library Instruction with Classroom Teaching at Plainview Junior High School.* Chicago: American Library Association, 1958.

Cleary, Florence Damon. *Discovering Books and Libraries.* New York: H. W. Wilson, 1966.

Cook, Margaret. *The New Library Key,* 3d ed. New York: H. W. Wilson, 1975.

Downs, Robert. *How to Do Library Research.* Urbana, Illinois: University of Illinois Press, 1966.

Gates, Jean Kay. *Guide to the Use of Books and Libraries,* 3d ed. New York: McGraw-Hill, 1974.

How to Use the Readers' Guide to Periodical Literature, rev. ed. New York: H. W. Wilson, 1973. Free class-size sets.

Rossoff, Martin. *The Library in High School Teaching,* 2d ed. New York: H. W. Wilson, 1961.

Rossoff, Martin. *Using Your High School Library,* 2d ed. New York: H. W. Wilson, 1964. (For high school students.)

Santa, Beauel and Lois Hardy. *How to Use the Library.* Palo Alto, Calif.: Pacific Books, 1966.

Teaching Reference Skills with the Random House Dictionary. New York: Random House, 1966 (an example of a teacher's guide produced by a publishing company). A student workbook is also available.

Chapter 12

DEVELOPING A SCHOOL-WIDE READING PROGRAM

Who should serve on a coordinating committee to design a school-wide reading program?

What kinds of decisions and recommendations should a coordinating committee make?

What are the major facets in a school-wide reading program? How is each organized, and how does each operate?

INTRODUCTION

If you have been reading carefully and thinking about what you have been reading, you know that all content area teachers must know what is involved in reading instruction and what they can do to help their students learn better through more efficient and enjoyable reading. All teachers who use printed materials must select them on the basis of their appropriateness to the students who will be using them. They must fuse the teaching of reading and study skills with the teaching of content if they are to foster optimal student achievement, development, and interest.

No longer can we justify the contention that "a child learns to read in grades one to three, and thereafter reads to learn" unless we define reading in the narrowest of terms, e.g., simple decoding. We know now that learning to read, like learning to think and enjoy, is a continuous process which does not begin and end at the elementary level, or any level, for that matter. Note, for example, the popularity of adult reading courses, and note that usually these are not remedial in nature. Also note the popularity of study skills and college reading courses for all types of readers—good and bad—in high schools and colleges, even in our best universities.

But content area teachers at all levels have a unique contribution to make. Their ability to make that contribution depends on their ability to recognize the kinds of reading and study skills that are necessary for success in reading and studying and enjoying the materials of their fields. They must be able to look at their materials to see which skills their students must have to read them with understanding. Then they must know how to teach these skills concurrently with their subject areas. Thus, they must know their students in order to know which skills they already have, which skills need reinforcement, and which skills need to be introduced and taught thoroughly.

Modern teachers cannot defend a lock-step position. They must be aware, alert, and alive to all kinds of students, and their approach must be fluid. Although many teachers accept this challenge, some of them do not know how to achieve such goals. Therefore, a school-wide program involving all students and providing for teacher training is essential.

LEADERSHIP IN THE PROGRAM

To make the attainment of goals a reality, certain considerations must be dealt with first. A major concern is identifying a person who is able to spearhead the program. This is followed by the need to identify faculty members and others who are willing and able to serve on a coordinating committee whose tasks are to share ideas, to determine a workable philosophy about reading instruction and ways of implementing this philosophy, to supply feedback to other faculty members, and to set things in motion.

If you are already a teacher, the present course work should help make you an invaluable contributing member to such a committee. If you are a preservice teacher, you should anticipate working on such a committee and seriously consider the kinds of school-wide contributions you will be able to make in the future.

Usually, the principal or another administrator takes the initiative in getting the program on its feet. A major decision an administrator may have to make when initially hiring reading personnel is whether to hire someone to help the teachers or someone to work directly with students. Since we are talking here about developing a school-wide program (which should be designed to help all students), we are talking about hiring a reading consultant, someone capable of promoting staff development rather than someone who will work principally or only with students. This person should have completed the recommended requirements for a reading consultant as set forth by the International Reading Association. The consultant should be especially well versed in developmental reading and in reading and study in the content areas and should be familiar with common remedial reading procedures.

The reading consultant may lay the groundwork for a school-wide program, but definitely needs a coordinating committee to assist in the implementation. This committee should be composed of people with a sincere interest in furthering the goals of reading instruction of various types, but especially in improving such instruction *in all classrooms,* i.e., in all content areas. In addition to the reading consultant, it is desirable to have the following personnel on the coordinating committee:

1. the principal
2. a representative from each department, including nonacademic departments
3. a guidance counselor
4. a school librarian
5. a member of the school board
6. others when needed: the school nurse, director of audiovisual instruction, students, parents, etc.

It might be apropos at this point to suggest that the administrator consider making provisions for a system-wide or school-wide materials sharing and production center. This center should be staffed by personnel who can aid the faculty in selecting and developing appropriate and attractive materials for all classrooms and for specific students in these classrooms. With the increased emphasis today on mainstreaming, it is becoming more and more apparent that teachers need help in adjusting to individual needs and interests of students.

DUTIES OF THE COORDINATING COMMITTEE

When the coordinating committee meets, its members must make the basic decisions that will govern the way the program will function. Such decisions normally include the following:

1. *determining a philosophy of reading.* What is reading? How important is it to build interests? What cognitive skills are important? What word-attack skills are necessary? How important is speed of comprehension?

2. *determining ways of diagnosing students' needs in reading skills.* What standardized tests should be given? What informal techniques should teachers use? How can we best train teachers to interpret these instruments and translate student needs to classroom practice?

3. *deciding what kinds of materials teachers should be encouraged to purchase.* Should multiple textbooks be adopted? Should teachers have classroom libraries? Should teachers be allowed to bring or send their students to the library at any time they wish? What supplementary materials should be made available?

4. *deciding on recommendations for school-wide grouping plans.* Should team teaching be used? Should multigrade classes be offered? Should there be achievement grouping?

5. *determining ways of helping teachers group students and individualize instruction in the classroom.* How can teachers best be taught techniques of grouping students according to skill needs, achievement, interests, social needs and desires, etc? How can teachers be taught to use the unit plan, to individualize instruction, etc?

6. *determining ways of showing teachers how to recognize the need for specific types of skill development and ways of showing them how to satisfy these needs.* How can teachers be taught which skills are important in understanding the materials used by their students? How can teachers be taught to develop these skills?

7. *determining ways of showing teachers the value of the Directed Reading Activity, SQ3R, and building interests, etc.* Can demonstration teaching be done? What else can be done to demonstrate the usefulness of these concepts?

8. *determining how the school-wide reading program can be coordinated and providing for such coordination.* Can a plan be made for developing reading skills, *possibly spirally,* from K–12? Can plans be made for developing interest in reading by using a wide variety of techniques? Can a plan be made relating services rendered in special reading classes with those in content area classes?

9. *determining methodology and materials to be used in evaluating the successes and failures of the program.* Who should test? Should standardized and/or informal techniques be used? What should be evaluated, etc.?

10. *determining policies to be used in in-service training.* Should there be released time? Should the whole faculty meet together at times? In departments at times? Who should be invited to guide in-service training?

AN IDEAL PROGRAM

The coordinating committee should attempt to design an ideal program for the school or the school system. Such a program might be three-faceted, providing for:

1. full participation by content-area teachers in the teaching of reading and study skills and the development of interests as they relate to each course of study
2. the development of units designed for the direct teaching of reading skills and the development of interests in English, or language arts, classes
3. special reading classes.

Let us look briefly at each of these elements.

Participation of Content Area Teachers

Ideally, all content area teachers will do all the right things. They will select materials appropriate to an individual student's reading achievement and, if possible, interests. They will know what skills are necessary for understanding these materials and will teach these skills at appropriate times. They will teach the vocabulary of their fields, use the Directed Reading Activity when they should, and get students involved affectively.

The ideal teacher will be aware that teaching such skills is not teaching an additional *something,* but rather "it is a *way* to teach—a way of teaching which advances not only the student's knowledge of subject matter but his ability to learn other subject matter independently and at will. [The ideal teacher's] aim, then, [would be] to unify knowledge learning and the skills of acquiring knowledge."[1] The ideal teacher is a paragon of virtue—and, amazingly, there are some of these people around.

However, although a growing number of concerned people feel that to certify a school teacher, including a middle grade or secondary school teacher, who has had no education in how to teach reading is indeed indefensible,[2] many teachers have never had a reading course, and they are not sure just what they should be doing. Many of these teachers are doing some reading tasks quite well, though they may not know what they are. (Some teachers think that teaching reading is just teaching word attack skills, etc. They are horribly misinformed!)

A good starting point in designing a school-wide reading program in the content areas is to discuss what is meant by reading. Directly before or after this, a survey form, such as the following, might be checked and analyzed. (The higher the score, the better.) Many teachers will find that they are doing more than they realize.

Survey Form*

Please circle 1, 2, 3, or 4 to indicate the frequency with which you use each of the given practices:

1. seldom or never	2. sometimes
3. most of the time	4. almost always

Practices Related to Reading in the Content Areas

1. I know the reading ability of my students from standardized tests, other evaluative materials, and/or cumulative records.	1	2	3	4
2. I know the reading level of the textbook(s) being used.	1	2	3	4
3. The materials used are suited in difficulty to the reading levels of my students.	1	2	3	4
4. Students are sometimes grouped within my classroom for differentiated instruction.	1	2	3	4
5. The course content is broader in scope than a single textbook.	1	2	3	4
6. Adequate reference materials are available.	1	2	3	4
7. Students are taught to use appropriate reference materials.	1	2	3	4
8. An adequate quantity of related informational books and other materials are available for students who read *below grade level, at grade level,* and *above grade level.*	1	2	3	4
9. I take advantage of opportunities that may arise to encourage students to read recreational as well as informational matter.	1	2	3	4
10. I encourage students through assignments to read widely in related materials.	1	2	3	4
11. At the beginning of the year, adequate time is taken to introduce the text(s) and to discuss how it (they) may be read effectively.	1	2	3	4
12. I am aware of the special vocabulary and concepts introduced in the various units.	1	2	3	4
13. Adequate time is given to vocabulary and concept development.	1	2	3	4
14. I know the special reading skills involved in my subject.	1	2	3	4
15. I teach adequately the special reading skills in my subject.	1	2	3	4

---

* This form is modified from Ira E. Aaron, "Check List of Practices Related to Reading in Content Areas." Used with permission of the author.

16. Provisions are made for checking the extent to which vocabulary, concepts, and other skills are learned, and reteaching is done when needed. 1 2 3 4

17. Time is allowed in class for reading pleasurable materials and for the informal sharing of ideas from these materials. 1 2 3 4

18. Provisions are made for checking the extent to which interests have been developed, and continued attempts are made to give breadth and depth to interests. 1 2 3 4

Following the completion of such a survey form, a brief discussion might be held which focuses on the desirability of implementing such practices and what it means to implement them. Teachers might be encouraged to discuss any special needs they feel they have.

At first, perhaps informally, the reading consultant may serve the faculty best by promoting awareness and sensitivity to the reading needs and interests of students. This might be done when the consultant talks with individual teachers or groups of teachers. Soon to evolve might be faculty awareness of the wide range of reading ability and interests among age-mates, the necessity for using multilevel materials in most classes, and an awareness of at least some of the types of reading skills necessary for reading various kinds of materials.

Teachers might begin to ask questions such as:

1. Why are students so different in reading achievement? in interests?
2. How can I select appropriate materials for my students? Will the school pay for a wide variety of materials? (See note 9, p. 119.)
3. How can I recognize the demands these materials make on the readers? How can I recognize whether the abilities of my students are sufficient in relation to these demands?
4. How can I instruct my students in areas in which they need help? How can I best facilitate their continuing growth, which will help them, in time, to read more difficult materials?
5. How can I recognize, develop, and capitalize upon their interests?

The reading consultant may then promote an awareness that these questions and their answers are multifaceted. To avoid overwhelming teachers, some simple answers might be given and some techniques demonstrated, perhaps in classrooms or in individual or group in-service work. Finally, some kind of master plan might evolve for individual and/or group in-service work, including proposed dates for such work. This plan should remain flexible and should constitute only part of the teacher education program. In addition, a continuing integral part of the work should be unstructured and informal—the day-by-day kind of thing a consultant can do when called upon by a teacher for guidance or assistance. At all times, efforts should be made to recognize exemplary procedures and techniques already used by teachers. These might be publicized to serve as models for other teachers.

Launching a reading program in the content areas may seem a formidable task, yet in reality it need not be so. With the coordinating committee at work and teachers cooperating, certain decisions can be made and implemented. It is, of course, important to be patient. A good reading program must evolve; it is not born in a day or even a year or two. It takes time and effort.

One school-wide program was begun in the following way:[3]

1. Priorities for skill development were established by testing students and analyzing their needs in the school system.
2. In-service work for teaching these skills was scheduled for specific content area departments at specific times. This work was of a practical nature.
3. All content area teachers were encouraged and taught how to use the D.R.A.
4. All content area teachers were shown interesting ways to teach the vocabulary necessary for understanding the ideas of their fields at all times.
5. All content area teachers were shown how to build interests in depth and/or breadth in topics related to their fields at regular times.

A block design was formulated, showing the dates that faculty in each department were to receive in-service work for teaching specific skills. Such a design, showing this program in action, is given in Table 12.1. You might be able to design such a program, or a better one. Why not try?

Other programs have been designed in which all teachers are taught how to teach the same skills at the same time. For example, during the first month of classes in the fall, all teachers might learn about the *preview* technique and/or SQ3R, or a variation of it. In addition, they might learn how to ask appropriate questions or how to state purposes for reading.

At another time they might study the teaching of outlining and/or other sequential translation activities: writing and reading graphs, maps, and charts in their content area materials. Also, they might focus on vocabulary development, building interest in reading, using the library, developing interpretive skills, critical-creative-evaluative skills, etc., in any order preferred. Table 12.2 illustrates such a plan.

Special Units in English Classes

Certain reading skills might be taught regularly as part of the English program.[4] For example, the multidimensional aspects of words might be explained in English class, as well as much of diachronic linguistics, certain aspects of semantics, and the basic skills of outlining. Yet, surely, English itself, like any other content-area subject, offers ample opportunity for the development of

Table 12.1 Design of school-wide reading program: In-service work for teachers

Skill	English	Social Studies	Science	Mathematics	Other (fill in department and month)
SQ3R	November April	September February	October March	January May	
Sequence and main idea	December January	October March	November April	September February	
Interpretations: a) anticipation b) cause-effect c) motives of characters and real people	October (anticipation) February (motives)	December (motives) April (cause-effect)	September (cause-effect) May (anticipation)	November (cause-effect) March (anticipation)	
Following directions: a) literal level; b) critical-creative level	November April	September February	October March	December May	
Analysis level: a) fallacies of reasoning; b) propaganda analysis; c) syllogistic reasoning; d) fact-opinion	October (propaganda) March (fallacies)	December (fallacies) April (propaganda)	September (fact-opinion) February (syllogistic reasoning)	November (syllogistic reasoning) January (fact-opinion)	
Synthesis level: a) unique communication; b) inductive/deductive reasoning	September May	November February	December March	October April	
Interest: emphasis on building interest, *per se*	September May	November February	December March	October April	
Developing flexibility of rate	whenever appropriate	whenever appropriate	whenever appropriate	whenever appropriate	

Table 12.2 Design of a school-wide reading program—In-service work for teachers

Areas for in-service work requested by teachers	Fall—Year 1	Spring—Year 1	Fall—Year 2	Spring—Year 2
Readability of materials	Teachers learned to use the Flesch and Fry formulas and/or the Dale-Chall and Spache formulas and applied them to random samples of their texts to determine readability of each text.	Teachers used formulas to help make their decisions about texts to be used the following year.		
Informal reading inventories		Teachers learned how to write an IRI using their content area texts to be used the following year. They learned to grade them and use diagnostic information from them.	Teachers used the IRIs with students in their classes to select the best level of materials for each student.	Teachers learned how to group students according to skill needs and how to design skill development centers for teaching necessary content related reading skills, e.g., a vocabulary center, sequence center, critical reading center in which materials which represent various points of view on a subject are found.
Directed reading activity and SQ3R	Teachers learned the importance of the following pre-reading lesson components: a) showing the structure of the assignment;		Teachers learned to use SQ3R, or a comparable study technique at appropriate times with their students.	

	b) stating purposes for reading; c) introducing vocabulary; d) exploring and building background for the assignment.			
Teaching vocabulary	Teachers learned to select words from students' reading materials and to use a variety of techniques to teach these words.		Teachers learned to select commonly used morphemes in their content areas and ways of making the learning of these interesting.	Teachers learned about connotative and figurative uses of language and ways words are used to influence people. They learned techniques for teaching these.
Teaching sequence and main idea		Teachers learned about the following patterns of organization: chronological, spatial, expository. They learned to compose charts appropriate for each pattern and to teach rhetorical signal words. They learned to use charts to show organizational pattern as a prereading activity.	Teachers learned how to teach students how to critique an author's pattern, how to reorganize it into another pattern, and how to organize using information from various sources.	
Developing interest in content related materials	Teachers learned several ways of developing interest: a) seeking, self-selection, pacing; b) time, materials, sharing; c) ring-a-bell, etc. The librarian gave help in selecting materials. The school began using the Read-In.	Teachers were given time and help in writing an Interest Inventory. They were encouraged to order trade books for their classroom.		

Table 12.2 Design of a school-wide reading program—In-service work for teachers (cont.)

Areas for in-service work requested by teachers	Fall—Year 1	Spring—Year 1	Fall—Year 2	Spring—Year 2
Selecting and comparing multiple sources on one topic				Teachers learned how to teach previewing information to determine general content of a source, bias of author, and completeness of information. They learned how to teach students to select materials which represent a variety of points of view on a topic.
Teaching critical creative reading			Teachers learned about propaganda analysis as it applies to advertisements and content related materials. They learned how to teach the difference between fact and opinion.	
Developing rate of reading				Teachers learned techniques to help students develop flexible roles of reading: skimming, scanning, previewing, reading for various purposes.

reading skills and interests that relate to the *content* of English. Interpretive skills, application skills, and critical-creative-evaluative reading all have a place ordained by the content of the course. It is important that these skills be taught well when they are needed for the understanding of such content. In addition, the English class is a marvelous place for the development of recreational reading interests—for free reading. Time should be allotted to reading for pure enjoyment, and no book reports should be required for such reading. There should be choral reading. The teacher should read to the class. There should be oral reading of plays. There should be *sharing* of a voluntary type. Units might be designed around themes of interest to the class, or there might be a completely free range in choice of materials. Something *must* be done to develop interest in reading for pleasure.

Special Reading Classes

Special reading classes of various types should be available to all students *on an elective basis—for credit.* The importance of making these classes elective cannot be overemphasized. Reading classes are not dumping grounds for students with complex problems, nor can such classes serve as a panacea. In a sense, a reading course is a skill course, as is a writing course, or even a typewriting course. Although society puts greater value on learning to read well than on learning to write or to typewrite well, success in learning to read will not solve most student problems. Of course, it might help solve them if the cause of the problem was inadequate reading, but this is not always so.

Students, even those in dire need of a reading course, should not be forced to take the course. The course is functioning poorly if such force is necessary. Students who do not read up to their ability level should be *invited* to take a special reading class. If they accept the invitation, they should be allowed to enroll. Other students who wish to take a reading class should also be allowed to enroll.

> When I began one of my high school jobs, my classes were filled with underachievers in reading who had been forced to take my course. It was a mess. Nobody *wanted* to be in the classes. Fortunately, most of the students found that reading class was not all that bad, but it was a difficult beginning for them and for me.
>
> The following semester I decided to accept only those students who personally asked me to be in one of my classes. I ruled out having a mother or father ask me. The school counselor, who gave the school-wide tests, extended the initial invitation to the students. All but two students who had been invited asked to be included, and one could not take reading because of a schedule conflict. My classes were filled, and I found I could take about twice as many students as I had taken the first semester because *they wanted to come.* There was an *esprit de corps.* And why not? There should be, if reading is taught correctly—cognitively *and* affectively.

Before talking about different kinds of reading classes that might be offered, we must first determine what kinds of readers we have. There are two broad categories: those students who read up to capacity, or almost up to capacity, are usually considered to be *developmental readers*. Those students who read well below their potential, or capacity, level are called *disabled readers*. The gap between potential and achievement widens from first grade to twelfth grade for students generally considered disabled.

A child who is reading one-half year below his or her potential level (see Chapter 1) in grades 1–3 is considered disabled and in need of special help in reading. In grades 4–6, the difference must be three-quarters of a year; in grades 7 and 8, one year; and in grades 9–12, two years. (Part of the reason for the broader range in the secondary school is that the error of measurement in most tests increases as the grade level increases, and such a span is necessary to be certain that there is a real disability.) Disabled readers should normally be encouraged to take remedial reading.

Developmental readers, or those who are making normal progress in reading in relationship to their intelligence, can be classified into three general categories:

1. *accelerated readers*—those students who are reading well above grade level and approximately at potential level. They need a rapidly paced program and should make more than a year's progress in a year's time.
2. *average developmental readers*—those students who are reading up to potential and are reading approximately at grade level. They need an average-paced program and should continue to make about one year's progress each year.
3. *slower than average learners*—those students who are reading well below grade level because they have low potential. They need a slowly paced program, often called an *adapted reading program*. If their I.Q. test scores are accurate, they will never read at grade level if they are socially promoted, even with excellent help from the school and cooperation and effort on their part. Normally, they make less than a year's progress in a year's time.

Ideally, all students who wish to should have the opportunity of enrolling in special reading classes. There should be *remedial reading classes* (though named something else) for disabled readers and *developmental reading classes* of various types for the developmental readers. Or, if the school's philosophy favors heterogeneous grouping, such clear lines need not be drawn.

I've always enjoyed having a few better readers included in classes which were principally remedial. Students enjoyed this, too. Instruction was individualized, so it really didn't matter. Also, if there is only one special reading teacher, such flexibility is needed to accommodate student schedules. These classes might meet daily for a semester or a year.

In addition to remedial and developmental classes in reading, there might be one or two *college prep* reading courses for accelerated readers in their senior year. (Average or slow-learning readers should take developmental reading.) These classes might meet twice a week for a semester or year.

Such a program has worked well for me. In another school, another plan might function better. Perhaps you can design a program you would prefer.

SUMMARY

If a school-wide reading program is to be effective, all teachers must participate. One or several reading teachers cannot accomplish the necessary goals, nor can one department. Furthermore, it is impossible to develop all desirable reading skills and interests at any one (or several) grade level. Learning to read, and to read better, is a never-ending task. And teaching students to improve their thinking skills and interests as they relate to reading materials is an integral part of good teaching in all subjects at all levels.

Designing a school-wide reading program, however, is not a simple task. A school or school system should have a *coordinating committee,* composed of a reading consultant, the principal, a guidance counselor, a librarian, a representative from each department, possibly a school board member, and other specialized personnel. *Duties of this coordinating committee* include determining a philosophy of reading acceptable to the school staff and the community and which relates to the best modern thought in reading education. This committee should also determine ways of implementing this philosophy.

The coordinating committee should develop an "ideal program" for the school or school system. Such a program should be three-faceted and provide for: (1) full participation by all content area teachers in the fusion of reading skills and interests with the teaching of content, (2) additional participation by English teachers in the development of units or lessons designed for the direct teaching of some reading skills and the development of interest in reading, and (3) organization of a variety of special reading classes.

NOTES

1 Jane H. Catterson. "Successful Study Programs." *Perspectives in Reading #4: Developing Study Skills in Secondary Schools,* Harold L. Herber, ed. Newark, Delaware: International Reading Association, 1965, pp. 158–159.

2 Paraphrased from Wayne Otto and Richard J. Smith. *Administering the School Reading Program.* Boston: Houghton Mifflin, 1970, p. 206.

3 *All Teachers Can Teach Reading,* 1951 Yearbook of the Secondary School Teachers Association, Plainfield, New Jersey.

4 See Margaret Early. "Reading: In and Out of the English Curriculum." *Bulletin of the National Association of Secondary School Principals,* **51** (April 1967): 47–59.

SUGGESTED ACTIVITIES

1. List the important reading skills students should have to facilitate their understanding of your content area ideas. If possible, compare this list with those written by your classmates or colleagues.

2. Plan, if possible, along with your classmates or colleagues, a design for a school-wide reading program for improving reading skills in all content areas. You may wish to design this in steps: first year, second year, third year, etc. What types of special reading classes would you hope to include in a school-wide program? What special personnel?

3. Define, in general terms and by using specific criteria, what is meant by the term *disabled reader.*

4. Define what is meant by *developmental* reading. Compare the approaches and materials teachers should use with the various kinds of developmental readers (slow learner, average learners, accelerated learners).

REFERENCES FOR FURTHER READING

Aaron, Ira, Byron Callaway, and Arthur V. Olson. *Conducting In-Service Programs in Reading.* Newark, Delaware: International Reading Association, 1965.

All Teachers Can Teach Reading, 1951 Yearbook. Plainfield, New Jersey: Secondary School Teachers Association.

Artley, A. Sterl. "Implementing a Developmental Reading Program on the Secondary Level," *Perspectives in Reading #2, Reading Instruction in Secondary Schools,* Margaret Early, ed. Newark, Delaware: International Reading Association, 1964.

Artley, A. Sterl. *Trends and Practices in Secondary School Reading.* Newark, Delaware: International Reading Association, 1968.

Austin, Mary and C. Morrison. *The First R: the Harvard Report on Reading in the Elementary Schools.* New York: Macmillan, 1963.

Beery, Althea, Thomas Barrett, and William Powell, (eds.). *Elementary Reading Instruction: Selected Materials.* Boston: Allyn and Bacon, 1969, Chapter 11.

Bond, Guy L. and Miles Tinker. *Reading Difficulties: Their Diagnosis and Correction.* New York: Appleton-Century-Crofts, 1967, Chapter 15.

Carlson, Thorsten R. (ed.). *Administrators and Reading.* New York: Harcourt Brace Jovanovich, 1972.

Catterson, Jane H. "Successful Study Skills Programs." *Perspectives in Reading #4: Developing Study Skills in Secondary Schools,* Harold Herber, ed. Newark, Delaware: International Reading Association, 1965.

Hafner, Lawrence E., (ed.). *Improving Reading in Middle and Secondary Schools, Selected Readings.* New York: Macmillan, 1974, Sections 10 and 12.

Harris, Theodore L., Wayne Otto, and Thomas C. Barrett. "Summary and Review of Investigations Relating to Reading." *Journal of Educational Research,* February or March yearly.

Herber, Harold. "Teaching Secondary Students to Read History," *Perspectives in Reading #2: Reading Instruction in Secondary Schools,* Margaret Early, ed. Newark, Delaware: International Reading Association, 1964.

Karlin, Robert. *Teaching Reading in High School.* Indianapolis: Bobbs-Merrill, 1964, Chapter 14.

Karlin, Robert, (ed.). *Teaching Reading in High School—Selected Articles.* Indianapolis: Bobbs-Merrill, 1969, Chapters 7, 12, and 14.

Marksheffel, Ned D. *Better Reading in the Secondary School.* New York: The Ronald Press, 1966, Chapters 3, 6, and 8.

Moburg, Lawrence G. *Inservice Teacher Training in Reading.* Newark, Delaware: International Reading Association, 1972.

National Society for the Study of Education. *Development in and Through Reading,* 60th Yearbook, Part I. Chicago: University of Chicago Press, 1961, Chapters 1, 4, and 5.

National Society for the Study of Education. *Innovation and Change in Reading Instruction,* 67th Yearbook, Part II. Chicago: University of Chicago Press, 1968, Chapters 8, 9, and 11.

Olson, Arthur V. and Wilber S. Ames, (eds.). *Teaching Reading Skills in Secondary Schools.* Scranton, Pa.: International Textbook Co., 1970, Sections 1, 2, 8, 10, and 11.

Otto, Wayne and Richard J. Smith. *Administering the School Reading Program.* Boston: Houghton Mifflin, 1970.

Robinson, H. Alan and Sidney Rauch. *Perspectives in Reading #6: Corrective Reading in the High School Classroom.* Newark, Delaware: International Reading Association, 1966.

Schell, Leo and Paul Burns, (eds.). *Remedial Reading—an Anthology of Sources.* Boston: Allyn and Bacon, 1968.

Strang, Ruth. *The Diagnostic Teaching of Reading.* New York: McGraw-Hill, 1969, Parts 3 and 4.

APPENDIX A

DALE-CHALL AND THE NEW SPACHE READABILITY FORMULAS

THE DALE-CHALL READABILITY FORMULA

The Dale-Chall readability formula is widely used for estimating the reading difficulty of printed materials at the fourth grade level and above.[1] Two factors are used to arrive at the score—*sentence length* and *word difficulty*.

It is necessary to refer to the original article for the list of easy words. With certain stipulations, as explained in the article, all other words are hard.

When the reader knows the number of hard words within a 100-word passage (i.e., the percentage of hard words) and the number of sentences totally within the 100-word passage, he or she can use the "Computation Ease" chart on the following page to find the grade level score.[2]

For example, suppose we are using the passage given in Chapter 2 of this book. There are 13 hard words within the 100-word sample: *Southwesterners, situation, area, perfect, skiers, enthusiasts, area, perfectly, groomed, slopes, accommodate, skiers, beginners.* There are three sentences completely *within* the 100 words.

Using the chart, we see that the *raw score* for the passage is 7.4 and that the *grade score* is 9–10.9. This overlaps somewhat with the Flesch score, which was 10–12.9. You may find that you prefer one formula to the other. You may wish to use a formula just to find the *relative difficulty* of materials.

THE NEW SPACHE READABILITY FORMULA

The Spache readability formula is widely used for estimating the reading difficulty of printed materials below the fourth grade level in difficulty.[3] Like the

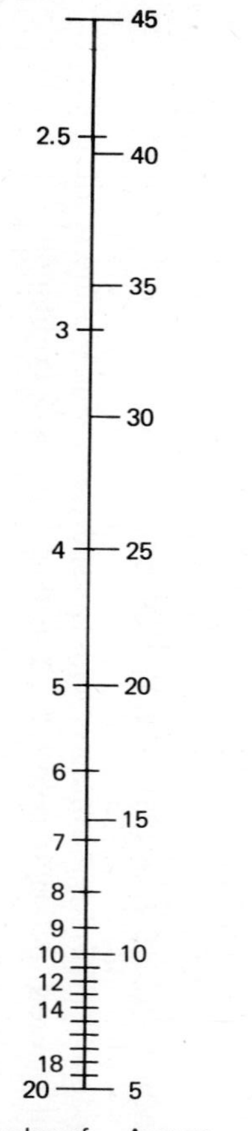

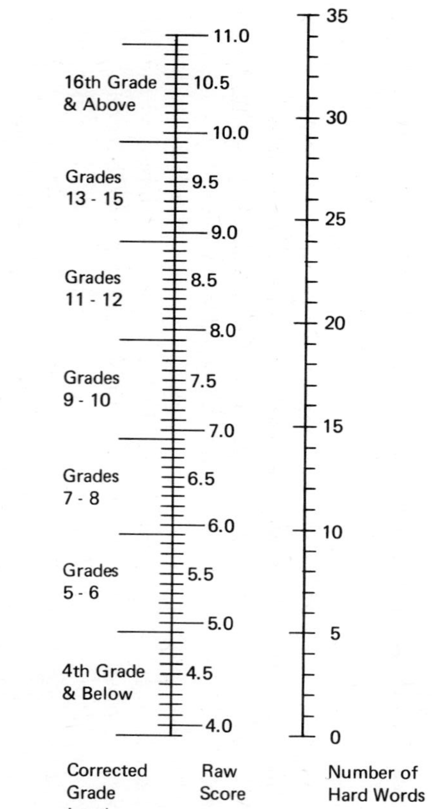

COMPUTATION EASE DIRECTIONS

To determine both the Dale-Chall raw readability score and the correspondent grade level placement:

1. Count a 100-word sample from the passage selected.
2. Count the number of sentences in the 100 words. Disregard the sentence in which the one hundredth word appears, i.e., count only those sentences which are completely within the 100-word sample.
3. Count the number of words in the 100-word sample which do not appear on the Dale List of 3,000 Words.
4. Lay a straight edge so that it touches (a) the number of sentences as shown on the left-hand column, and (b) the number of "Hard Words," i.e., those words not on Dale's list, as shown on the right-hand column.
5. Read (a) the Dale-Chall raw score and/or (b) the Grade Level at the point where the straight edge intersects the middle column.

Examples:

1. A 100-word sample with ten sentences and ten "Hard Words" has a raw score of 5.7 and a grade level designation of 5.6.
2. A sample with 20 sentences and seven "Hard Words" has approximately a 5.0 raw score and 5-6 grade level designation.

Fig. A.1 "Dale-Chall Readability Formula: A Computation Ease." (From "Another Practical Note on Readability Formulas," Karl Koenke, *Journal of Reading*, **15,** December 1971, p. 206. Reprinted with the permission of Karl Koenke and the International Reading Association.)

Sentence length	Percentage of Hard Words																					
	0	1	2	3	4	5	6	7	8	9	10	11	12	13	14	15	16	17	18	19	20	21
5	1.2	1.3	1.4	1.5	1.6	1.7	1.8	1.8	1.9	2.0	2.1	2.2	2.2	2.3	2.4	2.5	2.6	2.7	2.7	2.8	2.9	3.0
6	1.4	1.5	1.5	1.6	1.7	1.8	1.9	2.0	2.0	2.1	2.2	2.3	2.4	2.5	2.5	2.6	2.7	2.8	2.9	2.9	3.0	3.1
7	1.5	1.6	1.7	1.8	1.8	1.9	2.0	2.1	2.2	2.2	2.3	2.4	2.5	2.6	2.7	2.7	2.8	2.9	3.0	3.1	3.1	3.2
8	1.6	1.7	1.8	1.9	2.0	2.0	2.1	2.2	2.3	2.4	2.4	2.5	2.6	2.7	2.8	2.9	2.9	3.0	3.1	3.2	3.3	3.3
9	1.7	1.8	1.9	2.0	2.1	2.2	2.2	2.3	2.4	2.5	2.6	2.7	2.7	2.8	2.9	3.0	3.1	3.1	3.2	3.3	3.4	3.5
10	1.9	2.0	2.0	2.1	2.2	2.3	2.4	2.4	2.5	2.6	2.7	2.8	2.9	2.9	3.0	3.1	3.2	3.3	3.3	3.4	3.5	3.6
11	2.0	2.1	2.2	2.2	2.3	2.4	2.5	2.6	2.6	2.7	2.8	2.9	3.0	3.1	3.1	3.2	3.3	3.4	3.5	3.5	3.6	3.7
12	2.1	2.2	2.3	2.4	2.4	2.5	2.6	2.7	2.8	2.8	2.9	3.0	3.1	3.2	3.3	3.3	3.4	3.5	3.6	3.7	3.8	3.8
13	2.2	2.3	2.4	2.5	2.6	2.6	2.7	2.8	2.9	3.0	3.1	3.1	3.2	3.3	3.4	3.5	3.5	3.6	3.7	3.8	3.9	4.0
14	2.3	2.4	2.5	2.6	2.7	2.8	2.8	2.9	3.0	3.1	3.2	3.3	3.3	3.4	3.5	3.6	3.7	3.7	3.8	3.9	4.0	
15	2.5	2.6	2.6	2.7	2.8	2.9	3.0	3.0	3.1	3.2	3.3	3.4	3.5	3.5	3.6	3.7	3.8	3.9	4.0	4.0		
16	2.6	2.7	2.8	2.8	2.9	3.0	3.1	3.2	3.3	3.3	3.4	3.5	3.6	3.7	3.7	3.8	3.9	4.0				
17	2.7	2.8	2.9	3.0	3.0	3.1	3.2	3.3	3.4	3.5	3.5	3.6	3.7	3.8	3.9	3.9	4.0					
18	2.8	2.9	3.0	3.1	3.2	3.2	3.3	3.4	3.5	3.6	3.7	3.7	3.8	3.9	4.0							
19	2.9	3.0	3.1	3.2	3.3	3.4	3.5	3.5	3.6	3.7	3.8	3.9	3.9	4.0								
20	3.1	3.2	3.2	3.3	3.4	3.5	3.6	3.7	3.7	3.8	3.9	4.0										
21	3.2	3.3	3.4	3.4	3.5	3.6	3.7	3.8	3.9	3.9	4.0											
22	3.3	3.4	3.5	3.6	3.6	3.7	3.8	3.9	4.0													

Fig. A.2 "A Chart for the New Spache Formula." (From "A Chart for the New Spache Formula," by Lou E. Burmeister, *The Reading Teacher*, **29**, January 1976, p. 385. Used by permission of the International Reading Association.)

Dale-Chall formula, the Spache formula uses two factors to arrive at the score: average sentence length and difficulty of words (as indicated by presence or absence of each word on a word list).

One must refer to the original exposition of the new formula for directions and the word list. After the reader computes the *average sentence length* (by counting the number of sentences in a passage and dividing that number into the number of words) and the *percentage of difficult words* (as instructed by Spache), one need not do the computations. Instead, the reader can simply consult the following chart[4] and read to the point of intersection of the two figures to get the approximate grade level of the passage. For example, if the average sentence length were 12 words, and the percentage of difficult words were 10, the difficulty of the passage is 2.9.

NOTES

1 Edgar Dale and Jeanne Chall. "A Formula for Predicting Readability." *Educational Research Bulletin* (January 21, 1948): 11–20, 28.

2 Karl Koenke. "Another Practical Note on Readability Formulas." *Journal of Reading,* **15** (December 1971): 206.

3 George D. Spache. "The Spache Readability Formula." *Good Reading for Poor Readers.* Champaign, Illinois: Garrard Publishing, 1974, pp. 195–207.

4 Lou E. Burmeister. "A Chart for the New Spache Formula." *The Reading Teacher,* **29** (January 1976): 384–385.

APPENDIX B

INFORMAL READING INVENTORY— ORAL READING TEST

Sometimes a teacher wishing additional information about the reading achievement of one or more students may have time to administer individual oral reading tests. The kinds of errors a student makes on such a test may give the teacher clues to the type of reading instruction the student needs. Such an exam is especially appropriate for students who are reading below about seventh-grade level.

PROCEDURE

The teacher marks off a passage of about 100 words in a book or in a series of multilevel books. Students are asked to read the passage (or passages, beginning with the easiest) orally, individually, and in private with the teacher. As the student reads orally, the teacher records all errors that the student makes. Errors are usually of the following types:

1. mispronunciations—the teacher records the way the student mispronounced the word (dialectal variations are not errors);
2. substitutions—the teacher writes the substituted word above the word missed;
3. omissions—the teacher circles the word, or words, omitted;
4. insertions—the teacher uses a caret (∧) and writes in the extra word;

5. regressions (or repetitions of phrases)—the teacher draws a wavy line under the repeated phrase. A single word may be repeated without being counted as an error if it is finally pronounced correctly;

6. hesitations—if there is a hesitation of five or more seconds, the teacher writes "H" and then supplies the word.

It is important that the teacher record errors immediately—as they are made—and not trust to memory (see p. 363). It is wise to use a passage of exactly 100 words or exactly 200 words so that percentages can be computed easily. The passage need not end at the end of a sentence, though the student should read to the end of the sentence. When the student begins to make an excessive number of errors, i.e., over 6% to 8% errors, the oral testing is stopped.

The teacher's copy of the passage which the student reads orally may look like that shown on p. 363.

INTERPRETATION OF RESULTS

If the student scores 99%–100% correct in oral reading, i.e., up to one error in 100 words, the book is said to be on the student's *independent reading level.* If the student scores 95%–98% correct, i.e., up to one error in 20 words, the book is on the *instructional reading level.* If the student makes more than one error in 20 words (94% correct or lower), the book is on the *frustrational reading level.* (Some writers consider 91%–94% correct to be borderline.)

Name: John Sloan

Passage	Misp.	Sub.	Om.	Ins.	Reg.	Hes.
Humans are said to be "warm-blooded" because						
they maintain a relative(ly) constant body	1					
temperature regardless of the temperature of the						
environment. All mammals (mams) and birds	1					
are warm-blooded. All other animals,						
including insects, are said to be "cold-blooded"						
because their temperature changes with						
that of the environment. As body temperature						
changes, the rate of activi(ty) changes. You	1					
may have noticed that the chirping rate					1	
of crickets is related to the temperature.						
As the temperature drops, their chirp rate						
and body motions become noticeably slower.						
In late summer, one of the authors took						
some data on the chirp rate of tree						
crickets / (100 words) in some honeysuckle, using a						
tape recorder to be sure the results could						
be reexamined and measured accurately.						
Subtotal:	3				1	

Total = 4

Analysis:

Mispronunciations — 3: word endings

Regressions — 1

Levels	Errors
Independent	0–1
*Instructional	(2–5)
Frustrational	6 or more

APPENDIX C

MORPHEMES COMMONLY USED IN SPECIFIC CONTENT FIELDS

Table C.1 Morphemes in content areas—some are arbitrarily assigned

Morpheme and meaning	English	Social Studies	Science	Mathematics	Health and P.E.	Other
a (not, without)	alexia aphasia asyllabic athematic atonal achromatic	acephalous achronological aclinic atheist amnesty amoral anomie apathetic apolitical atypical asocial azoic agnostic	abranchiate acarpous achromatic aneroid aphonite apodal apterous aseptic asexual astatine atrophy	acentric asymptote asymmetric	achondioplasia amnesia apena arrhythmia asphyxiate ataracite	argon atemporal ascorbic a cappella
ambi (both)	ambiguous	ambivalent	ambilateral		ambidextrous	ambiversion
amphi (both, on both sides)	amphibolous amphibrach	amphictyony	amphibian amphibole amphicoelous amphipod amphibiotic amphibious		amphiarthrosis	amphiprostyle amphitheater
anim (life, mind, soul)	animation animator	anima unanimous	animal inanimate			magnanimous animate inanimate animosity equanimity

Table C.1 Morphemes in content areas (cont.)

Morpheme and meaning	English	Social Studies	Science	Mathematics	Health and P.E.	Other
ante (before)	antecedent anteclassical antepenult	antebellum antedate antemundane antediluvian	antebrachium antemortem anteorbital anterior	antemeridiem antenumber	antenatal	antechamber anteroom
anthropo (man, mankind)	anthropomorphism anthropopathism	anthropocentric anthropology anthropometry anthropophagi philanthropist	anthropogenesis anthropoid			misanthrope theanthropic
anti (against)	antagonist anticlimax antihero antithesis antonym	anticline antifederalist antipodes antipope antipoverty anti-Semitic antislavery antisocial antitrust antiwar	antibody anticatalyst antidote antimagnetic antiperiodic antitoxin antiseptic antibiotic	antiderivative antilogarithm	antienzyme antihistamine antiperspirant antiphlogistic antipyretic antacid	antiaircraft antifreeze antipathy antichrist antisubmarine
apo (away from, defense, off)	aphorism apothegm aposiopesis apostrophe	apostate apostle apotheosis	aphelion apochromatic apogee apophysis apogamy		apoplexy apothecary	apostasy apocalypse apology

arch (chief, principal)	archetype archimage	archduke archenemy archfiend archipelago archive autarchy matriarchy monarch oligarchy patriarch	archegonium	arch	archrival	architect architrave archangel archbishop
auto (self)	autobiography autocriticism autodidact autograph	autocracy autocrat autohypnosis autonomy autosuggestion	autoclave autolysis automation autonomic autoplasty autopsy autotomy autotrophic			automatic automobile autotransformer autoharp
bene (well, good)		benevolent	beneficiate benign			benediction benefactor beneficiary benefit
bi (two)	bilafial bilingual bilateral	bias bicameral bicentennial bigamy bilateral bipartisan biracial biannual bimonthly	biaxial bicentric biceps biconcave biconvex bifacial bifoliate bigeminal biped bipolar bivalve	biangular bilinear bimodal binomial bisect bimolecular binary bipinnate	bicuspid bifocals	bicolored bicycle binal biplane combine

Table C.1 Morphemes in content areas (cont.)

Morpheme and meaning	English	Social Studies	Science	Mathematics	Health and P.E.	Other
biblio (book)	bibliography bibliomania bibliophile bibliopole bibliotheca bibliotics	bibliotherapy				Bible bibliofilm
bio (life)	autobiography biography	biogeography biosocial biotic	amphibious antibiosis bioastronautics biochemistry biogenesis biology biolysis symbiosis		anabiosis	biodegradable
capt (head, chief; seize, take)	capitalize caption	capital capitalist capitol capitulation captive decapitate	capitate			captain
cent (hundred)	centenarian centennial	centenary centurial centurion	centigrade centipede	centavo centesimal centigram centimeter centinewton centipoise centner centuple centuplicate percent		century

cent- (center)	cento centum	centralism centrality centralize centrist egocentric	centrifugal centriole centipetal centrobaric centroid centrosome centrosphere epicenter	concentric		centerpiece
chrom (color)	achromatic	chromatic	achromatic chromoplast chromosome chromatophore chromosphere			autochrome bichromatic chrome chromolithograph monochrome polychrome
chron (time)	chronicle chronological	anachronism chronoscope	chronograph chronometer chronaxy synchronous		chronic	
cide (kill)		genocide homicide matricide patricide regicide suicide	ecocide insecticide			philocide
circum (around)	circumflex circumlocution	circa circumnavigate circumpolar circumvention	circulation circuit circumlunar	circumcenter circumference circumradius circumscribe		circumrotate circuitous circumcise circumfuse circumstance circumvolve circus circumspect

Table C.1 Morphemes in content areas (cont.)

Morpheme and meaning	English	Social Studies	Science	Mathematics	Health and P.E.	Other
co, con com (with, together)	coauthor collaborate colloquial compile concur consonant contemporary	coalition cobelligerent coexist coherence collateral compatriot confederate confront	coagulate cohesive compound	coefficient congruent correlation cosecant cosine cotangent	compete compress	coaxial component compose coadjutant coeducational coincide colleague companion cooperate copilot
contra (against, opposite)	contradiction contrast counterplot	contraband controversial counterattack counterproposal	contraorbital counterbalance counterearth	counterclockwise		counteract counterfeit countersign contrary counter encounter counterpoint contrapuntal
crat, cracy (government, rule)		democracy theocracy plutocracy monocracy Dixiecrat autocracy				plutocrat technocrat autocrat
cred (credit, to believe, to trust)	credulity	accreditation credentials credibility discredit				credo credulous credence incredible

cycle (circle)	cyclorama Cyclops encyclopedia	encyclical	cyclical cyclosis cyclotron epicycloid	epicycle cyclone hemicycle		bicycle
dec, deci (ten)				decimal	decathlon	decade
dem (people)		demagogue democracy demograph endemic	epidemic pandemic			demophobia
dia (across, through)	diachronic diacritical dialogue	dialecticism diatribe	diagnosis diagram diaphanous	diameter diagonal	diarrhea diathermal	diatonic diabetes
dic, dict (to speak)	contradiction dictation diction valedictorian dictionary dictate indicate	dictator dictum edict fatidic indictment jurisdiction verdict	addict			dictaphone dictograph benediction malediction predict
duc, duct (to lead)	adduce introduction inductive deductive	production subdue duke duchess	conductor inductor	deductive reducible inductive	reduce	conduct abduction induce seduce abduct educe educate

Table C.1 Morphemes in content areas (cont.)

Morpheme and meaning	English	Social Studies	Science	Mathematics	Health and P.E.	Other
epi (on, upon, over)	epic epicrisis epigram epilogue epithet epitome	epidemic	epicenter epicotyl epidermic epigastrium epigeal epiphysis	epicycle epicycloid epimorphism		epicure epigraph epistle epitaph episcopal
eu (well, good)	eulogy euphemism euphony	eugenics euthenics	euplastic eutectic euthanasia eutrophy		eupnea eurythmy	euphoria
fac, fic (to do, to make)	facsimile fictitious	malefactor factory faction fashion artifact	infections	factor	deficient	edifice facilitate benefactress beneficence efficient facile factotum proficient suffice difficulty
fin (to end, to limit)	finis definition	finance finalization		finite infinity		finale affinity
flex, flect (to bend)	inflection reflexive	genuflect	deflection flexor reflection			flexible

flu (to flow)	fluency mellifluous superfluous	affluence confluent flume fluvial reflux	effluvium fluid fluorescence	flu	effluence fluctuate flush influence influx
gamy (marriage)		bigamy misogamy monogamy polygamy	agamic allogamy autogamy cleistogamous dichogamous exogamy gamete gamopetalous gamosepalous heterogamy		
gen (to produce, to beget)	genitive genre	genealogy genesis genocide indigen primogeniture	congener epigene genotype genus progenitor homogeneous heterogeneous	congenital regenerate	photogenic degenerate generation ingenious miscegenation generate generous
gnos (knowledge)	cognitive cognition	diagnosis gnosis psychognosis	geognosy	physiognomy prognosis	agnostic ignorance recognize prognosticate recognize ignore
gogue, agogue (drive, lead)	antagonize protagonist	demagogue hypnagogic mystagogue pedagogue synagogue			

Table C.1 Morphemes in content areas (cont.)

Morpheme and meaning	English	Social Studies	Science	Mathematics	Health and P.E.	Other
graph (to write)	biography bibliography autograph monograph paragraph allograph grapheme digraph orthography	demography polygraph topography graffiti cryptography	oceanography photograph electrocardiograph electrograph graphite heliograph phototelegraph seismograph telegraph geography	graph	electroen- cephalograph	photograph telegraph stenography choreograph epigraph graphic lithograph photolithograph serigraphy phonograph pornography
gyn (woman, female)		misogyny gynarchy gynophore	gynandrous		gynecology	
hemi (half)	hemistich	hemisphere hemisfair	hemialgia hemiparasite hemiplegia	hemicycle hemispheroid		hemidemisemiquaver
hetero (other, different)	heteronym	heterodox heteronomous	heterocyclic heterogamous heteromorphic heterophylous heteropterous heterosexual			heterodyne heterochromatic heterogeneous

hyper (above, beyond, excessive)	hyperbole hypercorrection hypercritical hypermetric		hyperacid hyperbaric hyperemia hypermorph hypertrophy	hyperbola hypersphere	hyperventilate hyperactive hyperextension hyperglycemia hyperirritability hyperopia hypersensitive hypertension hyperthermia	
hypo (under, too little)	hypothesis	hypocrisy	hypochlorite hypobaric hypodermic hypogeal hypogene hypothermal	hypocycloid hypotenuse	hypoacidity hypochondriac hypoglycemia hypoxia hypoactive	hypogeum hypostyle
inter (among)	interjection interpretation interlude interview intermission	intercede intercontinental intercoastal intermarry intermediary international interracial interrogate interurban interstate intervene (-vention)	interbreed interplanetary interpolar internal interstellar	interaxial interpolate intersection interior interval	intercept intercollegiate interference	intercom interlock intermezzo interface interact interchange intermediate interrupt intersession interest interscholastic interim intertwine

Table C.1 Morphemes in content areas (cont.)

Morpheme and meaning	English	Social Studies	Science	Mathematics	Health and P.E.	Other
intra, intro (inside, within)	introduction	intrastate introspect	intracellular intravenous intracostal		intramural	intrinsic introvert intricate intrude
junc (to join)	conjugate conjunction subjoin juncture	conjoin injunction subjugate junta	jugular	juxtaposition		adjoining junction jugate juncture
leg, lig (to choose, to read)	lecture legend legible prelect sortilege dialect	election legislative selectivism legion sacrilege	collect			elegant elective eligible intelligent lectern select diligent neglect eclectic
log, logy (science of, study of)	dialectology phonology	anthropology criminology ethnology ideology psychology sociology ecology	biology ethology geology paleontology physiology radiology zoology methodology	horology logarithm topology		apology logic syllogism astrology

logy, loc, loq (to speak, speech)	trilogy colloquial colloquy elocution grandiloquence allocution magniloquent soliloquy eloquent epilogue prologue monologue dialogue	interlocutory				circumlocution loquacious obloquy ventriloquism
mal (bad, ill)	malapropism	malefactor malefaction malversation	malnutrition		malignant malady malaria maladroit malaise	malign maladjusted malevolent malice malformation
mania (madness for)		monomania kleptomania pyromania dipsomania megalomania				
meta (between, with, beside, after, transcending, reversed, behind)	metaphor metalinguistics	metazoan	metamorphosis metaphase metacarpus metachromatism metagenesis metabolism metacenter metagalaxy metastable	metamathematics		metaphysical metathesis

Table C.1 Morphemes in content areas (cont.)

Morpheme and meaning	English	Social Studies	Science	Mathematics	Health and P.E.	Other
meter, metr (measure)	dimeter hexameter metrical polymeter pentameter		barometer electrometer heliometer isometrics metric thermometer metrology	geometry chronometer diameter dimension parameter pseudometer trigonometry centimeter millimeter		diametric metronome
mono (one)	monograph monolingual monologue monosyllabic monodrama monothematic	monarchy monometallism monopoly monotheism monolith monocrat monogyny monogamy monopsony monomania	mononuclear monophobia monosymmetric monochromatic monodactyl monogenesis monomorphic	monomial	monocular mononucleosis monopade	monaural monophonic monochord monotone monocycle monogram monorail monocle monk monastery monoplane
morph (form, meaning)	morpheme morphology morphophone	anthropomorphic	metamorphic morphogenesis			amorphic
mov, mot (to move)	emotion motivation	commotion demobilize mobilization promotion remote	motile motion motoneuron			motor movable movie remove mobile momentum

multi (much, many)	multilingual	multilateral multipartite tumult multiuniversity	multicellular multiflorous multiped multipolar multivalent	multiangular multiform multinomial multiplicand multiplication multiply	multiparous	multiaddress multicolored multimedia multifold multitude multiplicity
non (not)	nonchalant nondescript nonfiction nonliterate nonobjective nonverbal	nonaggression nonaligned nonentity noncommittal noncompliance nonconformist nonintervention nonpartisan nonprofit nonviolent	nonconductor nonpolar nonreactive	non-Euclidean nonlinear nonnegative		nonflammable nonage nondenier nonnational nonexistent nonsense nonstop none
oid (likeness, similarity)	tabloid	anthropoid caucasoid mongoloid negroid schizoid paranoid	planetoid crystalloid celluloid lithoid alkaloid celluloid asteroid	ellipsoid trapezoid	hemorrhoid thyroid	
omni (all)	omnibus	omnidirectional omnirange	omnivorous			omnipotent omniscient omnipresent omnifarious omniumgatherum

Table C.1 Morphemes in content areas (cont.)

Morpheme and meaning	English	Social Studies	Science	Mathematics	Health and P.E.	Other
pan (all, every, universal)	panorama pantheon pantomime	Pan-American pandemic Pan-Germanism pandect	panchromatic pangenesis pancreas			panic panacea pandemonium panoptic pantheism panoply pan-Hellenic
para (beside)	parable paramilitary paramount paragraph paraphrase	parachronism paramilitary	paragenesis paramorph paranoia paraplegia parasite	parabola paraboloid parallel parallelogram parameter		paraprofessional parachute parapet paramour
ped (foot)	sesquipedalian	piedmont expediency	biped centipede pedate quadruped tripod pedometer		pedometer	pedicure pedal pedestal pedestrian tripedal pedigree impede expedite moped, i.e., (*mo*tor-*ped*al)
penta (five)	pentameter Pentateuch		pentadactyl pentamerous	pentagon pentahedron		pentad

phil (loving)	bibliophile	Anglophile Philadelphia philosophy	lyophilic philodendron photophilous			philharmonic philately philanthropy philology philander
phobia (fear)		xenophobia			hydrophobia	claustrophobia aquaphobia agoraphobia astraphobia acrophobia
phon (sound, voice)	aphonic phoneme phonetic phonogram phonology allophone		phonolite			symphonic cacophony euphony telephone phonograph
photo (light)		photogrammetry	photosynthesis photometer photonuclear photoperiod photosensitive phototaxis		photogene photokinesis phototherapy	photograph photolithograph photomontage photostat phototypesetter
poly (much, many)	polyphonic polyglot	polyethic polygraph polytheism polygamy	polysynthetic polyandrous polyatomic polychromatic polygenesis polyvalent polymeric	polycentric polygon polyhedron polynomial	polyphagia	polyphony polyester polytechnic

Table C.1 Morphemes in content areas (cont.)

Morpheme and meaning	English	Social Studies	Science	Mathematics	Health and P.E.	Other
post (after)	posthumous postscript	posthypnotic postwar	posterior postmortem postoperative	postmeridian postmultiply	postnasal	postdate postgraduate postpone preposterous posterity
pre (before)	preconceive preface prefix premise prerequisite pretest preview	preamble predecessor preempt prehistoric prejudice preliterate preside president	preaxial preclinical precipitate			prelude preamplifier prefabricate precook preadolescent precaution precede predestine predict prefer prevent precise presume
pro (forward)	proceed pronoun propose protagonist pronounce proverb	proclaim prohibition promontory promote prosecute proconsul		product protractor problem		prominent prospect procrastinate procreate project produce profess profile profit profuse progress protest protrude

proto- (first, earliest form)	proto-Germanic proto-Indo-European protagonist protolanguage	protocal protohistory protomartyr	protohuman protomorphic proton protonema protopathic prototrophic protozoa protamine			prototype protrude
pseudo (false)	pseudoclassic pseudonym	pseudoaggressive pseudoanarchical pseudoliberal pseudoconservative	pseudopodium pseudocare pseudomorph pseudoscience pseudocarp	pseudometric		pseudointellectual
psych (mind)		psychology psychometrics psychophysiology			psychiatry psychoanalysis psychodrama psychodynamics psychoneurosis psychopathy	psychic psychogenic psychosomatic psychotechnics
quad (four)		quadripartite quadroon quadrennial	quadruped	quadrangle		quadricentennial quadriplet
quin (five)			quinate			quintessence quintuplet
retro (backward)		retrocession retroactive	retrograde retrolental retrorocket			retroflex retrogress retrospect retroversion

Table C.1 Morphemes in content areas (cont.)

Morpheme and meaning	English	Social Studies	Science	Mathematics	Health and P.E.	Other
rupt (to break)	abrupt interruption	bankrupt corruption disruption irrupt	eruption rupture			disrupt
scrib, script (to write)	ascribe description inscription manuscript scribble scribe superscribe	conscription proscribe	prescription	circumscribe		transcribe postscript scripture subscribe
semi (half, partly)	semiabstract semicolon semidivine	semiliterate semipolitical semicivilized seminomad semitropical	semiaquatic semiconductor semiparasitic semipermeable semiprecious semisolid	semicircle semigroup semi-infinite	semiconscious	semiskilled semitone semiannual semiautomatic semiformal semifinal semiprivate
spect (to look)	aspect prospective respect spectacle	inspection introspect retrospective speculate suspect	spectrograph spectrum specimen		spectator	prospect circumspect expectation spy espionage conspicuous despise

stat (stable)	consistency	circumstance resistance statesmanship stature statute	astatic	constant		stator statement status ecstatic
sub (under, below)	subject subjunctive subplot subscript subscribe	subcommittee subconscious subcontinent subculture subjugate sublet submit subsoil subterranean subway	subatomic subhuman	subgroup subinterval subset		submarine subdivide subordinate subdue subnormal subservient subsidy submerge
super (over)	superlative superscribe	supersede superpatriotic	superclass superego supersonic superhuman supersaturate	superpose		supercharge superable superabundant supercilious superficial superstition superfluous superimpose superintendent supernatural superior supreme superb
sym, syn (together)	syncopate symposium synonym synopsis syntax symbolic symbolist	syndicate synthesis syncretism	syndactyl symbiosis symmetalism synapsis syngamy	symbol symmetric asymmetric	symptom syndrome sympathectonomy	symphony syncopate synagogue synod synthetic sympathy synchronize

Table C.1 Morphemes in content areas (cont.)

Morpheme and meaning	English	Social Studies	Science	Mathematics	Health and P.E.	Other
tang tact (touch)	tangible intangible	contingency	contact contagious	tangent		intact tactful tactile tactics tactless
tele (far off)	teleplay	teleology telepathy	phototelegraphy telemeter telephoto telescope			telecommunication telegram telepathic telephone telethon television
tetra (four)	tetralogy tetrameter	tetrarch	tetrapod tetratomic			tetrad
theo (God, god)	theogony	apotheosis monotheism theocentric theocracy theomania atheist pantheon polytheism				theobromine atheism theogony theologian theology theanthropic theosophy theophany
trans (across)	intransitive transitive translate transpose	transaction transcontinent transgress transient	transference transfusion transmit transplant	transformation transversal		transom transponder transatlantic transcend transcript transect transfer transpacific

tri (three)	trilogy	trinity triennial trilateral	triatomic trifoliate	triangle trisect		tricycle triad trio triplet tripod
ultra (beyond)		ultraconservative ultraism ultramontane ultranational	ultramundane ultrasonic ultraviolet ultramicroscopic ultracentrifuge			ultramarine ultramodern
uni (one)	unilingual unison univocal	unicameral unify unilateral unite	unicellular unifoliate universe	unimodular union uniplanar		unicorn unicycle unidirectional uniform unanimous unique unisexual
val (to be worth, to be strong)	evaluate	ambivalence devaluation prevail validation	bivalent bivalve valence	equivalent	convalesce	avail valiant validity valor valuable value invalidate
vert, vers (to turn)	advertise conversation converse diversity	controversy diversification extravert introvert reversion subversive ambivert	ambiversion converter diversiform irreversible	convergent divergent transversal vertex	conversion vertigo	convertible aversion divert versatile

Table C.1 Morphemes in content areas (cont.)

Morpheme and meaning	English	Social Studies	Science	Mathematics	Health and P.E.	Other
voc (to call, to voice)	equivocal evocative univocal vocabulary vocal nonvocal	advocacy convoke invoke provocation provoke revocation				vocation vocalist evoke revoke vociferous

NAME INDEX

SUBJECT INDEX

Overview